GW01017845

The tonic sol-fa music reader : a course of instruction and practice in the tonic sol-fa method of teaching singing, with a choice collection of music suitable for day schools and singing schools

Theodore F. 1835-1902 Seward, B C. 1843-1923 Unseld

PART I

THE
TONIC SOL-FA MUSIC READER

REVISED AND IMPROVED.

A COURSE OF INSTRUCTION AND PRACTICE IN THE

TONIC SOL-FA METHOD OF TEACHING SINGING,

WITH A

CHOICE COLLECTION OF MUSIC SUITABLE FOR DAY SCHOOLS AND SINGING SCHOOLS.

BY THEODORE F. SEWARD AND B. C. UNSELD.

APPROVED BY JOHN CURWEN.

The Biglow & Main Co., Publishers,

135 FIFTH AVENUE, NEW YORK. LAKESIDE BUILDING, CHICAGO

FOR SALE BY BOOKSELLERS AND MUSIC DEALERS GENERALLY.

PREFACE TO THE FIRST EDITION.

THE TONIC SOL-FA SYSTEM is presented by the authors of this book to the American public, in the firm belief that the introduction of the system will mark a new era in the musical history of this country. The TONIC SOL-FA SYSTEM presents two widely different characteristics, either one of which ought to commend it to all who are interested in music. Together they constitute an absolute demand for recognition. These characteristics are:

FIRST.—*It removes three-fourths of the difficulties of music from the path of the beginner; and,*

SECOND.—*It leads to far greater intelligence and appreciation in the advanced stages of study and practice.*

A scholarly American musician has recently written concerning TONIC SOL-FA:—"It is not only a method of making music easy, but for making it more truly and profoundly understood."

The TONIC SOL-FA SYSTEM is often called, by those who use it, "the natural method." The steps of progression are so easy and natural that both teachers and pupils find a pleasure in the study that they never realized before. It is so simple as to bring about a new departure in the teaching of music, in the following respect—*Those who know a little about music can teach that little without being compelled to master the whole science beforehand, as is necessary with the staff notation.* In this way a new class of teachers is developed wherever the TONIC SOL-FA SYSTEM is introduced, viz.: persons of education and culture who love music, but who have heretofore been deterred by its technical difficulties from devoting themselves to it. It has been a common experience in England for such persons to begin teaching the first steps by the SOL-FA method, and, becoming interested, they have gone on studying and teaching till they were led to devote themselves exclusively to music, and became among its most intelligent exponents and successful workers.

Try the system fairly. Do not omit the best points and fancy you know all about SOL-FA. The various devices and expedients presented in the system are not matters of theory, but the outgrowth of years of actual trial and experience by many of the best teachers of Great Britain.

It is important to state that the "TONIC SOL-FA MUSIC READER," is published with the full sympathy and approval of Mr. CURWEN, the founder of the system. The first steps were submitted to him for examination and were returned approved, with but few and unimportant changes. Since the recent death of Mr. CURWEN, his son, Mr. J. SPENCER CURWEN, who takes his place in directing the movement in England, has examined and approved the MS.

Orange, N. J.

THEO. F. SEWARD,
B. C. UNSELD.

PREFACE TO THE NEW EDITION.

When the Reader was first issued, in 1880, the TONIC SOL-FA system was almost unknown in America. It is now an acknowledged factor in our national education. Mr. Louis A. Russel, in the preface to his "Method of Solfeggio," says, "In America there has been no new thought or method in sight-singing for the last 20 years which cannot be traced more or less directly to Mr. Curwen's influence."

The advocates of the Staff Method cannot dismiss TONIC SOL-FA with a word, as they were able to do ten years ago. But their present attitude is, perhaps, as far as their influence extends, even more injurious to the interests of musical education. They freely acknowledge the merits of the system, but claim that its advantages can be secured by a direct application to the staff. This is a fatal fallacy. The blessing of TONIC SOL-FA to the world is in its notation. The devices which grow out of the notation can no more be educationally applied to the staff than the methods of modern arithmetic can be applied to the Roman system of numerals. The transforming power of TONIC SOL-FA is in its natural and philosophical method of representing the beautiful realities of the tone world.

The educational part of this book—the method proper—is drawn from Mr. CURWEN's various published works, but mainly from "The Standard Course." The authors claim no originality except in the manner of presentation. It has been prepared with great care, taking in every valuable point of the system, but rearranging and condensing for the special adaptation of the method to the musical needs of this country. The "Standard Course," which is Mr. CURWEN's most complete setting forth of the system, includes full instructions in vocal training, harmony, musical form, etc, etc. The "Tonic Sol-fa Music Reader" presents only the facts of time and tune, for the use of elementary classes. Part I, embracing the first four Steps of the method, contains the instructions and exercises needed to prepare pupils for the Junior and Elementary Certificates. Part II, embracing the Fifth and Sixth Steps and an introduction to the Staff notation, furnishes the material necessary for the preparation for the Intermediate Certificate. The two parts are also bound together in a complete edition.

New York, Jan., 1890.

THEO. F. SEWARD,
B. C. UNSELD.

The Certificates of the Tonic Sol-fa College.

Steps of the Method.

A great advantage of the Tonic Sol-fa method is that it is really a *system*, from beginning to end. One of the most useful features of the method is the arrangement of the course of instruction in a series of graded steps. The close of each step is intended as a point at which the work should be revised, and the standing of each pupil ascertained before proceeding to the next. Anything which is left dimly understood or imperfectly practiced in one step, is only a legacy of so much confusion, weakness and discouragement handed over to the next. How many *lessons* will be required to teach each step it is difficult to say, without knowing the kind of class. The teacher should be guarded against hurry rather than delay.

The Certificates.

The Tonic Sol-fa movement has been distinguished from all other efforts to promote music among the people by its System of Certificates, issued by the Tonic Sol-fa College of London. It is a complete system of examination upon an extensive scale. The special object of these certificates is to save the pupil from one-sidedness, and to secure an equality of progress in tune, time, memory, etc., as well as to promote private study and discipline at home. They insure an "all-roundness" of training and serve as a stimulus to the pupil. For the *true* pupil they find out (what he wants to know) his *weak places*, show him in what direction *self-teaching* is specially demanded, and give him the *confidence* of knowing that he has really and satisfactorily reached a certain stage. The ambition to obtain them promotes such an amount of home-work that it fully four-folds the work of the teacher.

American Tonic Sol-fa College.

The American Tonic Sol-fa Association and College of Music (Post office address, New York, N. Y.) was incorporated in 1889 under the laws of the State of New York. It acts in affiliation with the Tonic Sol-fa College of London, and its certificates are recognized as equivalent to its own. Information as to organization, postal courses, examinations, etc., may be obtained by writing to the above address.

Below are the requirements of the first two certificates.* The questions in Theory of the Second Grade are here omitted because of lack of space, but may be obtained from the College at 2 cents per copy, plus postage.

Manner of Teaching.

It is hardly necessary to say that the ways of presenting the various subjects in this book are not to be followed mechanically. They are illustrations of the manner in which the topics may be treated, but every teacher will have his own way of carrying out the details. See *Manual for Teachers of the School Series* (price, 12 cents, by mail) for other ways of teaching the various topics. One of the leading characteristics of this system is that so little time needs to be occupied with theory. "We learn to do by doing" is the grand motto of the Tonic Sol-faist. The new devices of the system—the Modulator, Manual Signs, Time-names, and even the doctrine of Mental Effects are all expedients for leading the student to *practice* more, to *think* more, to *remember* better; in other words, to increase his musical intelligence.

Requirements for the First Grade or Preparatory Certificate.

Examiners.—Those who hold the Second Grade or a higher certificate, with Theory, and who have been appointed to examine by the College of Music.

1. *Memory.*—Bring on separate slips of paper the names of three tunes, and *sol-fa* from memory, while pointing it on the modulator, one of these tunes chosen by lot.

2. *Time.—Taatai* once, and then *laa* on one tone in perfectly correct time, any of the rhythms Nos. 1, 3, 4, 5, 7, 9 or 11 (see pp. 107-8) which the Examiner may select. [Two attempts allowed; a different test to be given for the second trial.]

3. *Modulator.—Sol-fa* or *laa* from the Examiner's pointing on the modulator, a voluntary, moving at the rate of M.60, consisting of at least twenty-four tones, including leaps to any of the tones of the scale, but neither transition nor the minor mode.

4. *Tune.—Sol-fa* or *laa* at sight, from the tonic sol-fa notation, a phrase of eight tones, all in the common major scale, and no tones shorter than a pulse.

5. *Ear Test.*—The key-tone having been given, tell the sol-fa names of the tones of the Doh chord sung to *laa* or played in any order, also the phrases fah me and te, doh.

First Grade Musical Theory.

Answer any two or more of the following Questions, put by the Examiner:

1. Name the tones of the scale and their mental effects.

2. Name the tones of the Doh chord; of the Soh chord; of the Fah chord.

3. Name the little steps of the scale.

4. What is the time name of an undivided pulse?

5. What is the time name of a pulse divided into halves? into quarters?

6. Write in two-pulse measure an exercise of two measures: (*a*) In primary form. (*b*) In secondary form.

7. Write in three-pulse measure an exercise of two measures: (*a*) In primary form. (*b*) In secondary form.

Requirements for the Second Grade or Elementary Certificate.

Examiners.—Those who hold the Third Grade, or a higher certificate, with Theory, and who have been appointed to examine by the College of Music.

Before examination, Candidates must satisfy the Examiner that they hold the First Grade Certificate.

1. *Memory.*—Bring on separate slips of paper the names of six tunes, and *sol-fa* from memory, while pointing it on the modulator, one of these tunes chosen by lot.

2. *Time.—Taatai* at first sight and then *laa* in perfectly correct time, a test which may contain any of the quarter-pulse divisions. [Two attempts allowed; a different test to be given for the second trial.]

3. *Modulator.*—(*a*) Sing to *laa* to the Examiner's pointing on the modulator, a voluntary, including leaps to any of the tones of the scale, but neither transition nor the minor mode. (*b*) *Sol-fa* or *laa* a voluntary, containing transition of one remove in each direction.

4. *Tune.*—Pitch the key-tone by means of a given C; *sol-fa* once, then sing to *laa*, a sight test in tune containing leaps to any tones of the scale; but neither transition, nor minor mode, nor any divisions of time less than a full pulse.

Candidates may *laa* instead of *sol-faing* the test.

5. *Ear Test.*—Tell the notes of a phrase of three tones in smooth melodic progression. The Examiner will give the key-tone and sing the test to *laa*, or play it upon an instrument. [Two attempts allowed; a different test to be given for the second trial.]

The College will supply to the examiner the tests to be used in Nos. 2, 4 and 5

Note.—The registration fee for this Certificate is 15 cents, which is exclusive of Examiner's fee. Registration fee stamp may be purchased from the Examiner.

Mental Effects and Manual Signs of Tones in Key.

NOTE.—*The diagrams show the right hand as seen by pupils sitting in front of the teacher towards his left hand. The teacher makes his signs in front of his ribs, chest, face and head, rising a little as the tones go up, and falling as the tones go down.*

FIRST STEP.

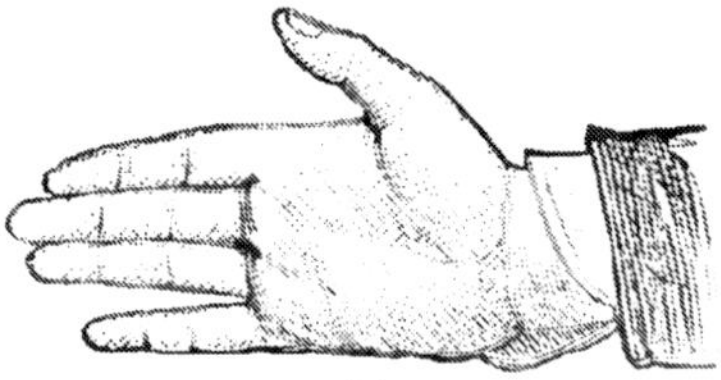

SOH.

The GRAND or *bright* tone.

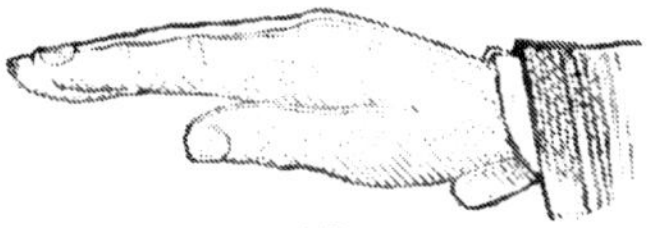

ME.

The STEADY or *calm* tone.

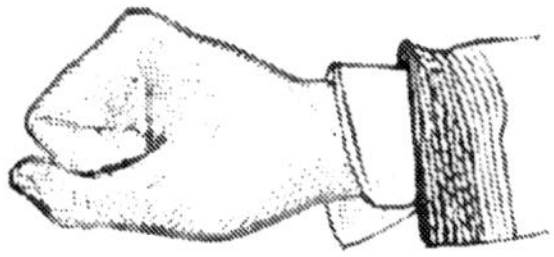

DOH.

The STRONG or *firm* tone.

SECOND STEP.

TE.

The PIERCING or *sensitive* tone.

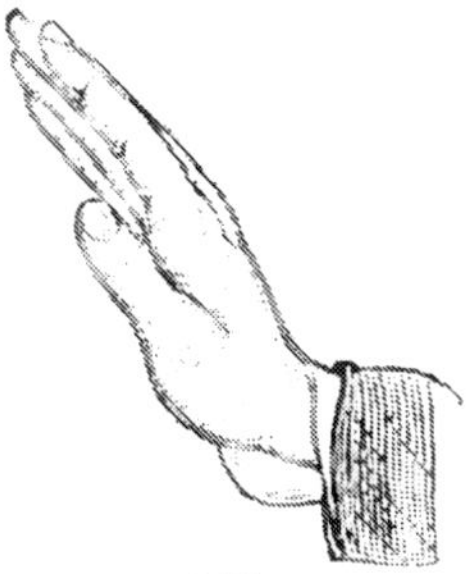

RAY.

The ROUSING or *hopeful* tone.

THIRD STEP.

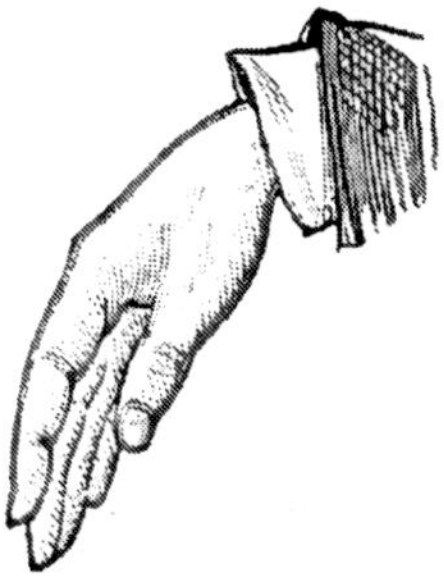

LAH.

The SAD or *weeping* tone.

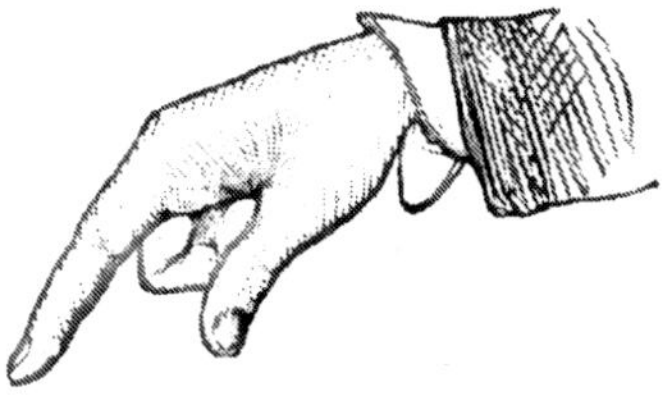

FAH.

The DESOLATE or *awe-inspiring* tone.

Mental Effects.—Some teachers are, at first, inclined to ignore this doctrine of the Sol-fa method, but it is a subject eminently worthy of the profoundest study. Mental effects are difficult to perceive because they *are* mental. Let not the teacher be discouraged if he does not at once grasp the whole matter. *The perception of mental effect is cumulative*, the more the subject is studied the plainer it becomes. The practice of teaching by mental effect has become so important in the Tonic Sol-fa method that the teacher cannot take too much pains to master it. *He should remember that these effects exist, whether he recognizes them or not*, and it is certainly wiser to utilize than to ignore them. The pamphlet "Studies in Mental Effects" furnishes a large variety of examples.

NOTE.—*These proximate verbal descriptions of mental effect are only true of the tones of the scale when sung slowly—when the ear is filled with the key, and when the effect is not modified by harmony.*

FINGER-SIGNS FOR TIME,

AS SEEN FROM THE PUPIL'S (NOT THE TEACHER'S) POINT OF VIEW.

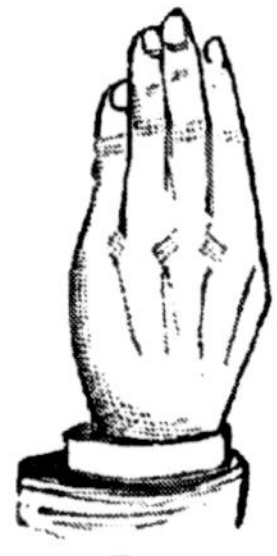

TAA.

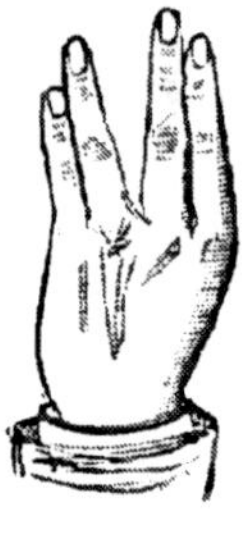

TAATAI.

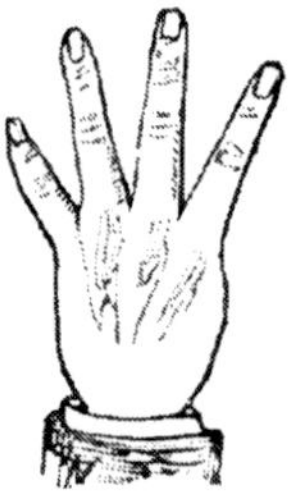

tafatefe.

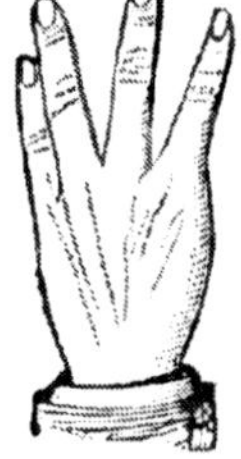

TAAtefe.

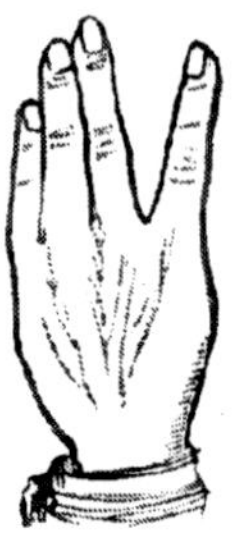

TAA-efe.

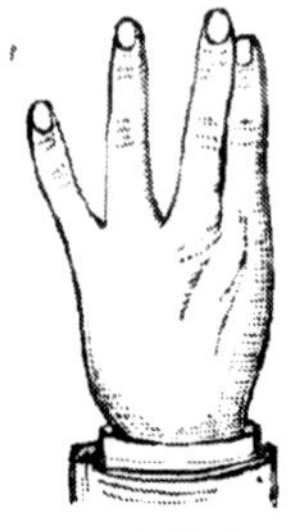

tafaTAI.

-AA.

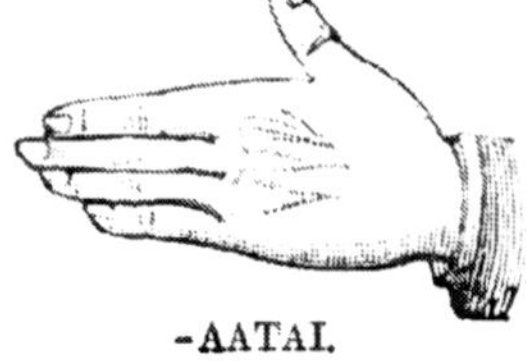

-AATAI.

SAA.

TAA*SAI.*

*SAA*TAI.

The Modulator, (see page 6). As the Sun is the centre of the Solar system so the Modulator is the centre of the Sol-fa system. The Modulator in the Tonic Sol-fa notation takes the place of the *Staff* in the common notation. It stands behind every note we see in the book. From habitual use of it, the Mind's eye always sees it there. It is our "pictorial symbol of tone relations." In the first steps it shows us the relations of tones in a single key, and at the fourth and other steps it shows the relations of keys to one another. A complete familiarity with the Modulator is of the utmost importance, for it is impossible to understand the notation properly until it is printed on the mind; in fact, until the letters of a tune become not merely a straight line, but "pointers" which at once carry the mind to the Modulator. It is to the Sol-fa singer what the key-board of the piano is to the player. It is not simply a diagram illustrating the intervals of the scale and related keys, to be used a few times and then laid aside. Its great value is in the means it affords for *drilling* the class on the tones of the scale. It will be observed that the syllables are spelled with the English sounds of letters instead of the Italian, as has heretofore been the usage. The open sound of *soh* is preferred to *sol* as being more vocal. The exchange of "te" for "se" (si) is a needed improvement for several reasons, viz.:—1. The use of the syllable "se" (si) twice, *i. e.*, as the seventh of the major scale and also of the minor. 2. The letter "s" has the most unpleasant sound in the language, and it should not occur more than once. 3. The change gives an additional consonant, and is useful for practice in articulation. 4. In the Sol-fa notation a different initial letter is needed for either *soh* or *se*.

NOTATION OF TIME.

The long heavy bar indicates a strong accent; the short, thin bar (|) a medium accent, and the colon (:) a weak accent.

Time is represented by the space between the accent marks. The space from one accent mark to the next represents a PULSE. (*Beat, or Part of the measure.*) The space between the strong accent marks (long bars) represents a measure.

TWO-PULSE MEASURE.	THREE-PULSE MEASURE.	FOUR-PULSE MEASURE.	SIX-PULSE MEASURE.
‖ : ‖	‖ : : ‖	‖ : | : ‖	‖ : : | : : ‖

The Tonic Sol-fa Method makes use of a system of *Time-names* to aid in the study of time. The Pulse is the unit of measurement, and a tone one pulse long is named TAA.

|d :d |d :d ‖
TAA TAA TAA TAA

The continuation of a tone through more than one pulse is indicated by a dash, and the time-name is obtained by dropping the consonant.

|d :d |d :— |d :— |— :— ‖
TAA TAA TAA - AA TAA - AA - AA - AA

A pulse divided into halves—half-pulse tones—is named TAATAI, and is indicated in the notation by a dot in the middle.
|d .d :d .d ‖
TAATAI TAATAI

A tone continued into the first half of the next pulse—a pulse-and-a half tone—is named and indicated thus:
|d :— .d ‖
TAA -AA TAI

A pulse divided into quarters is named *tafatefe*, and is represented by a comma in the middle of each half-pulse.
|d,d.d,d :d .d ‖
ta-fa-te-fe TAATAI

A pulse divided into a half and two quarters is named TAAtefe.
|d .d,d :d .d,d ‖
TAA - te-fe TAA - te-fe

A pulse divided into three quarters and a quarter is named TAA-efe, and is indicated by a dot and comma.
|d .,d :d .,d ‖
TAA -efe TAA -efe

Thirds of a pulse are named TAATAITEE, and represented by commas turned to the right.
|d ‘d ‘d :d ‘d ‘d ‖
taa-tai-tee taa-tai-tee

Silences (Rests) are named by substituting the letter S for T or t, thus—a full pulse silence is named *SAA*; a half pulse silence is named *SAA* on the first half of a pulse and *SAI* on the second half. Quarter pulse silences are named *sa* on the first half and *se* on the second. Silences are indicated by the absence of notes in the pulse divisions, *i. e.* vacant space.

|d : ‖
TAA *SAA*

|d . : .d ‖
TAA *SAI SAA* TAI

|d,d.d, : ,d.d,d ‖
ta-fa-te-*se* *sa*-fa-te-fe

THE MODULATOR.

NOTE.—AA has the sound of *a* in *father*; AI, as in *aid*; *e*, as in *effect*.

Minuter divisions of the pulse, sixths, eighths, ninths, are seldom used except in instrumental music. In the Sol fa notation no distinction is made between $\frac{2}{4}$, $\frac{2}{2}$, $\frac{3}{4}$, $\frac{3}{2}$ etc., there being but one way of writing the different *varieties* of measure.

THE TONIC SOL-FA MUSIC READER.

PART I.—INSTRUCTIONS AND EXERCISES IN THE FIRST, SECOND, THIRD AND FOURTH STEPS. COVERING THE JUNIOR AND ELEMENTARY CERTIFICATES.

FIRST STEP.

To recognize and produce the tones Doh, Me, Soh, the upper octave of Doh and the lower octave of Soh. To recognize and produce the strong and weak accent, and the simplest divisions of time, viz.—the Pulse, the half pulse, two pulse measure and three pulse measure.

The first lesson may begin by practicing a familiar tune, or by a few appropriate remarks by the teacher, after which he may say—

You may listen to me and be ready to sing the examples I give you.

He sings a tone which he considers in his own mind as *Doh*, the first tone of the scale, at about the pitch of D or E, clearly and firmly to the syllable *laa*.

You may all sing it.—

The Dash ——— will signify that a command is obeyed or a question answered. It may be necessary to repeat the example several times before the voices blend well.

NOTE.—The teacher should never sing *with* his pupils, but give examples or patterns carefully which they are to imitate. They should listen while he sings, and he listen while they sing. Mr Curwen says, "The first art of the pupil is to *listen well*. He that listens best, sings best." After this tone is sung correctly, the teacher may say—

Listen to me again.—

He now sings a tone a fifth higher, *Soh*, the fifth tone of the scale, to the syllable *laa*. The pupils imitate.

Now sing these two tones, after me, just as I sing them.

He sings the two tones in succession, to laa, in any order he chooses, but varies the manner of producing them, making them sometimes loud, sometimes soft, long or short, *changing the pitch of Doh frequently*, sometimes singing C and G, sometimes E and B, or D and A, etc., the pupils imitating each pattern. See examples below—Exs. 1 to 4.

SOH

We will now learn the names of these two tones.—
The lower tone is called *Doh*—What is it called?—
The upper tone is called *Soh*—What is it called?

NOTE.—In giving out a new fact or principle the teacher should always question the pupils, that they may not only hear it stated but be led to state it themselves. The teacher as he gives the names writes or "prints" them on the blackboard, *Soh* above *Doh*, leaving considerable space between them.

DOH

Now we will sing the tones to their names; repeat after me the tones I give you.

The following exercises are specimens of patterns which the teacher may give. The upright lines indicate how much of each exercise may be given as a pattern. The horizontal dash— shows that the tone should be prolonged.

1. KEYS D, F AND C.

|d d d — |s s s — |d d . s s d — ||

2.

|s s s — |d d d — |s s d s d ||

3.

|d d s — |s s d — |d d s s d ||

4.

|d — s — d — |s — d — s s d — ||

You may now sing as I point to the names on the blackboard and without a pattern from me.

They sing, to his pointing, exercises similar to those given above.

Sing again as I point, but this time sing the tones to laa.

He points to the names, they sing to laa. In all these exercises the teacher will frequently change his keytone, lest the pupils be tempted to try to sing by *absolute pitch* instead of giving their attention to the *relation* of tones.

Now I will sing *Doh* and you may sing the *Soh* to it.

He sings *Doh* and then gives them a signal to sing *Soh*.

I will take a different *Doh* and you may give me the *Soh* to it.

He takes a different pitch for *Doh* and they sing the *Soh* to it. This he does several times, always changing the keytone.

You may now name the tones as I sing them, I will sing to laa, and when I sing the lower tone, say *Doh* and when I sing the upper tone say *Soh*.

He sings the two tones in various successions, the pupils

calling out "Doh," "Soh," etc It may be well for him to sing each tone several times and not to change too quickly—for instance d d d d s s s d d s s d s d s s d, etc

Name them once more, and if I sing a different tone from these two, one that is neither *Doh* nor *Soh*, you may say *New-tone*

He sings as before, the class calling out the names, and after keeping them a little while in expectation, he sings the third tone of the scale—*Me*—(of course, to *laa*), which the pupils at once detect It is better to let the new tone come in after *Soh*, thus, d—s—m

Is the new tone higher or lower than *Doh?*	
Is it higher or lower than *Soh?*	SOH
The name of the new tone is *Me*	
What is its name?	ME
Where shall I write it on the board?	
See diagram	DOH
Imitate the patterns I give you	

He patterns the following, or similar examples, singing to the names, which the pupils repeat A narrower type and somewhat altered form is given to the letter m (m), for convenience in printing

5. KEYS D, F AND C.

|d s m — |m s d — |d s m s d ||

6.

|d m d — |s m s — |m d m — |m s m — ||

7.

|s d m — |m d s — |s s m s d ||

8.

|d m s — |s m d — |d s m d ||

Now sing as I point

The teacher should drill the class thoroughly on these three tones, singing them first to the names and afterward to laa

The pitch should be changed frequently

Thus far we have been studying the names and relative positions of these three tones, but now I want to call your attention to the most important and most interesting thing about them, and that is their characters, or the effects or impressions they produce upon the mind One of them is a strong, firm tone, another is a bright, clear grand tone, and another is a gentle, peaceful, calm tone I want you to find out the character of each tone for yourselves You may listen to me and, as I sing, give your attention specially to *Doh*, and then tell me which of these characters it has, whether it is calm and peaceful, or clear and grand, or strong and firm

Teacher sings the following phrases or something similar, bringing out strongly the character of *Doh*

|d :— |d .d |m .m |d — |d .m |s .m |s :s |d̍ :— ||

Is *Doh* calm and peaceful, or clear and grand, or strong and firm?

Now listen to *Soh* and tell me what character it has.

Teacher sings the following phrase:

|d .d |m .d |s .s |s .— |s .m |d .m |s :s |s :— ||

What kind of a tone is *Soh?*

Now listen to *Me*

Teacher sings the following phrase

:d |m .d |m :s |m :— |m .m |s :m |d .s |m :— ||

What is the character of *Me?*

What kind of tone is *Doh?*—*Soh?* *Me?*

I call your attention to these characters or mental effects of the tones not as a mere matter of curiosity, but as a real help in singing them As you try to sing a tone, think of its mental effect and that will help you to sing it correctly

Let us now learn to sing the tones from signs representing their mental effects The strong, firm tone is represented by the closed hand thus, (see manual signs). All make it

What kind of a tone is indicated by this sign?

What is its name?

The bright, clear, grand tone is represented by the open hand thus— All make it

What kind of a tone does this sign indicate?

What is its name?

And this sign (open hand, palm downwards), represents the calm, peaceful tone All make it

What kind of a tone is indicated by this sign?

And this?—and this?—etc, etc, etc

Give me the sign for the strong tone

The sign for the grand tone

The sign for the calm tone—Grand tone.—Strong tone, etc

You may sing the tones as I indicate them by the signs Think of their mental effects as you sing them

The teacher will give a good drill with the hand signs, pupils singing to the sol-fa names and also to laa

Listen to me and when I sing the grand tone, instead of telling me its name, you may give me its sign

Teacher sings the tones to laa, and each time he sings *soh* the pupils make the sign

Now give me the sign for the calm tone when you hear it.

Teacher sings as directed above, pupils make the sign.

Now give the sign for the strong tone

Teacher and pupils as directed as above

Now give the sign for each tone as I sing

Teacher sings to laa, pupils giving the sign for each tone

I will indicate the tones in yet another way. I will let d stand for *Doh*, m for *Me* and s for *Soh*

Teacher writes the following exercise or a similar one

d d s s m m d

You may sing the lesson as written and you will be singing from the Tonic Sol-fa Notation.

The following exercises may now be written upon the board and practiced, or they may be sung from the book—first to the syllables and then to laa "Key C," "Key G," etc, will tell the teacher where to pitch his *Doh*. Although there is no indication of time in these exercises, they all have a melodic form and should be sung with a rhythmic flow They may be sung as fast or as slow as the teacher likes, he can indicate the time by gentle taps on the table

9. KEY D.

d d m d m m s m s s m m s m d

10. KEY F.

d m s s m d s s m m s s m s d

11. KEY C.

d s m s d d m s m d m m s m d

12. KEY E.

s m d m s s s m s m d m s s d

13. KEY G.

m d s m m d s m m m s s m s d

14. KEY E.

m m m d m m m s m m s m d m d

15. KEY C.

d s m d m d s m d m d s m s d

16. KEY D.

d m s m s m d s m s d s d m d

The upper octave of *Doh* may now be taught by the same process as that used for *Me* When the pupils have discovered the new tone the teacher may proceed as follows

Is the new tone higher or lower than *Doh?*

Is it higher or lower than *Me?*

Higher or lower than *Soh?*

The name of the new tone is *Doh*. What is its name?

You may think it strange that we have two tones with the same name, but it will be explained a little later in the course

NOTE—The nature of octaves can be better explained after the complete scale has been taught

Where shall I write it on the board?

I need not write it in full; the first letter will be sufficient.

Teacher writes a d in the proper place

In writing, the Upper *Doh* is indicated by the figure 1 placed at the top of the letter thus, d^1, and is called *One-Doh* While we are practicing this new tone I want you to be thinking about its mental effect, compare the Upper *Doh* with the lower and notice whether it has the same effect, or if it is stronger or firmer.

Let the new tone be practiced in connection with the others, first by patterns from the teacher, and then from the teacher's pointing Then let the teacher by questioning develop the fact that its mental effect is the same as the lower *doh*, only stronger or more positive The manual sign for d^1 is the same as for d with the hand raised The following exercises are given as specimen patterns for the teacher Sing them first to the sol-fa syllables, and afterwards to laa.

d^1

SOH

ME

DOH

Exercise 17 consists of short phrases, intended as patterns, to be given by the teacher.

17. KEYS C AND D.

| d m s d^1 | d^1 s m d | d^1 s d^1 — | d^1 s m — | m d^1 s — | s m d^1 — |

| d^1 m s — | s d^1 m — | m d d^1 — | d^1 d m — | m d^1 d | d d^1 s m d |

After a thorough drill upon the tones by pattern, from the Modulator, Hand-Signs, and so on, the following exercises may be written upon the blackboard and practiced or they may be sung from the book.

18. KEY D.

d d m m d m s s d^1 d^1 s m s m d

19. KEY C.

d s m s d^1 s d^1 s m m s s m s d^1

20. KEY C.

d^1 s m m d^1 m s s d^1 m s m s d^1 d

21. KEY D.

d m s d^1 d^1 s s m d m s m d^1 s d

d^1

SOH

ME

DOH

s_1

The teacher may now explain the lower octave of *Soh* by simply stating that as we have an Upper *Doh*, so we may also have a Lower *Soh*. It is indicated in the notation by the figure 1 placed at the bottom of the letter thus s_1, and is called *Soh-One*. Its mental effect is the same, only somewhat subdued. The hand sign for s_1 is the same as for s with the hand lowered. Let *Soh-One* be practiced after the same manner as that pursued with the *One-Doh*, only taking a higher pitch for the key tone.

The following exercises are patterns for the teacher

22. KEYS F, A and G.

| d s_1 d — | d m s_1 d | d s_1 m d |

| d m s s_1 d | d s_1 s m d |

The class is now ready to practice the following exercises.

23. KEY F.

d s_1 d m s s m d d s_1 d m s s_1 d

24. KEY A.

d d m d s_1 s_1 m d m m s m d s_1 d

25. KEY G.

m m d s_1 s s m d s m d s_1 m s_1 d

26. KEY F.

s s m d s_1 s_1 m d s s m d s_1 s d

TIME AND RHYTHM.

NOTE.—The Tonic Sol fa treatment of the subject of Time (Rhythmics), differs essentially from that which has usually prevailed in this country. Here the *measure* has been regarded as the standard or unit. In the Sol-fa method, the *pulse*, which corresponds to our *beat* or *part of the measure*, is treated as the unit, and time is measured by a regular recurrence of accent. This is undoubtedly the true philosophy. In fact some prominent teachers in this country have already developed this theory in their later works. There are several ways in which this subject may be presented to a class. The following will serve as an illustration of one way, which the teacher may vary, or condense or enlarge as he may deem best. For another method, see *Teacher's Manual of the Tonic Sol fa School Series*, published by Biglow & Main.

Listen to me, I will sing a familiar tune, and as I sing I wish you to observe that their will occur in your minds, at regular intervals, a throb or pulsation of some kind that keeps time with the music.

The teacher sings to laa a familiar tune, such as "Haste thee, Winter,"—

|d :d |s :s |l .l |s :— |f .f |m :m |r :r |d :— || etc

or "Vesper Hymn,"—

|m :s |f .s |m .s |r :s |m :s |f :r |d :t_1 |d :— ||

bringing out the strong accent.

Those who noticed the throbs or pulsations may hold up hands.

I will sing again and will indicate these pulsations by taps upon the table, and you may indicate them by some motion of your hands.

He sings again, giving a tap for each *strong* accent, the pupils making, perhaps, a downward motion of the hand.

These throbs or heavy tones are called accents. What are they called?

I will sing again and you will notice that after each of these accents there occurs a second pulsation, but of less force.

He sings again, giving a heavy tap for the strong accent and a light tap for each weak accent.

How many noticed the light throbs?

The heavy pulsations are called strong accents, and the light ones are called weak accents.

How many kinds of accents have we?

I will sing again and you may indicate every accent, strong or weak, by some motion of your hand.

The pupils may be directed to make a downward motion for the strong accent and an upward motion for the weak accent. These motions are not absolutly essential and they are not intended as an exercise in beating time, but merely as a means for the pupils to show to the teacher that they recognize the accents.

Listen again—this time I will occasionally stop singing to show you that the accents may go on in the mind without the music.

In this exercise the teacher will occasionally stop singing for a measure or two but keeps on tapping in regular time.

I will now show you that the accents will move quickly or slowly as the music goes fast or slow.

Teacher illustrates this.

You learn from all these examples that time in music is measured by regularly recurring accents.

How is time measured in music?

The time from one strong accent to the next strong accent is called a Measure.

What is it called?

What is a Measure?

The time from any accent, strong or weak, to the next is called a Pulse.

What is it called? What is a Pulse?

Listen to me.

He sings a number of measures to laa, two tones to each measure, accenting distinctly, thus, LAA *laa*, LAA *laa* etc.

After each strong pulse how many weak pulses were there?

Yes, they were regularly STRONG, *weak*, STRONG, *weak*, etc.

Listen again.

This time he accents the first in every three, thus, LAA *laa laa*, LAA *laa laa*, etc.

How many weak pulses followed each strong pulse?

Yes, they were regularly STRONG, *weak*, *weak*, STRONG, *weak*, *weak*, etc.

Different arrangements of the order of accents make different kinds of measure.

What makes different kinds of measure?

A measure consisting of two pulses, one strong and one weak, is called Two-pulse measure. What is it called?

A measure consisting of three pulses, one STRONG and two *weak*, is called Three-pulse measure. What is it called?

Listen to me, and tell me which kind of measure you hear.

Teacher sings a number of measures to laa, accenting distinctly, changing occasionally from two-pulse to three-pulse measure and back again, the pupils calling out "two-pulse," "three-pulse," at each change. Or he may sing a familiar tune in each kind of measure and require the pupils to tell which kind of measure the tune is in.

NOTE.—In the Standard Course of the Tonic Sol fa Method the pupils are not taught to beat time until the Fourth Step. Mr Curwen says—"Pupils should not be allowed to "beat" time until they have gained *a sense* of time * * * Because no one can well learn two things at once, and, consequently those who try to do so are constantly found beating to their singing instead of singing to an independent, steady beat * * * *Beating* time can be of no use—is only a burden to the pupil in *keeping* time, till it has become almost automatical, until 'the time beats itself' " and you know that your beating *will* go right whatever becomes of the voice. Then, and not till then, the beating becomes *an independent test* of the singing."

American teachers however, are so accustomed to teaching counting and beating time from the beginning that the teacher may introduce it here if he prefers—not as a test in singing but as a separate exercise as a means or a help in developing the sense of time In two pulse measure the countings are *one* two, *one* two etc , and the motions of the hand are *down* up *down* up, etc In three pulse measure the countings are *one* two three, *one* two three, etc , and the motions are *down* left up, *down* left up, etc or *down* right up, etc

In practicing exercises in time it is useful to have names for the different lengths The time-name of a tone one pulse long is TAA

The "AA" is pronounced as "a" in father

You may sing in two-pulse measure, one tone to each pulse, thus TAA TAA, TAA TAA, etc

If preferred by the teacher, the syllable TRAA may be used for the strong accent Let this be kept going until all get into the "swing" of the rhythm—alternate measures may then be sung by the teacher and class, or by two divisions of the class, being careful to keep a steady rate of movement Then let it be done with a different rate

Let us try two pulse measure again, but this time begin with the weak pulse, thus, TAA TAA, TAA TAA, etc

Let this be practiced as above

When the measure begins with a strong pulse it is called the Primary Form of the measure What is it called?

When is a measure in the Primary Form?

When the measure begins with a weak pulse it is called the Secondary Form What is it called? When is a measure in the Secondary Form?

Three pulse measure may next be practiced with the same process as that just given to the two pulse measure, or it may be deferred until later

I will now write a number of pulses on the blackboard and you may sing them as I direct

Teacher writes thus —

TAA TAA TAA TAA TAA TAA TAA TAA

You may sing them in two-pulse measure commencing with a strong pulse —

Teacher indicates the time by a gentle tap of the pointer on each pulse

Again, commencing with a weak pulse

Teacher, if he chooses, may have them sung in three pulse measure

You see that as the exercise now stands there is nothing on the board to tell us which are the strong and which are the weak pulses In the Sol-fa notation an upright bar (|) shows that the pulse following it is to have the strong accent; the weak accent is indicated by two dots ( ) and the Double Bar (||) shows the end.

Teacher while he is making the above statement inserts the accent marks as follows —

| TAA TAA | TAA :TAA | TAA TAA | TAA .TAA ||

What does the bar indicate?

How is the weak accent indicated?

What does the double bar show?

The accent marks are placed at equal distances of space and thus represent the equal divisions of time

The space from one accent mark to the next, strong or weak, represents the time of a pulse, and the space between the bars represents the time of a measure

What represents the time of a pulse?

What represents the time of a measure?

You may now sing the exercise as written

After it is sung correctly, at different rates of movement, the teacher will write an exercise, beginning with the weak pulse, thus —

TAA | TAA TAA | TAA TAA | TAA TAA | TAA ||

Let this be practiced at different rates of movement from the teacher's patterns Then each exercise should be sung to laa, teacher writing an "l" under each *laa* Then erasing the "ls" and putting a d in each pulse, sing *doh* Then again with the following or similar successions

TAA .TAA	TAA ·TAA	TAA TAA	TAA TAA	
d d	s s	m m	d d	

Teacher will next erase the Sol-fa notes, leaving the taas

I will sing the exercise, and if I make a mistake, you may say wrong

Teacher sings it the first time correctly, second time with wrong accent, and the third time he makes a mistake in the second measure—prolonging the tone through both pulses, at which the pupils will say "wrong"

Which measure was wrong?

How many tones are indicated in the second measure?

How many did I sing?

Was it a long tone or a short tone? How long was it?

Yes, I continued the tone through the second pulse—made it two pulses long It is called a two-pulse tone. What is it called?

When a tone is continued from one pulse to the next the continuation is indicated by a horizontal line, thus, — The time-name for continuations is obtained by dropping the consonant, thus, TAA-AA

The teacher, as he makes these statements, changes the second and fourth measure so they appear thus —

| TAA TAA | TAA : -AA | TAA TAA | TAA : -AA ||

Teacher pointing to the continuation mark, asks —

What does this horizontal line indicate?

How are the time-names for continuations obtained?

How long must this tone be?

What is the time-name of a two-pulse tone?

A convenient short name for two-pulse tones is Twos What will be a good short name for one-pulse tones?

In the lesson now on the blackoard what kind of tones are required in the first and third measures? *Ones*

In the second and fourth? *Twos*

I will sing the lesson first and then you may try it.

If the pupils fail to prolong the tones their full length, the vowel AI (as in "aid") may be added thus, | TAA-AI -AA-AI. When the lesson has been sung correctly to the time-names and at different rates, it should be sung to laa, the teacher indicating laa by an l under the time-names

Then he may change the measures so as to obtain the following or similar rhythms Each exercise should be sung several times—to the time-names to laa—and at different rates of speed They may also be sung in tune, the teacher writing the Sol-fa letters under the time names as has been already suggested

27.

|TAA TAA |TAA TAA |TAA -AA |TAA -AA ||
|l :l |l :l |l :— |l :— ||

28.

|TAA -AA |TAA TAA |TAA TAA |TAA -AA ||
|l :— |l :l |l :l |l :— ||

29.

|l :— |l :— |l :l |l :— ||

30.

|l :— |l :l |l :— |— :— ||

31.

:l |l :l |l :l |l :— |— ||

32.

:l |l :— |l :l |l :— |— ||

It is not important to *dwell* on the *secondary* forms of the measure or on three-pulse measure at this point. To practice three-pulse measure the teacher will write the following exercise on the board

| TAA TAA TAA | TAA TAA TAA | TAA TAA TAA | TAA TAA TAA |

Let it be sung with clear accent to the time-names and to the laa, then the teacher will change the measures so as to obtain the following rhythms Each exercise should be sung to the time-names, to laa, etc

33.

|TAA TAA TAA |TAA -AA -AA |TAA TAA TAA |TAA -AA -AA ||
|l :l :l |l :— :— |l :l :l |l :— :— ||

34.

|l :l :l |l :— :l |l :l :l |l :— :— ||

35.

|l :— :l |l :— :l |l :l :l |l :— :— ||

36.

:l |l :l :l |l :— :l |l :l :l |l :— ||

The pupils are now prepared to take up the following lessons. It will be observed that here is an abundance of exercises, but the teacher must not feel compelled to dwell upon *all* that are here given,he selects only such as his class may require. A bright, smart class may sing through all of these exercises to advantage, while a dull, slow class will positively need them.

Two-part Singing. It is at first very difficult for pupils to sing independently one of another. The simplest form of two-part singing is that in which one divison of the class repeatedly strikes the same tone ("tolls the bell"), while another divison sings the tune as in exercise 37. Each part should be sung seperately by all the class before singing the two together. These early exercises are best suited for those classes in which the voices are all of the same sort, that is, all men's voices, or else all woman's or children's voices. If, however, the class is a mixed one, the ladies may take one part and the gentlemen the other, or, better still, half the gentlemen and half the ladies may sing each part. As soon as an exercise is sung, it should be sung over again, exchanging the parts.

The teacher will explain that Braces are used both at the beginning and ending of lines to show what parts of the music may be sung together.

The teacher may explain that music is naturally divided into short portions or *phrases*. Just before beginning a phrase is, *musically considered*, the best place to take breath. Where words are sung, the breath must be taken with reference to the sense of the words. More on this subject in the following steps. The dagger (†) shows where breath may be taken.

37. KEY D.

d :d	m :m	s :s	m :—	† d' :d'	s :m	s :s	d :—
d :d	d :d	d :d	d :—	d :d	d :d	d :d	d :—

38. KEY D.

d :m	s :m	s :m	d' :—	† d' :s	m :s	s :m	d :—
d :d	d :—	m :m	m :—	m :m	m :m	d :d	d :—

39. KEY F.

d :—	m :—	s :s	m :—	† m :—	d :—	s :m	d :—
d :d	d :d	m :m	d :—	d :d	m :d	s_1 :s_1	d :—

40. KEY C.

d :d	m :m	s :s	d' :s	† d' :s	m :—	† m :s	d :—
Great and	good is	God our	Fa - ther,	Great and	good,	great and	good.
Trees and	birds and	flow'rs de -	clare Him	Great and	good,	great and	good.
d :d	d :d	m :m	m :m	m :m	d :—	d :m	d :—

41. KEY D. Round for four parts.

d' :s	m :d	m :s	d' :d'	† * s :s	s :s	s :—	s :— †
Join in	sing - ing	Hal - le -	lu - jah!	Hal - le -	lu - jah!	A - -	men.
m :—	m :—	† m :m	m :m	d :m	s :m	d :—	d :—
A - -	men,	Hal - le -	lu - jah!	Hal - le -	lu - jah!	A - -	men.

When the first division reaches the note under the asterisk (*) the second division strikes in at the beginning; the third division begins when the second has reached the asterisk, and so on

42. Key D.

				†				
d :d :d	m :m :m	d :m :s	d' :— :—	d' :d' :d'	s :s :s	d' :s :m	d :— :—	‖
d :d :d	d :— :—	m :m :m	m :— :—	m :m :m	m :— :—	m :m :m	d :— :—	‖

43. Key C.

		†		†				
d :d :d	m :— :—	m :m :m	s :— :—	s :s :s	d' :d' :d'	s :s :s	d :— :—	‖
d :— :d	d :— :—	d :— :d	m :— :—	m :— :m	m :— :m	m :— :m	d :— :—	‖

44. Key G. Round in four parts.

:s,	d :— :d	s, :— :s, *	m :— :m	d :— :m
Now	sing a	loud, your	voic - - es	raise ! To

s :m :d	s :m :d	s, :— :s,	d :—	‖
join in the	cho - rus of	grate - - - ful	praise.	

Half-pulse Tones may now be taught, or if the teacher prefers, they may be transfered to the next step.

The following lesson may be written on the board,

|1 :1 |1 :1 |1 :1 |1 :1 ‖

and after it is sung correctly the teacher may say:

I will sing the lesson and if I make a mistake you may say wrong.

He may sing it correctly the first time; with wrong accent the second, and the third time he sings two tones in the first pulse of the second measure at which the pupils will say "wrong."

Which measure was wrong?

Which pulse of that measure?

How many tones are indicated in that pulse?

How many did I sing?

Two tones sung in the time of one pulse are called Half-pulse Tones or Halves.

What are they called?

The time-name of the first half is Taa—of the second half Tai. What is the time-name of the first half? Second half?

The sign for an equally divided pulse is a dot in the middle, thus, | . :

The teacher changes the measures to obtain the following rhythms. They should be practiced carefully—from the teacher's patterns—to the time-names—to laa, etc.

The Finger Signs for time (Taa, Taatai and Taa-aa) may be introduced here with good effect. These signs are generally given with the left hand, to distinguish them from the Hand Signs for Tune, which are chiefly given with the right. Of course the teacher may use his right hand if he finds it easier. The back of the hand is toward the pupils, and the thumb should not be seen, for we never divide a pulse into five equal parts. The time may be marked either by slight forward and backward movements of the hand, or by the right hand tapping the pulses on the top of the left or beating Time in the regular way close by.

The Time Chart also affords a most excellent means for drilling a class in time. It is to Time what the modulator is to Tune.

45.

Taa Taa	Taa - tai Taa	Taa Taa	Taa -aa	
1 :1	1 .1 :1	1 :1	1 :—	‖

46. Key D.

Taa Taa	Taa - tai Taa	Taa - tai Taa - tai	Taa -aa	
1 :1	1 .1 :1	1 .1 :1 .1	1 :—	‖
d :m	s .s :m	s .s :m .m	d :—	‖
d :s	m .s :d	m .d :s .m	d :—	‖

47. KEY F.

TAA - TAI TAA	TAA - TAI TAA	TAA - TAI TAA - TAI	TAA - TAI TAA
l .l :l	l .l :l	l .l :l .l	l .l :l
s_1 .d :d	s_1 .d :d	s .m :s .m	d .d :d

Taatai-ing in tune.—By "taataing" is meant singing an exercise (on one tone) to the time-names, just as "Sol-fa-ing" is singing to the Sol-fa syllables. "Taataing in tune" is singing the *tune* to the time names. Mr. Curwen says, "*Laaing* on *one* tone helps to form that *abstract* idea of a rhythm which is desired. But such an idea is never truly established until the ear can recognize a rhythm as the *same*, though all the various *disguises* which different tune-forms put upon it. To learn the abstract you must recognize it in *many* concretes * * * As a help to this distinct conception of rhythm, it is useful to *taatai* each time-exercise on various tune-forms."

After the above time-exercises have been sung to the time-names and to laa, let them be sung to the *tunes* printed under each, and lastly let the tunes be sung to the time names.

Exercises 48 to 52 introduce half-pulse tones in two-pulse measure. Each exercise should be *taataid* on one tone to secure correct rhythm.

48. KEY D.

d .m :m	d .m :m	s :s	m :—	m .s :s	m .s :s	d^1 :s	d^1 :—
d :d	d :d	d .m :m	d :—	m :m	m :m	m .s :s	m :—

49. KEY C.

d :d	m :d	s .s :m .s	d^1 :—	† d^1 .s :m .s	d^1 :m	s :s	d :—
d :d .d	d :d .d	m .m :m .m	m † :m .m	m :m .m	d :d .d	m .m :s .s	d :—

50. KEY D.

d .d :d .d	m .m :m .m	s .m :d .m	s :—	m .m :m .m	s .s :s .s	d^1 .s :m .s	d :—
d .d :d .d	d .d :d .d	m .m :m .m	s :—	d .d :d .d	m .m :m .m	m .m :m .m	d :—

51. KEY G. Round in four parts. T. F. S.

d .d :d .d	d .d :d .d	* m .m :m .m	m .m :m .m
What a clat - ter!	What's the mat - ter!	John-ny's gone and	spilt the bat - ter
s .s :s .s	s :s_1	s :s_1	s :—
On my nice new	clothes, oh,	dear! oh,	dear!

52. KEY G. Round in three parts.

d :d	s_1 :s_1	m :—	d :—	* m :m	d :d	s :—	m :—
Roam-ing	o - ver	mead -	ows,	Sing - ing	ev - er	gai - -	ly,

s .s :s .s	s :s	s_1 .s_1 :s_1 .s_1	s_1 :s_1
Tra la la la	la la,	Tra la la la	la la.

Modulator Voluntaries.—At every lesson the teacher should drill the class in following his pointing on the Modulator, *without a pattern.* This exercise is called a *Voluntary.* The pupils must be taught to follow promptly, and to hold the tones as long as the pointer stays on a note. The teacher must be careful not to vary from the "Step" at which the class is engaged; that is, in the first step he must use only the tones **d m s d' s,**; in the second step he may use the tones **d m s t r** and their replicates, but not **f** and **l**. The *Step Modulators* are recommended for the early work, as they prevent the teacher going out of the step in which the class is studying. The teacher must follow his own fancy in his voluntaries, taking care to adapt them to the capacity of his class, not to make them too difficult nor too easy, but progressive as his pupils gain facility. He should make them as beautiful and attractive as he can, introducing snatches of familiar tunes now and then; and above all things he must avoid falling into self-repeating habits, that is, constantly repeating favorite phrases which the pupils come to know by heart. The teacher is recommended to *practice* his voluntaries at home; write them down, if necessary, and commit them to memory. See the pamphlet, "Hints for Voluntaries."

The Time Chart is intended to be used for *time-voluntaries* in the same way that the Modulator is used for tune-voluntaries.

The Hand-Signs, in connection with mental effects, are to be used at every lesson. *The Finger-Signs for Time* are also considered very useful for exercises in time.

Mental Effects should be frequently reviewed, accompanied with fresh illustrations. It is only in this way the impression can be deepened. The perception of mental effect is at first very dim, but it is cumulative, and the more attention given to it the clearer and stronger it becomes. See pamphlet, "Studies in Mental Effects."

Ear Exercises.—At every lesson the teacher will exercise his class in naming the tones he sings. There are several ways in which this may be done. First way, teacher sings several tones to figures and requires the pupil to tell him to which figure or figures he sung **s** or **m**, etc. Thus, "Tell me to which figure I sing **s**"—

Sings **d m m s d**— or **d d m d s m d**— or **m d s m**, etc.
1 2 3 4 5 — 1 2 3 4 5 6 7 — 1 2 3 4

"Tell me to which figure I sing **d**"—

Sings **s m s d m**— or **m s d m d s m**, etc.
1 2 3 4 5 — 1 2 3 4 5 6 7

The same process is given to other tones. Another way, the teacher sings the tones to laa and the pupils make the manual sign for the tone required. Again, the teacher gives the key-tone and chord and after a slight pause sings to *laa, lo, loo, lai* or any vowel either **d m s d'** or **s,** and requires the pupils to tell him what tone he sung, thus:—

|d :— |s :m |d :— |s (loo) :— ||

Again, the teacher sings to laa and the pupils name or give the hand signs for all the tones. Again, the teacher sings two or three or four or more tones to laa, as, **d m d s**, etc., which the pupils repeat after him, first to laa, then to the Sol-fa syllables. When the pupils can do this quite readily they will then be required to simply give the names without singing the tones. The teacher may then sing to different vowels, as,

s m s d
lo lo lai laa

and the pupils give the names.

In *time* ear-exercises the teacher sings two, three or four measures on one tone to laa, and requires the pupils to tell him the length of the tones in each measure, or they may *Taatai* or write what the teacher sings. Again the teacher *sol-fas* a short exercise which the pupils *taatai in tune.* It is a great advantage when the answers to these ear-exercises can be *written* by the pupils and afterward examined by the teacher or his assistants. The answers should come from *all* the pupils, not merely from a few. See pamphlet, "Hints for Ear Exercises."

Writing Exercises.—Notation is best taught by writing, and the thing *noted* is more quickly and easily practiced when the notation is clear and familiar to the mind. Hence the value of the writing exercises. The teacher instructs his pupils to draw on slate or paper four (or eight or sixteen) measures in the primary (or secondary) form, thus:—

| : | : | : | : | etc., or : | : | : | : | ||

and then dictates the notes to be written in each pulse, or he may write them on the blackboard for the pupils to copy.

Dictation.—The time-names furnish a means of dictating, by very brief orders, *one pulse at a time*, "Accent," "Time," and "Tune" at once. The following example would be dictated thus: "Prepare four two-pulse measures, secondary form." "TAA *soh-one*," "TRAA *doh*," "TAATAI *me doh*," "TRAA *soh-one*," "TAA *doh*," "TRAATAI *me doh*," "TAA *soh*," "TRAA *doh*."

:s, |d :m .d |s, :d |m .d :s |d ||

Pointing from Memory.—At the close of each lesson the pupils should take pride in showing their teacher how many of the previous exercises they can point on the Modulator and Sol-fa from memory. Musical memory should be cultivated from the first, because it will greatly facilitate the progress of the pupil in future steps, and will be of constant service in after life. To encourage this exercise the pupils should be provided with small modulators upon which they can practice pointing at home. Where it is feasible the whole class should be supplied with "Hand Modulators" and point and sing together, holding their modulators in such way that the teacher can overlook all.

Writing from Memory.—Pupils should also be well practiced in writing tunes from memory. Even where it is difficult for a whole class to point on their modulators from memory at the same moment, so as to be seen by the teacher it is not difficult to engage a whole class at the same moment in writing from memory the tunes they have learned. At the close of every lesson, one or two of the exercises should be chosen for the memory exercise of the next meeting. The pupil (at home) should copy that exercise six or ten times from the book, until he finds by testing himself that he can write it from memory.

Keep within the Step.—The teacher must fully understand that in all these exercises he must keep within the step at which the class is engaged. All the topics of the step should be mastered before the next step is entered. For instructions in *Voice Training*, Breathing, etc., belonging to this Step, the teacher will consult the Standard Course.

QUESTIONS FOR WRITTEN OR ORAL EXAMINATION.

DOCTRINE.

1. What are the first three tones you have learned thus far?
2. Which of these is the lowest tone? The next higher? The highest?
3. Which is the more important, the relative position of these tones or their mental effects?
4. What is the mental effect of *Doh?* Of *Me?* Of *Soh?*
5. How are these mental effects represented to the eye?
6. Besides the hand signs and the modulator what other way have we of indicating or writing the tones?
7. What letter represents *Doh? Me? Soh?*
8. What is this method of musical notation called?
9. What other tones have you learned beside *Doh, me, soh?*
10. What is the mental effect of *one-doh?*
11. What is its hand-sign?
12. How is it indicated in the notation?
13. What is the mental effect of *soh-one?*
14. What is its hand sign?
15. How is it indicated in the notation?
16. How is time in music measured?
17. How many kinds of accents have you learned?
18. What is the time from one strong accent to the next strong accent called?
19. What is the time from any accent to the next called?
20. Is there but one order of arrangment of accents or may there be different arrangements?
21. What do different arrangements of accents produce?
22. How many kinds of measure have you learned and what are they?
23. What is the order of accents in two-pulse measure? Three pulse measure?
24. When is a measure in its primary form? Secondary?
25. How is the strong accent indicated in the notation? The weak accent?
26. What represents the time of a pulse? Of a measure?
27. What is the time-name of a one-pulse tone?
28. How is the strong accent indicated in the time-names?
29. When a tone is continued from one pulse into the next, how is the continuation marked?
30. How are the time-names for continuations obtained?
31. When two tones are sung in the time of one pulse, what are they called?
32. What is the time name of the first half of a pulse? The second?
33. How are half-pulse tones indicated in the notation?
34. How is the end of an exercise indicated?

PRACTICE.

35. Sing to *laa* the *Soh* to any *Doh* the teacher gives.
36. Sing in the same manner the *Soh-one.*
37. Sing in the same manner the *One-Doh.*
38. Sing in the same manner the *Me.*
39. Sing in the same manner *Soh* to any *One-Doh* the teacher gives.
40. Sing in the same manner the *Me.*
41. Sing in the same manner the *Doh.*
42. Taatai the upper part in one of the Exs. 48, 49, or 50.
43. Taatai in tune one of the Exs. 48, 49, or 50, but not the same as in the last requirement, chosen by the teacher.
44. Point on the modulator from memory any one of the Exs. 40, 41, 42, 44, chosen by the teacher.
45. Write from memory another of these exercises.
46. From any phrase (belonging to this step), sung to figures, tell your teacher or write down which figure was sung to *Me.*
47. Ditto *Soh.*
48. Ditto *Doh.*
49. Ditto Soh_1.
50. Having heard the chord, tell or write down which tone was sung to *laa*
51. Follow the teacher's pointing on the modulator in a new voluntary, containing *Doh, Me, Soh,* Doh^1, and Soh_1, TAA, TAA-AA and TAATAI.
52. Write from dictation and afterwards sing a similar exercise.

This tune properly belongs in the Third Step, but is inserted here on account of space.

53. KEY F. DENNIS. S. M. NAEGELI.

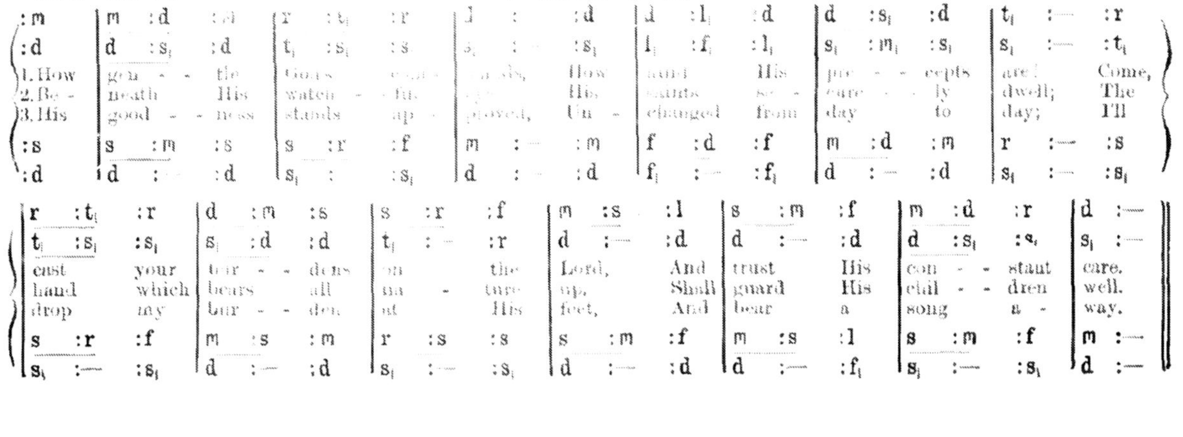

SECOND STEP.

In addition to the tones d, m, s, d' *and* s, *to recognize and produce Ray and Te To distinguish and produce the medium accent and the four-pulse and six-pulse measures The whole-pulse silence, half-pulse tones in three pulse measure, pulse and-a-half tones and quarter-pulse tones in their simplest forms*

To introduce *Ray* and *Te* the teacher may proceed somewhat as follows After reviewing the tones already taught, and a short drill from the Modulator or hand-signs, he may say —

Name the tones I sing and if I sing a different tone from those you have learned, one that is not d, m, or s, you may say *new tone*

The teacher sings the tones to *laa*, pupils calling out "Doh," "Soh" and so on, and after keeping them a moment or two in expectation he sings *Ray* the second tone of the scale (of course, to *laa*), which the pupils at once detect as a new tone

Is the new tone higher or lower than *Doh?*

Is it higher or lower than *Me?*

If the answers are not prompt and correct the exercise must be repeated

The name of the new tone is *Ray*

He writes it on the board or shows it on the Modulator

As we have an upper *Doh* so also we can have an upper *Ray*, and there is also an upper *Me* and an upper *Soh* They are called *one-Ray, one-Me* and *one-Soh*

He writes them on the board or shows them on the modulator

Name the tones again, and if I sing a tone you have not heard before, say *new tone*

He sings the tones to laa as before pupils calling out the names, and after a moment or two he sings *Te* the seventh tone of the scale He questions the class as to the position of the new tone writes its name on the board or shows it on the modulator, and also its lower octave See diagram He then patterns and points on the modulator such exercises as these—

m'
r'
DOH'
TE
SOH
ME
RAY
DOH
t,
s,
m,

54. KEY C.

{|d m |s .—|s :t |r' ·—|r' :t |s ·d' |s :m |d :—||

55. KEY F.

{,d :m |s .m |s, .t, |r .t, |s, :s |m .s |d .—||

56. KEY A.

{|d ·m |d :s, |t, .r |t, .s, |d .s, |m ·s, |d :—||

57. KEY F.

{|s :m |d :m |s :r |t, :r |s :m |s :s, |d :—||

58. KEY D.

{|m :d |m :s |r :t, |r :s |m :s |r :s |d :—||

The teacher next brings up in review the mental effects of *doh, me* and *soh*, and then proceeds to develope the mental effects of *ray* and *te*, somewhat as follows

Now give your attention to the mental effect of *ray* in the examples I shall sing, and notice first whether *ray* gives a feeling of rest, of satisfaction, or whether it is the reverse of that, is restless, expectant, unsatisfied

Teacher sings in any key suited to his voice, the following exercises, making a slight pause before the last tone.

|d' ·s |m :s |d' .r' |r' ·— ||

All sing it —

Are you satisfied to stop on that tone or do you expect something else?

Listen again

Teacher sings.

|d' :s |m :s |d' r' |m' :— ||

All sing the same —

Is that as satisfactory as the former or more so?

Listen again

Teacher sings

|d' :s |m :s |m' :r' |r' :— ||

All sing it —

Satisfactory or expectant?

Listen again

Teacher sings

|d' s |m :s m' :r' |d' :— ||

All sing it —

Satisfactory or expectant?

You learn from these examples that *ray* is a restless, moving, expectant tone, that it leans upon *doh* or *me* But listen again and notice whether it has a depressing, desponding, hopeless effect, or whether it is hopeful, rousing, animating

Teacher sings the following which the pupils may repeat

:s .d' |r' .d' .t |d' :s .d' |r' ·m' .r' |d' ||

What is its effect, depressing and hopeless, or hopeful, rousing, animating?

It will be well to sing the exercise again, substituting *doh* for *ray*, thus,

:s .d' |d' :d' .t |d' :s .d' |d' :m'.d' |d' ||

and again with *ray* as at first, this will produce a contrast that will make *ray* stand our very clearly The following examples will illustrate the mental effect of *te*. The teacher may use them in his own way, to show that *te* is a restless tone, with an intense longing for *doh*, an urgent, sharp, sensitive piercing effect.

|d :m |s :d' |t :— |d' :— ||

:d' |s :m |r :t |t :— |d' ||

In the following exercise m and s are substituted for t to produce a contrast

.d' |s :m |r .m |m :— |d' ||

Sing it again with t and then as follows—

.d' |s :m |r .s |s :— |d' ||

and finally with t as above

The manual sign for the rousing, hopeful tone is this —. All make it.—

The sign for the sensitive, piercing tone is this —, pointing up to *doh*, the tone to which it so strongly leans. All make it.—

The teacher now proceeds to drill the class thoroughly in the new tones by means of the modulator, hand-signs, ear-exercises, etc , during which practice he will have the tones d m s sung together as a chord.

This may be done by dividing the class into three sections, one section to sing *doh*, another *me*, and another *soh*. First let *doh* and *soh* be sung together, then *doh* and *me*; then *me* and *soh*, and then *doh*, *me* and *soh* all at once. The teacher will explain that when tones are combined in this way, the combination is called a chord. This particular chord, formed of the tones of d m s is called the chord of DOH, or Tonic Chord. The chord of DOH may be taught in the first step, if the teacher prefers The tones s t r' should next be combined in the same way They form the chord of SOH, or Dominant Chord. The class is now prepared to take up the study of the following exercises.

59. KEY F. Round for three parts

|d :d |m :r |d :t, |d :— |†* m :m |s :s |
Af - ter la - bor we shall find, Mu - sic will re

|m :r |m :— |† s :m |d :t, |d :s, |d :— ||
lieve the mind, And our hearts to - - geth - er bind

60. KEY G. Round for four parts

|s, :s, |d :d |† s, :s, |d :d |†* r :— |m :— |† r :— |m :— |†
Scotland's burn - ing, Scot land's burn-ing, Look out, Look out,

|s :— |† s :— |† s :— |† s :— |† t, :r |d :d |† t, :r |d :d ||
Fire! Fire! Fire! Fire! Pour on wa - ter, pour on wa - ter

61. KEY D. Round for three parts — A L. C.

|d :t, |d :— |r :r |m :— |†* m :r |m :d |
"Here I go, sure and slow," Says the tur - tle

|d :t, |d :— |† s .s :s |s .d' :m |† s .s :s .s |d' :— ||
down be - - low "Not so I, swiftly fly," Sings the bird on high.

62. KEY C. Round for four parts. — T. F. S.

|s .s :m |s .s :r |* m .m :d |r .s :s .s |
Hur - ry now, hur - ry now, Come a - long, Won't you hur - ry?

|d' :— |t :— |d' :s |s :— ||
No, no, Wait a - - while.

Tuning Exercises are designed for the purpose of teaching voices singing different parts *to study one another*, and to chord well together. To some extent this is done in every exercise, but it requires also separate study. The teacher, in these exercises endeavors to secure from the class a uniformly clear, *soft* tone—making a signal to any one whose voice is so prominent as to stand out from the rest,—and to maintain the perfect *tuning into each other* of all the parts of the chord. For some time the accord of the voices will be very rough and imperfect, but *soft singing* and listening will amend the fault. The exercises may be sung from the book, but a better plan is to sing them from the blackboard, as in this way a correct position of the pupil is secured, and the teacher can readily call the attention of all, in a moment, to any point in the exercise. Ex. 63 may be sung as follows—By three sections of women's voices, one section singing the first part, another the second and another the third. When moderately well done, the parts should be exchanged, those who sang the first part taking the second, the second taking the third and the third the first. At the next change the same process is repeated. The exercise may then be sung in the same manner by three sections of men's voices. Boys whose voices have not changed will sing with the women. Again, let all the men sing the third part, and two sections of women take the first and second; again, all the women sing the first part, and the men in two sections taking the second and third. Again, all the women sing the second part, and the men in two sections the first and third.

To be sung first to the sol-fa syllables, then to *laa* and to *loo*.

TUNING EXERCISES.

63. KEYS F AND G.

1st.	d :—	m :—	s :s	m :—	s :—	— :—	m :s	s :—
2d.	d :—	m :—	m :m	d :—	s :—	m :—	d :m	m :—
3d.	d :—	— :—	d :d	d :—	s :—	m :—	d :s_1	d :—

For the following exercises in four parts the class should be divided into four sections, two sections of ladies taking the two upper parts and two sections of gentlemen taking the two lower parts. This division of the voices must not be considered as a final classification into Soprano, Contralto, Tenor and Base. That will come later in the course. The top line is the Soprano (marked S), the next lower is the Contralto (C); the next below the Contralto is Tenor (T), and the lowest is the Base (B).

64. KEY C.

Sing first as written. Second time, Soprano and Tenor change parts. Third time, Soprano and Contralto change parts, Contralto singing d t_1 d instead of d^1 t d^1.

S.	d :—	s :m	d :—	m :—	s :—	d^1 :—	d^1 :t	d^1 :—
C.	d :—	s :m	d :—	m :—	— :—	— :—	m :r	m :—
T.	d :—	s :m	d :—	m :—	s :—	— :—	s :s	s :—
B.	d :—	s :m	d :—	— :—	— :—	— :—	s :s	d :—

65. KEY F.

First as written. Second time, Soprano take Tenor, Tenor take Contralto, singing s instead of s_1, Contralto take Soprano. Third time, Soprano and Contralto change parts, Soprano singing s instead of s_1.

d :—	s_1 :m	d :—	m :—	s_1 :—	d :—	d :t_1	d :—
d :—	s_1 :m	d :—	m :—	s_1 :—	— :—	s_1 :s_1	s_1 :—
d :—	s_1 :m	d :—	m :—	— :—	— :—	m :r	m :—
d :—	s_1 :m	d :—	— :—	— :—	— :—	s_1 :s_1	d :—

66. KEY C.

First as written. Second time, Soprano and Tenor change parts. Third time, Soprano take Contralto—Contralto take Tenor, singing t_1 instead of t—Tenor take Soprano.

d :—	m :d	s :—	:	:	s :—	s :s	s :—
d :—	m :d	s :—	:	r :—	— :—	m :r	m :—
d :—	m :d	s :—	t :—	— :—	— :—	d^1 :t	d^1 :—
d :—	m :d	s :—	— :—	— :—	— :—	s :s	d :—

67. KEY F.

First as written. Second time, Soprano take Tenor—Tenor take Contralto, singing s instead of s_1. Contralto take Soprano. Third time Soprano and Contralto change parts, Soprano singing s instead of s_1.

d :—	m :d	s_1 :—	t_1 :—	— :—	— :—	d :t_1	d :—
d :—	m :d	s_1 :—	:	:	s_1 :—	s_1 :s_1	s_1 :—
d :—	m :d	s_1 :—	:	r :—	— :—	m :r	m :—
d :—	m :d	s_1 :—	— :—	— :—	— :—	s_1 :s_1	d :—

Breathing Places.—It was taught in the first step that the best places to take breath, *musically considered*, are at the beginning of the musical phrases. But the sense of the words is of more importance than musical phrasing. It frequently happens that the phrasing of the words and phrasing of the music do not agree. In such cases breath must be taken where it will not destroy the sense of the words. In the following example the musical phrasing would allow a breath to be taken at the dagger (†), and this would suit the first verse; but it would not do for the second verse; and the breathing places neither of the first nor second verses would answer for the third.

KEY G.

		†		
d :s_1 .s_1	d :— .d	r :t_1	d :—	‖
1. Light of the	world, O	Sav - iour	dear!	
2. Son of the	Fa - ther	Lord most	high.	
3. Je - sus is	from the	proud con -	cealed.	

To take breath before a strong pulse the time of the breath must be taken from the end of the previous weak pulse; to take breath before a weak pulse the time of it may be taken from the beginning of the same pulse. It is not only convenient but necessary to take breath before all long sustained tones or long connected phrases.

It is recommended that before singing the words of a tune they should be studied separately. The teacher may read the portion of words from one breathing place to another, which the pupils are to repeat after him and mark the breathing place with pencil. In this exercise particular attention should be given to pronunciation; the vowels should be clear and pure and the consonants sharp and distinct.

Expression is such a use of *loudness* and *softness* in singing as tends to make the music more expressive. Even in the earliest steps, pupils enjoy thus embellishing their music. Here it is enough to draw attention occasionally to what is indeed the chief part of expression—that which is suggested by the words. First there must be fixed the *medium* or normal degree of force proper to the *general sentiment* of the piece,—then whatever words are printed in the common type are to be sung with that appropriate medium force, whatever words are printed in SMALL CAPITALS are to be sung louder, and whatever words are printed in *italics* are to be sung more *softly*. Many of the pieces in this book are left to be marked by the pupils under the direction of the teacher. A single line drawn under the words by pen or pencil will indicate italics, and a double line small capitals.

SWELL THE ANTHEM.

68. KEY G.

SOPRANO.	d :d	d :s_1	d :m	s :—	s :s	s :m	r :d	t_1 :—
CONTRALTO.	s_1 :s_1	s_1 :m_1	s_1 :d	t_1 :—	t_1 :t_1	d :d	t_1 :d	s_1 :—
	1. Swell the	an - them,	raise the	song;	Prais - es	to our	God be -	long;
	2. Hark! the	voice of	na - ture	sings,	Prais - es	to the	King of	kings;
TENOR.	m :m	m :d	s :m	r :—	r :r	m :s	s :m	r :—
BASE.	d :d	d :d	m :d	s_1 :—	s_1 :s_1	d :d	s_1 :s_1	s_1 :—

d :d	d :s_1	d :m	s :—	s :s	s :m	r :r	d :—
s_1 :s_1	s_1 :m_1	s_1 :d	t_1 :—	t_1 :t_1	d :d	d :t_1	d :—
Saints and	an - gels	join to	sing,	Prais - es	to the	heav'n - ly	King.
Let us	join the	cho - ral	song,	And the	grate - ful	tones pro -	long.
m :m	m :d	s :m	r :—	r :r	m :s	s :s	m :—
d :d	d :d	m :d	s_1 :—	s_1 :s_1	d :d	s_1 :s_1	d :—

ff **69.** KEY F.

		f		*m*		*p*	
s :s	s :m	d :m	s :—	d :m	s :—	d :m	s :—
TRY THE	ECH - OES	AS WE	GO,	as we	go,	*as we*	*go,*

f		*m*		*p*		*pp*	
m :m	m :r	d :r	m :—	d :r	m :—	d :r	m :—
HEAR THEM	AN - SWER	soft and	low,	*Soft and*	*low,*	*soft and*	*low.*

The Slur is a horizontal line drawn under two or more notes and shows that one syllable of the words is to be sung to as many notes as are thus connected.

CHEERFUL LABOR.

70. KEY D.

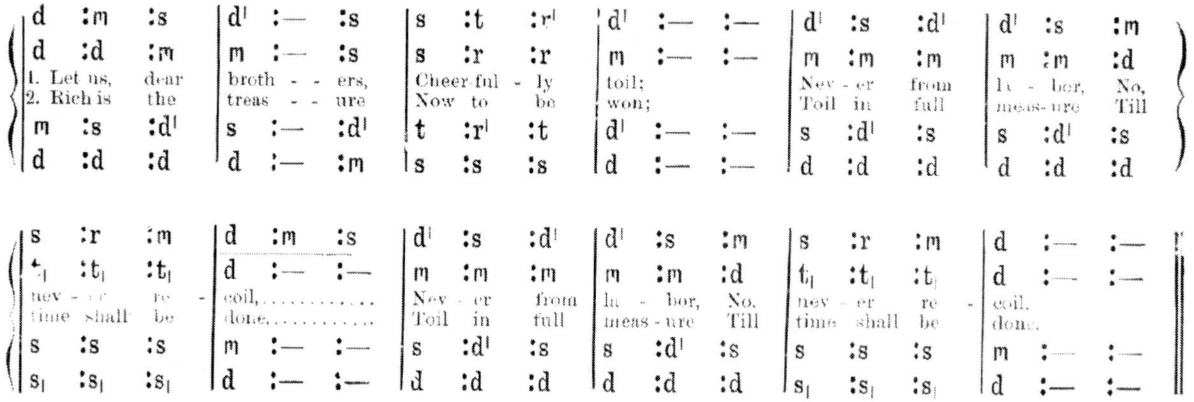
1. Let us, dear broth - - ers, Cheer-ful - ly toil; Nev - er from la - bor, No, nev - er re - coil,.......... Nev - er from la - bor, No, nev - er re - coil.
2. Rich is the treas - - ure Now to be won; Toil in full meas - ure Till time shall be done,.......... Toil in full meas - ure Till time shall be done.

LONGINGS.

71. KEY E♭.

B. C. U.

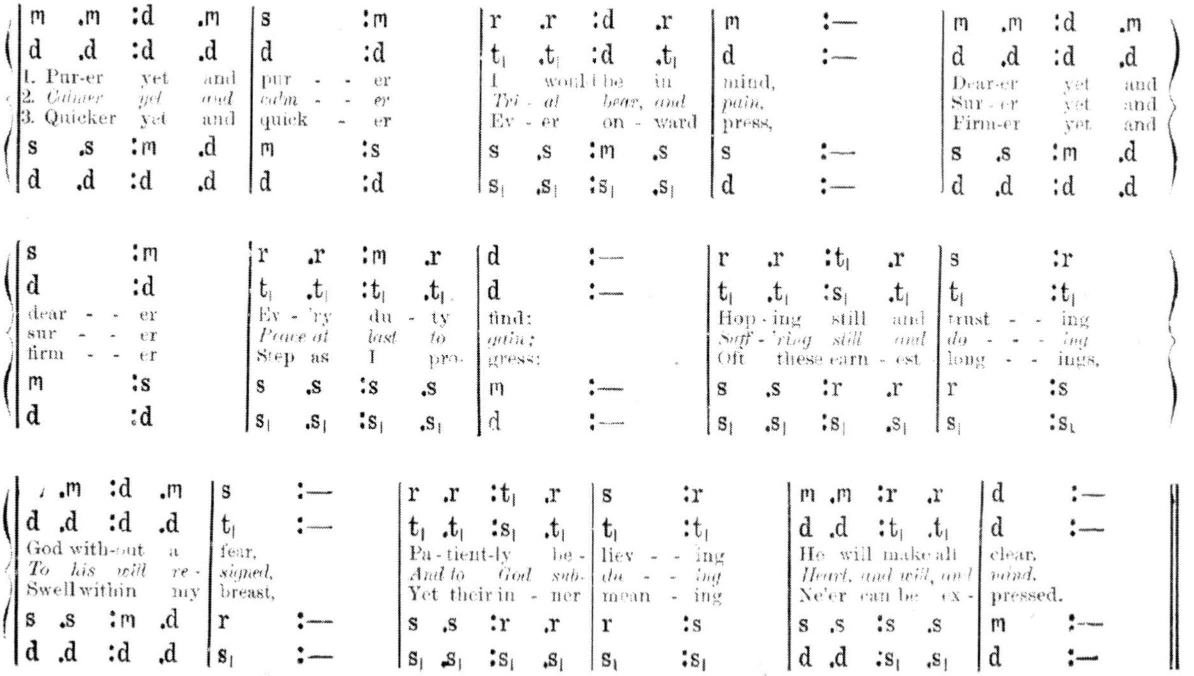
1. Pur-er yet and pur - - er I would be in mind, Dear-er yet and dear - - er Ev - 'ry du - ty find: Hop - ing still and trust - - ing God with-out a fear, Pa - tient-ly be - liev - - ing He will make all clear.
2. *Calmer yet and calm - - er Trial bear, and pain, Sur - er yet and sur - - er Peace at last to gain; Suff - 'ring still and do - - - ing To his will re - signed, And to God sub - du - - ing Heart, and will, and mind.*
3. Quicker yet and quick - er Ev - er on - ward press, Firm-er yet and firm - - er Step as I pro - gress; Oft these earn - est long - - ings, Swell within my breast, Yet their in - ner mean - ing Ne'er can be ex - pressed.

The Medium Accent should now be explained One or more of the following tunes may be sung by the teacher (to *laa*), first in two-pulse measure with every other accent strong and heavy, and then in four-pulse measure by changing every alternate strong accent into a medium It may be well to let the pupils imitate the teacher's examples

:s, |d .d |m :m |r .d |r :m |r .d |m :r |d ||

|d .d |r .r |m :m |r :r |m :s |f .m |r r |d — ||

|m :s |f .s |m .s |r :s |m :s |f .r |d .t, |d :— ||

Also the following, first in three-pulse measure, as written, and then in six-pulse measure by changing every alternate strong accent into a medium.

|m :— :m |m :— :d |r :— :r |r :— :— |m :— :m |s :— :f |

|m :— :— |r :— :— |d :— :— || or |s, :s, :s, |s, :s, :s, |

|s, :d :r |m :— .— |r :r :r |r :r :d |m :m :r |d :— :— ||

Also the following time-exercises may be written on the blackboard and sung first as written, and then with every other strong accent made medium.

TWO-PULSE MEASURE
FOUR-PULSE MEASURE
|l :l |l :l |l :l |l :l ||

THREE-PULSE MEASURE
SIX-PULSE MEASURE
|l :l :l |l :l :l |l :l :l |l :l :l ||

When the pupils have distinguished the medium accent and can produce it, the teacher will explain that the medium accent changes two two-pulse measures into a four-pulse measure, and two three-pulse measures into a six-pulse measure In four pulse measure the accents are arranged in the order—**strong**, *weak*, MEDIUM, *weak* (as in the words "**MO**-*men*-TA-*ry*," "**plan**-*e*-TA-*ry*") In six-pulse measure the accents are arranged in the order **strong**, *weak*, *weak*, MEDIUM, *weak*, *weak* (as in the words "**spir**-*it*-*u*-AL-*i*-*ty*" "**im**-*m*-*u*-*ta*-BIL-*i*-*ty*") The medium accent is indicated in the notation by a short thin bar. In the time-names the medium accent is indicated, when necessary (as in dictation exercises), by the letter L, thus, TLAA, TLAATAI, etc In Taataing, the L is not useful The teacher must not expect too great a nicety of distinction at first. The finer points both of time and tune require much practice.

The following time-exercises may now be practiced from the teacher's pattern, first with the time-names and then to *laa*.

It will be well in exercises 72 and 74 to sing each measure four times, as a separate exercise, before singing the four measures continuously In exercises 73 and 75 the portions marked off by the dagger (†) should be treated in the same way. Additional time-exercises are obtained by Taataing the rounds and tunes on one tone.

72.

|l :l |l :l |l :— |l :l |l :— |l :— |l :— |— :— ||
TAA TAA TAA TAA TAA-AA TAA TAA TAA-AA TAA-AA TAA-AA-AA-AA

73.

:l |l :— |l :l |l :— |— :l† |l :l |l :l |l :— |— ||
TAA TAA-AA TAA TAA TAA-AA-AA TAA TAA TAA TAA TAA TAA-AA-AA

74. First slowly, beating six times to the measure, then quickly, beating twice

|l :l :l |l :l :l |l :— :— |l :— :— |l :l :l |l :— :l |l :— :— |— :— :— ||
TAA TAA TAA TAA TAA TAA TAA-AA-AA TAA-AA-AA TAA TAA TAA TAA-AA TAA TAA-AA-AA-AA-AA-AA

75.

:l |l :— :l |l :l :l |l :— :— |l :— :l† |l :l :l |l :— :l |l :— :— |— :— ||
TAA TAA-AA TAA TAA TAA TAA TAA-AA-AA TAA-AA TAA TAA TAA TAA TAA-AA TAA TAA-AA-AA-AA-AA

76. KEY E♭. Round in four parts.

| d :d |d :d |r :r |r :r |m :m |m :m |s :— |— :— |
When the pan - sies' pur - ple buds Came forth in ear - ly Spring,

| s :s |s :s |t :t |t :t |d' :s |m :d |s, :— |— :— ||
Na - ture from her sleep did wake To greet the blos - som - ing.

77. KEY F. Round in four parts.

:s |m :m |m :r |d :d |d :t, |d :s, |d :r |m :m |m ||
Now we are met, let mirth a - bound, And let the catch and glee go round.

78. KEY C. Round in four parts.

| m :m |r :— |d :m |s :— |d' :d' |t .d' :r' .t |d' :s |s :— ||
Come, let's laugh, come, let's sing, Win - ter shall as merry be as Spring.

79. KEY G. Round in four parts.

| d :d .d |t, :t, |d :d |s, :— |d .r :m .d |r :s, .s, |s :s |s :— ||
Come, merry men, the horn doth blow, Follow, follow me, and a - way we'll go.

HAPPY HOME.

80. KEY C. B. C. U.

| s :s |m :s |d' :— |— :— |t :d' |r' :s |m' :— |— :— |r' :r' |r' :s
| m :m |d :m |m :— |— :— |r :m |s :s |s :— |— :— |s :s |s :s
Sing we now of home, hap - py, hap - py home; Sing we now of
| d' :d' |s :d' |s :— |— :— |s :d' |t :t |d' :— |— :— |t :t |t :t
| d :d |d :d |d :— |— :— |s :s |s :s |d :— |— :— |s :s |s :s

| r' :r' |r' :s |m' :r' |d' :t |d' :— |— :— |t :t |t :t |d' :d' |d' :d'
| s :s |s :s |s :s |m :r |m :— |— :— |r :r |r :r |m :m |m :m
hap - py home, of hap - py, hap - py home. Yes, with heart and voice un - tir ing,
Love, that bright-ens ev - 'ry pleas - ure,
Bless-ings ev - er new in - vite us,
Love with last - ing bonds shall bind us,
| t :t |t :t |d' :t |d' :s |s :— |— :— |s :s |s :s |s :s |s :s
| s :s |s :s |s :s |s :s |d :— |— :— |s :s |s :s |s :s |s :s

| t :t |t :t |d' :d' |d' :d' |t :d' |r' :s |m' :— |— :— |m' :m' |r' :r' |d' :— |— :— ||
| r :r |r :r |m :m |m :m |r :m |s :s |s :— |— :— |s :s |s :s |m :— |— :— ||
We will join the strain in - spir-ing, Sing-ing now of home, hap-py, hap - py home.
Brings us more than gold - en treas-ure,
Joy and so - cial mirth de - light us,
While the fleet-ing mo-ments find us,
| s :s |s :s |s :s |s :s |s :d' |t :t |d' :— |— :— |d' :d' |t :t |d' :— |— :— ||
| s :s |s :s |s :s |s :s |s :s |s :s |d' :— |— :— |d' :d' |s :s |d :— |— :— ||

81. Key C. Round in two parts.

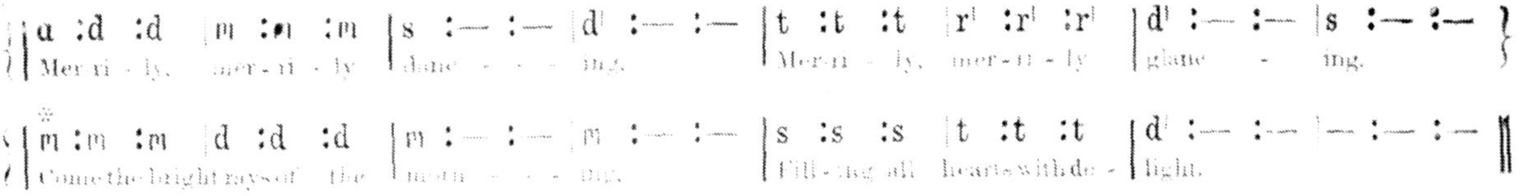

82. Key G. Round in two parts.

83. Key D. Round in four parts.

BOUNDING SO MERRILY ONWARD.

84. Key G. Arr. from H. R. Palmer.

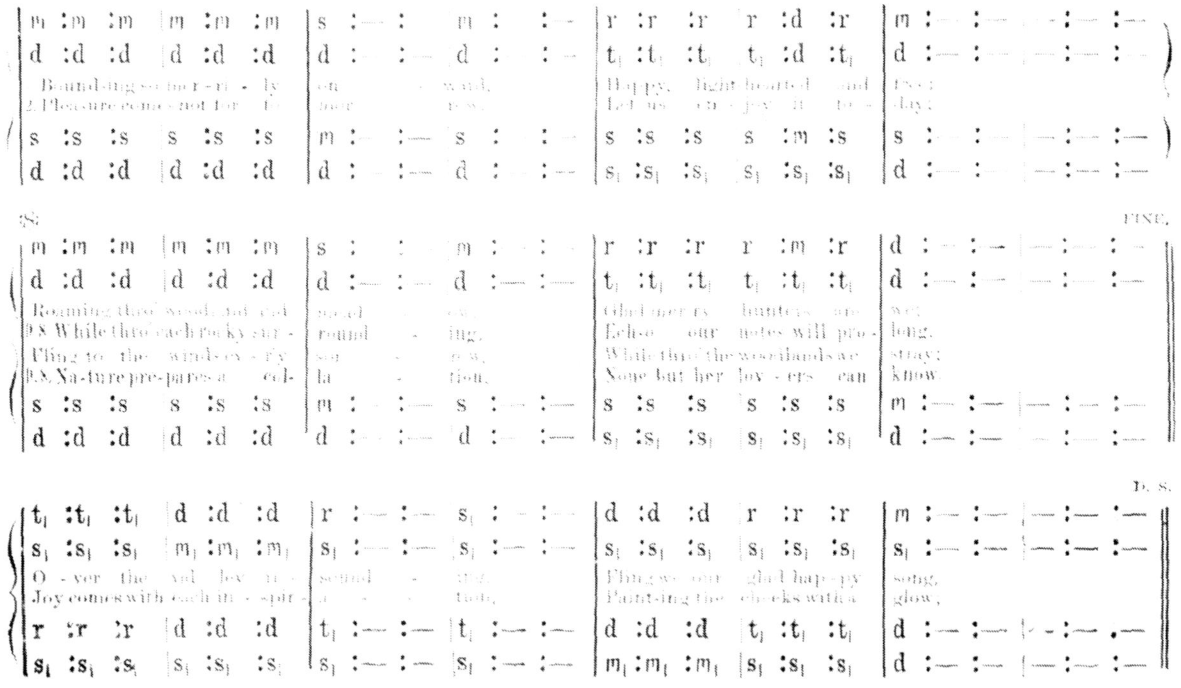

Silent Pulse.—The following exercises inclnde the practice of the one-pulse silence. The teacher mav explain this in his own way. A very good way is th n whic. two-pulse tones, and half-pulse tones were taught in the first step—that is, by singing a simple time-exercise and making a mistake, passing over a pulse in silence, the pupils calling out, *wrong*, etc. The time-name of a silent pulse is *SAA*, and to further distinguish the silence names they are printed in *italics*. In taataing, the silent pulses are to be passed in a whisper—that is, the time-name *SAA* is to be whispered. Some teachers prefer the name [TAA] placed in brackets or printed in italics, *Taa*, and sung in a whisper. The teacher must not allow the pupils to exaggerate the hissing sound of the S. The silent pulses may at first be passed in a whisper, but they should finally be done in absolute silence, the pupils being told to close the lips firmly and *think* the name. The following exercises should be Taataied and *laa-ed* on one tone and then taataid in tune:

85. KEY D.

				*			
TAA :TAA	TAA :*SAA*	TAA :TAA	TAA :*SAA*	TAA :*SAA*	TAA :*SAA*	TAA :TAA	TAA :*SAA*
d :d	d :	m :m	m :	s :	s :	m :s	d' :
Now we	sing,	now we	rest;	Sing,	rest,	do your	best.

86 KEY A.

				*			
d :	s, :	d :s,	d :	d :d	t, :t,	d :t,	d :
March,	march,	march a -	long,	Brave - ly	for - ward	all day	long.

87. KEY F.

				*			
d :d	*SAA* :*SAA*	m :m	:	s :	m :	:s, .s,	d :
On - ward,		Up - ward,		March,	march,	forward	march.

88. KEY G. Round in four parts. U.

				*			
d :	s, :	d :s,	d :	d :d	t, :t,	d :t,	d :
March,	march,	march a -	way,	Who are	read - y	for the	fray;
m :m	r :r	m :r	m :	s :s	s :s	s, :s,	:s
Fal - ter	not for	foe - man's	ire,	Now make	read - y,	aim and	shoot.

89. KEY C. Round in two parts. T. F. S.

				*			
s :d' :	s :d' :	t :t :t	d' :— :	s :m :d	s :m :d	r :r :r	m :— :
Cuc-koo	cuc-koo,	list to the	song;	Sweetly it	floats o'er the	meadows a -	long.

f **90.** KEY C.

	m		*p*		*pp*		
:d' | t :	| :t	d' :	| :d'	t :	| :t	d' :	| :
Who's THERE?	I'm	sure	I	*heard*	*a*	*sound;*	
: |	*m* :s | s :		*p* :d | d :		*pp* :s | s :		*f* :d | m :s
	Don't speak,		keep still,		*hush, hush,*		O YES, 'TIS

f							
	:d' | d' :		:d' | d' :		:d' | r' :t	d' :— | —
	AH YES,		who sing		this lit - tle	song.
d' :	| :d'	s :	| :s	m :m	| r :s	d :— | —
WE	who	sing,	who	sing this	lit - tle	song.

SWEET EVENING HOUR.

91. Key F. A. L. Cowley.

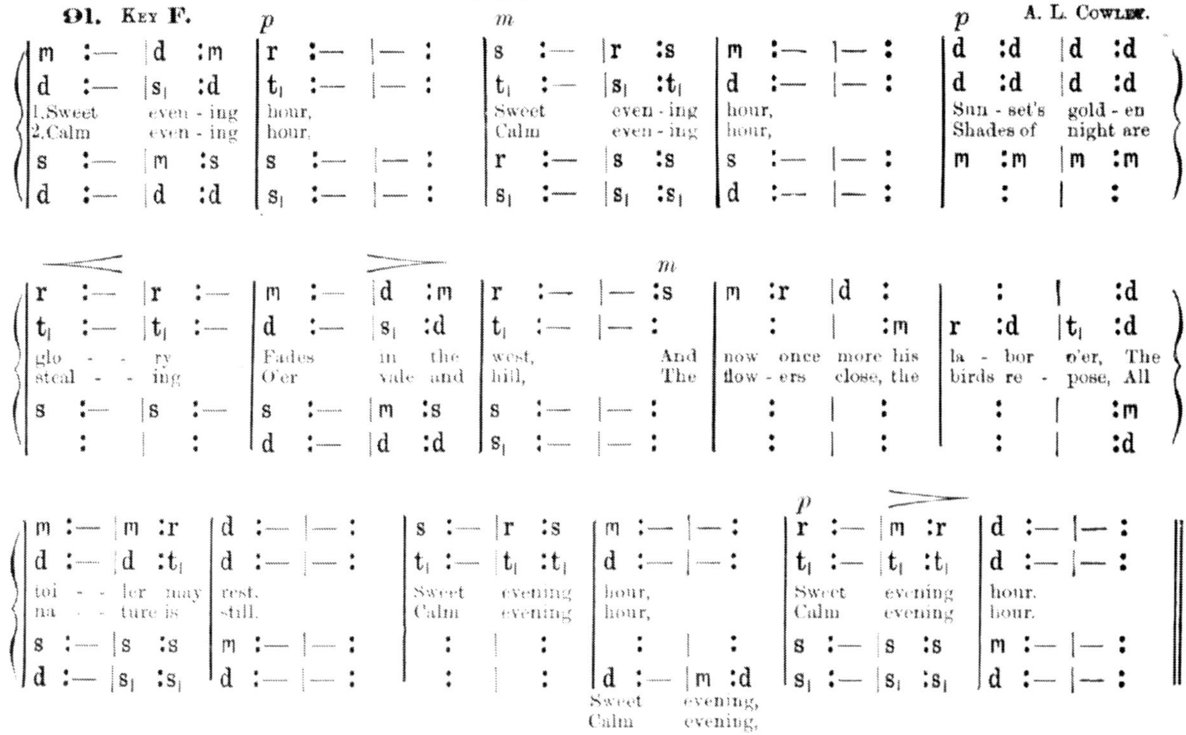
1. Sweet even-ing hour, Sweet even-ing hour, Sun-set's gold-en glo-ry Fades in the west, And now once more his la-bor o'er, The toi-ler may rest. Sweet evening hour, Sweet evening, Sweet evening hour.
2. Calm even-ing hour, Calm even-ing hour, Shades of night are steal-ing O'er vale and hill, The flow-ers close, the birds re-pose, All na-ture is still. Calm evening hour, Calm evening, Calm evening hour.

OVER THE SNOW.

92. Key E. R. S. Taylor.

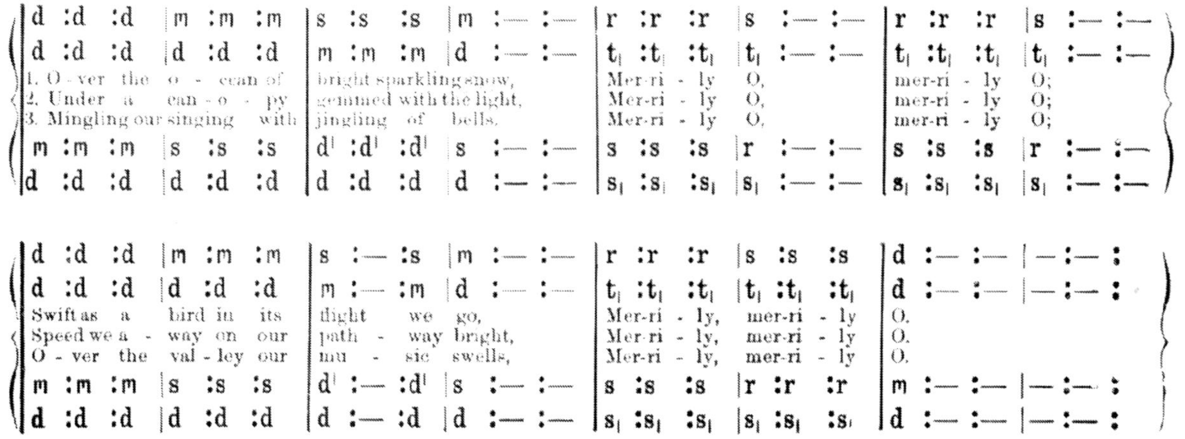
1. O-ver the o-cean of bright sparkling snow, Mer-ri-ly O, mer-ri-ly O; Swift as a bird in its flight we go, Mer-ri-ly, mer-ri-ly O.
2. Under a can-o-py gemmed with the light, Mer-ri-ly O, mer-ri-ly O; Speed we a-way on our path-way bright, Mer-ri-ly, mer-ri-ly O.
3. Mingling our singing with jingling of bells, Mer-ri-ly O, mer-ri-ly O; O-ver the val-ley our mu-sic swells, Mer-ri-ly, mer-ri-ly O.

92. CHORUS.

```
{ s :s :s | s :s :s | s :— :— | d¹ :— : ‖ m :m :m | m :m :m | m :— :— | s :— : }
{ m :m :m | m :m :m | m :— :— | — :— : ‖ d :d :d | d :d :d | d :— :— | m :— : }
  Mer - ri - ly,   mer - ri - ly   O,              Mer - ri - ly,   mer - ri - ly   O;
{ : : | : : | : : | : : ‖ s :s :s | s :s :s | s :— :— | d¹ :— : }
{ d :d :d | d :d :d | d :— :— | — :— : ‖ d :d :d | d :d :d | d :— :— | — :— : }
  O - ver the snow,
```

D. S.

```
{ : : | : : | m :m :m | m :— :— ‖ r :r :r | s :s :s | d :— :— | — :— : }
{ : : | : : | d :d :d | d :— :— ‖ t₁ :t₁ :t₁ | t₁ :t₁ :t₁ | d :— :— | — :— : }
                        Swift - ly we go,   Mer - ri - ly, mer - ri - ly O.
{ : : | : : | : : | : : ‖ s :s :s | r :r :r | m :— :— | — :— : }
{ d :d :d | d :— :— | — :— :— | — :— : ‖ s₁ :s₁ :s₁ | s₁ :s₁ :s₁ | d :— :— | — :— : }
```

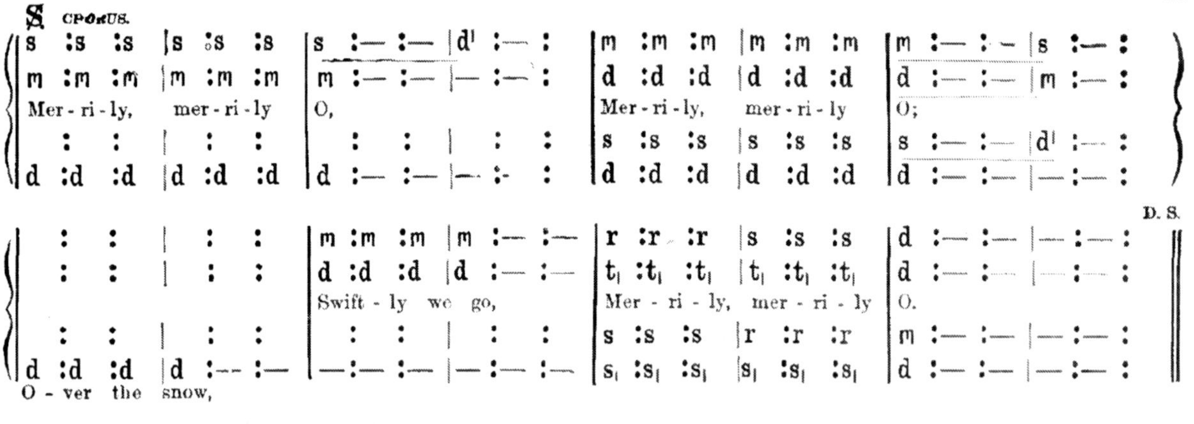

STILL LIKE DEW.

93. KEY F.

B. C. UNSELD.

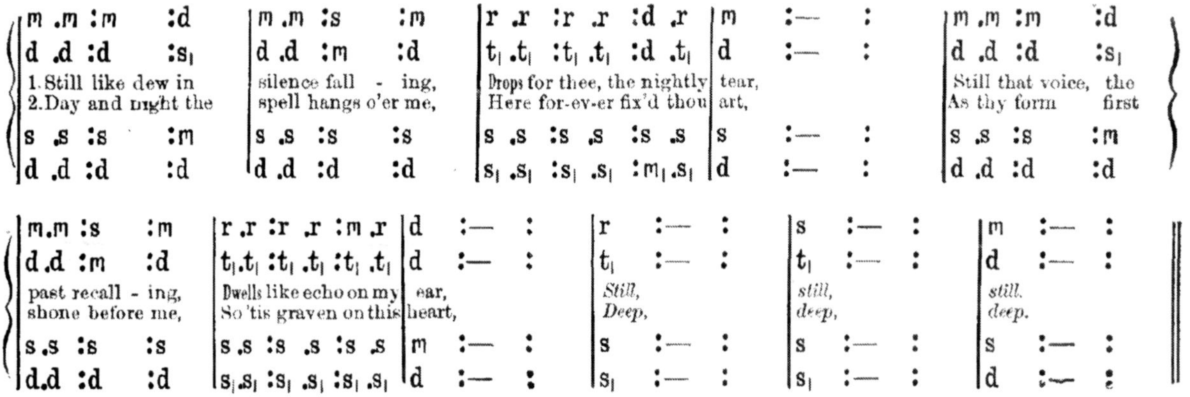

```
{ m .m :m | :d | m .m :s | :m | r .r :r .r :d .r | m :— : | m .m :m | :d }
{ d .d :d | :s₁ | d .d :m | :d | t₁ .t₁ :t₁ .t₁ :d .t₁ | d :— : | d .d :d | :s₁ }
  1. Still like dew in   silence fall - ing,   Drops for thee, the nightly tear,   Still that voice, the
  2. Day and night the   spell hangs o'er me,   Here for-ev-er fix'd thou art,   As thy form   first
{ s .s :s | :m | s .s :s | :s | s .s :s .s :s .s | s :— : | s .s :s | :m }
{ d .d :d | :d | d .d :d | :d | s₁ .s₁ :s₁ .s₁ :m₁ .s₁ | d :— : | d .d :d | :d }
```

```
{ m .m :s | :m | r .r :r .r :m .r | d :— : | r :— : | s :— : | m :— : }
{ d .d :m | :d | t₁ .t₁ :t₁ .t₁ :t₁ .t₁ | d :— : | t₁ :— : | t₁ :— : | d :— : }
  past recall - ing,   Dwells like echo on my ear,   Still,   still,   still.
  shone before me,   So 'tis graven on this heart,   Deep,   deep,   deep.
{ s .s :s | :s | s .s :s .s :s .s | m :— : | s :— : | s :— : | s :— : }
{ d .d :d | :d | s₁ .s₁ :s₁ .s₁ :s₁ .s₁ | d :— : | s₁ :— : | s₁ :— : | d :— : }
```

ff **94.** KEY C.

```
{ d¹ :s | m :s | d¹ :t | d¹ :— | d :r | m :r | m :s | d :— }
  LOUD AND   STRONG THE   STORM-WINDS   BLOW,   Soft and   sweet the   breez - es   flow.
```

pp

pp **95.** KEY G.

```
{ d :d | s₁ :s₁ | d :t₁ | d :— | m :m | s :m | d :r | d :— }
  Soft and   sweet the   breez - es   flow,   LOUD AND   STRONG THE   STORM - WINDS   BLOW.
```

ff

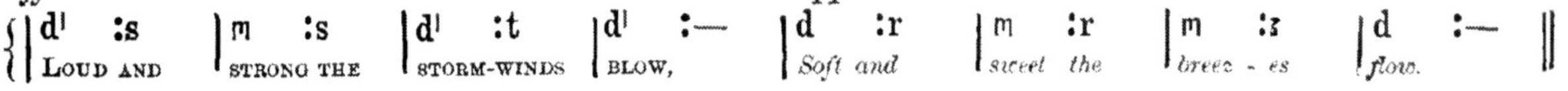

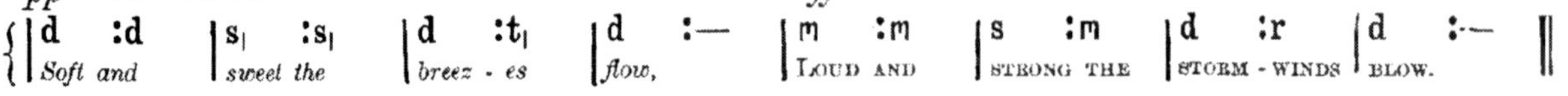

Pulse and half tones may be taught as follows. The teacher writes the following exercises on the board:

```
TAA   TAATAI TAA   TAA   TAA   TAATAI TAA   TAA
|1   :1 .1 |1   :1   |1   :1 .1 |1   :1   ‖

TAA   TAATAI TAA   TAA   TAA   TAATAI TAA   TAA
|1   :1 .1 |1   :1   |1   :1 .1 |1   :1   ‖
```

And when they are sung correctly he changes the second one to

```
TAA - AA TAI TAA   TAA   TAA - AA TAI TAA   TAA
|1   :— .1 |1   :1   |1   :— .1 |1   :1   ‖
```

and explains that in the first and third measure the tones are to be continued from the first pulse into the first half of the second, making the tone a pulse and a half long. The exercise is then to be taataid and laa-ed from the teacher's pattern. The two exercises may then be sung alternately.

The following exercises are to be taataid and laaed on one tone and taataid in tune:

96. Key G.

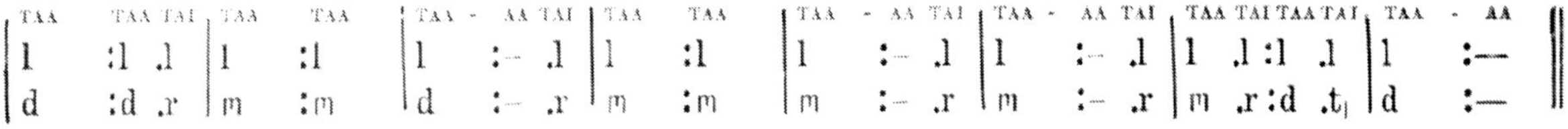

97. Key D.

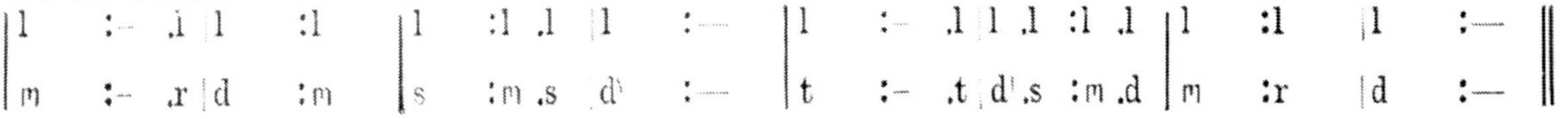

98. Key F.

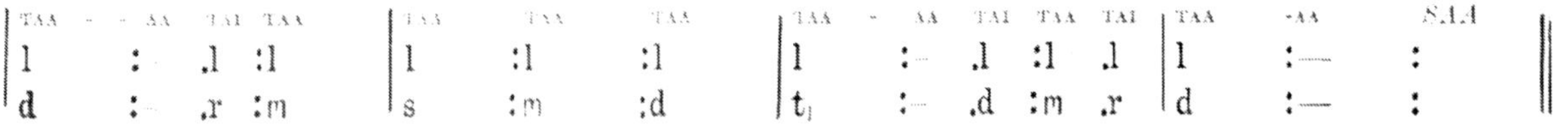

99. Key G.

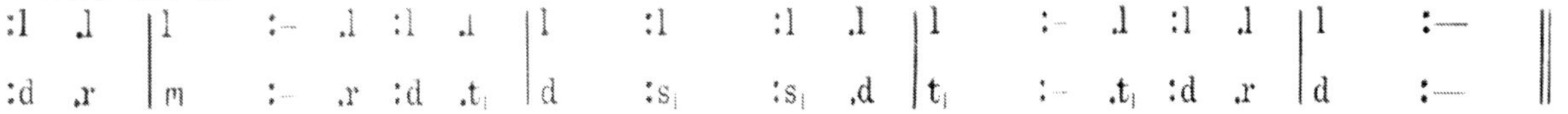

100. Key F. Round for three parts.

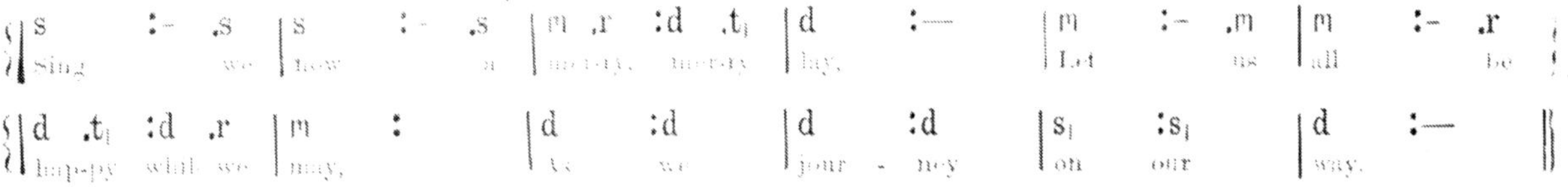
Sing we now a merry, merry lay, Let us all be
hap-py while we may, As we jour - ney on our way.

A. S. Kieffer.

GENTLE SPRING IS HERE AGAIN.

101. Key G.

B. C. Unseld.

1. Gen - tle spring is here a - gain, Bring - ing mirth and glad - - - ness;
2. Years a - go her gen - tle voice, Filled my heart with pleasure - - - ure,
3. All a - lone she calm - ly sleeps, Un - der - neath the wil - - - low;
And the sing - ing birds have come, Chas - ing gloom and sad - - - ness,
And life's lot was full of joy, With this sin - gle treas - - - ure;
And the hare - bells mute - ly weep, Tears up - on her pil - - - low;

```
| r  :- .r | r   :r  | t₁ :d  | r  :-  | m  :- .m | m  :m  | d  :r  | m  :- |
| t₁ :- .t₁| t₁  :t₁ | s₁ :m₁ | s₁ :-  | s₁ :- .s₁| s₁ :s₁ | s₁ :s₁ | s₁ :- |
```
But   my heart is   sad and lone,   Though the win - try   days have flown,
But   no joy earth   now can give,   Tempt - ing with the   wish to live,
But   her face still   bright - ly beams,   Com - ing to me   in my dreams—
```
| r  :- .r | r   :r  | r  :d  | t₁ :-  | d  :- .d | d  :d  | d  :t₁ | d  :- |
| s₁ :- .s₁| s₁  :s₁ | s₁ :s₁ | s₁ :-  | d  :- .d | d  :d  | m₁ :s₁ | d  :- |
```

```
| s₁ :- .s₁| d  :d  | r  :d .r | m  :-  | s  :- .s | s  :m  | r  :-  | d  :  |
| m₁ :- .m₁| s₁ :d  | t₁ :d .t₁| d  :-  | d  :- .d | d  :d  | t₁ :-  | d  :  |
```
For   I miss the   lov - ing tone,   Which could bring it   glad - - - ness.
And   I lin - ger   but to grieve,   For the dear lost   treas - - - ure.
Like   an an - gel's   still it seems —   Bend - ing o'er my   pil - - - low.
```
| d  :- .d | m  :m  | s  :s  | s  :-  | m  :- .m | m  :s  | s  :-  | m  :  |
| d  :- .d | d  :d  | s₁ :m₁ .s₁| d :-  | d  :- .d | d  :d  | s₁ :-  | d  :  |
```

BANISH SORROW.

202. Key E.   B. C. U.

```
```
1 Ban-ish all   despending sor - row,   Tho' the skies   may frown to-day;   Shall not sun - shine with to-
2 Here's a hand for ev - 'ry broth-er, Working stout - ly, climbing slow,   Here's a will   to help each
3 Join we, then, in bravest cho - rus,   Sing-ing all   our pains to rest   While the heav'n gleams kind-ly

mor - row,   O'er its a - - - zure beauty play?   Life must bring   its toils and trou-bles,   But the
oth - - er, In the doubt   we all must know.   Hopes are cheered and loads are light - ened   By the
o'er   us,   Light and joy   shall make us blest.   Strength shall stoop   to lift the weak - est,   Love the

heart that fears and faints, Makes the heav - y bur-den dou - ble, Heap-ing care with vain com plaints.
mag - ic of a word, Dusk - y day by smiles are bright ened, Ere the friend - ly tone is heard.
low - est grief shall see, Pride no more shall spurn the meek - est; Broth-ers firm and true are we.
```
```

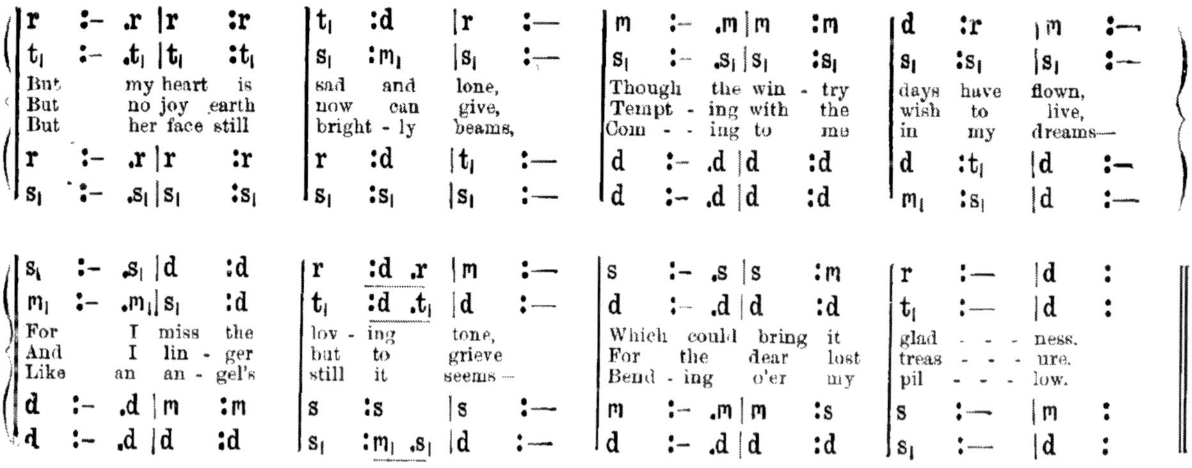

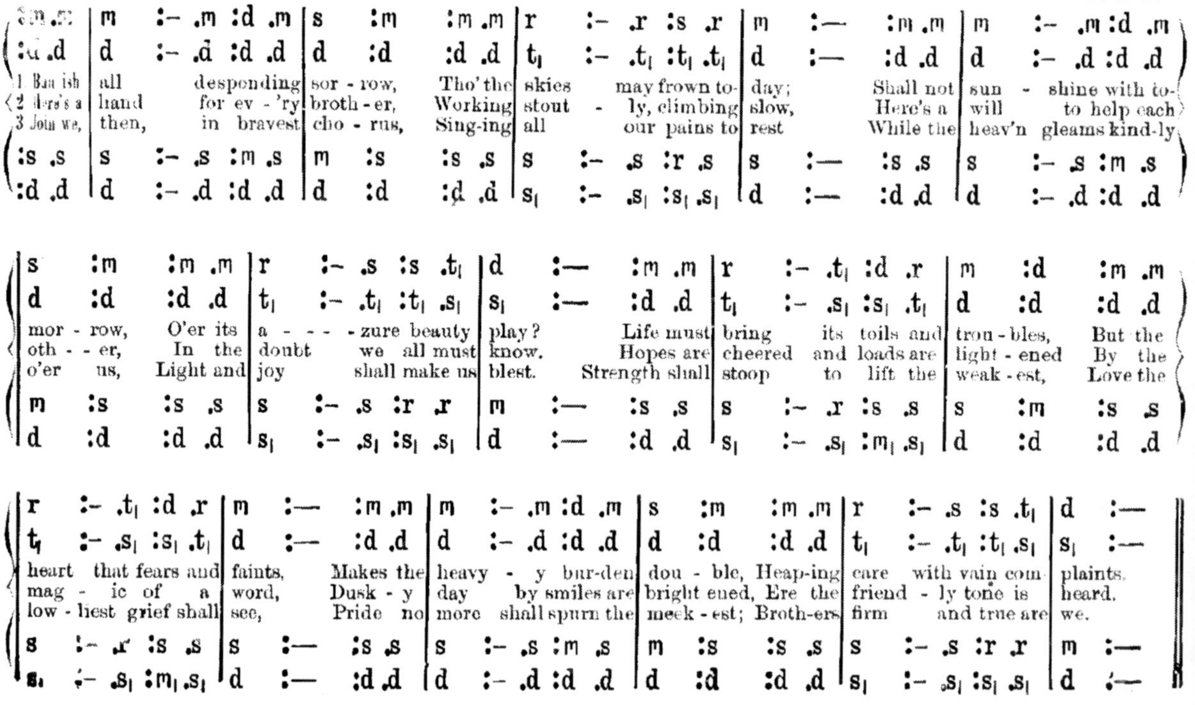

Quarter-pulse tones are to be taught next. The method for doing this need not be described—the same process pursued with half-pulse tones may be used or they may be taught at once by pattern from the Time Chart or Finger-signs or from the exercises below. They are named *tafatefe*. They are indicated in the notation by a comma in the middle of each half-pulse, thus, |l ,l .l ,l :
ta fa te fe

Exercises to be taataid and laa-ed and taataid in tune:

103. Keys C, G.

TAA TAI ta-fa-te-fe | TAA TAI TAA | ta-fa-te-fe TAA TAI | ta-fa-te-fe TAA
l .l :l ,l .l ,l	l .l :l	l ,l .l ,l :l .l	l ,l .l ,l :l
d .d :m ,m .m ,m	d .m :s	s ,s .s ,s :m .s	s ,s .s ,s :d'
d .t_1 :d ,r .m ,r	d .t_1 :d	r ,d .t_1 ,d :r .r	m ,r .d ,r :m

ta-fa-te-fe TAA TAI | ta-fa-te-fe TAA | ta-fa-te-fe ta-fa-te-fe | TAA TAI TAA
l ,l .l ,l :l .l	l ,l .l ,l :l	l ,l .l ,l :l ,l .l ,l	l .l :l	
d' ,d' .d' ,d' :t .t	d' ,d' .d' ,d' :s	s ,s .s ,s :m ,m .m ,m	s .t :d'	
m ,r .d ,t_1 :d .s_1	d ,t_1 .d ,r :m	m ,r .d ,r :m ,r .d ,r	d .t_1 :d	

104. Key G. Round in three parts. A. L. C.

| d :d | d :d | t_1 .t_1 :t_1 | d .d :d | * m :m | m :m | r .r :s | m .m :m |
One, two, three, four, keep the time, keep the time, One, two, three, four, Voices chime, voices chime,

| s ,s .s ,s :s .m | d .m :s | s_1 ,s_1 .s_1 ,s_1 :s_1 .s_1 | d :— ||
Tra la la la la la la la la, Tra la la la la la la

105. Key D. Round in three parts.

| d :d .d | r :r .r | m :r | d :— |
Come with the reap - - ers this sun - ny morn,

*
| m :m | s :s | s .s :s .s | m :— |
Hear them sing a - - mong the yel - low corn,

| s ,s .s ,s :s | t ,t .t ,t :t | d' ,d' .d' ,d' :d' .t | d' :— ||
Merri - ly they sing, mer-ri - ly they sing, Tra la la la la la la.

106. Key F. Round in four parts. U.

| d ,d .d ,d :m .m | r .r :m | * m ,m .m ,m :s .s | t_1 .t_1 :d |
Mer-ri - ly the bells are ring - ing near; Cheeri-ly the birds are sing - ing here.

| s ,s .s ,s :s .s | s ,s .s ,s :s | d ,d .d ,d :d .d | s_1 ,s_1 .s_1 ,s :d ||
Listen to the bells! how merri - ly they ring! Listen to the birds! how cheeri-ly they sing.

A. S. KIEFFER.

LOVELY MAY.

B. C. UNSELD.

107. KEY C.

s	.s	:s	s ,s .s ,s :s	s	.m	:s*	.d¹	d¹	:t
m	.m	:m	m ,m .m ,m :m	m	.d	:m	.m	m	:r
1. Love-ly		May,	mer-ry, mer-ry May!	Bird - lets	now	are	sing	-	ing;
2. Hap-py		May,	mer-ry, mer-ry May!	With our	songs	we	greet		thee;
3. Balm-y		May,	mer-ry, mer-ry May!	How we	love	thy	glad	-	ness;
d¹	.d¹	:d¹	d¹,d¹.d¹,d¹:d¹	d¹	.s	:d¹	.s	s	:s
d	.d	:d	d ,d .d ,d :d	d	.d	:d	.d	s	:s

r¹	.r¹	:r¹	r¹,r¹.r¹,r¹:r¹	m¹	.r¹	:d¹	.t	d¹	:—
s	.s	:s	s ,s .s ,s :s	s	.s	:m	.r	m	:—
Ev - ery - where,			thro' the balmy air,	Songs of	pleas - ure	ring!		
On the	hill,		by the shining rill	Now we	wel - come	thee.		
Buds and	flow'rs		thro' the sunny hours	Ope their	scent - ed	leaves.		
t	.t	:t	t ,t .t ,t :t	d¹	.t	:d¹	.s	s	:—
s	.s	:s	s ,s .s ,s :s	s	.s	:s	.s	d	:—

s	.s	:m	.m	s	.s	:d¹	t ,t .t ,t :r¹	d¹,d¹.d¹,d¹:m¹
m	.m	:d	.d	m	.m	:m	r ,r .r ,r :r	m,m .m ,m :m
Wel - come, wel - come,				love - ly		May,	Merry, merry May,	merry, merry May;
d¹	.d¹	:s	.s	d¹	.d¹	:s	s ,s .s ,s :s	d¹,d¹.d¹,d¹:d¹
d	.d	:d	.d	d	.d	:d	s ,s .s ,s :s	d,d .d ,d :d

s	.s	:m	.m	s	.s	:m¹	m¹,m¹.m¹,m¹:r¹ ,r¹ .r¹ ,r¹	d¹	:—
m	.m	:d	.d	m	.m	:s	s ,s .s ,s :s ,s .s ,s	m	:—
Wel - come, wel - come,				love - ly		May,	Merry, merry, merry, merry	May.	
d¹	.d¹	:s	.s	d¹	.d¹	:d¹	d¹,d¹.d¹,d¹:t ,t .t ,t	d¹	:—
d	.d	:d	.d	d	.d	:d	s ,s .s ,s :s ,s .s ,s	d	:—

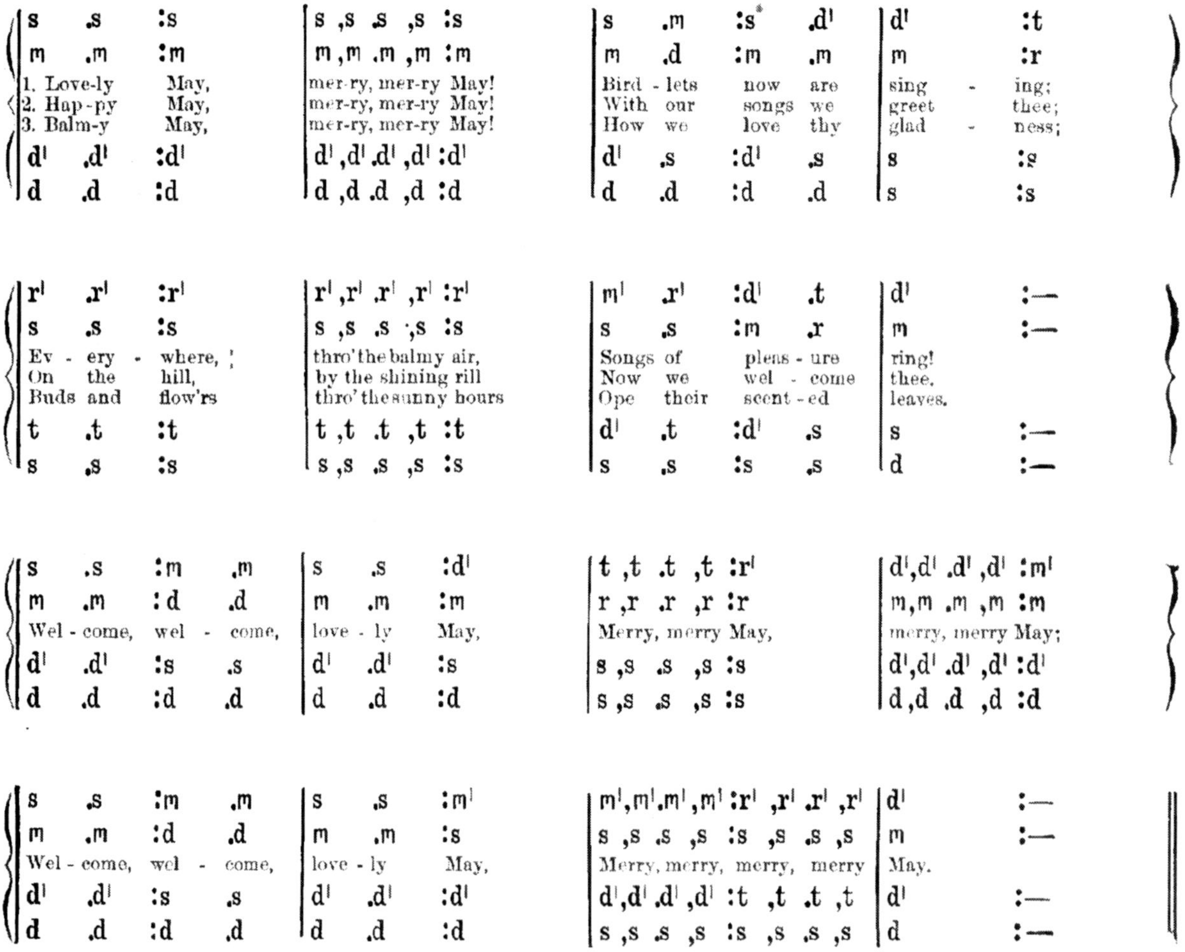

Modulator Voluntaries, EAR EXERCISES, DICTATION, *Pointing* and *Writing from Memory*, as described in the first step are to be practiced regularly at every lesson. Pulse-and-a-half tones, quarter pulse tones and silences, as in the following example—

d	:—	.r	m	:		m,m.m,m: m	.r	d	:—	‖

would be dictated thus, "TRAA d," "—AATAI r," "TLAA m," "SAA,"

"tafatefe m m m m," "TAATAI m r," "TLAA-AA d."

Certificates.—Pupils now begin to make up their list of three tunes for the Junior School Certificate or six tunes for the Elementary Certificate. No tune of less than eight four-pulse measures or sixteen two-pulse measures should be accepted. For instructions in *Voice Training, Breathing, Harmony*, etc., belonging to this step, the teacher will consult the Standard Course.

QUESTIONS FOR WRITTEN OR ORAL EXAMINATION.

DOCTRINE.

1 What two new tones have you learned in this step?
2 What is the relative position of *Ray* to *Doh?*
3 What is the relative position of *Te* to *Doh?*
4. What is the mental effect of *Ray?*
5. What is the mental effect of *Te?*
6. What is the manual sign for *Ray?* For *one Ray?*
7 What is the manual sign for *Te?* For *Te one?*
8 What chord is formed of the tones d m s?
9 What chord is formed of the tones s t r?
10 What new kind of accent have you learned in this step?
11 How is the medium accent indicated in the notation?
12 How is the medium accent indicated in the time names?
13 What two new kinds of measure have you learned in this step?
14 What is the order of accents in four pulse measure?
15 What is the order of accents in six pulse measure?
16 What is the time-name for a silent pulse?
17 How is it indicated in the notation?
18 What is the time-name of a pulse and a-half tone?
19 How is it indicated in the notation?
20. What is the time-name of four quarter pulse tones?
21 What is the time-name of the first quarter of a pulse? The second? The third? The fourth?
22. How are quarter pulses indicated in the notation?

PRACTICE.

23 Sing to *laa* the *Ray* and the *Te*, to any *Doh* the teacher gives
24 Ditto the *Ray'* and *Te* to any *Doh'*
25 Taatai from memory any one of Exs 85 to 89, 96 to 99 chosen by the teacher
26 Taatai the upper part of one of the Exs 103 or 107, chosen by the teacher
27 Taatai in tune the upper part of Exs 102 or 107, chosen by the teacher
28 Point on the Modulator (sol faing) any one of the following four Exs 60 61, 78 79, chosen by the teacher
29 Write from memory any other of these exercises chosen by the teacher
30 Follow the teacher's pointing in a new voluntary containing *Doh Me, Soh, Te* and *Ray*, but no difficulties of time
31 From any phrase (belonging to this step) sung to figures, tell your teacher (or write down) which figure was sung to *Ray*,—to *Ray'*,—to *Te*—to *Te,*
32 Having heard the tonic chord tell your teacher (or write down) which tone (*Doh Me, Soh, Te* or *Ray*) was sung to *laa* Do this with two different tones
33. Taatai any Rhythm of at least two measures belonging to this step which the teacher shall *laa* to you He will first give you the measure and rate of movement by taataing two plain measures and marking the accent by *r* and *l* without beating time, but the two measures you have to copy he will simply *laa* on one tone
34 Taatai in tune any Rhythm of at least two measures belonging to this step which after giving the measure and rate as above, the teacher may sol fa to you

pp **108.** KEY C.

| m :m :m | f :f :m | r :m :f | m :— :— |
| *Wand - 'ring in* | *dark - ness and* | *grop - ing our* | *way;* |

ff

| d' :d' :d' | r' :r' :d' | t :d' :r' | d' :— :— ‖
| LIGHT WILL BE | WEL - COME, YES, | WEL - COME THE | DAY. |

p **109.** KEY D.

| d .d :d | r .r :r | *m* m .d :r .m | f :— | *f* s .s :s |
| *Soft - ly now,* | *soft - ly now,* | Lightly raise the | song, | LOUDER NOW, |

| l .l :l | *ff* t .s :l .t | d' :— | *ff* d' .d' :d' | t .t :t |
| LOUDER NOW, | LOUD AND VER - Y | STRONG | LOUD AND STRONG, | LOUD AND STRONG, |

| *f* l .d' :t .l | s :— | *m* f .f :f | m .m :m | *p* r .f :m .r | d :— ‖
| NOW LESS LOUD AND | STRONG | Soft-er now, | soft-er now, | *Soft ly end our* | *song.* |

THIRD STEP.

The prominent topics of the Third Step are as follows—The tones FAH and LAH, completing the Scale. The Standard Scale. To pitc tunes. Classification of voices. The Metronome. The Half-pulse Silence. Various combinations of Quarter-pulses. Modification o mental effects.

s¹

f¹

m¹

r¹

DOH¹

TE

The tones *Fah* and *Lah* are now to be taught. The method for doing this need not be described, the same process which was used for r and t will be used for the new tones, see p. 19. The mental effect of *Fah*, a gloomy, serious, desolate tone, and of *Lah*, a sorrowful, weeping tone, may be shown by the following examples.

KEY C OR D.

|d :s |m :d |f :— |d :— ‖

|d¹ :m |s :d¹ |f :— |m :— ‖

|d :m |r :s |f :— |m :— ‖

KEY G.

|d :s |m :d |{f :— |d :— ‖
           |f₁ :— |d :— ‖}

KEY C OR D.

|d :m |s :m |l :— |s :— ‖

|d :m |s :m |d¹ :t |l :— ‖

KEY G.

|d :m |r :l₁ |d :t₁ |l₁ :— ‖

|d :r |m :d |l₁ :— |s₁ :— ‖

After the mental effects of the new tones are developed and their appropriate hand-signs taught, the tones are then to be thoroughly practiced, from the modulator, hand-signs, ear exer cises, etc. The chord of FAH, or *Sub-Dominant*, consisting of the tones f l d¹, may be brought out. See chords of DOH and SOH page 20. The chord of *Seven-Soh* (7S) or *Dominant Seventh*, con sisting of the tones s t r f, although belonging to the Fourth Step, may be taught at this point.

The following exercises should be carefully taught by pat tern from the modulator.

LAH

SOH

FAH

ME

RAY

DOH

t₁

l₁

s₁

110. KEY C.

{|d :m :s |f :l :d¹ |s :t :r¹ |d¹:—:— |r¹ :t :s |d¹:l :f |s :r :m |d :—:— ‖

111. KEY C.

{|d :m |s :m |f :l |d¹ :l |s :t |r¹ :t |d¹ :— |— :— }

{|d¹ :s |m :s |d¹ :l |f :l |d¹ :s |t :r¹ |d¹ :— |— :— ‖

112. KEY A.

{|d :m :d |l₁ :f₁ :l₁ |s₁ :t₁ :r |d :—:— |d :s₁ :m₁ |d :l₁ :f₁ |r :t₁ :s₁ |d :—:— ‖

113. KEY G.

{|d :s₁ |m :d |d :l₁ |f :l₁ |s₁ :t₁ |r :f |m :— |— :— }

{|m :d |s₁ :d |f :d |l₁ :d |t₁ :r |f :t₁ |d :— |— :— ‖

The Scale. After the tones **d r m f s l t d'** have been sung in successive order, the teacher will explain that this series of tones is called the Scale. Each tone of the scale differs from the others in pitch. By "pitch" is meant the highness or lowness of tones. It may be observed that the eighth tone above or below any given tone has the same mental effect and the same name. The two tones are so nearly alike in character that the ear accepts them as relatively the same notwithstanding the difference of pitch. They are Replicates or Octaves one of the other. The word octave sometimes means a *set* of eight tones, sometimes the eighth tone and sometimes the difference of pitch or distance between the two tones. The teacher will question the class thoroughly in regard to the scale—"Which is the third tone?" Me. "The fifth tone?" Soh. "The second tone?" "Ray—and so on, also questions in regard to the mental effects and hand-signs. He will explain that **d m** and **s** are readily distinguished as the strong, bold tones of the scale, and **r f l** and **t** as the leaning tones. **t** and **f** have the strongest leaning or leading tendency, **t** leading upward to **d** and **f** leading downward to **m**. The most important tone of the scale, the strongest, most restful, the governing tone, is called the Key-tone. A key tone, with the tones related to it or belonging to it, is called a key. A distinction is made between "key" and "scale." A Key is a family of related tones, consisting of a key-tone with six related tones and their replicates. A scale is the tones of a key arranged in successive order, ascending or descending. The intervals of the scale, large and small steps, etc., will be explained in the Fourth Step.

The Standard Scale. The teacher will show by practical examples that the scale may be sung at different pitches. Any conceivable pitch may be taken as the key-tone, and the other related tones will readily take their proper places. It is necessary to have one particular scale of pitch as a standard from which all the others are to be reckoned. This scale is called The Standard Scale (commonly known as Natural Scale). The particular degree of pitch which is taken as the key-tone of the Standard Scale is named C, *Ray* is D, *Me* is E, *Fah* is F and so on, as shown in the diagram. These pitch names (letters) of the Standard Scale should be thoroughly committed to memory. The correct pitch of this scale may be obtained from a piano or organ, or any of the common musical instruments properly tuned, or, for ordinary vocal purposes from a C' tuning fork. It is a great advantage to have one tone in absolute pitch fixed on the memory, and it is more easy to do this than is commonly supposed. The teacher will frequently ask the pupils to sing C' (which in a man's voice is really C) and then tests them with the tuning-fork. In this way the power of recollection is soon developed. In estimating the chances of certainty however, we should always bear in mind that any bodily or mental depression has a tendency to flatten even our recollection. Any pitch of the Standard Scale may be taken as a key tone. A scale or key is named from the letter taken as the key-tone. The different keys are indicated in the notation by the signatures "Key C," "Key G," and so on.

To pitch tunes. Up to this point the teacher has fixed the pitch of the key-tone. The pupils themselves should now learn to do it in turn. The pupil strikes the C' tuning-fork, and taking the tone it gives, sings down the scale to the tone he wants. This tone he swells out and then repeats it to the syllable *doh*, and perhaps sings the scale or chord of DOH to confirm the key. Further instructions on pitching tunes in the Fourth Step.

d'—C'
t—B

l—A

s—G

f—F
m—E

r—D

d—C

114. KEY G. Round in three parts.

|d :d |f :m |r :s |m :— |d :d |l_1 :d |t_1 :t_1 |d :— |d :d |f_1 :f_1 |s_1 :s_1 |d :— ||
Come now let us mer-ry be, Fill our souls with mirth and glee, Hearts and voices all a - gree

115. KEY B♭. Round in four parts.

:s_1 |d :d |r :r |m :m |d :d' |l_1 :l_1 |t_1 :t_1 |d :— |—
If hap - pi - ness has not her seat And cen - tre in the breast,

:s_1 |f_1 :f_1 |f_1 :f_1 |m_1 :s_1 |d :s_1 |l_1 :f_1 |r_1 :s_1 |d_1 :— |— ||
We may be wise or rich or great, But nev - er can be blest.

116. KEY D. Round in two parts. T. F. S.

|m :m |f :m |m :m |f :m |m :m |f :m |d :r |m :
If the weath - er keeps so storm - y, and the rain comes down like that,

|s :s |l :s |s :s |l :s |s :s |l :s |m :s |d' : ||
I shall nev - er have the priv - i - lege of wear - ing my new hat.

117. KEY F. Round in three parts. T. F. S.

s :— :l	s :— :m	s :— :l	s :— :m	s :f :m	r :m :f	m :— :—	— :— :—
With the	Spring - time	comes the	rob - - in,	Singing his	cheer-ful re -	frain;	
*m :— :f	m :— :d	m :— :f	m :— :d	m :r :d	t_1 :d :r	d :— :—	— :— :—
Sing a -	way you	hap - py	bird - ling,	Bring us the	Spring-time a -	gain:	
d :— :	d :— :	d :— :	d :— :	s_1 :s_1 :s_1	s_1 :s_1 :s_1	d :— :—	— :— :— ‖
Hark!	hark!	hark!	hark!	Hear the mel -	o - di - ous	strain.	

118. KEY C. T. F. S.

:s	l :s	m :s	l :s	m :s	l :l	t :t	d^1 :—	—
1.O	sweet to	me the	gen - tle	spring, When	earth is	robed in	flowers,	
2.The	plow - man	drives his	shin - ing	share A -	cross the	mel - low	lea.	
:m	f :m	d :m	f :m	d :m	f :f	r :r	m :—	—
:d^1	t :l	s :d^1	t :l	s :l	s :m	f :s	m :—	— ‖
And	beau - ti -	- ful the	sum - mer	time, With	all its	leaf - y	bowers.	
And	lays the	fur - rows	broad and	fair, As	waves up -	on the	sea.	
:m	s :f	m :m	s :f	m :f	m :d	r :m	d :—	— ‖

119. KEY G. T. F. S.

m :— :m	s :— :m	d :— :d	m :— :d	l_1 :— :d	f :— :l_1	s_1 :d :m	r :— :—
All that	now so	dark ap -	pears, While	earth's dark	shad - ows	dim the	sight,
d :— :d	m :— :d	m_1 :— :m_1	s_1 :— :m_1	f_1 :— :l_1	l_1 :— :f_1	m_1 :s_1 :d	t_1 :— :—
m :— :m	s :— :m	d :— :d	m :— :d	l_1 :— :d	f :— :l_1	s_1 :m :r	d :— :— ‖
All our	doubts and	all our	fears Will	be made	clear in	heav - en's	light.
d :— :d	m :— :d	m_1 :— :m_1	s_1 :— :m_1	f_1 :— :l_1	l_1 :— :f_1	m_1 :s_1 :f_1	m_1 :— :— ‖

Tuning Exercises.—See page 21. To be *Solfa-ed*, *laa-ed* and then sung very softly to *loo*.

Sing Ex. 120 first as written. Second time, Soprano take the Tenor, Tenor take the Contralto, singing d^1 instead d, Contralto take the Soprano. Third time Soprano and Contralto change parts, Soprano singing d^1 instead of d. In the key G the Tenor and Contralto change parts, Contralto singing l_1 instead of l, and Base will take f_1 instead of f.

120. KEYS C, E♭ AND G.

d :—	m :d	f :—	:	:	f :—	f :f	m :— ‖
d :—	m :d	f :—	:	d :—	— :—	d :d	d :— ‖
d :—	m :d	f :—	l :—	— :—	— :—	l :l	s :— ‖
d :—	m :d	f :—	— :—	— :—	— :—	f :f	d :— ‖

121. KEY C. Sing only as written.

d :—	m :d	s :—	:	:	f :—	m :r	m :—
d :—	m :d	s :—	:	r :—	— :—	d :t_1	d :—
d :—	m :d	s :—	t :—	— :—	— :—	d^1 :s	s :—
d :—	m :d	s :—	— :—	— :—	— :—	s :s_1	d :— ‖

122. KEY E♭.

d :—	m :d	s :—	:	:	f :—	m :r	d :—
d :—	m :d	s_1 :—	t_1 :—	— :—	— :—	d :t_1	d :—
d :—	m :d	s :—	:	r :—	— :—	s :f	m :—
d :—	m :d	s_1 :—	— :—	— :—	— :—	s_1 :s_1	d :—

123. KEY F.

d :—	m :d	s :—	:	r :—	— :—	d :t_1	d :—
d :—	m :d	s_1 :—	t_1 :—	— :—	— :—	d :s_1	s_1 :—
d :—	m :d	s :—	:	:	f :—	m :r	m :—
d :—	m :d	s_1 :—	— :—	— :—	— :—	s_1 :s_1	d :—

COMING NIGHT.

124. KEY F. M. 86. B. C. U.

d :d	t_1 :t_1	l_1 :l_1	s_1 :—	d :d	r :m	s :m	r :—
s_1 :s_1	s_1 :s_1	f_1 :f_1	m_1 :—	s_1 :d	t_1 :d	d :d	t_1 :—
1. Slow-ly,	gen - tly	comes *the*	*night,*	With its	heav - y	*e - bon*	*pall,*
2. O, the	won - drous	brow *of*	*night,*	Beau - ti -	ful with	moon and	*star,*
m :m	r :r	d :r	m :—	m :m	s :s	s :s	s :—
d :d	s_1 :s_1	l_1 :t_1	d :—	d :d	s_1 :d	m :d	s_1 :—

m :m	f :f	s :d^1	l :—	l :s	s :m	m :r	d :—
d :d	t_1 :t_1	d :d	d :—	d :d	t_1 :d	d :t_1	d :—
But the	cres - cent	RIS - ING	CLEAR,	Sheds a	mel - low	*light o'er*	*all,*
Send - ing	forth its	SIL - VER	LIGHT,	O'er the	dark - 'ning	*shades a -*	*far,*
s :s	s :s	s :s	f :—	f :s	s :s	s :f	m :—
d :d	r :r	m :m	f :—	f :m	r :d	s_1 :s_1	d :—

SILENT VALE.

p **125.** KEY E♭. M. 76. B. C. U.

s :s | l :l	s :m | s :m	d :d | r :r	*m* m :s | r :—	s :s | l :l
d :d | d :d	d :d | d :d	d :d | t_1 :t_1	d :d | t_1 :—	d :d | d :d
1. *Si - lent vale! where*	love and pleas - ure	Ev - er round our	cot - tage flow'd,	Beauteous as the
2. *Fare ye well, ye*	love - ly shad - ows,	Which have shielded	oft our head;	Still be green ye
m :m | f :f	m :s | m :s	l :m | s :s	s :s | s :—	m :m | f :f
d :d | d :d	d :d | d :d	l_1 :l_1 | s_1 :s_1	d :m | s :—	d :d | d :d

d^1 :l | s :m	s :s | d :d	m :r | d :—	*p* f :f | l :l	m :m | s :—
d :d | d :d	d :d | d :d	d :t_1 | d :—	d :d | d :d	d :d | d :—
WESTERN EVENING,	Love-ly as the	*sun-lit cloud,*	*Peaceful as the*	*ves - per bell,*
LOVE - LY MEADOWS,	Fields with brightest	*flow'rs be spread;*	*Fields where oft the*	*ves - per song.*
l :f | m :s	m :m | m :m	s :f | m :—	l :l | f :f	s :s | m :—
d :d | d :d	d :d | l_1 :l_1	s_1 :s_1 | d :—	f :f | f :f	d :d | d :—

m s :m |s :m	d :r |m :—	s :m |s :m	*p* s :— |s :—	s :— |— :—
d :d |d :d	d :t, |d :—	d :d |d :d	d :— |t, :—	d :— |— :—
Thee we bid a	long fare - well,	Thee we bid a	*long fare -*	*well.*
Swelled in ech - oes	sweet and long,	Thee we bid a	*long fare -*	*well.*
m :s |m :d	m :s |s :—	m :s |m :s	m :— |r :—	m :— |— :—
d :d |d :d	l, :s, |d :—	d :d |d :d	s, :— |s, :—	d :— |— :—

SONG OF THE AUTUMN.

126. Key C. M. 76. Words and Music by H. R. Palmer, by per.

d' :d' :d' |t :t :t	l :l :l |s :s :s	f :f :f |m :m :m	r :— :— |— :— :—
m :m :m |s :s :s	f :f :f |m :m :m	r :r :r |d :d :d	t, :— :— |— :— :—
1.Beauti - ful morning, the	au-tumn a - dorn-ing, Oc -	to - ber's as pleasant as	May;
2.Let us be straying, no	time for de - lay - ing, Oc -	to - ber's as pleasant as	May;
s :s :s |s :s :s	s :l :t |d' :d' :d'	s :s :s |s :s :s	s :— :— |— :— :—
d :d :d |d :d :d	d :d :d |d :d :d	t, :t, :t, |d :d :m	s :— :— |— :— :—

r' :r' :r' |d' :d' :d'	t :t :t |l :l :l	s :s :s |l :l :l	s :— :— |s :l :t
f :f :f |m :m :m	r :r :r |m :m :m	r :r :r |r :r :r	r :— :— |r :m :f
Long tho' the shadows Thrown	out on the meadows, The	for - ests are ro - sy and	gay; Mer - ri - ly
Nuts we will gath - er To	cheer wintry weather; A -	way to the for - ests, a -	way; Cheerful - ly
t :t :t |d' :d' :d'	r' :r' :r' |d' :d' :d'	t :t :t |d' :d' :d'	t :— :— |t :d' :r'
s :s :s |s :s :s	s :s :s |d :d :d	r :r :r |r :r :r	s :— :— |f :m :r

d' :d' :d' |t :t :t	l :l :l |s :s :s	f :f :f |m :m :m	r :— :— |— :— :—
m :m :m |s :s :s	f :f :f |m :m :m	r :r :r |d :d :d	t, :— :— |— :— :—
birds are now filling the	air with their trilling, Let	us be as joy - ful as	they;
squirrels are chipping in	time with our tripping, They	of - fer to show us the	way;
m' :r' :d' |s :s :s	s :l :t |d' :d' :d'	s :s :s |s :s :s	s :— :— |— :— :—
d :d :d |d :d :d	d :d :d |d :d :d	l, :t, :d |r :m :f	s :— :— |— :— :—

r' :r' :r' |d' :d' :d'	t :t :t |l :l :l	s :l :s |f :m :r	d :— :— |— :— :—
f :f :f |m :m :m	r :r :r |m :m :m	r :r :r |t, :t, :t,	d :— :— |— :— :—
Fling a-way sor - row, Ne'er	grieve for the morrow, Oc -	to - ber's as pleasant as	May.
Fling a-way sor - row, Ne'er	grieve for the morrow, Oc -	to - ber's as pleasant as	May.
t :t :t |d' :d' :d'	r' :r' :r' |d' :d' :d'	t :t :t |s :s :f	m :— :— |— :— :—
s :s :s |s :s :s	s :s :s |d :d :d	r :r :r |s, :s, :s,	d :— :— |— :— :—

MOTHER, CHILDHOOD, FRIENDS AND HOME.

127. KEY F. M. 76. CHESTER G. ALLEN.

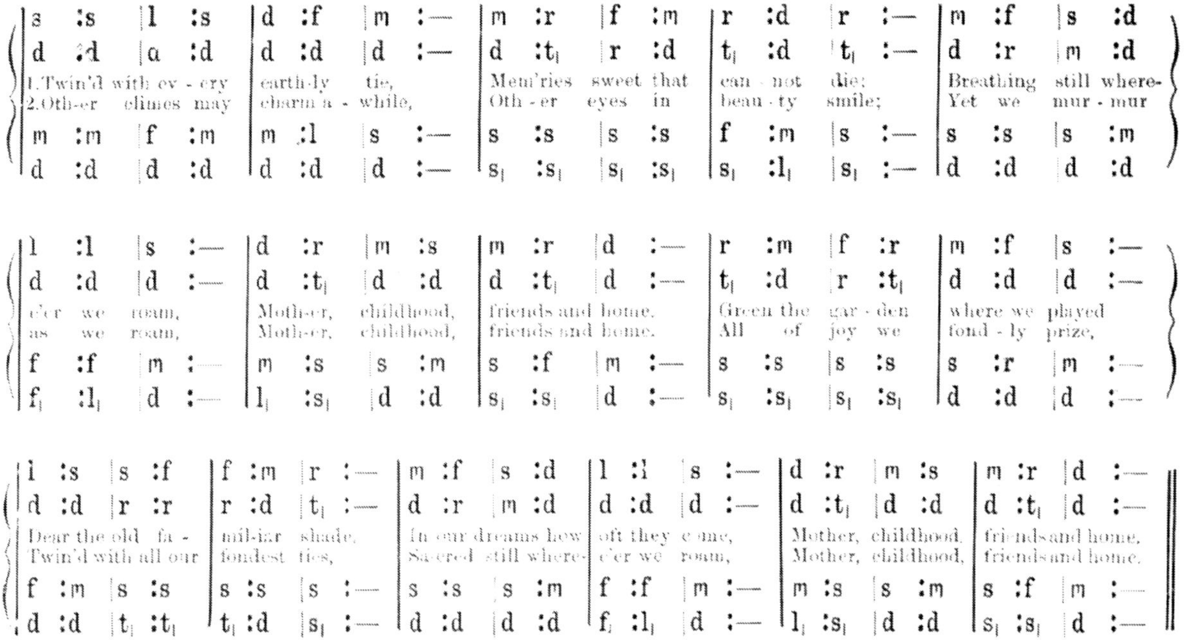
1.Twin'd with ev - ery earth-ly tie, Mem'ries sweet that can - not die; Breathing still where-
2.Oth-er climes may charm a - while, Oth - er eyes in beau - ty smile; Yet we mur - mur
e'er we roam, Mother, childhood, friends and home. Green the gar - den where we played
as we roam, Mother, childhood, friends and home. All of joy we fond - ly prize,
Dear the old fa - mil-iar shade, In our dreams how oft they come, Mother, childhood, friends and home.
Twin'd with all our fondest ties, Sacred still where-e'er we roam, Mother, childhood, friends and home.

THE WAYSIDE WELL.

128. KEY D. B. C. UNSELD.

1.Oh! the pret - ty way-side well, Wreath'd a - bout with ros - - es, When be-guiled with
2.Treads the drov-er on the sward, Comes the la - b'rer to thee, Free as gen - tle -
3.Fair the greet-ing face as - cends, Like a na - iad daugh - ter, When the pea - sant
sooth-ing spell, Wea-ry foot re - pos - es; With a wel - come fresh and green,
man or lord, From his steed to woo thee; Thou from parch-ing lips dost earn,
las - sie bends, To the trem-bling wa - ter; When she leans up - on her pail,

l .l :d' .l | l :s | d' .d' :s .s | m .f :s | l .s :m .d | r :d ||
f .f :l .f | f :m | m .m :m .m | d .r :m | f .m :d .d | t, :d ||
Wave thy bor-der | grass - es, | By the dust - y | trav-'ler seen, | Sigh-ing as he | pass - es.
Many a murmured | bless - ing, | And en - joy - est | in thy turn, | In - no - cent ca - | ress - ing
Glanc-ing o'er the | mead - ow, | Sweet shall fall the | whispered tale, | Soft the doub-le | shad - ow.
d' .d' :d' .d' | d' :d' | s .s :d' .d' | s .s :d' | t .d' :s .m | f :m ||
f .f :f .f | d :d | d .d :d .d | d .d :d | s, .s, :s, .s, | s, :d ||

MUSIC EVERYWHERE.

129. Key G. M. 90. — Chester G. Allen, by per.

d .d :t, .l, | s, :d | r .r :d .t, | d :— | d .d :t, .l,
m, .m, :s, .f, | m, :s, | l, .l, :s, .s, | s, :— | m, .m, :s, .f,
1. Mu-sic in the | spring - time, | Wak-ing up the | flowers; | Mu - sic in the
2. Mu-sic in the | rain - drops, | Fall-ing in the | night; | Mu - sic in the
d .d :d .d | d :m | f .f :m .r | m :— | d .d :d .d
d .d :d .d | d :d | f, .f, :s, .s, | d :— | d .d :d .d

s, :d | r .r :d .t, | d :— | r .m :r .d | t, :d
m, :s, | l, .l, :s, .s, | s, :— | t, .d :t, .l, | s, :s,
green trees, | Mu - sic in the | bowers; | Mu - sic in the | cot - - tage,
young birds, | When the day is | bright; | Mu - sic in the | crick - et,
d :m | f .f :m .r | m :— | s .s :s .r | r :m
d :d | f, .f, :s, .s, | d, :— | s, .s, :s, .s, | s, :s,

r .m :f .m | r :— | d .d :t, .l, | s, :d | r .r :d .t, | d :— ||
t, .d :r .d | t, :— | s, .s, :s, .f, | m, :s, | l, .l, :s, .s, | s, :— ||
Mu-sic in the | lea, | Mu-sic in the | south wind, | Mu-sic o'er the | sea,
Chirping loud and | clear, | Mu-sic in the | spring time, | Mu-sic all the | year,
s .s :s .s | s :— | m .m :d .d | d :m | f .f :m .r | m :— ||
s, .s, :s, .s, | s, :— | d .d :d .d | d :d | f, .f, :s, .s, | d :— ||

130. Key D. Crescendo and Diminuendo.

p d :r | m :r | m :f | s :— | *m* s :s | l :s | l :t | d' :—
See the | *sun* in | glo - ry | rise | From the | o - cean's | HEAV - ING | BREAST,

f d' :t | l :s | l :l | s :— | *m* s :f | m :f | m :r | d :— ||
THEN MOVE | O'ER the | bound-less | skies, | Sink - ing | soon *be* - | *neath the* | *West.*

SKATING GLEE.

131. Key C. M. 100 beating twice. A. S. Kieffer.

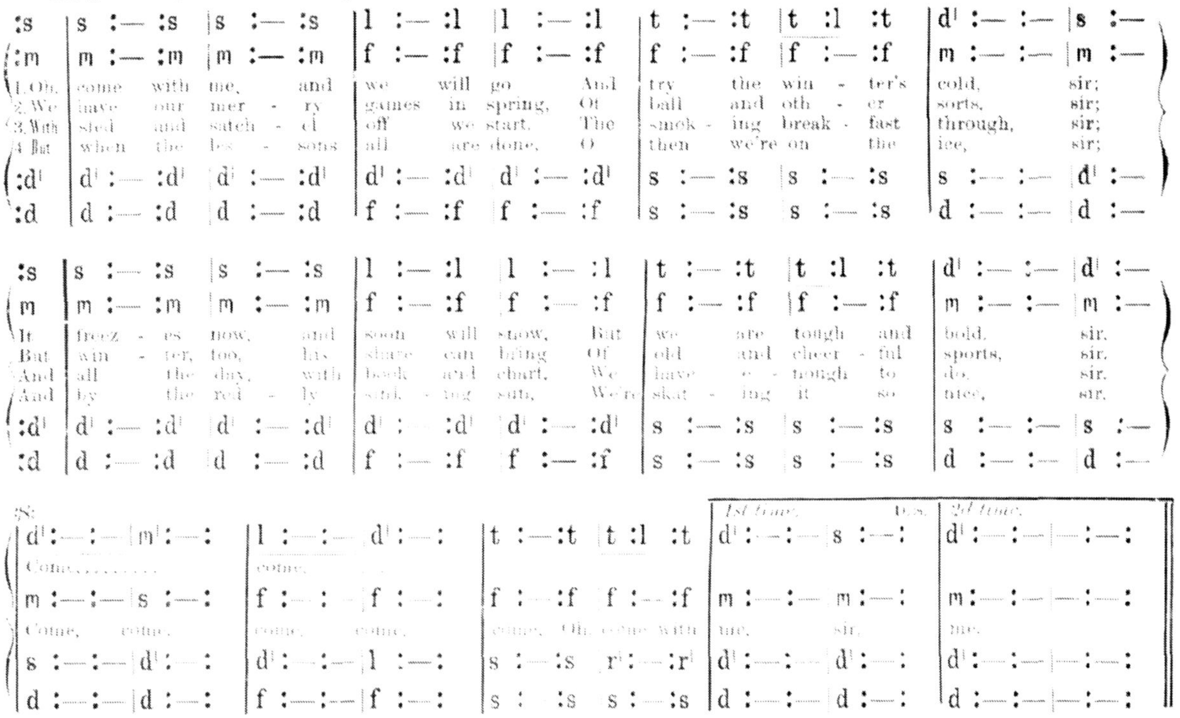
1. Oh, come with me, and we will go And try the win - ter's cold, sir;
2. We have our mer - ry games in spring, Of ball and oth - er sorts, sir;
3. With sled and satch - el off we start, The smok - ing break - fast through, sir;
4. But when the les - sons all are done, O then we're on the ice, sir;
It freez - es now, and soon will snow, But we are tough and bold, sir.
But win - ter, too, has share can bring Of old and cheer - ful sports, sir.
And all the day, with book and chart, We have e - nough to do, sir.
And by the red - ly sink - ing sun, We're skat - ing it so nice, sir.
Come, come.
Come, come, come, come, come, Oh, come with me, sir.
1st time. D.S. 2d time.
me.

LO! THE GLAD MAY MORN.

132. Key D. M. 120. *Brightly.* From the German.

1. Lo! the glad May morn, With her rosy light is breaking, O'er the hills so love - ly and fair;
2. O'er the rus - tic wild, When the gentle winds are blowing, We will roam with pleas - ure to - day;
3. Oh, the glad May morn, Like a child she comes to meet us, With her brow all cov - er'd with flow'rs;
And the pure young buds, From their dewy sleep awaking, Mirth and mu - sic float in the air.
On the mos - sy bank, Where the crystal brook is flowing, We will crown our queen of the May.
And she calls the birds, All the merry birds to greet us, And the laugh-ing, bright summer hours.

cres - cen - - - - - - - - - - - - - - - - do.

|:d .m|s .s :s .s|s :d¹ .:|l .l :l .l|l :r¹ .d¹|t :s|s :l .t|d¹ :— ||
|:d .d|m .m :m .m|m :m .s|f .f :f .f|f :f .f|f :m|f :f|m :— ||

Then a- way, a-way, a-way, Then a- way, a-way, a-way, And a - May - ing we will go.

|:m .s|d¹.d¹:d¹ .d¹|d¹ :d¹ .d¹|d¹.d¹:d¹ .d¹|d¹ :l .l|s :s|t :d¹ .r¹|d¹ :— ||
|:d .d|d .d :d .d|d :d .m|f .f :f .f|f :f .f|s :s|s₁ :s₁|d :— ||

MERRILY THE CUCKOO.

133. Key **D.** M. 80.

CHESTER G. ALLEN.

|s .s .s .s :s .m|d¹ .l :s|r .m :f .l|s :m|
|m .m .m .m :m .d|m .f :m|t₁ .d :r .f|m :d|

1. Merri-ly the cuck - oo in the vale To the morn is sing - ing,
2. Pleasantly the sun, with gold-en light, Wakes the earth to glad - ness,

|d¹.d¹ .d¹ .d¹:d¹ .s|s .d¹ :d¹|s .s :s .t|d¹ :s|
|d .d .d .d :d .d|d .d :d|s₁ .s₁ :s₁ .s₁|d :d|

|s .s .s .s :s .m|d¹ .l :s .d¹|t .s :l .t|d¹ :d¹ .s|
|m .m .m .m :m .d|m .f :m .m|f .f :f .f|m :m .m|

Cheeri-ly the ech - o's fair - y tale By sil - ver fount is ring - ing. A -
Happi - ly we roam till dew - y night With out a thought of sad - ness. A -

|d¹.d¹ .d¹ .d¹:d¹ .s|s .d¹ :d¹ .d¹|r¹ .t :d¹ .r¹|d¹ :s .s|
|d .d .d .d :d .d|d .d :d .d|s .s :s .s|d :d .d|

|f .m :r .l|s .f :m .s|f .m :r .l|s .f :m|
|r .d :t₁ .f|m .r :d .m|r .d :t₁ .f|m .r :d|

way, a - way, with foot - steps free, We'll chase the shad - ows o'er the lea:
way, a - way, with foot - steps free, We'll chase the shad - ows o'er the lea:

|s .s :s .t|d¹ .d¹ :d¹ .s|s .s :s .t|d¹ .d¹ :d¹|
|s₁ .s₁ :s₁ .s₁|d .d :d .d|s₁ .s₁ :s₁ .s₁|d .d :d|

:S:

|s .s .s .s :s|l .l .l .l :l|l .r¹ :d¹ .t|d¹ :—|
|m .m .m .m :m|f .f .f .f :f|f .f :m .r|m :—|

Merri - ly we go, Merri - ly we go, None so gay as we.
Merri - ly we go, Merri - ly we go, None so gay as we.

|d¹.d¹ .d¹ .d¹:d¹|d¹.d¹ .d¹ .d¹:d¹|l .l :s .s|s :—|
|d .d .d .d :d|f .f .f .f :f|f .r :s .s₁|d :—|

D.S.

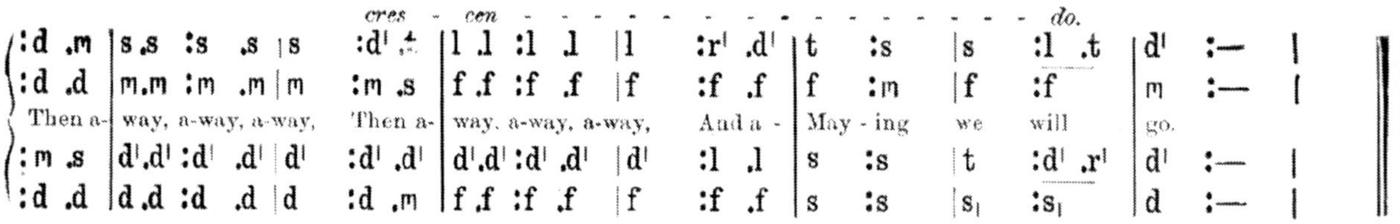

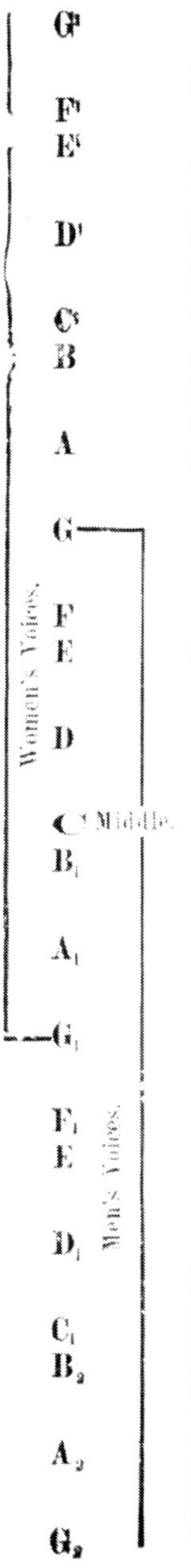

Classification of Voices. The teacher may now proceed to a more definite classification of the voices. He will first explain the difference of pitch between the voices of men and the voices of women. This may be done by having the women sing the scale of C several times alone, and then let the men sing it alone. Most of the men will think they sang the same tones the ladies sang. To prove they did not, let the ladies sing d (C) and sustain it, while the men sing from *their* d up to d', when they reach their d' they will be in exact unison with the ladies. It will thus be seen that the voices of men are naturally an octave lower than the voices of woman. This pitch C, which was just sung in unison, and which stands high in a man's voice and low in a woman's—is called middle C. It is about the middle tone of the usual vocal compass and is common to nearly all musical instruments. The diagram on the left will show the usual vocal compass, male and female. The teacher may find it useful to draw this diagram on the blackboard and have the tones sung at their proper pitch to his pointing. Let all begin at Middle C, the voices of the men and women in exact unison, then, as the teacher points, sing up the scale together. At G the men will stop, many of them will have to stop before reaching that tone, the woman continue up to G'. Then, descending, the men will join in at G (at the proper pitch) and together descend to to G,, at this tone the women will stop, the men continuing down to G₂. Returning upwards, the women will join in at G, and so on.

134. Key C.

LADIES.	d	:d	d	:d	d	:d	d	:d
	Now	our	voic -	es	all	u -	nit -	ed;
GENTLEMEN.	d'	:d'	d'	:d'	d'	:d'	d'	:d'

m	:m	s	:s	d'	:d'	t	:—
Let	us	see	why	they	a -	gree:	
d'	:d'	t	:t	l	:l	s	:—

t	:t	d'	:s .f	m	:f	s	:m
'Tis	be -	cause	when	first	we	start -	ed
s	:f	m	:r	d	:r	m	:d

s	:f	m	:r	d	:d	d	:—
We	were	sing -	ing	Mid -	dle	C.	
m	:f	s	:l .t	d'	:d'	d'	:—

The teacher may next examine the women's voices and classify them into high voices called Soprano and low voices, called Contralto. The high voices of men are called Tenor—the low voices of men are called Base. Each voice should be examined individually. To examine the women's voices the teacher gives G (first G above middle C) as a key-tone and requires the pupil to sing the scale, first upward as high as she can go, and then downward as low as she can go. If the fuller, more beautiful and more easily produced tones of her voice lie above G it may be classed as a high voice. If the best tones lie below G, then it may be called a low voice. The men's voices may be examined in the same way by taking G, (first G, below middle C), as a key-tone. It is the *quality* of the voice, not the compass, that decides the question. Cultivation may afterwards make a difference, but this simple mode of classification will answer for the present purpose. The diagram on the right shows the usual easy compass of the different voices.

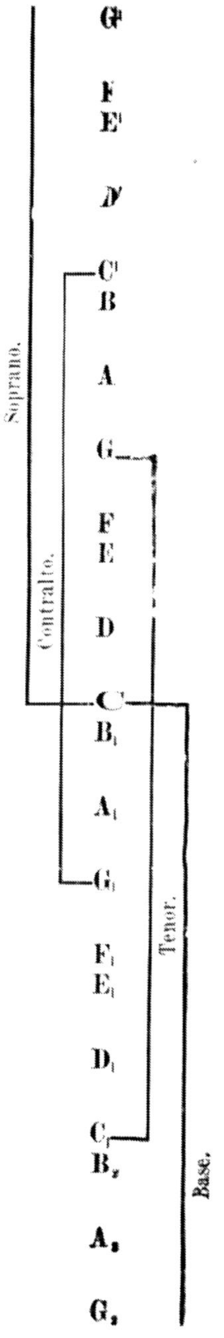

G'	d'
	t
F'	
E'	l
D'	s
C'	f
B	m
A	r
G—	d
	t,
F	
E	l,
D	s,
C	f,
B,	m,

Octave Marks. The pitch of the key-tone of any key is always taken from the unmarked octave of the Standard Scale, and this *doh*, whatever pitch it may be, with the six tones above it are without octave marks. For instance, for the key G, the unmarked G of the Standard Scale is taken as *doh*, this *doh* with the six tones above, **r m f s l t**, are without octave mark; the scale below would have the lower octave mark. This may be illustrated by the following diagram. To save the unnecessary multiplicity of octave marks, both in writing and printing, the Tenor and Base parts are always written an octave higher than they are sung. In quoting octave marks, as in dictation, the upper octave marks are distinguished by naming them before the note, the lower by naming them after—thus, C' is "one-C," d' is "*one-doh*," G, is "G-one," s, is "*soh-one*." It will help the memory to notice that the higher comes first. Thus, we say that the easy Base Compass is, as above, "from G-two to C," that of Contralto "from the G-one to one-C," that of the Tenor "from C-one to unmarked F," that of the Soprano "from unmarked C to one-F."

135. Key C.

SOPRANO.	d :—	d :d	d :—	d :d	m :m	s :s	d' :—	— :s
CONTRALTO.	d :—	d :d	d :—	d :d	m :m	s :s	m :—	— :m
	Once	more u -	nit -	ed, And	then in	four parts	sing;	The
TENOR.	d' :—	d' :d'	d' :—	d' :d'	d' :d'	s :s	s :—	— :d'
BASE.	d' :—	d' :d'	d' :—	d' :d'	d' :d'	s :s	d :—	— :d

	l :l	l :l	s :—	d' :d'	t :t	t :t	d' :—	— :—
	f :f	f :f	m :—	m :m	r :r	r :r	m :—	— :—
	measure	gen - tly	flow -	ing, The	pleas-ant	tones will	ring.	
	d' :d'	d' :d'	d' :—	s :s	s :s	s :s	s :—	— :—
	f :f	f :f	d :—	d :d	s :s	s :s	d :—	— :—

Unison really means two or more voices singing the same identical tone, as in the first two measures of No. 135, but it is generally used to mean that men and women sing the same part, *i. e.*, the men an octave lower than the women, as in the first two measures o No. 136.

SONGS OF PRAISE.

136. Key C. H. R. Palmer.

d :- .m	s :s	l :d'	d' :—	m' :- .f'	m' :d'	t :d'	r' :—
d :- .m	s :s	l :d'	d' :—	s :- .l	s :m	f :m	s :—
1.Songs of	praise the	an - gels	sang,	Heav'n with	hal - le -	lu - jahs	rang,
2.Heav'n and	earth must	pass a -	way;	Songs of	praise shall	crown the	day;
d :- .m	s :s	l :d'	d' :—	d' :- .d'	d' :d'	r' :d'	t :—
d :- .m	s :s	l :d'	d' :—	d' :- .d'	d' :d'	s :s	s :—

d :- .m	s :s	l :d'	d' :—	m' :- .r'	d' :r'	d' :t	d' :—	d'	d'
d :- .m	s :s	l :d'	d' :—	s :- .f	m :f	m :r	m :—	f	m
When Je-ho -	vah's	work be -	gun,	When He	spake, and	it was	done.	A -	men
God will	make new	heav'ns, new	earth, —	Songs of	praise shall	hail their	birth.		
d :- .m	s :s	l :d'	d' :—	d' :- .t	d' :l	s :s	s :—	l	s
d :- .m	s :s	l :d'	d' :—	d' :- .s	l :f	s :s	d :—	f	d

CHRISTMAS SONG.

137. Key C. L. M. Gordon, by per.

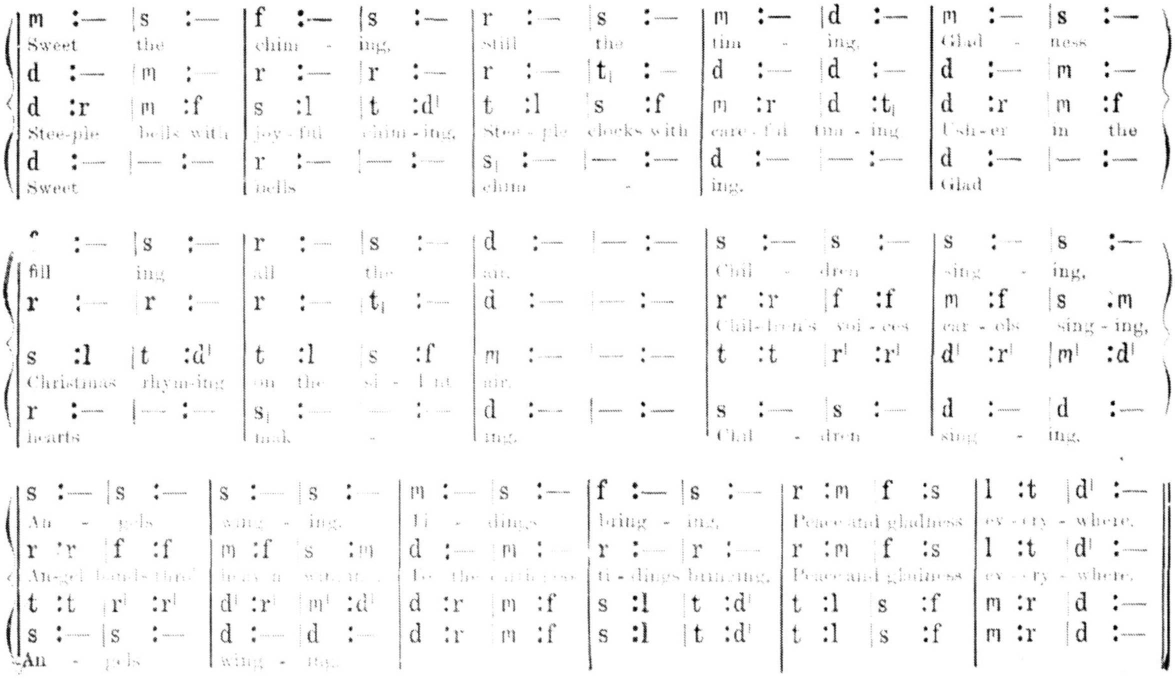
Sweet the chiming, still the timing, Gladness filling all the air.
Steeple bells with joyful chiming, Steeple clocks with careful timing, Usher in the Christmas rhyming
Children singing, Angels winging, Tidings bringing, Peace and gladness every-where.
Peace and gladness every-where.

NEVER SAY FAIL.

138. Key D. Chester G. Allen.

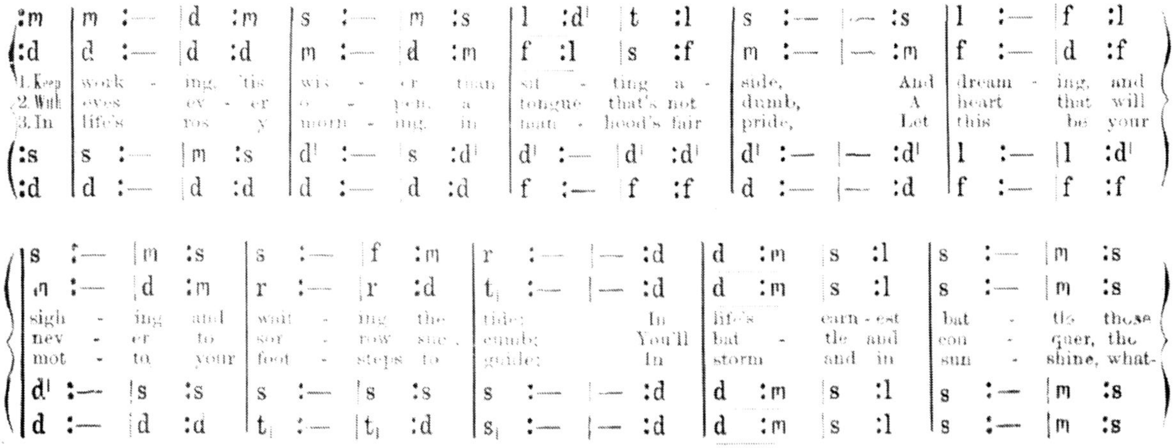
1. Keep working, 'tis wiser than sitting aside, And dreaming and sighing and waiting the tide; In life's earnest battle those
2. With eyes ever open, a tongue that's not dumb, A heart that will never to sorrow succumb; You'll battle and conquer, the
3. In life's rosy morning, in manhood's fair pride, Let this be your motto your footsteps to guide; In storm and in sunshine, what-

{| l :s |m :d | r :— |— :r | m :— |f :s | l :— |d¹ :l | s :— |l :t | d¹ :— |— :|| }
{| l :s |m :d | t₁ :— |— :t₁ | d :— |t₁ :d | d :— |f :f | m :— |f :f | m :— |— :|| }

on - ly pre - vail,	Who	dai - ly march	on - ward and	con - quer, and	nev - er say	fail.
thous - ands as - sail,	We'll	on - ward and	con - quer, and	nev - er say	fail.
ev - er as - sail,	Then	nev - er, oh,	nev - er, oh,	nev - er say	fail.

{| l :s |m :m | s :— |— :s | s :— |s :s | f :— |l :d¹ | d¹ :— |r¹ :r¹ | d¹ :— |— :|| }
{| l :s |m :d | s₁ :— |— :s₁ | d :— |r :m | f :— |f :f | s :— |s₁ :s₁ | d :— |— :|| }

MORNING HYMN.

139. KEY C.   T. F. SEWARD.

{| :d | m :— |m :f | s :— |m :s | l :— |— :l | d¹ :— |t :l | s :— |s :m |
{| :d | d :— |d :r | m :— |d :m | f :— |— :f | l :— |s :f | m :— |m :d |

1. Our	Fa - ther we	thank thee for	sleep,	For	qui - et and	com - fort and
2 Our	voic - es would	ut - ter thy	praise,	Our	hearts would o'er -	flow with thy
3. So	long as thou	deem - est it	right,	That	here on the	earth we should

{| :m | s :— |s :d¹ | d¹ :— |s :d¹ | d¹ :— |— :d¹ | d¹ :— |d¹ :l | d¹ :— |d¹ :s |
{| :d | d :— |d :d | d :— |d :d | f :— |— :f | f :— |f :f | d :— |d :m |

{| r :— |— :d | m :— |m :f | s :m |f :s | l :— |— :l | s :— |d¹ :m¹ |
{| t₁ :— |— :d | d :— |d :r | m :d |r :m | f :— |— :f | m :— |m :s |

rest,	We thank thee for	lov - ing to	keep	Thy chil - dren from
love,	O teach us to	walk in thy	ways,	And fit us to
stay,	We pray thee to	guard us by	night,	And help us to

{| s :— |— :m | s :— |s :d¹ | d¹ :— |d¹ :d¹ | d¹ :— |— :d¹ | d¹ :— |d¹ :s |
{| s :— |— :d | d :— |d :d | d :— |d :d | f :— |— :f | s :— |s :s |

{| r¹ :— |d¹ :t | d¹ :— |— :d¹ | d¹ :— |t :l | d¹ :— |t :l | s :— |m :f |
{| f :— |m :r | m :— |— :m | l :— |s :f | l :— |s :f | m :— |d :r |

be - ing dis - tressed.	O	how in their	weak - ness can	crea - tures re -
meet thee a - bove.	The	heart's pure af -	fec - tion is	all we can
serve thee by day.	And	when all the	days of our	earth - life are

{| s :— |s :s | s :— |— :d¹ | d¹ :— |d¹ :d¹ | d¹ :— |d¹ :d¹ | s :— |s :d¹ |
{| s₁ :— |s₁ :s₁ | d :— |— :d | f :— |f :f | f :— |f :f | d :— |d :d |

{| s :— |— :d¹ | m¹ :— |r¹ :d¹ | m¹ :— |r¹ :d¹ | t :— |l :t | d¹ :— |— :|| }
{| m :— |— :m | s :— |f :m | s :— |f :m | r :— |d :r | m :— |— :|| }

pay	Thy	fath - er - ly	kind - ness by	night and by	day.
give:	In	love's pure de -	vo - tion O	help us to	live.
past,	Re -	ceive us in	heav - en to	praise thee at	last.

{| d¹ :— |— :d¹ | d¹ :— |s :s | d¹ :— |s :s | s :— |s :s | s :— |— :|| }
{| d :— |— :d | d :— |d :d | d :— |d :d | s₁ :— |s₁ :s₁ | d :— |— :|| }

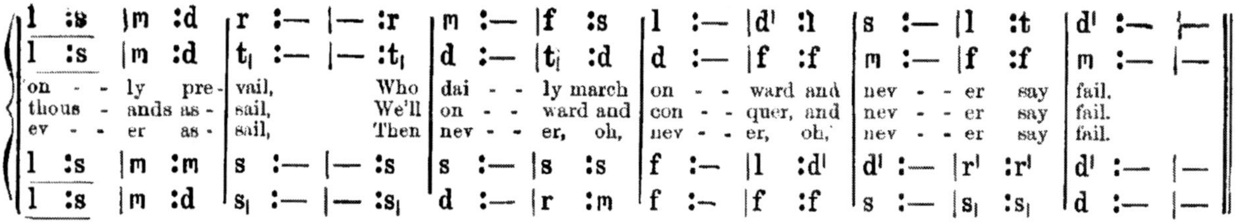

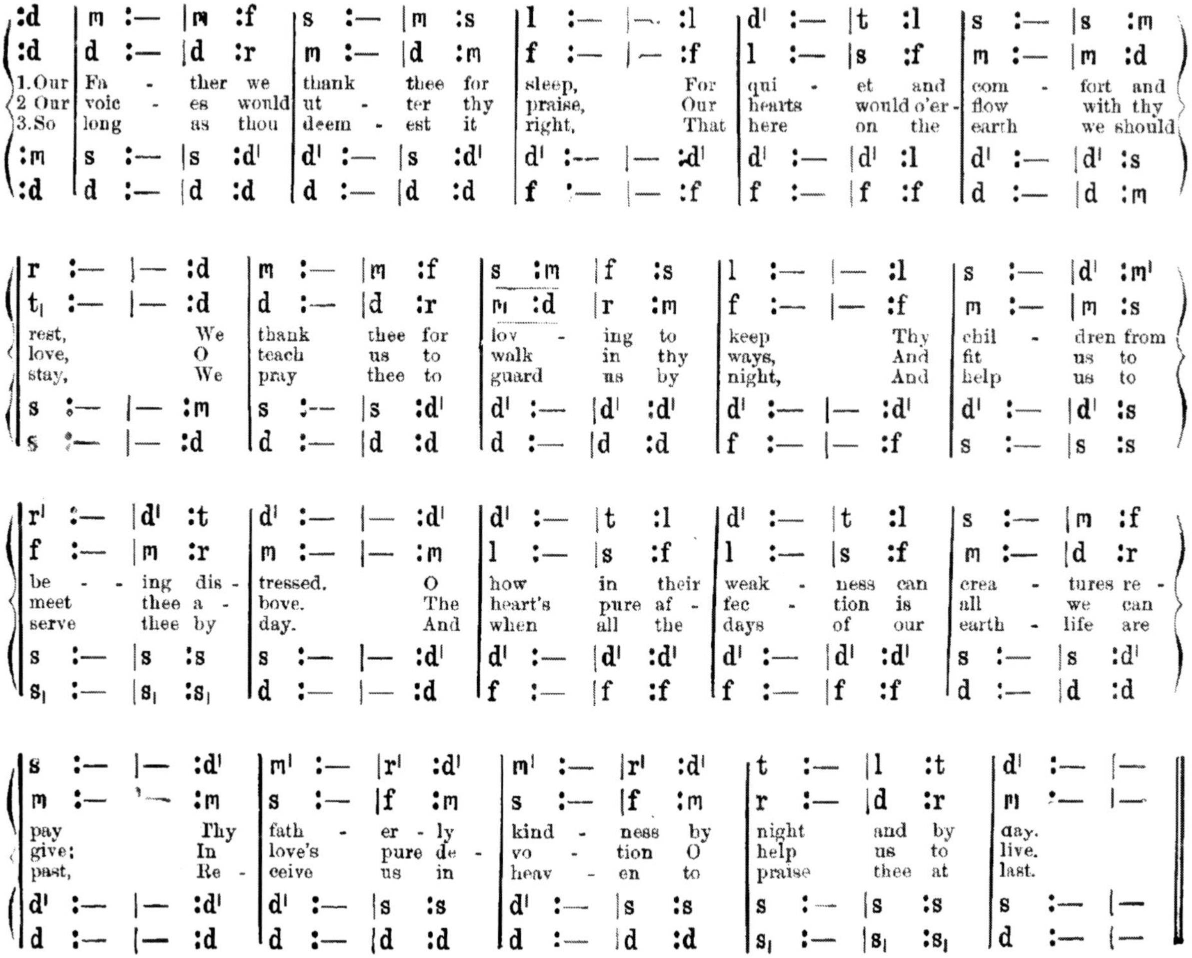

HOW SWEET TO HEAR.

140. Key D.

T. F. Seward.

:d	m :- :f	s :- :	: :	: :s	d¹ :- :s	s :f :m	r :-	- :- :r	s :- :l	t :-
:d	d :- :r	m :- :	: :	: :m	m :- :m	m :r :d	t₁ :-	- :- :t₁	t₁ :- :r	s :-

1. How sweet to hear, When ring - ing clear, At eve or ear - ly morn, Borne on the breeze
2. A - bove doth float The cuc - koo's note, O'er fields of wav - ing corn, But sweet - er still,
3. With flow - ers sweet This gay re - treat Kind na - ture doth a - dorn, And oft we come,

:	: :	: :d	m :- :f	s :- :s	s :- :d¹	d¹ :- :s	s :-	- :- :	: :
:	: :	: :d	d :- :r	m :- :d	d :- :d	d :- :d	s₁ :-	- :- :	: :

:	: :	: :t	t :- :t	t :l :t	d¹ :-	- :- :-	- :- :	: :	:
:	: :	: :r	r :- :r	r :d :r	m :-	- :- :m	m :- :m	f :- :f	m :-

Thro' rust - ling trees, The mel - low, mel - low horn, The mel - low, mel - low horn.
O'er vale and hill Re - sounds the mel - low horn, The mel - low, mel - low horn.
When la - bor's done, To hear the mel - low horn, The mel - low, mel - low horn.

:r	s :- :l	t :- :s	s :- :s	s :- :s	s :- |- :- :s	d¹ :- :d¹	l :- :l	s :- |- :- :
:r	t₁ :- :r	s :- :s₁	s₁ :- :s₁	s₁ :- :s₁	d :- |- :- :-	- :- :	- :- :-	- :- :- :-

141. Key D.

m   *p*

s :f	m :-	f :m	r :-	r :m	f :f	s :f	m :-
m :r	d :-	r :d	t₁ :-	t₁ :d	r :r	m :r	d :-

Fall - ing leaves, fall - ing leaves, Tell how sad - ly na - ture grieves;

p   *f*   *m*   *p*

m :f	s :s	l :t	d¹ :-	d¹ :l	s :-	s :f	m :-
d :r	m :m	f :f	m :-	m :f	m :-	m :r	d :-

While the au - tumn breez - es blow, Soft and low, soft and low.

142. Key D. Staccato and Legato.

Staccato.   *Legato.*

s :s	s :s	d¹ :l	s :	l :s	f :m	r :- |- :
La la	la la	la la la,		La		

r :r	r :m	f :m	r :	s :f	m :r	d :- |- :
La la	la la	la la la,		La		

143. Key A.

s₁ :l₁ :t₁	d :	:t₁,l₁	s₁ :l₁ :t₁	d :	:	s₁ :l₁ :t₁	d :t₁ :d	r :m :r	d :- :-
Trip, trip, trip, trip,	Lightly	trip, trip, trip,	trip,	Glide a -	long in	dance and	song.

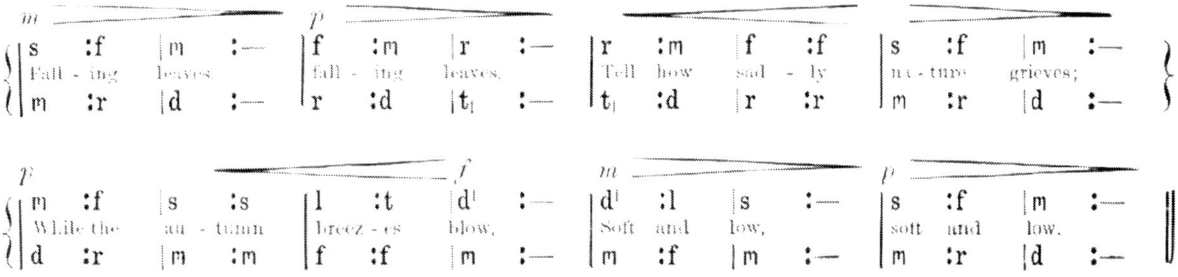

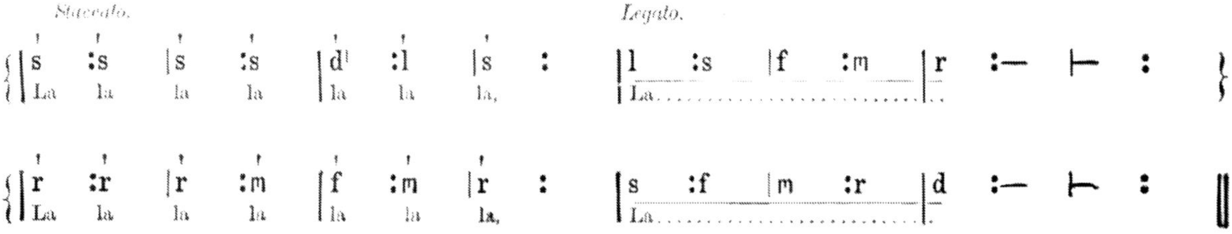

MY MOUNTAIN HOME.

144. Key D. M. 90, beating twice.　　　　　　　　Words and Music by A. S. Kieffer, by per.

```
:s  |s  :m :s  |l :— :s  |s :— :— |— :r .m|f :m :f |l :— :s  |m :— :— |— :—
:m  |m :d :m  |f :— :m  |m :— :— |— :— :t| |r :d :r |f :— :m  |d :— :— |— :—
```

1. I love my mount - ain home, Where wild winds love to roam!
2. For here the wild flow'rs sweet Spring up a - round my feet,
3. 'Tis sweet to wan - der here, By fount - ains cool and clear,
4. My mount - ain home for me, Where wild winds wan - der free,

```
:d¹ |d¹ :— :d¹ |d¹ :— :d¹ |d¹ :— :— |— :— :s  |s :— :s |s :— :s |s :— :— |— :—
:d  |d :— :d  |d :— :d  |d :— :— |— :— :s| |s| :— :s| |s| :— :s| |d :— :— |— :—
```

```
:m .f|s :— :s  |d¹ :— :d¹.d¹|r¹ :— :d¹ |l :— :l  |s :— :m |s :f :r |d :— :— |— :—
:d .r|m :— :m  |m :— :m.m |f :— :f  |f :— :f  |m :— :d |t| :— :t| |d :— :— |— :—
```

Where the cy - press vine and the whisp 'ring pine A - dorn each gran - ite dome.
And the lau - rel blows 'mid the cy - press gloom Of many a sweet re - treat.
And talk of love where the coo - ing dove A - lone may see and hear.
With my own true love, who will nev - er rove, My mount - ain home for me.

```
:s s|d¹ :— :d¹ |s :— :s.s  |l :— :l  |d¹ :— :d¹ |d¹ :— :s |s :— :f |m :— :— |— :—
:d .d|d :— :d  |d :— :d.d  |f :— :f  |f :— :f  |s :— :s |s| :— :s| |d :— :— |— :—
```

CHORUS.

```
:s  |s :m :s  |d¹ :— :t  |d¹ :— :— |— :s :— :m |l :— :s |f :— :m |r :— :— |— :—
:m  |m :d :m  |m :— :r  |d :— :— |— :m :— :d |f :— :m |d :— :d |t| :— :— |— :—
```

I love my mount - ain home,.............I love my mount - ain home.
　　　I love my mount - ain home, I love my mount - ain home,

```
:   |:   :d¹ |s :— :f  |m :— :s |d¹ :— :  |:  :m |l :— :s |s :t :r¹ |s :— :
:   |:   :d  |d :— :d  |d :— :d |d :— :  |:  :d |d :— :d |s| :— :s| |s| :— :
```

```
:f  |m :r :m  |s :— :s  |l :— :f |d¹ :t :l |s :— :m |s :f :r |d :— :— |— :—
:r  |d :t| :d |m :— :m  |f :— :f |l :s :f |m :— :d |t| :— :t| |d :— :— |— :—
```

Where skies are blue, and hearts are true, I love my mount - ain home.

```
:s  |s :— :s  |d¹ :— :d¹ |d¹ :— :l |f :— :l |d¹ :— :s |s :— :f |m :— :— |— :—
:s| |d :— :d  |d :— :d  |f :— :f |f :— :f |s :— :s |s| :— :s| |d :— :— |— :—
```

145. Key C. Round for two parts.　　　　　　　　　　　　　　　T. F. S.

```
:s :— :d¹ |t :— :l |s :— :l |s :— :m |f :— :f |f :m :f |l :— :s |s :— :—
```
Will the vio - let bloom a - gain, Where now the drift - ed snow is piled;

```
*
m :— :m |s :— :f |m :— :f |m :— :d |r :— :r |r :d :r |f :— :m |m :— :—
```
On the hill - side, in the glen, Where blows the wind so bleak and wild?

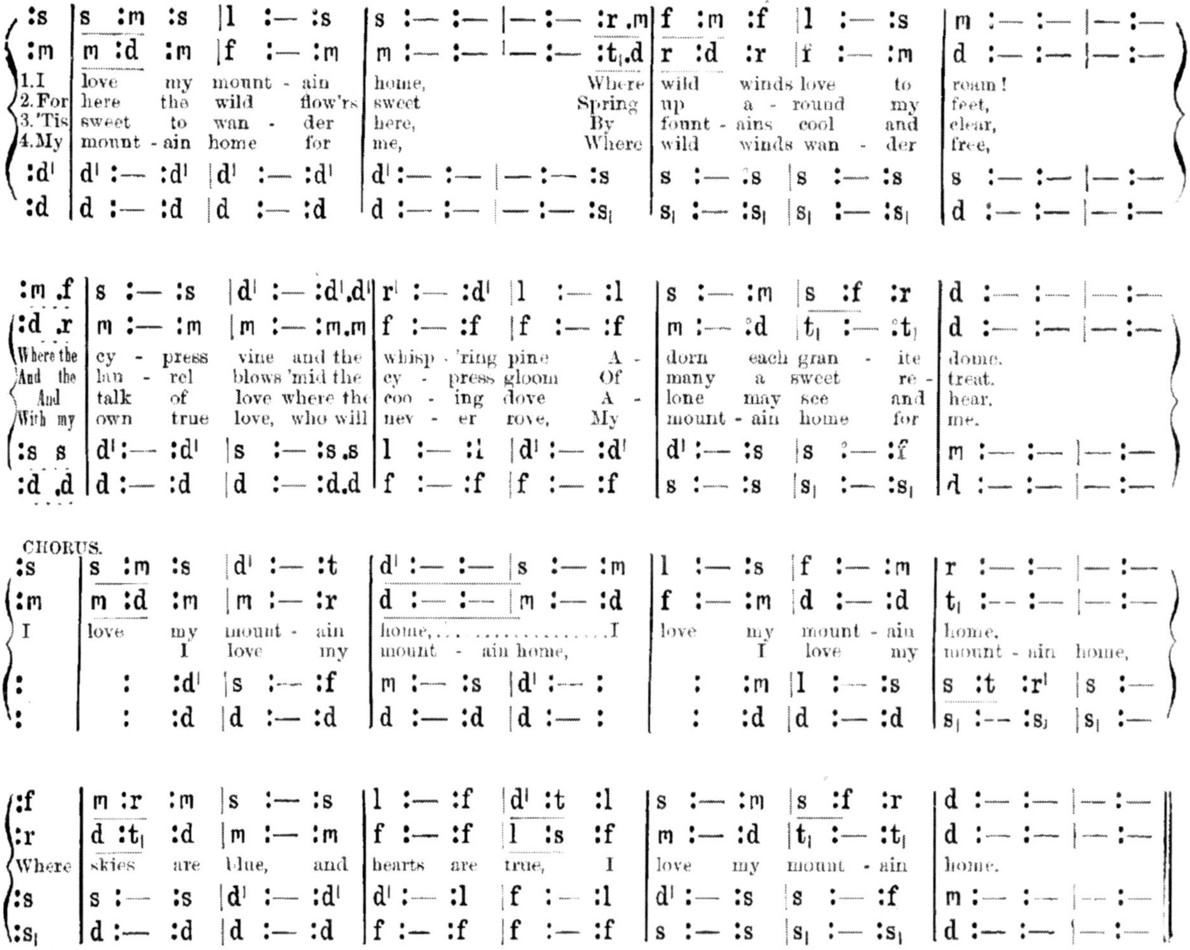

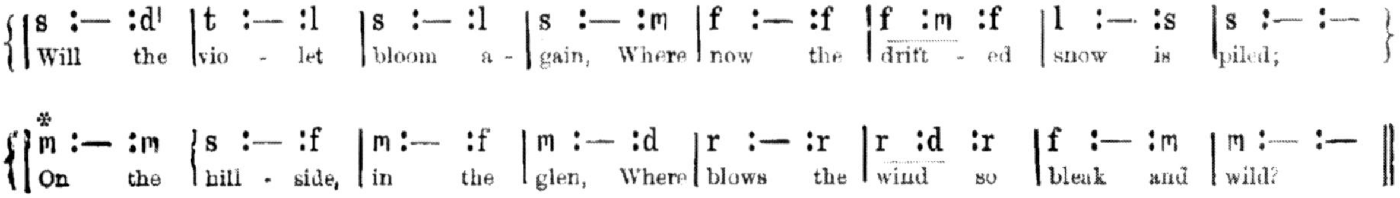

SUNSHOWER.

146. KEY A. M. 72. T. W. DENNINGTON, by per.

1. Sparkling in the sunlight, Dancing on the hills, Tapping at my win - dow, Singing in the rills;
2. Clouds are flying swiftly, Sunlight breaking through, Everything is shin - ing, As with morning dew;
Comes the pleasant sunshower Like a glad surprise, While I gaze with wonder At the changeful skies.
Falling on the mount - ain, In the fer-tile vale, Giving joy and glad - ness, Comes the gentle rain.
Pat - ter, pat - ter, hear the rain, Gen - tle spring has come a - - gain;
Patter, patter, patter, patter, Listen to the rain, Patter, patter, patter, patter, Spring has come again;
Pat - ter, pat - ter, soft re - frain, Tap - ping on the win - dow - pane,
Patter, patter, patter, patter, hear the soft refrain, Tapping, tapping, tapping, tapping on the window pane.

147. KEY D. Round for three parts.

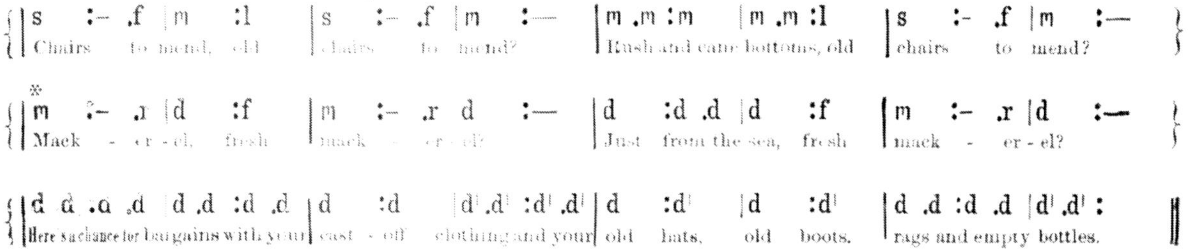
Chairs to mend, old chairs to mend? Rush and cane bottoms, old chairs to mend?
Mack - er - el, fresh mack - er - el? Just from the sea, fresh mack - er - el?
Here's a chance for bargains with your cast - off clothing and your old hats, old boots, rags and empty bottles.

148. KEY A. M. 72. **SERENADE.**

:m .m	m :d :d .d	d :s, :s, .s,	s, .s, :s, :s,	s, :—
:s, .s,	s, :m, :f, .f,	m, :m, :m, .f,	s, .s, :s, :f,	m, :—
1.Sleep on,	dear - est, while a -	round thee All is	wrapt in si - lence	deep;
2.To the	cham - ber of her	dwell - ing, Where my	love in slum - ber	lies;
3.And the	woo - ing night wind	bears them Far a -	way o'er dis - tant	plain;
:d .d	d :s, :l, .l,	s, :d :d .r	m .m :m :r	d :—
:d, .d,	d, :d, :d, .d,	d, :d, :	d, .m, :s, .s, :s, .s,	d, :—
			All is wrapt in si - lence	deep;
			Where my love in slum-ber	lies;
			Far a - way o'er dis - tant	plain;

:s, .s,	l, :— .d :t, .l,	s, :d :d .m	*f* s :— .f :m .r	m :—
While the	chains of sleep have	bound thee, God doth	con - stant vig - ils	keep,
Thro' the	trees in love-tones	tell - ing, As on	gold - en lad - ders	rise,
And the	dream - - ing fair one	hears them, Hears and	sweet - ly dreams a -	gain,
:m, .m,	f, :— .l, :s, .f,	m, :m, :m, .s,	t, :— .t, :d .s,	s, :—
:	d .d :d .d :d .d	d :s, :	r .r :r .r :d .t,	d :—
	While the chains of sleep have	bound thee,	God doth constant vig - ils	keep,
	Thro' the trees in love-tones	tell - ing,	As on gold - en lad - ders	rise,
	And the dream-ing fair one	hears them,	Hears and sweetly dreams a -	gain,
:	f, .f, :f, .f, :f, .f,	d, :d, :	s, .s, :s, .s, :s, .s,	d, :—

Dim.

:m .m	d :— :d	d :— :d .d	s, :— :s,	s, :—
Con-stant	vig - - - ils	keep, Con - stant	vig - - - ils	keep.
As on	lad - - - ders	rise, As on	lad - - - ders	rise.
Sweet-ly	dreams a - -	gain, Sweet-ly	dreams a - -	gain.
:	f, .f, :l, .l, :s, .f,	m, :— :	r, .m, :s, .f, :m, .r,	m, :—
	God doth constant vig - ils	keep,	God doth constant vig - ils	keep.
	As on gold - en lad - ders	rise,	As on gold - en lad - ders	rise.
	Hears and sweetly dreams a -	gain,	Hears and sweetly dreams a -	gain.
	l, .l, :d .d :t, .l,	s, :— :	t, .d :m .r :d .t,	d :—
:	f, .f, :f, .f, :f, .f,	d, :— :	s, .s, :s, .s, :s, .s,	d, :—

149. KEY A♭. **EVAN. C. M.** W. H. HAVERGAL.

:s,	s, .d :m :r	d .l, :s, :s,	s, .d :m :d	r :—
:m,	m, .m, :s, :f,	m, .f, :m, :m,	m, .m, :m, :m,	s, :—
1.Lord,	I be - lieve a	rest re - mains To	all Thy peo - - ple	known;
2.A	rest where all our	soul's de-sire Is	fixed on things a - -	bove,
3.Oh,	that I now the	rest may know, Be - -	lieve and en - ter	in;
:d	d .d :d :t,	d .d :d :d	d .d :d :d	t, :—
:d,	d, .d, :d, :s,	l, .f, :d, :d,	d, .d, :l, :l,	s, :—

:f	m .r :d :r	m .d :l, :s,	s, .d :m :r	d :—
:s,	s, .f, :m, :s,	s, .s, :f, :r,	m, .m, :s, :f,	m, :—
A	rest where pure en - -	joyment reigns, And	thou art loved a -	lone.
Where	fear, and sins, and	grief ex - pire, Cast	out by per - fect	love.
Now,	Sav-iour, now the	pow'r be-stow, And	let me cease from	sin.
:r	d .t, :d :t,	d .d :d :t,	d .d :d :t,	d :—
:s,	d, .s, :l, :s,	d, .m, :f, :s,	d, .l, :s, :s,	d, :—

CANON. NOW THE EVENING FALLS.

150. KEY B♭. M. 104. May be sung in two, three or four parts. BEETHOVEN.

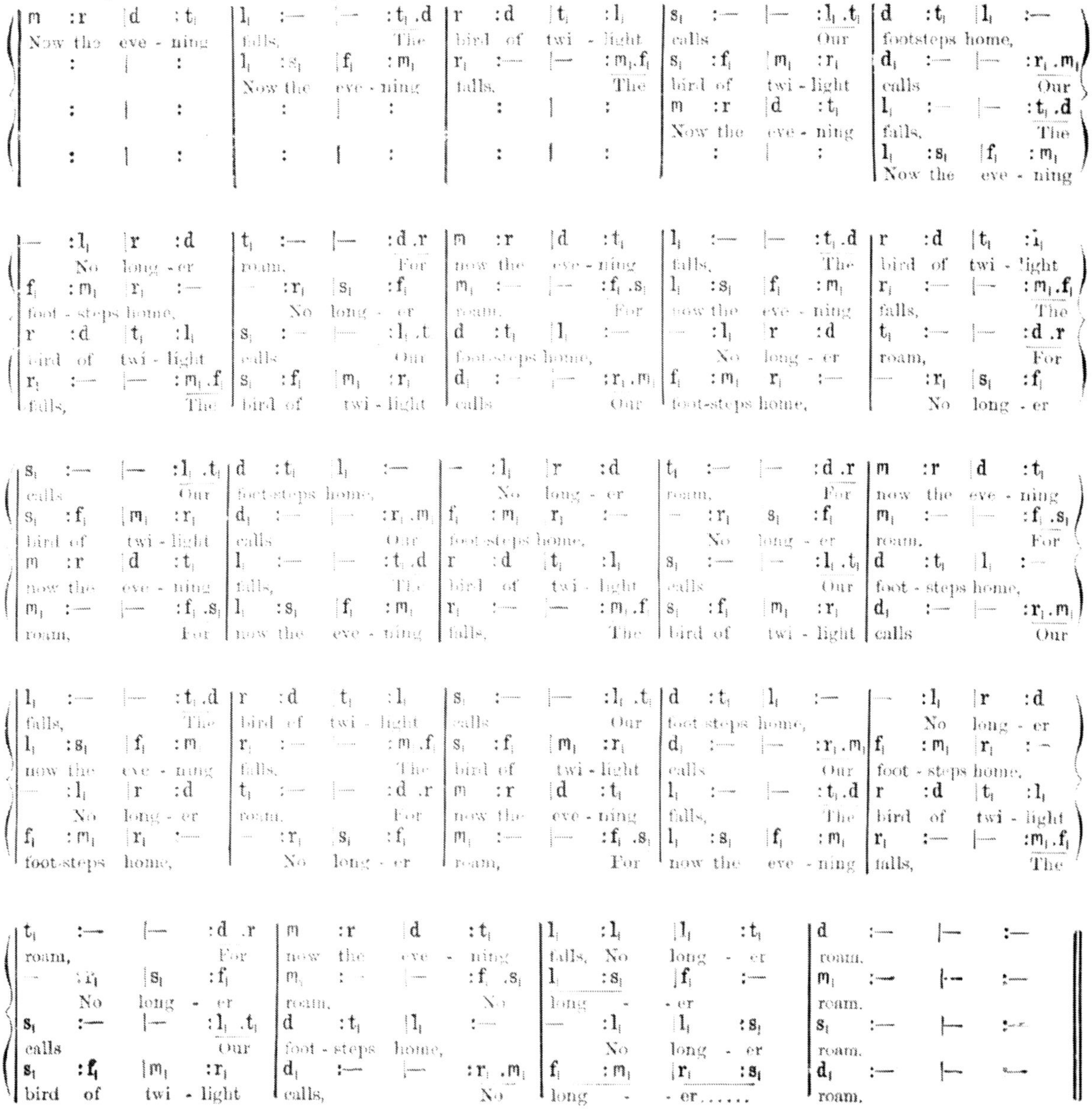
Now the eve - ning falls, The bird of twi - light calls Our footsteps home,
Now the eve - ning falls, The bird of twi - light calls Our
Now the eve - ning falls, The
Now the eve - ning
No long - er roam. For now the eve - ning falls, The bird of twi - light
foot - steps home, No long - er roam. For now the eve - ning falls, The
bird of twi - light calls Our foot-steps home, No long - er roam, For
falls, The bird of twi - light calls Our foot-steps home, No long - er
calls Our foot-steps home, No long - er roam, For now the eve - ning
bird of twi - light calls Our foot-steps home, No long - er roam. For
now the eve - ning falls, The bird of twi - light calls Our foot - steps home,
roam, For now the eve - ning falls, The bird of twi - light calls Our
falls, The bird of twi - light calls Our foot-steps home, No long - er
now the eve - ning falls, The bird of twi - light calls Our foot - steps home,
No long - er roam. For now the eve - ning falls, The bird of twi - light
foot-steps home, No long - er roam, For now the eve - ning falls, The
roam, For now the eve - ning falls, No long - er roam.
No long - er roam. No long - - er roam.
calls Our foot - steps home, No long - er roam.
bird of twi - light calls, No long - - er...... roam.

EVENING PRAYER.

151. KEY A♭.

J. H. TENNEY.

```
{ s₁ :- .s₁ :s₁ .d | m :— :r | d :— :— | d :t₁ :l₁ | s₁ :— : }
{ m₁ :— .m₁ :s₁ .s₁ | s₁ :— :f₁ | m₁ :— :— | l₁ :s₁ :f₁ | m₁ :— : }
  1.God,   who madest earth   and   heaven,        Dark-ness and   light,
  2.Guard  us when we sleep   or    wake,          And  when  we   die,
{ d :- .d :d .m | d :— :t₁ | d :— :— | d :d :d | d :— : }
{ d₁ :- .d₁ :m₁ .d₁ | s₁ :— :s₁ | d₁ :— :— | f₁ :f₁ :f₁ | d₁ :— : }
```

```
{ s₁ :- .s₁ :s₁ .d | m :— :r | d :— :— | r :d :t₁ | d :— :t₁ .d }
{ m₁ :— .m₁ :s₁ .s₁ | s₁ :— :f₁ | m₁ :— :— | l₁ :s₁ :f₁ | m₁ :— :s₁ .s₁ }
  Who     the day for toil    has   given,       For  rest  the   night:   May thine
  Wilt    thou then in mer  - cy    take         Our  souls on    high?    When the
{ d :- .d :d .m | d :— :t₁ | d :— :— | f :m :r | d :— :r .d }
{ d₁ :- .d₁ :m₁ .d₁ | s₁ :— :s₁ | l₁ :— :— | f₁ :s₁ :s₁ | d₁ :— :s₁ .m₁ }
```

```
{ r :— :r :m :r | r :d :d .r | m :— .m :f .m | m :r :r .r }
{ s₁ :— .s₁ :s₁ .f₁ | f₁ :m₁ :m₁ .f₁ | s₁ :— .s₁ :s₁ .s₁ | s₁ :s₁ :s₁ .s₁ }
  an -    gel guard de-  fend   us,   Slumber sweet     thy mercy  send   us,   Ho-ly
  last    dread call shall wake us,   Do  not thou,     our Lord, for- sake us,   But to
{ t₁ :— .t₁ :d .t₁ | d :d :d .d | d :— .d :r .d | d :t₁ :t₁ .t₁ }
{ s₁ :— .s₁ :s₁ .s₁ | d₁ :d₁ :d₁ .d₁ | d :— .d :t₁ .d | s₁ :s₁ :s₁ .s₁ }
```

```
                                           f    :m   :r      d   :—  :—
{ r :— .r :d .r | m :d : | l₁ :s₁ :s₁ | s₁ :— :— }
{ s₁ :— .s₁ :s₁ .s₁ | s₁ :l₁ : | f₁ :s₁ :f₁ | m₁ :— :— }
  dreams and   hopes at- tend   us       This  live - long   night.
  reign  in    glo-ry   take    us       With  thee   on     high.
{ t₁ :— .t₁ :d .t₁ | d :d : | d :d :t₁ | d :— :— }
{ s₁ :— .f₁ :m₁ .r₁ | d₁ :f₁ : | f₁ :m₁ :r₁ | d₁ :— :— }
                                           l₁  :s₁  :s₁
```

Small notes for second verse.

152. KEY **F.** Round for three parts.

T. F. S.

```
{ s :f :m | m :f :s | l :— :— | l :— :— | f :m :r | r :m :f | s :— :— | s :— :— }
  Banish all trouble and  sor  -  row,        Why should we foolishly borrow
```

```
* 
{ m :r :d | d :r :m | f :— :— | f :— :— | r :d :t₁ | t₁ :d :r | m :— :— | —:—:— }
  Care that is coming to- mor  -  row?        Let us be happy  and  gay;
```

```
{ s₁ :s₁ :s₁ | d :d :d | l₁ :— :— | d :— :— | s₁ :s :s | f :m :r | d :— :— :—:—:— }
  Don't be a slave to the  mor  -  row,       Losing the joy of to- day.
```

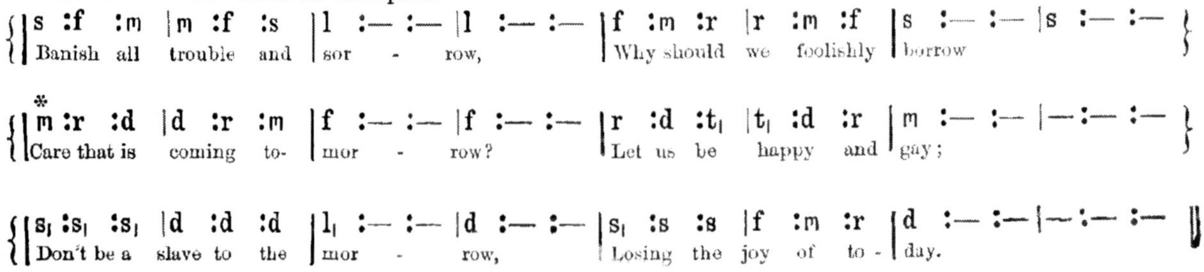

WAKE THE SONG OF JUBILEE.

153. Key D. M. 112. *Boldly, without dragging.* Chester G. Allen, by per.

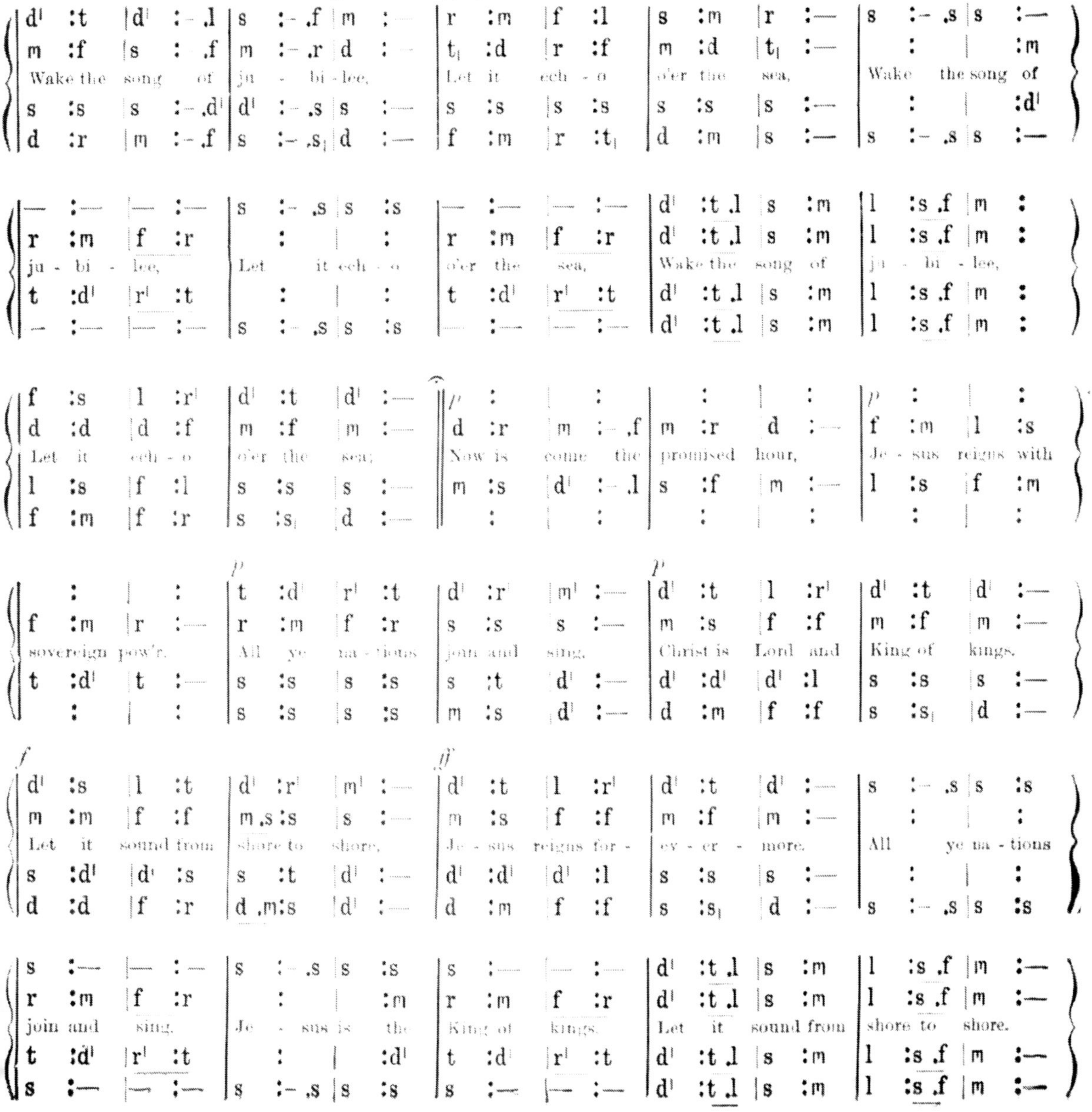
Wake the song of ju - bi - lee, Let it ech - o o'er the sea, Wake the song of
ju - bi - lee, Let it ech - o o'er the sea, Wake the song of ju - bi - lee,
Let it ech - o o'er the sea; Now is come the promised hour, Je - sus reigns with
sovereign pow'r. All ye na - tions join and sing, Christ is Lord and King of kings.
Let it sound from shore to shore, Je - sus reigns for - ev - er - more. All ye na - tions
join and sing, Je - sus is the King of kings. Let it sound from shore to shore.

```
|f  :s  |l  :r' |d' :t  |d' :—  ‖  :  |  :  |  :  |  :  |  :  |  :  |  :
|d  :d  |d  :f  |m  :f  |m  :—     :  |  :  |  :  |  :  |  :  |  :  |  :
```
Je - sus   reigns for   ev - er - more.
```
|l  :s  |f  :l  |s  :s  |s  :—     :  |  :  |  :  |  :  |  :  |  :  |  :
|f  :m  |f  :r  |s  :s, |d  :—  mezzo. |d  :r  |m  :d  |f  :m ,r |d :— |l, :t, |d :m
```
                                        Now   the   des - ert   lands re - joice,   And   the   isl - ands
```
‖  :  |  :  |  :  |  :  |  :  |  :  |  :  |  :
   :  |  :  |  :  |  :  |  :  |  :  |  :  |  :
   :  |  :  |  :  |  :  |  :  |  :  |  :  |  :
|r  :d  |s, :—  |f  :m  |r  :d  |l  :s .f |m  :—  |f  :r  |m  :f  |s  :s, |d  :—
```
join their voice,   Yea, the whole cre - a - tion sings,   Je - sus   is the   King of kings!
```
   :  |  :  |  :  |r' :d' |t  :—  |  :  |  :  |r' :d' |t  :—
   :  |  :  |  :  |f  :m  |r  :—  |  :  |  :  |f  :m  |r  :—
```
                     lands re - joice,   join their voice;
```
|s  :— .s |s  :s  |s  :—  |—  :—  |s  :— .s |s  :s  |s  :—  |—  :—
```
Now   the des - ert lands,   And   the isl - ands join
```
|s  :— .s |s  :s  |s  :—  |—  :—  |s  :— .s |s  :s  |s  :—  |—  :—
```

```
 f
|d' :t .l |s  :m  |l  :s .f |m  :—  |f  :s  |l  :r' |d' :t  |d' :—  ‖
|d' :t .l |s  :m  |l  :s .f |m  :—  |d  :d  |d  :f  |m  :f  |m  :—
```
Yea, the whole cre - a - tion sings,   Je - sus   is   the   King of   kings.
```
|d' :t .l |s  :m  |l  :s .f |m  :—  |l  :s  |f  :l  |s  :s  |s  :—
|d' :t .l |s  :m  |l  :s .f |m  :—  |f  :m  |f  :r  |s  :s, |d  :—
```

THE LORD'S PRAYER.

154. Key F.

```
   d           |t, :d  |r  :—  ‖      r       |m  :r  |d  :t, |d :—
   s,          |s, :s, |t, :—         t,       |d  :l, |s, :s, |s, :—
```
1. Our Father who art in heaven, hallowed be Thy | name; | Thy kingdom come, Thy will be done on | earth as it | is   in | heaven;
2. Give us this day our .... dai - ly | bread; | And forgive us our trespasses as we for- | give.. | them that | trespass a- | gainst us.
3. And lead us not into temptation, but | | | For Thine is the kingdom, and the power, | | |
   deliver................................ us from | evil; | and the.................................... | glory, for- | ever. A - | men.
```
   m           |f  :m  |s  :—         s        |s  :f  |m  :r  |m :—
   d           |r  :d  |s, :—         s,       |d  :f, |s, :s, |d :—
```

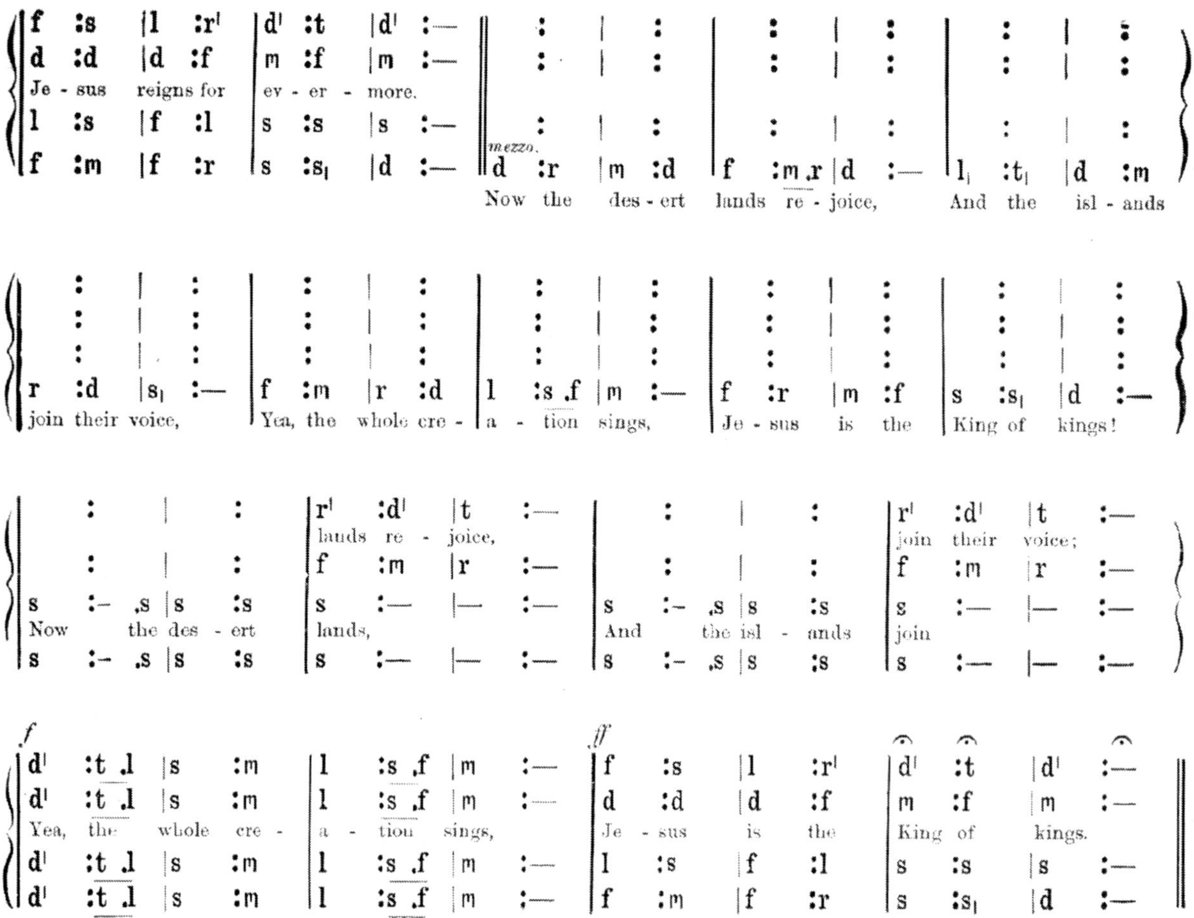

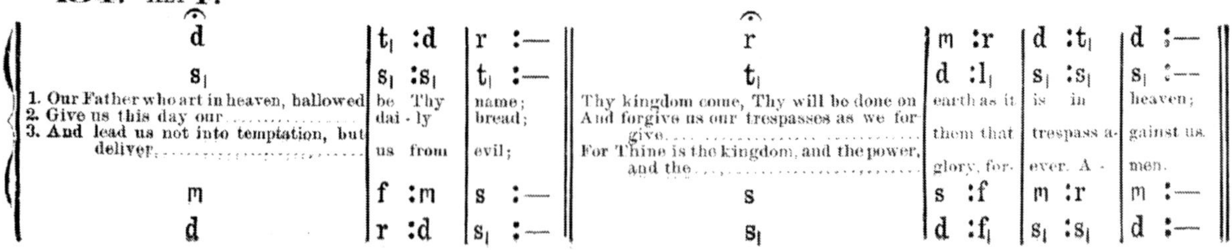

The Metronome is an instrument for regulating the rate of movement in a piece of music. It is a pendulum which can be made to swing at various rates per minute. M. 60 (Metronome 60), in the Tonic Solfa notation means, "Let the *pulses* of this tune move at the rate of 60 in a minute." In the case of very quick six-pulse measure, the metronome rate is made to correspond, not with pulses, but with half measures—"beating twice in the measure."

A cheap substitute for the costly clockwork metronome is a string with a weight attached to one end—a common pocket tape-measure is the most convenient. The following table gives the number of inches of the tape required for the different rates of movement. The number of inches here given is not absolutely correct, but is near enough for ordinary purposes.

M. 50........	Tape 56 inches.
M. 56........	" 47 "
M. 60........	" 38 "
M. 66........	" 31 "
M. 72........	" 27 "
M. 76........	" 24 "
M. 80........	" 21 "
M. 88........	" 17 "
M. 96........	" 13½ "
M. 120........	" 8½ "

Remembering M. 60. Just as it is useful to remember one tone in absolute pitch, so also, is it useful to remember one rate of movement. The rate of M. 60 is to be fixed in the mind as a standard; then twice that speed, M. 120; or a speed half as fast again, M. 90, are easily conceived. To fix M. 60 in the mind, the teacher will frequently ask the pupils to begin *Taataing* at what they consider to be that rate, and then test them with the metronome. The recollection of rate of movement is, like the recollection of pitch, affected by temperament of body or mood of mind. But these difficulties can be conquered, so that depression of either kind shall not make us sing too slowly.

Sustaining the Rate of Movement. The power of sustaining a uniform speed is one of the first and most important musical elements. To cultivate this faculty the teacher requires the pupils to taatai on one tone a simple measure, thus:

```
| TAA    : TAA    | TAA    : TAA    ||
```

repeating it steadily six or eight times *with* the metronome, so as to get into the swing. He then stops the metronome while they continue taataing for several measures, then starts it again, on the first pulse of the measure, and the class can see immediately whether the rate has been sustained.

The Half-Pulse Silence is indicated by the blank space between the dot (which divides the pulse into halves) and the accent mark. It is named *SAA* on the first half of the pulse, and *SAI* on the second half, thus:

```
|     .l     : or |l     .     :
 SAA   TAI         TAA    SAI
```

In taataing, the silent half-pulses are passed, by whispering the time-name.

155. Key F.

```
 TAA TAI TAA SAI | TAA TAI TAA SAI | TAA SAI TAA SAI | TAA  .  AA
|l  .l  :l  .    |l  .l  :l  .    |l  .   :l  .    |l     :—    ||
|m  .r  :d  .    |f  .m  :r  .    |m  .   :d  .    |s     :—    ||
|d  .r  :m  .    |r  .m  :f  .    |m  .   :s  .    |d     :—    ||
```

156. Key D.

```
 TAA TAI SAA TAI | TAA TAI SAA TAI | TAA SAI SAA TAI | TAA  .  AA
|l  .l  :   .l   |l  .l  :   .l   |l  .   :   .l   |l     :—    ||
|d  .d  :   .r   |m  .m  :   .f   |s  .   :   .f   |m     :—    ||
|m  .m  :   .r   |d  .d  :   .t1  |d  .   :   .r   |d     :—    ||
```

157. Key D.

```
 TAI | TAA      TAA TAI | TAA  SAA TAI | TAA TAI TAA TAI | TAA  SAA TAI | TAA TAI TAA TAI | TAA  SAA TAI | TAA      TAA TAI |
 .l  |l        :l  .l   |l     :   .l  |l  .l   :l  .l   |l     :   .l  |l  .l   :l  .l   |l     :   .l  |l        :l  .l   |l  .  :  .||
 .s  |d'       :s  .m   |d     :   .d  |m  .m   :d  .m   |s     :   .s  |d' .d'  :s  .s   |m     :   .m  |d        :m  .s   |d' .  :  .||
```

158. Key A.

```
 TAI  TAA  TAI | TAA   -AA TAI  TAA  TAI | TAA   -AA TAI  TAA  TAI | TAA   TAA   TAA TAI | TAA   -AA
 .l   :l   .l  |l     :—  .l   :l   .l   |l     :—  .l   :l   .l   |l     :l    :l  .l   |l     :—  .||
 .s1  :s1  .s1 |d     :—  .t1  :l1  .t1  |d     :—  .t1  :d   .r   |m     :d    :r  .t1  |d     :—  .||
```

159. Key D. Round in two parts.

```
{|d'   .d'   :d'   .    |t    .t    :t    .    |d'   .t    :l    .s    |l    .t    :d'   .    }
 |Mer - ry    May,       |mer - ry    May,       |How   I     love  the   |mer - ry    May:

*
{|d    .d    :d    .    |r    .r    :r    .    |m    .     :m    .    |f    .f    :m    .    ||
 |Mer - ry    May,       |mer - ry    May;       |Yes,        yes,       |mer - ry    May.
```

YES, OR NO.

160. Key G. M. 96.   Lowell Mason.

```
| d   :d  .d | d  .d  :  .s₁ | d    :m  | r   :   | m    :f  .m
| s₁  :s₁ .s₁| s₁ .s₁ :  .s₁ | s₁   :s₁ | s₁  :   | s₁   :s₁ .s₁
```
1. Short speech suf - fi - ces deep thought to show, When you, with
2. Time nev - er lin - gers, moves nev - er slow, While he per-
3. Deep may the im - port for joy or woe, Be in the
```
| m   :m  .m | m  .m  :  .s₁ | s₁   :d  | t₁  :   | d    :r  .d
| d   :d  .d | d  .d  :  .s₁ | m₁   :d₁ | s₁  :   | d    :t₁ .d
```

```
| r  .d :l₁ | r  :  .t₁ | d   :   | s    :l  .s | s    :m
| s₁ .m₁:l₁ | l₁ :  .s₁ | s₁  :   | d    :d  .d | d    :d
```
wis-dom, say Yes, or No. Save me from speech - es
mits it, say Yes, or No. If he es - capes you,
lit - tle words, Yes, or No. But if the utt'r - ance
```
| t₁ .d :d | f  :  .r | m   :   | m    :f  .m | m    :d
| s₁ .l₁:f₁| r₁ :  .s₁| d₁  :   | d    :d  .d | d    :d
```

```
| s   :l  .s | s  :  | m    :f  .m | r  .d :l₁ | r  :  .t₁ | d  :
| d   :d  .d | d  :  | s₁   :s₁ .s₁| s₁ .m₁:l₁ | l₁ :  .s₁ | s₁ :
```
long, dull and slow, Oh, how much bet-ter plain Yes. or No.
ne'er can you know If you a - gain may say, Yes, or No.
you would fore- go, Eyes, ev - en eyes, may say, Yes, or No.
```
| m   :f  .m | m  :  | d    :r  .d | t₁ .d :d | f  :  .r | m  :
| d   :d  .d | d  :  | d    :t₁ .d | s₁ .l₁:f₁| r₁ :  .s₁| d₁ :
```

ROBBINS. C. M.

161. Key B♭.   Darius E. Jones.

```
| .s₁ :l₁ .l₁ | s₁ :— .d :d .d | d   :— :r | m .r :d :m
| .m₁ :f₁ .f₁ | m₁ :— .m₁:f₁.f₁| m₁  :— :s₁| s₁ .s₁:s₁ :s₁
```
1. Thy home is with the hum - ble, Lord, The sim - plest and the
2. Dear Com-fort - er, e - ter - nal Love. If thou wilt stay with
3. Who made this beat - ing heart of mine? But thou, my heaven - ly
```
| .d :d .d | d :— .s₁:l₁ .l₁| s₁  :— :t₁| d .t₁:d :d
| .d₁:d₁.d₁| d₁:— .d₁:d₁.d₁| d₁  :— :s₁| d .s₁:m₁ :d₁
```

```
| r  :— .s₁:l₁ .l₁| s₁ :— .d :d .d | d  :— .m :d .l₁| s₁ :— :s₁ | s₁ :—
| s  :— .m₁:f₁ .f₁| m₁ :— .m₁:f₁.f₁| m₁ :— .s₁:s₁ .f₁| m₁ :r₁:f₁ | m₁ :—
```
best; Thy lodging is in child-like hearts, Thou makest there...... thy rest.
me, Of low-ly thoughts and sim-ple ways, I'll build a house...... for thee.
guest; Let no one have it then but thee. And let it be...... thy rest.
```
| t₁ :— .d :d .d | d  :— .s₁:l₁ .l₁| s₁ :— .d :d .d | d  :t₁:r | d  :—
| s₁ :— .d₁:d₁.d₁| d₁ :— .d₁:d₁.d₁| d₁ :— .d₁:m₁.f₁| s₁ :— :s₁| d₁ :—
```

KEOKUK. C. M.

162. KEY C.

WM. B. BRADBURY.

.s	s	.s:s .s	s	:d¹	t	: .t	d¹.l :s .f	m	: .m	m .m.m.s	s .f:f .r
.m	m	.m:r .r	d	:s	s	: .f	m.f:m .r	d	: .d	d .d:d .m	m .r:r .t₁
.d¹	d	.d¹:t .t	d¹	:m¹	r¹	: .r¹	d¹.d¹:d¹.s	s	:	:	:
.d	d	.m:s .f	m	:d	s	: .s	l .f:s .s₁	d	:	:	:

1. Ye trembling souls, dis-miss your fears, Be mercy all your theme, Mer-cy which like a river flows In
2. Fear not the powers of earth and hell, Thos' powers will God re-strain; His arm shall all their rage repel, And
3. Fear not the want of out - ward good: For His He will pro-vide: Grant them supplies of daily food, And

r .r:s .f	m	: .s	s .s :d¹ .d¹	m¹	:d¹	d¹	:l	s .s:s .t	d¹	: - .¹
t₁.t₁:t₁ .r	d	: .m	m .m:s .s	s	:s	l	:f	m .m:r .f	m	: - .¹
:	:	.d¹	d¹ .d¹:m¹.m¹	d¹	:d¹	d¹	:d¹	d¹ .d¹:t .r¹	d¹	: - .¹
:	:	.d	d .d:d .d	d	:m	f	:f	s .s:s .s	d	: - .¹

one perpetual stream; Mer-cy which like a ri - ver flows In one perpetual stream.
make their efforts vain; His arm shall all their rage re-pel And make their efforts vain.
all they need be-side; Grant them supplies of dai - ly food, And all they need be - side.

A pulse divided into two quarters and a half, is named tafaTAI. A half and two quarters are named TAA-tefe. They are indicated thus:

.l	.l	:		.l	.l	:
tafa	TAI			TAA	tefe	

A pulse divided into three quarters and a quarter is named TAA-efe. The quarter-pulse continuation, like all other con-tinuations, is properly represented by a dash, (a) but in order to save space the dash is omitted and the dot and comma placed close together. (b):

(a) .l	. .l	:		(b) .l	. .l	:
TAA	- efe			TAA	- efe	

The time name TAA-efe must not be pronounced TAA-effe, the inter-vening "e" is not to be sounded, but the "AA" continued up to the "f" thus, TAA-afe or TAA-fe.

163. KEYS D, G. TafaTAI

TAA	TAI	ta fa TAI	TAA	TAI	ta fa TAI	ta fa TAI	ta fa TAI	ta fa TAI	ta fa TAI	ta fa TAI	ta fa TAI
l	.l	:l .l.l	l	.l	:l .l.l	l .l.l	:l .l.l	l .l.l	.l:l .l.l		
d	.d	:d .d.d	m	.m	:m .m.m	s .s.s	:m .m.m	s .s.s	.s:d¹.d¹.d¹		
d	.s₁	:l₁ .t₁.d	m	.r	:m .f.s	s .f.m	:f .m.r	m .r.d	.t₁:l .t₁.d		

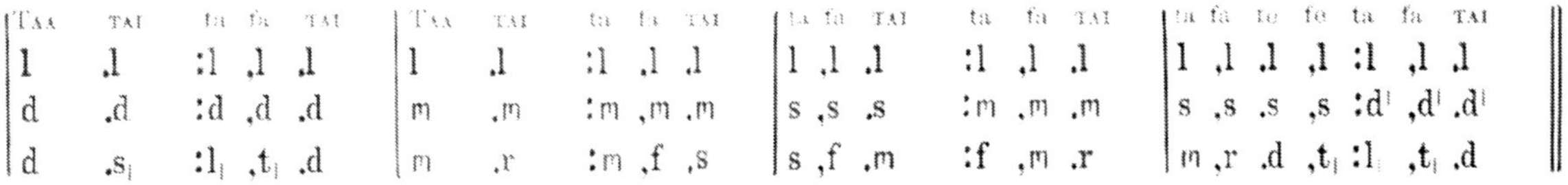

164. KEYS D, F. TAAtefe.

TAA	te fe TAA	TAI	TAA	te fe TAA	TAA	te fe TAA	te fe	ta fa te fe TAA
l	.l .l :l	.l	l	.l .l :l	l	.l .l :l	.l .l	l .l .l .l :l
s	.s .s :d¹	.s	m	.d .m :s	d¹	.s .s :d¹	.s .s	m .m.m .m:d
m	.m .r :d	.s₁	d	.d .r :m	m	.r .m:f	.m .f	s .f .m .r :d

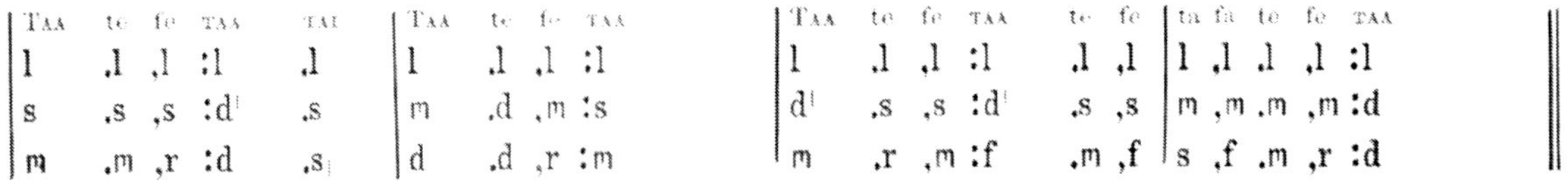

165. KEY F. HALVES AND QUARTERS. Round in four parts.

d	.r	:m	.r	d	.t₁	:d	m	.f	:s	.f	m	.r	:m
All	to -	geth -	er	let	us	sing.	We	will	make	the	wel - kin		ring;

s	.s .s	:s .s .s	s .s .s	:s	d	.d .d :d	.d	s₁	.s₁ .s₁:d
Gentlemen,		gentlemen,	gentlemen	sing,	Sing.	la-dies, sing,	now	sing	ladies, sing.

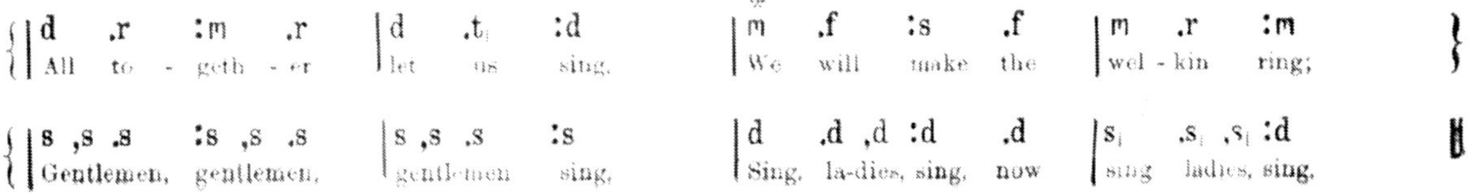

166. KEYS C, A. Taa-efe

Taa tai taa te fe	Taa tai taa	Taa tai taa- efe	Taa tai taa
l .l :l .l ,l	l .l :l	l .l :l .,l	l .l :l
m .m :d .d ,m	s .s :s	s .s :m .,s	d' .d' :d'
d .t, :d .d ,r	m .f :s	d .t, :d .,r	m .r :d

l .,l :l .l	l .,l :l	l .,l :l .,l	l .l :l
d' .,d' :s .s	m .,m :d	d .,d :m .,m	s .s :d'
m .,r :d .r	d .,l, :s,	s, .,l, :t, .,d	r .m :d

167. KEYS F, C.

l :l .,l	l :l	l :l .,l	l :—	l :l .,l	l :l	l :—	— :
d :d .,r	m :s	d :m .,m	r :—	t, :t, .,d	r :m	d :—	— :
s :l .,s	m :s	d' :r' .,d'	l :—	s :s .,s	l :t	d' :—	— :

168. KEY G. Round for three parts.

| m :m .,m | m .m :m .m | r :s .,f | m :— | *d :d .,d | d .d :d .d |
Bim, bome, the bells are ring-ing, Come, come a - way; Hark! to their distant ring-ing,

| t, :m .,r | d :— | s :s, | d :— | s :s, | d :— |
Come, come a - way. Bim, bome, bell, Bim, bome, bell.

169. KEY D. Round for four parts.

| d . :d . | d . :d . | *d .,r :m .f | m .r :d | m .,f :s .l | s .f :m | d' :— | d' :— |
Tick, tock, tick, tock, Hear the clock, it seems to say, One more hour is pass'd away, Ding, dong.

ANTWERP. L. M.

170. KEY A. T. F. SEWARD.

| d :s, .,s, | d :— .d | r :t, | d :— | m :d .,r | m :— .m | f :m | r :— |
| m :m, .,m, | m, :— .m, | f, :f, | m, :— | s, :m, .,f, | s, :— .s, | s, :s, | s :— |

1. Light of the soul, O Sav - iour blest! Soon as thy pres - ence fills the breast,
2. Son of the Fa - - ther Lord most high: How glad is he who feels thee nigh;
3. Je - sus is from the proud con - cealed, But ev - er - more to babes re - vealed,

| d :d .,d | d :— .d | t, :r | d :— | d :s, .,s, | d :— .d | r :d | t, :— |
| d :d .,d | d :— .d | s, :s, | d, :— | d, :d, .,d, | d, :— .d | t, :d | s, :— |

| r :t, .,d | r :— .m | f .s :m .f | r :— | m .r :f .m | s .f :m .r | d :t, | d :— |
| s, :s, .,s, | s, :— .s, | s, :s, | s, :— | s, .f, :l, .s, | s, :s, .l, | s, :f, | m, :— |

Darkness and guilt are put to flight, All then is sweet - ness and de - light.
Come in thy hid - - den maj - es - ty, Fill us with love, fill us with thee.
Through him unto the Fa - ther be Glo - ry and praise e - - ter - nal - ly,

| t, :s, .,l, | t, :— .d | r .m :d .r | t, :— | d :d .d | m .r :s .f | m :r | m :— |
| s, :s, .,s, | s, :— .s, | s, :s, | s, :— | d, :d, .d, | d, .r, :m .f, | s, :s, | d, :— |

OH! THE SPORTS OF CHILDHOOD.

171. KEY C. *Smoothly; in swinging style.* M. 104. O. R. BARROWS.

1. Oh, the sports of child - hood! Roaming thro' the wild - wood, Run-ning o'er the mead - ows, Hap - py and free; How my heart's a - beat - ing, Thinking of the greet - ing, Swinging 'neath the old ap - ple tree.
2. Swaying in the sun - beams, Floating in the shad - ow, Sail - ing on the breez - es, Hap - py and free; Chas - ing all our sad - ness, Shout-ing in our glad - ness, Swinging 'neath the old ap - ple tree.
3. Oh, the sports of child - hood! Roaming thro' the wild - wood, Sing - ing o'er the mead - ows, Hap - py and free; But my heart's a - beat - ing, For the old time greet - ing, Swinging 'neath the old ap - ple tree.
CHORUS.
Swing - ing, swing - ing, Swing - ing, swing - ing, Lull - ing care to rest 'neath the old ap - ple tree; Swing - ing, swing - ing, Swing - ing, swing - ing, Swinging 'neath the old ap - ple tree.

TWILIGHT IS STEALING.

A. S. KIEFFER. B. C. UNSELD.

172. KEY G. M. 72.

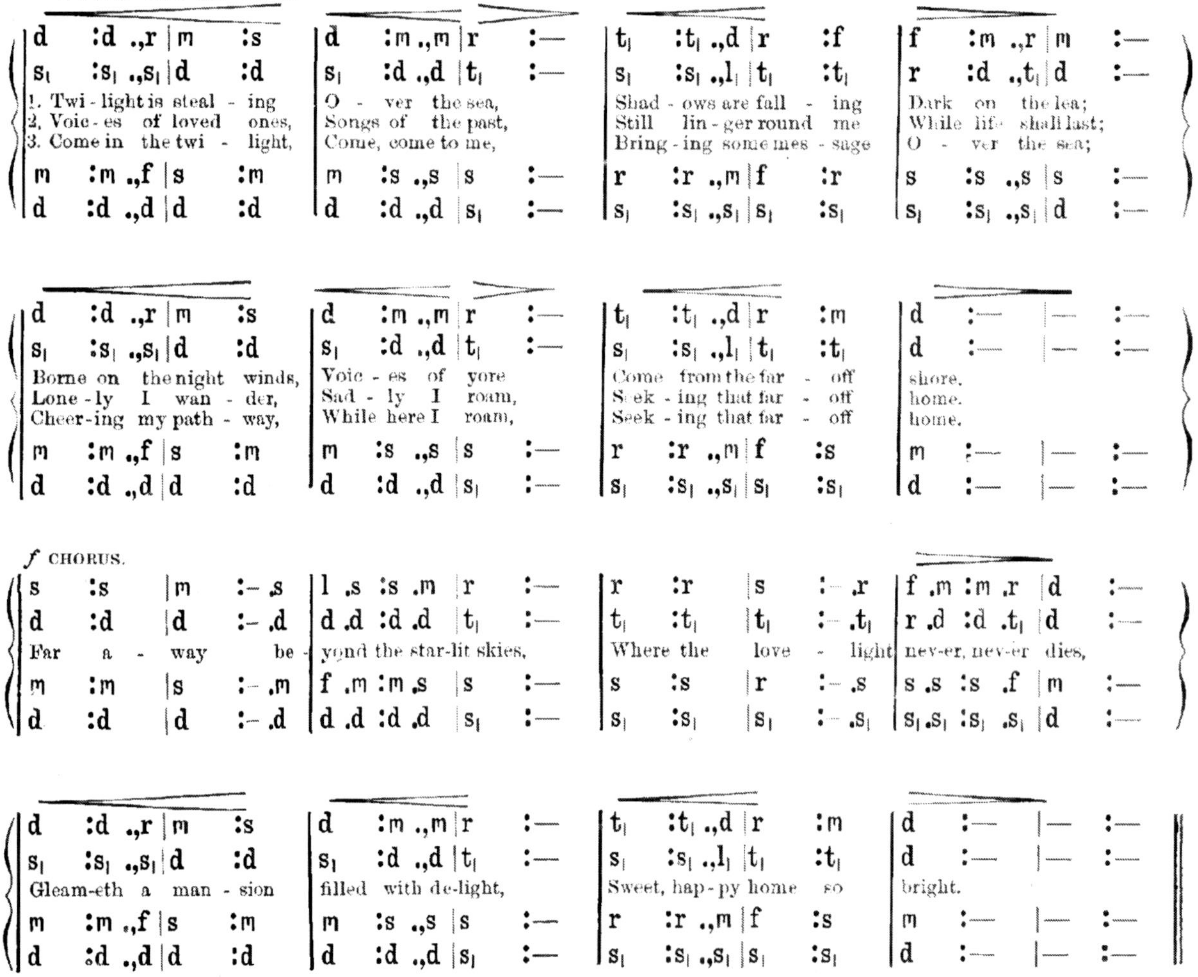
1. Twi - light is steal - ing O - ver the sea, Shad - ows are fall - ing Dark on the lea;
2. Voic - es of loved ones, Songs of the past, Still lin - ger round me While life shall last;
3. Come in the twi - light, Come, come to me, Bring - ing some mes - sage O - ver the sea;
Borne on the night winds, Voic - es of yore Come from the far - off shore.
Lone - ly I wan - der, Sad - ly I roam, Seek - ing that far - off home.
Cheer - ing my path - way, While here I roam, Seek - ing that far - off home.
f CHORUS.
Far a - way be - yond the star-lit skies, Where the love - light nev-er, nev-er dies,
Gleam-eth a man - sion filled with de-light, Sweet, hap - py home so bright.

173. KEY G. Round for three parts. T. F. S.

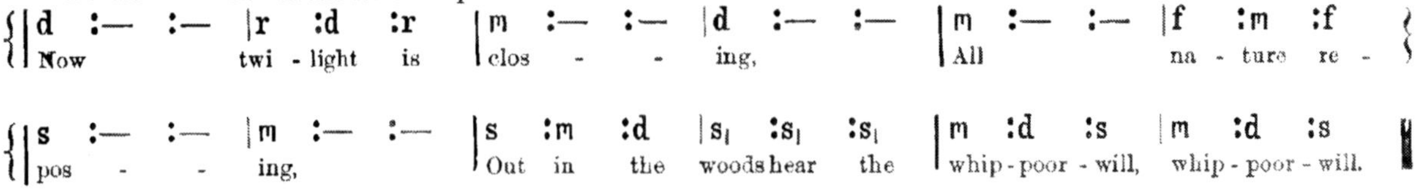
Now twi - light is clos - - ing, All na - ture re - pos - - ing, Out in the woods hear the whip - poor - will, whip - poor - will.

LOUD THROUGH THE WORLD PROCLAIM.

f **174.** KEY C. M. 104.

C. HUNTING.

| s :m .,r\|d :m | s :— \|— :d¹ | t :r¹ \| d¹ :t | d¹ :d¹ \| :s | s :d¹ \| t :l |
| s :m .,r\|d :m | s :— \|— :m | r :f \| m :r | m :m \| :m | m :m \| s :f |

Loud thro' the world pro- claim   Je - ho - vah's high-est prais-es,   Je - ho - vah's high-est

| s :m .,r\|d :m | s :— \|— :s | s :s \| s :s | s :s \| : | : \| : |
| s :m .,r\|d :m | s :— \|— :d | s :s \| s :s | d :d \| : | : \| : |

| f¹ :— \|m¹ :r¹ | d¹ :m¹ \| r¹ :t | d¹ :— \| d¹ :s | l :— \| r¹ :— | d¹ :— \| t :— |
| l :— \|s :f | m :s \| f :r | m :— \| m :m | f :— \| f :— | m :— \| r :— |

prais - es, Je - ho-vah's high-est prais - es, Je - ho - vah's high - est

| : \| : | : \| : | : \| :d¹ | d¹ :— \| l :— | s :— \| s :— |
| : \| : | : \| : | : \| :d | f :— \| f :— | s :— \| s₁ :— |

| d¹ :d¹ \| : | : \| s :m | m :— \| f :l | s :— \| s :m | r :— \| f :f |
| m :m \| : | : \| m :d | d :— \| r :f | m :— \| m :d | t₁ :— \| r :r |

praises   Bow-ing low   at   his   throne, with the an - gels a -

| s :s \| : | : \| : | : \| : | : \| : | : \| : |
| d :d \| : | : \| : | : \| : | : \| : | : \| : |

| m :— \| s :m | m :— \| f :l | s :— \| s :s | l :— \| t :t | d¹ :— \|— :— |
| d :— \|m :d | d :— \| r :f | m :— \| m :m | f :— \| f :f | m :— \|— :— |

dore; Bow - ing low   at   his throne with the an - gels a - dore;

m¹ :— | m¹ :—	f¹ :f¹ .f¹| r¹ :r .r¹	d¹ :— | d¹ :f¹	m¹ :r¹ | :s
s :— | s :—	l :l .l | s :s .s	m :f .s| l :l .l	s :s | :m
d¹ :— | d¹ :—	d¹ :d¹ .d¹| t :t .t	d¹ :— | d¹ :d¹	d¹ :t | :
d :— | d :—	f :— | s :s	d :r .m|f :f .f	s :s | :

For   he   liv - eth and reign-eth for-ev - - er and ev - er; Re -

m¹ :— |— :d¹	s :— |— :s	l :f¹ .r¹|d¹ :t	d¹ :— |— :s	m¹ :— |— :d¹
s :— |— :s	m :— |— :m	f :l | s :f	m :— |— :m	s :— |— :s
:d¹ | s :m	d¹ :— |— :d¹	d¹ :r¹ | m¹ :r¹	d¹ :— |— :	*p* :d¹ | s :m
: | :	:s | m :d	f :— | s :—	d :— |— :	: | :

joice,   re - joice,   re - joice and praise his name;   Re - joice,   re -
Re - joice, re - joice,   Re - joice, re -
                    Re - joice and praise his   name;

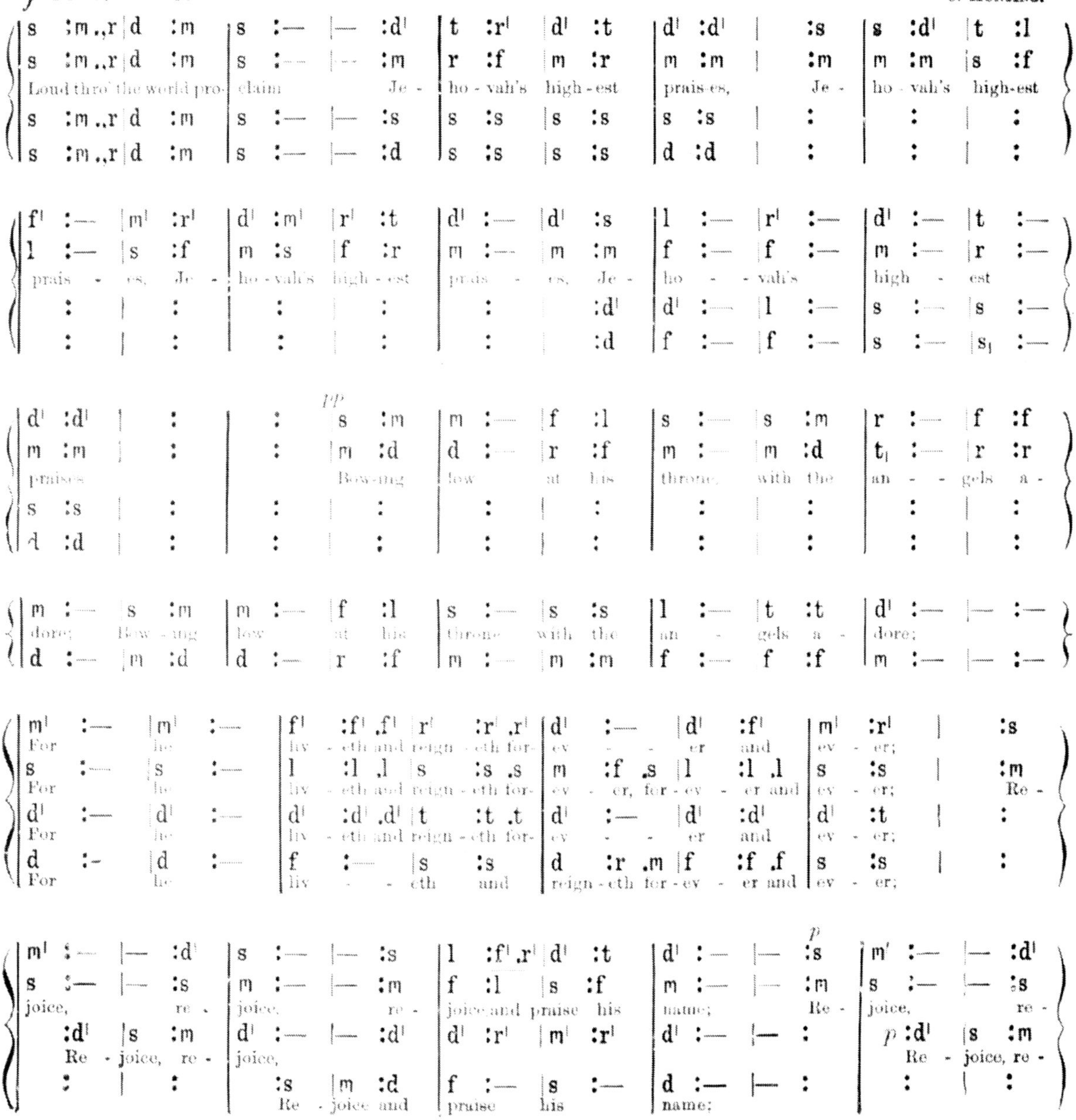

```
                                                  f
s  :—  |—  :s   |l  :f'.r'|d' :t   |d' :—  |   :   |s  :m.,r|d  :m   |s  :—  |—  :d'
m  :—  |—  :m   |f  :l    |s  :f   |m  :—  |   :   |s  :m.,r|d  :m   |s  :—  |—  :m
joice,     re - |joice and praise his|name.          |Loud thro' the world pro-|claim   Je -
d' :—  |—  :d'  |d' :r'   |m' :r'  |d' :—  |   :   |s  :m.,r|d  :m   |s  :—  |—  :s
p :s   |m  :d   |f  :—    |s  :—   |d  :—  |   :   |s  :m.,r|d  :m   |s  :—  |—  :d
  Re - joice and|praise    his     |name.

t  :r' |d' :t   |d' :d'  |   :s    |m' :—  |—  :d'  |s  :—  |—  :s   |l  :f'.r'|d' :t
r  :f  |m  :r   |m  :m   |   :m    |s  :—  |—  :s   |m  :—  |—  :m   |f  :l    |s  :f
ho - vah's high-est|prais-es;  Re -|joice,      re - |joice,     re - |joice and praise his
s  :s  |s  :s   |s  :s   |   :     |   :d' |s  :m   |d' :—  |—  :d'  |d' :r'   |m' :r'
                                      Re - joice, re - |joice,
s  :s  |s  :s   |d  :d   |   :     |   :   |—  :    |   :s  |m  :d   |f  :—    |s  :—
                                                          Re - joice and|praise    his

d' :—  |—  :d'  |d' :—   |—  :d'   |d' :—  |—  :f'  |m' :m' |r' :r'  |d' :—  |—  :
           Je - |ho  -  -  vah     |reigns,     Re - |joice and praise his|name.
m  :—  |—  :m   |f  :f   |f  :m    |f  :f  |f  :l   |s  :s  |s  :f   |m  :—  |—  :
name;      Je - |ho-vah reigns, Je -|ho - vah reigns, Re -|joice and praise his|name.
d' :—  |—  :s   |l  :l   |l  :s    |l  :l  |l  :d'  |d' :d' |t  :t   |d' :—  |—  :
d  :—  |—  :d   |f  :f   |f  :d    |f  :f  |f  :f   |s  :s  |s, :s,  |d  :—  |—  :  ||
```

Modifications of Mental Effect. Thus far we have studied the mental effect of tones when sung slowly. All these effects are greatly modified by pitch, by harmony, by quality of tone, but chiefly by speed of movement. Highness in pitch favors the brightness and keenness of effect, makes *ray* more rousing, and *te* more piercing. Lowness in pitch favors the depressing emotions, makes *fah* more desolate, and *lah* more sad. Quick movement makes the strong tones of the scale (**d m s**) more bold, and the emotional tones (**r f l t**) gay and lively. Let the pupils sing any exercise containing *fah* and *lah* very slowly indeed, and notice how their mental effects are brought out. Then let them sing the same piece as quickly as they can, keeping the time and observing the change. *Fah* and *lah* are now gay and abandoned instead of weeping and desolate in their effect, and the other tones undergo a similar modification. The tune Manoah will afford a very good illustration. Let it be sung first very slowly and then very quickly. Let the pupils try in the same way other tunes which are deemed most characteristic.

KEY G.

```
:d .r |m   :—  :r   |d   :—  :t,  |t,  :—  :l,  }
|l,  :—  :r.m|f   :—  :m   |r   :—  :d   |d   :—  :—  }
|t,  :—  :s, |m   :—  :r   |f   :—  :m   |l   :—  :m  }
|s  :f  :r  |d  :—  :s,  |m  :—  :r  |d  :—  :—  |—  :—  ||
```

"Elementary Rhythms" required for the time exercise of the Elementary Certificate, should be carefully taught by the teacher and diligently practiced by the pupils at home.

Modulator Voluntaries, Ear Exercises, *Pointing and Writing from Memory* are still to be practiced at every lesson. The exercises becoming more and more difficult as the pupils gain facility. The voluntaries will now include *laa-ing* as well as *solfa-ing,* to the teacher's pointing. A few two-part Ear Exercises, as in "Hints for Ear Exercises," can now be wisely introduced, but only to quick and observant classes. To others, each "part" of the exercise will serve as a separate exercise.

Examinations for the Certificate may begin six weeks before the close of the term. All the requirements need not be done at one interview; as soon as a pupil is prepared in any one requirement, he may be examined in that, but all the requirements must be done within six weeks, or else the examination begins again. The examination may be conducted before the whole class, or in private, as suits the convenience of the teacher and pupils.

For instructions in *Voice Training, Breathing, Harmony,* etc., belonging to this step, the teacher will consult the Standard Course.

QUESTIONS FOR WRITTEN OR ORAL EXAMINATION.

DOCTRINE

1. What two new tones have you learned in this step?
2 Between what two tones does *Fah* come?
3 Between what two tones does *Lah* come?
4 What is the relative position of *Fah* to *Doh*?
5 What is the relative position of *Lah* to *Doh*?
6 What is the mental effect of *Fah*? Of *Lah*?
7 What is the manual sign for *Fah*? For *Lah*?
8 What chord is formed of the tones f l d?
9 What is the series of tones, d r m f s l t d', called?
10 Which is the fifth tone of the scale? The third? The sixth? (The teacher will supply additional questions and also questions on the mental effects and hand signs.)
11 Each tone of the scale differs from the others, in what?
12 What is meant by "pitch?"
13 What is the eighth tone above or below any given tone called?
14 How is the octave above any tone indicated in the notation?
15 How is the octave below indicated?
16 How is the second octave indicated?
17 Which are the strong bold tones of the scale?
18 Which are the leaning tones?
19 Which two tones have the strongest leaning or leading tendency?
20 To what tone does t lead?
21 To what tone does f lead?
22 What is the most important the strongest, the governing tone of the scale called?
23 What is a family of tones consisting of a key tone and six related tones, called?
24 When the tones of a key are arranged in successive order ascending or descending, what do they make?
25 Must the scale always be sung at the same pitch or may it be sung at different pitches?
26 What is the name of that scale from which all the others are reckoned?
27. What is the name of the pitch that is taken as the key tone of the Standard Scale?
28 Name the pitches of the Standard Scale?
29 What pitch is *Soh*? *Ray*? *Lah*? (The teacher will supply similar questions.)
30 In the absence of a musical instrument how may the correct pitch of the Standard Scale be obtained?
31 From what is a scale or key named?
32 How are the different keys indicated in the notation?
33 What is the difference of pitch between the voices of men and the voices of women?
34 What is the name of the pitch that stands about the middle of the usual vocal compass?
35 Is middle C a high or a low tone in a man's voice?
36 Is it a high or a low tone in a woman's voice?
37 What are the high voices of women called?
38 What is the usual compass of the Soprano?
39 What are the low voices of women called?
40 What is the usual compass of the Contralto?
41 What are the high voices of men called?
42 What is the usual compass of the Tenor?
43 What are the low voices of men called?
44 What is the usual compass of the Base?
45 From what octave of the Standard Scale is the pitch of the key-note of any key taken?
46 How is this tone and the six tones above it marked?
47 In the Key G the unmarked G of the Standard Scale is *doh* what is the unmarked A? The unmarked E?
48 How would that *lah* be marked?
49 With what octave marks are the Base and Tenor parts written?
50 How is the exact rate of movement of a tune regulated?
51 What does M 60 indicate?
52 How is the rate of very quick, six pulse measure marked?
53 What is the time name of a silence on the first half of a pulse? On the second half?
54 How are half pulse silences indicated in the notation?
55 What is the time name of a pulse divided into two quarters and a half?
56 How are they indicated in the notation?
57 What is the time name of a half and two quarters?
58 How are they indicated in the notation?
59 What is the time name of a pulse divided into a three quarter pulse tone and a quarter?
60 How are they indicated in the notation?
61 By what chiefly, is the mental effect of tones modified?
62 How does a quick movement effect the strong tones of the scale? The emotional tones?

PRACTICE.

63 Sing from memory the pitch of d' of the Standard Scale, and sing down the scale
64 Strike, from the tuning fork, the pitch of d' of the Standard Scale, and sing down the scale, as above
65. Pitch, from the tuning fork, Key D—G—A—F
66 Sing to *laa* the *Fah* to any *Doh* the teacher gives
67 Ditto *Fah*$_1$, Ditto *Lah* Ditto *Lah*$_1$ Ditto any of the tones of the scale the teacher may choose
68 Taatai, with accent, a four-pulse measure, at the rate of M. 60 from memory At the rate of M 120
69 Taatai, with accent *eight* four pulse measures, sustaining the rate of M 60 The rate of M 120
70 Taatai from memory any one of the Exs 155 to 158 and 163 to 167, chosen by the teacher, the first measure being named
71 Taatai on one tone any one of the Exs 165, 168, 169, chosen by the teacher
72 Taatai, in tune any one of the Exs 165, 168, 169, chosen by the teacher
73 Follow the examiner's pointing in a new voluntary containing all the tones of the scale but no difficulties of time greater than the *second* step
74. Point and Solfa on the modulator, from memory, any one of the following four Exercises, 115, 116, 118, 119, chosen by the examiner.
75 Write from memory any other of these four Exercises, chosen by the examiner
76 Tell which is *lah*, which is *fah*, as directed on page 34, question 31
77 Tell what tone of all the scale is sung to *laa*, as on page 34 question 32
78 Taatai any rhythm of two four pulse measures belonging to this step, which the examiner shall *laa* to you, see page 34, question 33
79 Taatai in tune any rhythm of two four-pulse measures belonging to this step, which the examiner Solfas to you. See page 34, question 34

FOURTH STEP.

The Intervals of the Scale. Transition to the First Sharp and the First Flat Keys; its process and mental effect. The tones Fe and Ta. Chromatic effect Cadence, Passing and Extended Transition. Pitching Tunes. Thirds of a Pulse. Beating Time. Syncopation.

The Intervals of the Scale. In the art of singing, this subject is not now deemed so important as it once was, for attention is now directed immediately to the character and mental effect of a tone in the scale, rather than to its distance from any other tone. In an elementary class the subject need not be dwelt upon—merely the main facts briefly presented. The teacher or student who wishes an exhaustive treatment of the matter, is referred to Musical Theory, Book I, by John Curwen.

The Tonic Sol-fa statement of the scale-intervals is as follows:

t to **d**......Little Step......5 Kommas.
l to **t** .....Greater Step....9 Kommas.
s to **l**......Smaller Step....8 Kommas.
f to **s** .....Greater Step ...9 Kommas.
m to **f**.....Little Step......5 Kommas.
r to **m**.....Smaller Step....8 Kommas.
d to **r**......Greater Step....9 Kommas.

Thus the scale contains Three Great Steps, Two Small Steps and Two Little Steps. The difference between a Greater and a Smaller Step is called a Komma; a Greater Step consisting of nine Kommas; a Smaller Step, eight Kommas, and a Little Step, five Kommas. Ordinarily, no distinction is made between the Greater and Smaller Steps, they are simply called Steps, and the Little Step is commonly called a Half-Step.

Intervals are also named Seconds, Thirds, Fourths, Fifths, Sixths, Sevenths, Octaves, and so on. The interval from any tone to the next in the scale is called a Second; from any tone to the third tone is called a Third; to the fourth tone a Fourth, and so on. A Second that is equal to a Step is called a Major Second; a Second that is equal to a Little Step is called a Minor Second. A third that is equal to two Steps is called a Major third—as from **d** to **m**—**f** to **l**—or **s** to **t** A Third that is equal to one full Step and one Little Step (a Step and a Half) is called a Minor Third—as from **r** to **f**—**m** to **s**—**l** to **d'**—or **t** to **r'**.

Fah and *Te* are separated by a peculiar interval, called the **Tri-tone**—equal to three full Steps—it is the only one found in the Scale. Thus **f** and **t** become the most marked characteristic tones of the scale. From their mental effects **t** may be called the *sharp* tone of the scale, and **f** the *flat* tone. We shall presently see how the whole aspect of the scale changes when **f** is omitted and a new **t** put in its place, or when **t** is omitted and a new **f** is taken instead.

Transition is the "passing over" of the music from one key into another. (Heretofore this has been called modulation—but in the Tonic Sol-fa system "modulation" has a different meaning.) Sometimes, in the course of a tune, the music seems to have elected a new governing or key-tone tone; and the tones gather, for a time, around this new key-tone in the same relationship and order as around the first. For this purpose one or more new tones are commonly required, and the tones, which do not change their absolute pitch, change, nevertheless, their "mental effect" with the change of key-relationship. To those who have studied the mental effect of each tone, the study of "transition" becomes very interesting. At the call of some single new tone, characteristically heard as it enters the music, the other tones are seen to acknowledge their new ruler, and, suddenly assuming the new offices he requires, to minister in their places around him.

The musical *fact*, thus didactically stated, may be set before the minds of pupils in some such way as the following: First bring up the scale in review, questioning the class as to the mental effects of the tones, the intervals, and the two most marked characteristic tones of the scale. The teacher may then say:

Listen to me while I sing a tune, and notice whether I stay in the same key all through the tune, or whether I go out of it at any point.

Teacher sings the following example to *laa*.

I. Key **C.**

{|d	:m	|s	:m	|l	:l	|s	:—	}				
{|s	:s	|d'	:t .l	|s	:f	|m	:—	||				

Did I stay in the one key all the time, or did I go out of it at any point?

Listen again, and raise your hands when you feel the key has changed.

Teacher now sings, still to *laa*, example II.

II. Key **C.**

{|d	:m	|s	:m	|l	:l	|s	:—	}
{|s	:s	|d'	:t .l	|s	:fe	|s	:—	||

When the teacher strikes the tone *fe* the pupils will, without doubt, hold up their hands—if they do not, then both examples must be repeated.

You feel that the music has "passed over" into a new key. This change of key during the progress of a tune is called Transition.

It may be well now to repeat the two examples to *laa*, pupils imitating.

Let us now learn what has caused this transition, or change of key. You may sing (solfa-ing) as I point.

The teacher points on the modulator the example I above.

Did you make a transition then, or stay in the same key?

Try it again, as I point

This time he changes second phrase, thus

III. Key **C.**

{|d :m |s :m |l :l |s :— }

{|s :s |d' :t .l |s .f |s :— ||

Did you make a transition then, or stay in the same key?

Listen to me

Teacher sings example **II** to *laa*, pointing as he sings, and at *fe* he points to *fah*, on the modulator, but sings *fe*

Did I sing *fah*, then, or a new tone?

Was the new tone higher or lower than *fah?*

Was it higher or lower than *soh?*

The new tone is a **Little** Step below *soh*, and is called *fe*, it is to *soh* exactly what *te* is to *doh* Now sing as I point, listen to the mental effect of *soh*, and tell me whether it still sounds like *soh*

Pupils sol-fa, to the teacher's pointing example II, page 65

What did the last *soh* sound like? What did the *fe* sound like?

Yes, *soh* has changed into *doh, fe* is a new *te, lah* is changed into *ray, te* into *me*, and so on

The teacher may illustrate this further if he thinks best

You see that the transition is caused by omitting *fah*, the *flat* tone of the old key, and taking *fe*, the *sharp* tone of a new key, in its place *Fe* thus becomes the *distinguishing* tone of the new key The new key is called the "Soh Key," or (on account of the *sharp* effect of the distinguishing tone), the First *Sharp* Key The new key is shown on the modulator on the right of the old key You see the new *doh* is placed opposite the old *soh;* the new *ray* opposite the old *lah*, the new *me* opposite the old *te*, and so on

The teacher will now pattern and point on the modulator example II, going into the side column, as indicated in example IV, following

IV. Key **C.**

{|d :m |s ·m |l :l |s ·— }

G.t

{|sd ·d |f .m r |d ·t_1 |d ·— ||

Now for another experiment Instead of putting a *sharp* tone under *soh*, in place of *fah*, let us put a *flat* tone under *doh*, in place of *te*, and see what the effect will be

Teacher sings, and points on the modulator, example **V**, which the pupils may sing after him.

V. Key **C.**

{|d :m |s :m |l :l |s :— }

{|s :s |d' :s .l |t :l .s |f :— ||

Have we made a transition or not?

Has the mental effect of any of the tones changed?

Listen again, and in place of *te* we will put a new tone called *ta**, now notice the mental effect of *fah*

Teacher repeats example V, singing *ta* in the place of *te*—pupils imitating

Fah has become *doh, soh* has become *ray, lah* has become *me, ta* is a new *fah*, and so on We have made a transition into a new key, but a *different* new key The *distinguishing* tone of this new key is *ta* It is called the "Fah Key," or (on account of the *flat* effect of its distinguishing tone), the First *Flat* Key The Fah Key is represented on the modulator on the left of the old, or Doh Key

Teacher will now pattern and point example V, going into the side column, as indicated in example VI.

VI. Key **C.**

{|d :m |s ·m |l l |s :— }

f **F.**

{|sr .r |s :r .m |f :m r |d .— ||

It will be interesting now to review examples **I, II, IV, V** and **VI**

Adjacent Keys in Transition. Such transitions as have just been studied are called transitions of one remove, because only one change is made in the pitch tones used When **s** becomes **d** the music is said to go into the *first sharp key*, or key of the Dominant When **f** becomes **d** the music is said to go into the *first flat key*, or key of the Sub-Dominant Eighty per cent of all the transitions of music are to one or the other of these two keys, and that to the Dominant is the one most used The relation of these two adjacent keys should be very clearly understood by the pupil, and he should be led to notice how the pitch tones change their mental effect, as described in the following table

Piercing	t	*becomes*	Calm	m.
Sorrowful	l	"	Rousing	r
Grand	s	"	Strong	d
Desolate	f	*is changed for*	Piercing	t
Calm	m	*becomes*	Sorrowful	l
Rousing	r	"	Grand	s.
Strong	d	"	Desolate	f

* For pronunciation, see Chromatic Effects, page 67.

Returning Transition. As a rule, all tunes go back again to their principal key, but the returning transition is not always taken in so marked a manner as the departing transition, because the principal key has already a hold on the mind, and the ear easily accepts the slightest hint of a return to it. Commonly, also, it is in the departing transition that the composer wishes to produce his most marked effect, and in which he therefore makes his chords decisive, and his distinguishing tones emphatic. Let it be carefully noticed, that the return to the orignal key is the same thing in its nature, as going to the first flat key so that a study of the mutual relation of these two keys is the ground work of all studies in transition. The pupils should be taught to draw a diagram of a principal key, with its first sharp key on the right, and its first flat key, on the left, observing carefully the shorter distances between m f and t d', and to learn, by rote, the relations of their notes. Thus, let him say aloud, reading from the middle column to the right, "d f, r s, m l, fe t, s d," and so on; and from the middle column to the left, "d s, r l, m t, and so on. It may be interesting to mention, that in passing to the first sharp key, the old l requires to be raised a komma to make it into a new r; and in passing to the first flat key the old r is lowered a komma, to make a new l. These changes need not trouble the learner, his voice will naturally make them without any special effort.

Notation of Transition. Tonic Sol-faists always prefer that their notes should correspond with the mental effect of the tones they represent. We therefore adopt the plan of giving to some tone, closely preceding the distinguishing tone, *a double name.* We call it by its name in the old key as well as by that which it assumes in the new, pronouncing the old name slightly, and the new name emphatically, thus: *S' Doh, L' Ray, T'' Me,* etc. These are called *bridge-tones;* they are indicated in the notation by *double notes,* called *bridge-notes,* thus: sd, lr, tm, etc.; the small note on the left giving the name of the tone in the old key, and the large note its name in the new key. But when the transition is very brief, less than two measures long, it is more convenient not to alter the names of the tones, but to write the new t as *fe,* and the new f as *ta.* The notation of transition by means of bridge-notes is called the "perfect" notation, because it represents the tones according to the new character and mental effect which they have assumed. The notation by accidentals," as *fe* and *ta,* is called the "imperfect" notation.

The Signature of the New Key is placed over every transition, when written in the "perfect" way. If it is a *sharp* key (*e. i.* to the *right* on the modulator) the new distinguishing tone is placed on the *right* of the key-name, thus, G. t. If it is a *flat* key (*e. i.* to the *left* on the modulator) the new distinguishing tone is placed to the *left,* thus, f. F; and so on. By this the singer knows that he has a new t or a new f to expect. More distant removes would have their two or three distinguishing notes similarly placed, for which see Sixth Step.

Mental Effects of Transition. The most marked effects of transition arise from the distinguishing tones which are used. Transition to the first sharp key naturally expresses excitement and elevation; that to the first flat key depression and seriousness.

Manual Signs. It is not advisable to use manual signs in teaching transition, because they are apt to distract attention from the modulator, with its beautiful "trinity of keys." The greatest effort should be made to fix the three keys of the modulator in the mind's eye. But if, on occasion, it is wished to indicate transition by manual signs, the teacher may, to indicate transition *to the right* on the modulator, use his *left* hand (which will be to the pupil's right), thus: When with the right hand he reaches a bridge-tone, let him place his left hand close beside it, making the sign proper to the new key, then withdrawing his right hand, let him proceed to signal the music with his left. He can use the reverse process in the flat transition.

Cadence Transition. The most frequent transitions are those which occur in a cadence, that is, at the close of a musical line. When these transitions do not extend more than a measure and a half, they are called Cadence Transitions, and are commonly written in the "imperfect way," that is, by using *fe* or *ta.* Cadence transitions are most frequently made by *fe.* In singing, emphasize this *fe* and the first f that follows it.

Passing Transition is one which is not in a cadence and does not extend more than two or three pulses. The commonest form of the transition to the first flat key, is that in which it makes a *passing* harmonic ornament in the middle of a line, or near the beginning. It is written in the "imperfect" manner.

Extended Transition is that which is carried beyond a cadence. The first sharp key is much used in this way in hymn tunes, often occupying the second or third lines, and sometimes the greater part of both.

Missed Transitions. If one "part" is silent while another changes key *twice*—when the silent "part" enters again, it is necessary, for the sake of the solitary singer, to give *both* bridge-notes, thus, rsd. But the chorus singer must *disregard* these marks and tune himself from the other parts. Such bridge-notes are commonly enclosed in brackets.

Chromatic Effects. The tones *fe* and *ta* are frequently introduced in such a way as *not* to produce transition. When thus used they are called *chromatic tones,* and are used to *color* or ornament the music. Chromatic tones may also be introduced between any two tones of the scale which form the interval of a step. These tones are named from the scale-tone below, by changing the vowel into "e," as *doh, de, ray, re,* etc.; or, from the scale-tone above, by changing the vowel into "a," as *te, ta, lah, la.* The customary pronunciation of this vowel in America is "ay," as in "say;" in England it is pronounced "aw."

Such exercises as the following should be carefully taught by *pattern,* from the modulator. Let them be first sol-faed, and afterward sung to *laa.* In fact, all the early transitions, and all the more difficult transitions, following later, should be well taught from the modulator. If this is not done, transition will become a confusion instead of a beauty and a pleasure to the learner.

In the following exercises the two methods of representing transition are shown. The small notes under the middle phrase showing the "imperfect" method of notation. Sing each exercise first by the "perfect" notation, and then by the "imperfect" method.

175. KEY D. A.t. f D.

|d :m |s :m |f :l |s :— |sd :d |t, :d |m :r |d :— |ds :l |s :m |f :r |d :— ||
|s :s |fe :s |t :l |s :— |

176. KEY C. G.t f C.

|m :r |d :m |s :f |m :— |ml, :t, |d :m |r :r |d :— |ds :s |l :l |s :f |m :— ||
|m :fe |s :t |l :l |s :— |

177. KEY F. C.t f F.

|d :r |m :d |f :m |r :— |rs :l |s :d' |d' :t |d' :— |d's :f |m :f |m :r |d :— ||
|r .m |r .s |s :fe |s :— |

178 KEY C. G.t. f C.

|s :f |m :s |d' :t |l :— |lr :m |f :r |d :t, |ds :— |s :m |f :r |d :t, |d :— ||
|l .t |d' l |s :fe |s .— |

179. KEY G. D.t f G.

|m :f |s :m |d :r |t, :— |t,m :f |m :d |r :t, |ds, :— |s, :f, |m, :s, |l, :t, |d :— ||
|t, :d |t, .l, |s, .fe, |s, :— |

180. KEY F. C.t f F.

|m :f |s :m |f :r |d :— |df :m |f :l |s :t |d's :— |m :f |m :r |l, :t, |d :— ||
|d t, |d .m |r fe |s |

181 KEY C. G.t f C.

:s |s :m |f :s |l :— |— :lr |r :m |r :t, |ds :— |— :m |f :m |m :r |d :— |— ||
.l |l :t |l :fe |s :— |— |

182. KEY D. A.t f D.

:d |m :r |d :m |s :f |m :ml, |s, :d |t, :d |m :r |ds :f |m :m |f :m |r :r |d ||
.m |r .s |fe :s |t :l |s |

Extended transition to the first flat key seldom occurs, so that it is not necessary to give more than one or two examples of it.

183. KEY C. f F. C.t

|s :f |m :s |d' :t |l :— |lm :f |m :r |d :t, |d :— |df :f |m :s |l :t |d' :— ||
|l .ta |l :s |f :m |f :— |

184. KEY G. f C. G.t.

|m :r |d :t, |d :l, |s, :— |s,r :m |f :r |d :r |m :— |ml, :l, |s, :d |d :t, |d :— ||
|s, l, |ta, .s, |f, :s, |l, :— |

185. Key D. A.t. f.D.

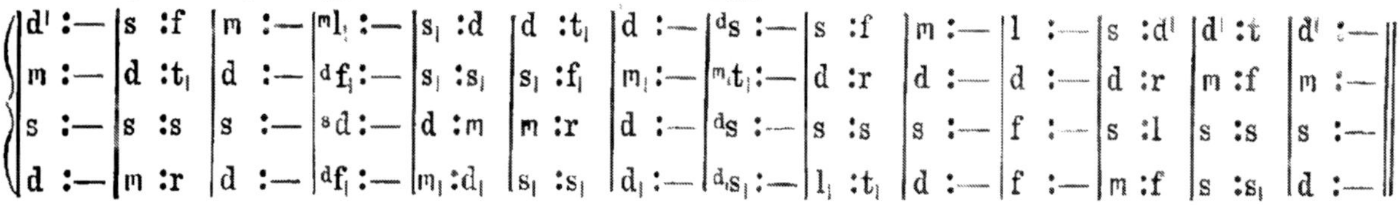

THE BRIGHT NEW YEAR.

186. Key F. *Joyously.* Hubert P. Main.

1.Ver - nal spring and ro - sy sum - mer, Gold - en au - tumn all are past;
2.Slid - ing, skat - ing, laugh-ing, shout-ing, Down the rug - ged hill we go.
3.Tho' the for - est shades are si - lent, And the birds have flown a - way;
C.t.
O'er the face of na - ture frown-ing, Lone - ly win - ter comes at last;
Hark! the sleigh-bells gai - ly peal - ing, O'er the white and down - y snow;
We can war - ble sweet-est mu - sic, We can sing as light as they:
f.F.
Yet she brings us many a pleas-ure, Many a scene of fes - tive cheer,
Can we think the win - ter drear - y, When such mer - ry tones we hear?
Hap-py sea - son, hap - py greet - ing, Friends and kindred far and near;
Now with joy our hearts are glow-ing. While we hail the bright New Year, While we hail the bright New Year.
Now the cup of pleas-ure spar-kles, While we hail the bright New Year, While we hail the bright New Year.
Take our best and kind-est wish - es, While we hail the bright New Year, While we hail the bright New Year.

Bridge-tones approached by the interval of a Second.

187. KEY F. — C.t. — f.F.

| d :m | r :f | m :r | d :— | ^{t}m :f | s :s | l :t | d^1 :— | $^{d^1}$s :m | r :f | m :r | d :— ||

188. KEY F. — C.t. — f.F.

| m :f | s :m | d :r | m :— | ^{r}s :s | d^1 :t | d^1 :l | s :— | ^{l}m :r | m :s | f :r | d :— ||

189. KEY F. — C.t. — f.F.

| s :f | m :s | f :m | r :— | ^{m}l :t | d^1 :l | s :f | m :— | ^{f}d :t_1 | d :r | m :f | m :— ||

Bridge-tones approached by Leaps of a Third, Fourth and Fifth.

190. KEY D. — A.t. — f.D.

| m :r | d :m | s :f | m :— | ^{s}d :t_1 | d :s_1 | l_1 :t_1 | d :— | ^{l_1}m :f | m :r | d :t_1 | d :— ||

191. KEY C. — G.t. — f.C.

| d^1 :s | m :f | s :l | s :— | $^{m}l_1$:t_1 | d :d | m :r | d :— | ^{m}t :t | d^1 :s | f :s | m :— ||

192. KEY G. — D.t. — f.G.

| m :r | d :t_1 | d :l_1 | s_1 :— | ^{d}f :m | f :r | d :t_1 | d :— | ^{f}d :m | r :f | m :r | d :— ||

193. KEY G. — D.t. — f.G.

| m :d | s_1 :m_1 | s_1 :f_1 | m_1 :— | ^{l}r :d | t_1 :d | r :f | m :— | ^{l}m :m | f :m | r :t_1 | d :— ||

194. KEY G. — D.t. — f.G.

| d :t_1 | d :l_1 | s_1 :f_1 | m_1 :— | ^{t}m :f | m :d | r :t_1 | d :— | ^{s}r :t_1 | d :f | m :r | d :— ||

GRACIOUS PROMISE.

195. KEY D. — A.t. — B. C. U.

| s :m .f | s :d^1 | l :t | d^1 :— | ^{t}m :m .f | s :f | m :r | d :— |
| d :d .t_1 | d :m | f :f | m :— | $^{r}s_1$:l_1 | s_1 :l_1 | s_1 :f_1 | m_1 :— |

1. Wait, my soul, up - on the Lord, To his gra - cious prom-ise flee;
2. If the sor - rows of thy case Seem pe - cul - iar still to thee;

| m :s | d^1 :s | l :s | s :— | ^{s}d :d | d :d | d :t_1 | d :— |
| d :d .r | m :d | f :r | d :— | ^{s}d :l_1 | m_1 :f_1 | s_1 :s_1 | d_1 :— |

f.D.

| ^{d}s :m .f | s :m | r :m | f :— | m :m .f | s :f | m :r | d :— |
| ^{f}d :d .t_1 | d :d | d :d | t_1 :— | d :d .t_1 | d :r | d :t_1 | d :— |

Lay - ing hold up - on his word, "As thy days thy strength shall be."
God has prom - ised need - ful grace, "As thy days thy strength shall be."

| ^{l}m :s | d' :s | l :s | s :— | s :s | s :l | s :f | m :— |
| ^{f}d :d .r | m :d | f :m | r :— | d :d .r | m :f | s :s_1 | d :— |

NEW HOPE.

T. J. Cook.

196 Key A. — E.t. — f.A.

| s_1 :m_1 .f_1 | s_1 :d | d .l_1 :l_1 .d | s_1 :— | ^{t}m :m .f | s :m | s .f :m .r | $^{d}s_1$:— |
| m_1 :d_1 .r_1 | m_1 :s_1 | l_1 .f_1 :f_1 | m_1 :— | ^{s}d :d .t_1 | d :d | t_1 :d .t_1 | $^{d}s_1$:— |

1. Sweet peace of conscience, heaven-ly guest, Come, fix thy man - sion in my breast;
2. Come, smiling hope, and joy sin - cere, Come, make your constant dwell - ing here;

| s_1 :s_1 .s_1 | d :d | d :d | d :— | ^{r}s :s .s | s :s | s :s .f | $^{m}t_1$:— |
| d_1 :d_1 .d_1 | d_1 :m_1 | f_1 :f_1 .l_1 | d :— | ^{s}d :d .r | m :d | s_1 :s_1 | $^{d}s_1$:— |

| s_1 :l_1 .t_1 | d :r | m .s :f .m | m :r .r | d :t_1 .l_1 | s_1 :d .r | d :t_1 | d :— |
| f_1 :f_1 .f_1 | m_1 :s_1 | s_1 :s_1 | s_1 :— .f_1 | m_1 :s_1 .f_1 | m_1 :s_1 .l_1 | s_1 :s_1 .f_1 | m_1 :— |

Dis - pel my doubts, my fears con - trol, And heal the an - guish of my soul.
Still let your pres - ence cheer my heart, Nor sin com - pel you to de - part.

| t_1 :d .r | d :t_1 | d :t_1 .d | d :t_1 .t_1 | d :d | d :d .f | m :r | d :— |
| s_1 :s_1 .s_1 | l_1 :s_1 | d_1 .m_1 :r_1 .d_1 | s_1 :— .s_1 | l_1 :f_1 | d_1 :m_1 .f_1 | s_1 :s_1 | d_1 :— |

197. Key D. Chromatic Fe.

| d :m | s :— | s :fe | s :— | s :fe | s :f | m :r | d :— |

198. Key G.

| m :d | s_1 :fe_1 | s_1 :l_1 | s_1 :— | m :d | s :fe | s :f | m :— |

199 Key F.

| d :m | r :m | f :fe | s :— | m :f | fe :s | f :r | d :— |

200. Key D.

| m :s | l :s | s :fe | f :— | m :s | l :s | fe :f | m :— |

201. Key C.

| s :fe :s | m :f :fe | s :l :s | m :— :— | s :fe :s | d' :t :d' | s :fe :f | m :— :— |

202 KEY C. Passing Transition to the first flat key. CHROMATIC TA.

| d^1 :s | l :ta | l :l | s :— | s :l | ta :l | l :t | d^1 :— ‖

203. KEY C.

| m :s | d^1 :ta | l :d^1 | s :— | s :ta | l :f | m :r | m :— ‖

204. KEY A.

| m :d | s_1 :ta_1 | l_1 :t_1 | d :— | d :ta_1 | l_1 :r | d :t_1 | d :— ‖

205. KEY D.

| s :m | d :ta_1 | l_1 :t_1 | d :— | d :m | s :ta | l :t | d^1 :— ‖

206. KEY A.

| s_1 :m | r :d | t_1 :ta_1 | l_1 :— | l_1 :ta_1 | t_1 :d | m :r | d :— ‖

207. KEY C.

| s :f | m :l | s :fe | s :— | d^1 :ta | l :r^1 | d^1 :t | d^1 :— ‖

208. KEY C.

| s .s :fe .f | m :r | r .m :f .s | m :— | d^1 .d^1 :t .ta |
| Soh, soh, fe, fah, | me, ray, | That's the way it | goes. | Now we'll try to - |

| l :s | fe .s :f .s | m :— .s | fe .s :f .s | m :— ‖
| geth - er, | Fe, soh, fah, soh, | me; Yes, | that's the way it | goes. ‖

209. KEY D. FE and TA as bridge-tones.

| d :m | s :m *or* { f :l / r :m } | { s :— / f :— } | A.t ${}^{fe}t_1$:d | m :r | d :t_1 | d :— | f D. ^{ta_1}f :m | r :f | m :r | d :— ‖

210. KEY F.

| m :r | d :m *or* { s :f / f :m } | { m :— / r :— } | C.t. ^{fe}t :t *or* { d^1 :t / d^1 :l } | { d^1 :l / s :f } | { s :— / m :— } | f F. ^{ta}f :m | f :r | s :f | m :— ‖

VIRTUE WOULD GLORIOUSLY.

211. Key C.

:		:	:		:	:		:	d¹ :—	t :s
									Vir - - - tue	would

s °—	m :d	l :l	l :s	f :m .f	s :f	m :fe	s :s
Vir - - - tue would	glo - ri - ous - ly	and for - ev - er	shine By her own

m¹ :m¹	m¹ :r¹	d¹ :t .d¹	r¹ :d¹	t :s	d¹ :—	l :— .l	l :l
glo - ri - ous ly	and for - ev - er,	ev - er shine	By her ra - diant

s :s	d¹ :t	l :s	f :fe	s :—	d :—	f :f	f :r
ra - diant light, By	her own ra - diant	light, Though	sun and moon and

r¹ :—	— :d¹	t :d¹	r¹ :	:	:	d¹ :—	t :s
light, her	ra - diant light,		Though moon and

r :r	m :fe	s :l	t :	d¹ :—	t :s	m¹ :—	:r¹
stars were in the	deep sea sunk,	Though moon and	stars, Though

m¹ :—	:d¹	f¹ :—	m¹ :—	r¹ :—	:r¹	d¹ :—	:
stars were	in the	deep sea	sunk.

d¹ :s	d¹ :ta	l :t	d¹ :—	— :d¹	t :t	d¹ :—	:
moon and stars were	in the deep,	the deep sea	sunk.

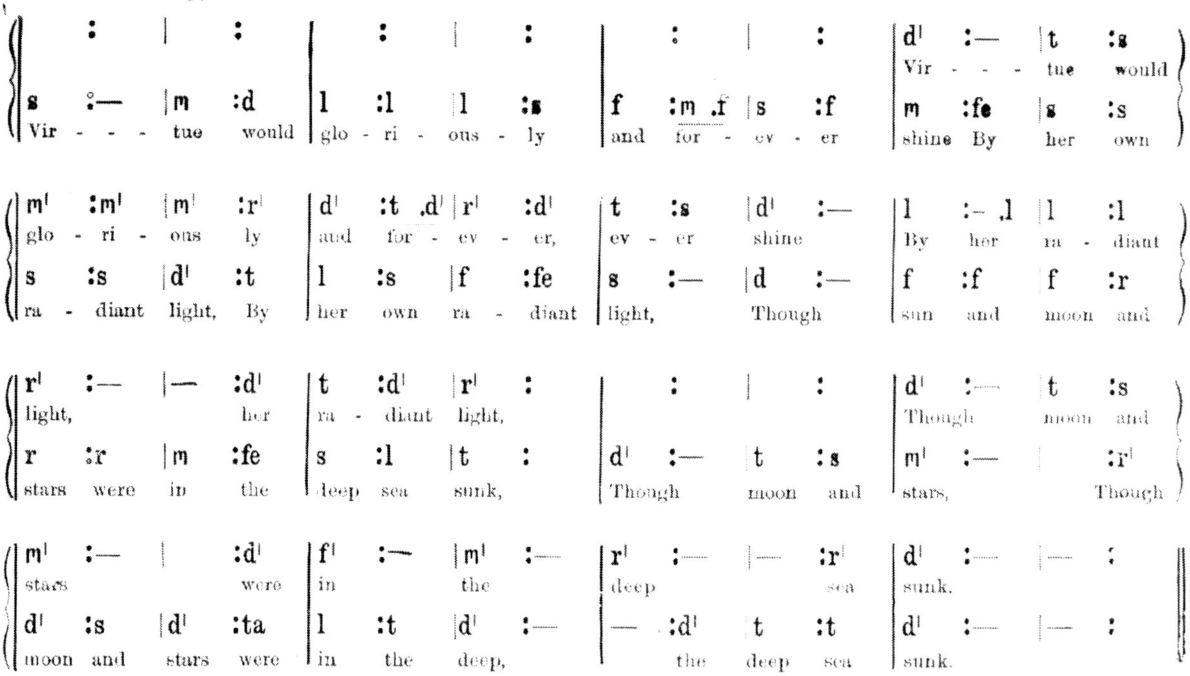

GENTLY EVENING BENDETH.

212. Key A♭

C. H. Rink

Sweetly.

m :m	r :r	d :	s₁ :	l₁ :t₁	d :m	r :—	— :

d :d	t₁ :s₁	s₁ :—	m₁ :	f₁ :f₁	s₁ :d	t₁ :—	:
1. Gen - tly even - ing	bend - - - eth,	O - ver vale and	hill,
2. Save the wood - brook's	gush - - - ing,	All things si - lent	rest;
3. And no even - ing	bring - - - eth,	To its life re -	lease;
4. Rest-less thus life	flow - - - eth,	Striv - eth in my	breast;

d₁ :m₁	s₁ :f₁	m₁ :—	d₁ :—	f₁ :r₁	m₁ :d₁	s₁ :—	— :

m :m	f :m	r :—	s :—	d :f	m :r	d :—	— :

d :d	r :d	t₁ :—	d :ta₁	l₁ :r	d :s₁	m₁ :—	— :
Soft - ly peace de -	scend - - eth,	And the world is	still.
Hea - its rest - less	rush - - ing,	On t'ward o - - cean's	breast.
And no sweet bell	ring - - eth,	O'er its wave - lets	peace.
God a - - lone be -	stow - - eth	Tran - quil even - ing	rest.

d :l₁	r₁ :m₁ .f₁	s₁ :f₁	m₁ :—	f₁ :r₁	s₁ :s₁	d₁ :—	— :

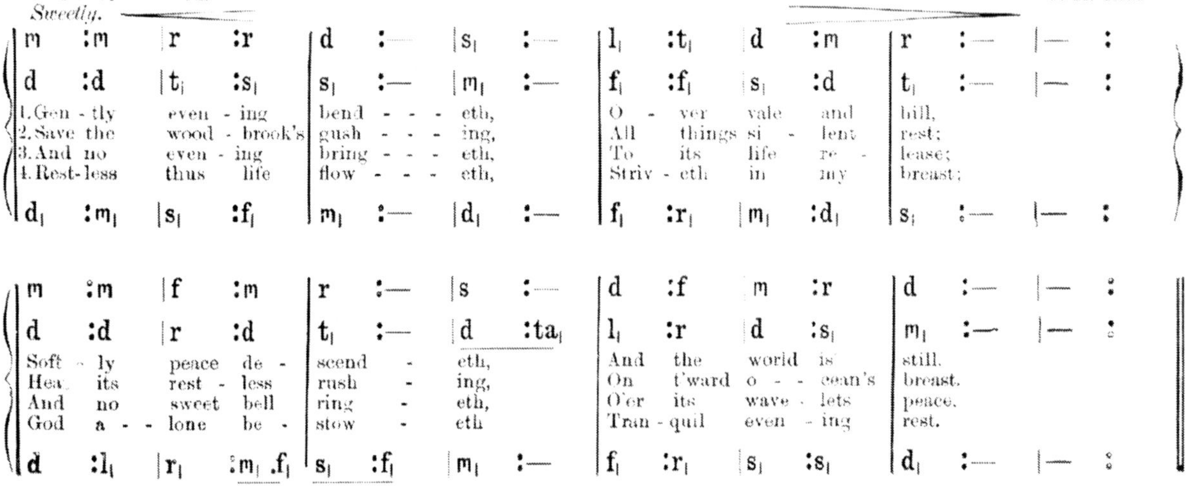

ANYWHERE.

213. Key E♭. B. C. Unseld.

m :m |s :m |m :r |r :— |f :f |s :r |m :— |— :
d :d |m :d |d :t, |t, :— |r :r |t, :t, |d :— |— :
1. A - ny lit - tle cor - ner, Lord, In thy vine - yard wide;
2. Where we pitch our night - ly tent, Sure - ly mat - ters not;
3. All a - long the wil - der - ness, Let us keep our sight;
s :s |s :s |s :s |s :— |s :s |s :s |s :— |— :
d :d |d :d |s, :s, |s, :— |s, :s, |s, :s, |d :— |— :

s :s |l :s |s :m |r :— |r :s |t :l |s :— |— : |s :s |l :d'
m :m |f :m |m :d |t, :— |t, :r |r :d |t, :— |— : |d :d |d :d
Where thou bid'st me work for thee, There I would a - bide; Mir - a - cle of
If the day for thee is spent, Blessed is the spot; Quickly we our
On the mov - ing pil - lar fixed, Con - stant day and night. Then the heart will
d' :d' |d' :d' |d' :s |s :— |s :s |s :fe |s :— |— : |m :m |f :l
d :d |d :d |d :d |s, :— |s, :t, |r :r |s, :— |— : |d :d |f :f

d' :l |s :— |s :s |l :d' |d' :l |s :m |s :m |r :— |m :r |d :—
d :d |d :— |d :d |d :d |d :d |d :— |m :d |t, :— |t, :t, |d :—
sav - ing grace, That thou giv - est me a place A - ny - where, A - ny - where.
tent may fold, Cheerful march thro' storm and cold, With thy care, With thy care.
make its home, Will-ing, led by thee, to roam A - ny - where, A - ny - where.
l :f |m :— |m :m |f :l |l :f |m :s |s :s |s :— |s :f |m :—
f :f |d :— |d :d |f :f |f :f |d :— |d :d |s, :— |s, :s, |d :—

THE LOVELY LAND.

214. Key E♭. R. Lowry, by per.

:s |d' :t |d' :s |l :l |l .t :d' |s :s .f |m :r |d :— |—
:m |m :f |s :m |d :d |d :d |m :m .r |d :t, |d :— |—
1. There is a land of pure de - light, Where saints im - mor - tal reign;
2. There ev - er - last - ing spring a - bides, And nev - er fad - ing flowers;
3. Sweet fields a - mong the swell - ing flood Stand dressed in liv - ing green;
:s |s :s |s :s |f :f |f .s :l |d' :s |s :f |m :— |—
:d |d :r |m :d |f :f |f :f |s :s |s, :s, |d :— |—

:s |d' :t |d' :s |l :l |l .t :d' |s :s .f |m :r |d :— |— :
:m |m :f |s :m |d :d |d :d |m :m .r |d :t, |d :— |— :
In - fin - ite day ex - cludes the night, And pleas - ures ban - ish pain;
Death, like a nar - row sea, di - vides This heaven-ly land from ours;
So to the Jews old Ca - naan stood, While Jor - dan rolled be - tween;
:s |s :s |s :s |f :f |f .s :l |d' :s |s :f |m :— |— :
:d |d :r |m :d |f :f |f :f |s :s |s, :s, |d :— |— :

s :- .m	l :s	m :r	d :r	m :d' .,d'	t .l :s .fe	s :—	—
m :- .d	f :m	d :t_1	d :t_1	d :m .,m	r :r	r :—	—
Oh! the land,	the	love - ly	land, The	land o - ver	Jor - dan's	foam;	
s :- .s	d' :d' .s	s :f	m :s	s :s .,s	s :t .l	t :—	—
d :- .d	d :d	s_1 :s_1	d :s_1	d :d .,d	r :r	s_1 :—	—

:s .s	d' :t	d' :s .,s	l .l :l .l	l .t :d'	s :s .,f	m :r	d :—	—
:m .m	m :f	s :m .,m	d .d :d .d	d :d	m :m .,r	d :t_1	d :—	—
On the	gold - en	strand, Wait the	happy, happy	band, To	wel - come the	ransomed	home.	
:d' .d'	s :s	s :s .,d'	d'.d' :d'.d'	d'.t :d'	s :s .,s	s :f	m :—	—
:d .d	d :r	m :d .,d	f .f :f .f	f :f	s :s .,s	s_1 :s_1	d :—	—

MAY IS HERE.

215. KEY A.

s_1 .,s_1 :m :- .r	d .m_1 :l_1 :s_1	s_1 .,s_1 :l_1 :t_1	d .,r :m :d	s_1 .,s_1 :m :- .r
m_1 .,m_1 :s_1 :- .f_1	m_1 .m_1 :f_1 :m_1	s_1 .,s_1 :fe_1 :f_1	m_1 .,f_1 :s_1 :m_1	m_1 .,m_1 :s_1 :- .f_1
1. May is here, the	world re-joic - es,	Earth puts on her	smiles to greet her,	Grove and field lift
2. Birds, thro' ev - ery	thicket call - ing,	Wake the woods to	sounds of glad - ness,	Hark! the long - drawn
3. Earth to heav'n lifts	up her voic - es,	Sky, and fields, and	woods, and riv - er,	With their heart our
d .,d :d :- .d	d .d :d :d	t_1 .,t_1 :d :r	d .,d :d :d	d .,d :d :- .d
d_1 .,d_1 :d_1 :- .d_1	d_1 .d_1 :d_1 :d_1	s_1 .,s_1 :s_1 :s_1	d .,d :d :d	d_1 .,d_1 :d_1 :- .d_1

d .,m_1 :l_1 :s_1	s_1 .,s_1 :l_1 :t_1	d .,r :m :d	l .,s :r :—	f .,m :d :—
m_1 .,m_1 :f_1 :m_1	s_1 .,s_1 :fe_1 :f_1	m_1 .,f_1 :s_1 :m_1	t_1 .,t_1 :t_1 :—	d .,d :d :—
up their voic - es,	Leaf and flow'rs come	forth to meet her.	Happy May,	blithesome May,
notes are fall - ing,	Sad, but pleas - ant	in their sad - ness.	Happy May,	blithesome May, &c.
heart re joic - es,	For his gifts we	praise the Giv - er.	Happy May,	blithesome May, &c.
d .,d :d :d	t_1 .,t_1 :d :r	d .,d :d :d	r .,r :f :—	d .,d :m :—
d_1 .,d_1 :d_1 :d_1	s_1 .,s_1 :s_1 :s_1	d .,d :d :d	s_1 .,s_1 :s_1 :—	d .,d :d :—

m .,r :l_1 :t_1	d .,r :m :f	l .,s :r :—	f .,m :d :—	m .,r :l_1 :t_1	d .,m :d :—
s_1 .,f_1 :f_1 :f_1	m_1 .,f_1 :s_1 :—	t_1 .,t_1 :t_1 :—	d .,d :d :—	s_1 .,f_1 :f_1 :f_1	m_1 .,s_1 :m_1 :—
Winter's reign has	passed away;	Happy May,	blithesome May,	Winter's reign has	passed away.
s .,s :r :r	d .,d :d :r	r .,r :f :—	d .,d :m :—	s .,s :r :r	d .,d :d :—
s_1 .,s_1 :s_1 :s_1	d .,d :d :—	s_1 .,s_1 :s_1 :—	d .,d :d :—	s_1 .,s_1 :s_1 :s_1	d_1 .,d_1 :d_1 :—

ONWARD, CHRISTIAN SOLDIERS.

216. Key F. M. 120.   A. S. Sullivan, Mus. Doc.

```
{| s  :s  | s  :s  | s  :-.l | s  :—  | r  :r  | d  :r  | m  :—  | — :—  | d  :m  | s  :d¹ |
 | m  :m  | m  :m  | f  :—   | f  :—  | t₁ :t₁ | l₁ :t₁ | d  :—  | — :—  | d  :d  | d  :d  |
   1.Onward,  Chris-tian   sol - - - diers,    March-ing  as  to    war,              With the   cross of
   2.Onward,  then  ye     faith - - ful,      Join our   hap - py   throng.           Blend with ours your
 | d  :m  | s  :d¹ | d¹ :—  | t  :—  | s  :s  | s  :s  | s  :—  | — :—  | s  :s  | s  :m  |
 | d  :d  | d  :d  | r  :—  | s₁ :—  | s  :f  | m  :r  | d  :—  | — :—  | m  :m  | m  :m  |}

{| d¹ :—  | t  :—  | l  :l  | m  :fe | s  :—  | — :—  | r  :r  | s  :r  | m  :—.f | m  :—  |
 | r  :—  | r  :—  | d  :d  | d  :d  | t₁ :—  | — :—  | t₁ :t₁ | r  :t₁ | d  :—.r | d  :—  |
   Je - - - sus        Go - ing  on  be - fore:                 Christ, the  Roy - al   Mas - - ter,
   voic - - es         In   the   tri - umph song:              Glo - ry,   land and   hon - - or
 | s  :-.l | s  :—  | fe :fe | s  :l  | s  :—  | — :—  | s  :s  | s  :s  | s  :—  | s  :—  |
 | r  :—  | r  :—  | r  :r  | r₁ :r₁ | s₁ :—  | — :—  | s₁ :s₁ | t₁ :s₁ | d  :—  | d  :—  |}

{| s  :s  | d¹ :s  | l  :—  | — :—  | l  :s  | f  :s  | l  :s  | f  :s  | l  :s  | f  :m  |
 | d  :d  | d  :d  | d  :—  | — :—  | d  :d  | d  :d  | d  :—  | d  :—  | d  :d  | r  :d  |
   Leads a - gainst the  foe:           For - ward  in - to   bat - - tle,       See his   ban - ners
   Un - to   Christ the  King:          This, through countless  a - - - ges,     Men and   an - gels
 | m  :m  | s  :m  | f  :—  | — :—  | f  :m  | f  :m  | f  :m  | f  :m  | f  :m  | r  :r  |
 | d  :d  | m  :d  | f  :—  | — :—  | f  :d  | l₁ :d  | f  :d  | l₁ :d  | f₁ :f₁ | f₁ :f₁ |}

{| r  :—  | — :—  | d  :d  | d  :d  | d  :t₁.l₁ | t₁ :d  | r  :r  | r  :d.r |
 | t₁ :—  | — :—  | s₁ :s₁ | s₁ :s₁ | s₁ :—    | s₁ :—  | s₁ :s₁ | s₁ :s₁ |
   go,              On - ward,  Chris-tian   sol - - - diers,      March-ing   as   to
   sing.           On - ward,  Chris-tian   sol - - - diers,      March-ing   as   to
 | s  :—  | — :—  | m  :m  | m  :m  | f  :—  | f  :—  | f  :f  | f  :f  |
 | s₁ :—  | — :—  | d  :s₁ | d  :s₁ | r  :s₁ | r  :s₁ | t₁ :s₁ | t₁ :s₁ |}

{| m  :—  | — :—  | s  :s  | d¹ :t | d¹ :—  | s  :—  | f  :m  | r  :—.d | d  :—  | — :—  |
 | s₁ :—  | — :—  | m  :m  | f  :f  | m  :—  | d  :—  | d  :d  | t₁ :—.d | d  :—  | — :—  |
   war,            With the   cross of   Je - - - sus      Go - ing  on    be - fore.
   war,            With the   cross of   Je - - - sus      Go - ing  on    be - fore.
 | m  :—  | — :—  | d¹ :d¹ | s  :s  | s  :—  | s  :—  | l  :s  | f  :—.m | m  :—  | — :—  |
 | d  :—  | — :—  | d  :d  | r  :r  | m  :—  | m₁ :—  | f₁ :f₁ | s₁ :—.s₁ | d  :—  | — :—  |}
```

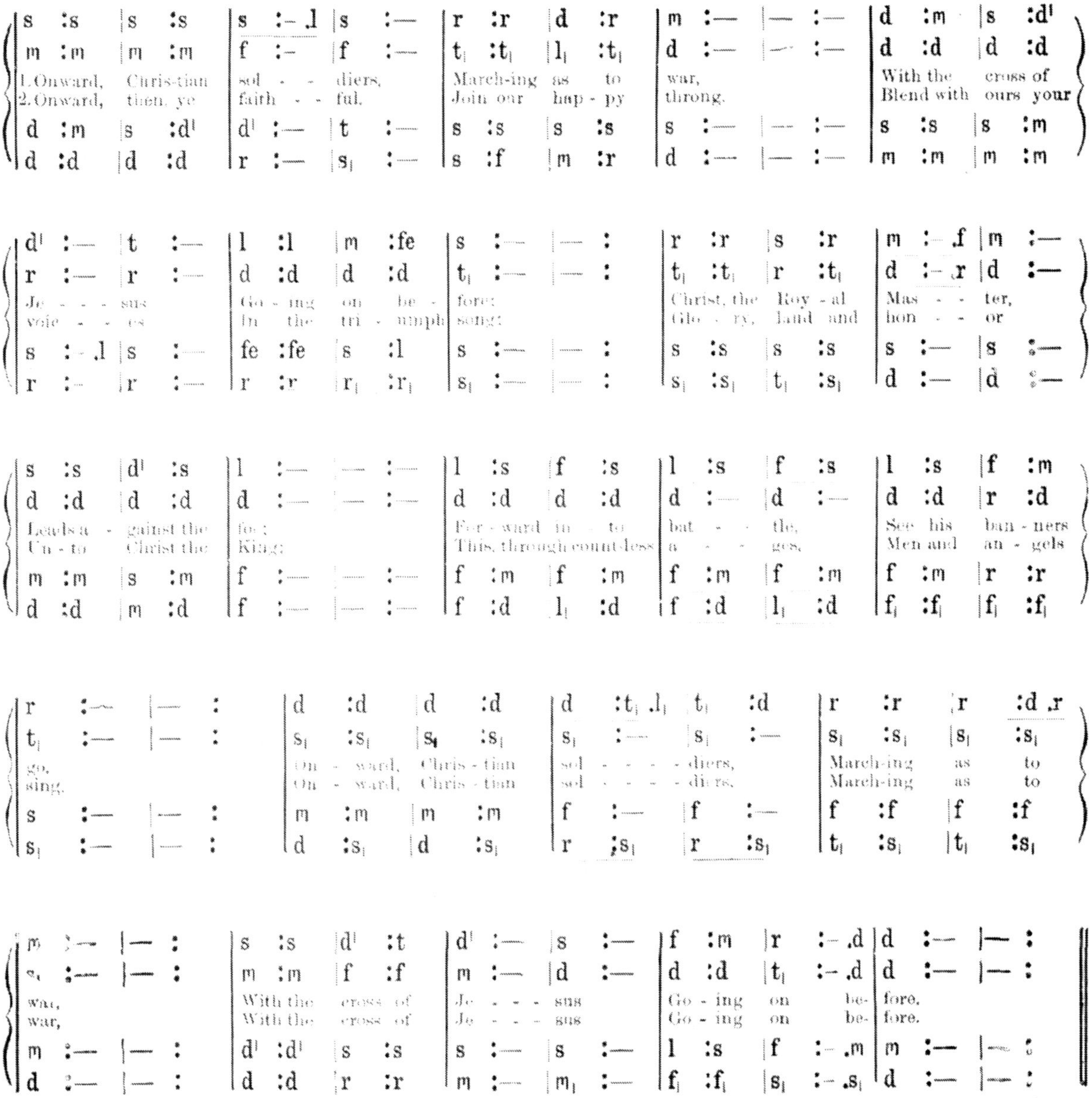

FATHER OF MERCIES.

217. KEY E.

BERNARD SCHMIDT.

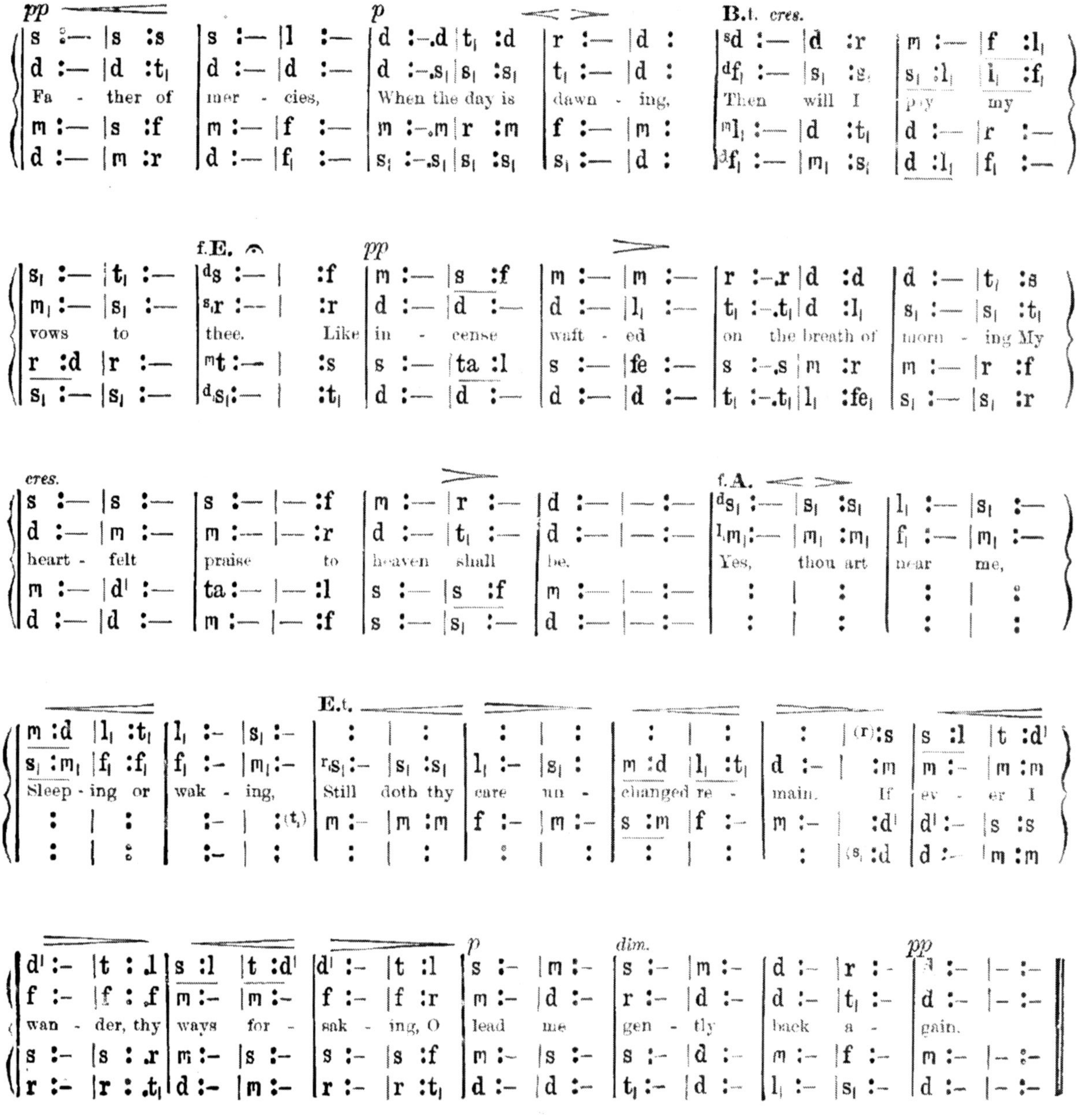

Fa - ther of mer - cies, When the day is dawn - ing, Then will I pay my
vows to thee. Like in - cense waft - ed on the breath of morn - ing My
heart - felt praise to heaven shall be. Yes, thou art near me,
Sleep - ing or wak - ing, Still doth thy care un - changed re - main. If ev - er I
wan - der, thy ways for - sak - ing, O lead me gen - tly back a - gain.

HURRAH FOR THE SLEIGH-BELLS!

FANNY J. CROSBY. T. F. SEWARD.

218. KEY G.

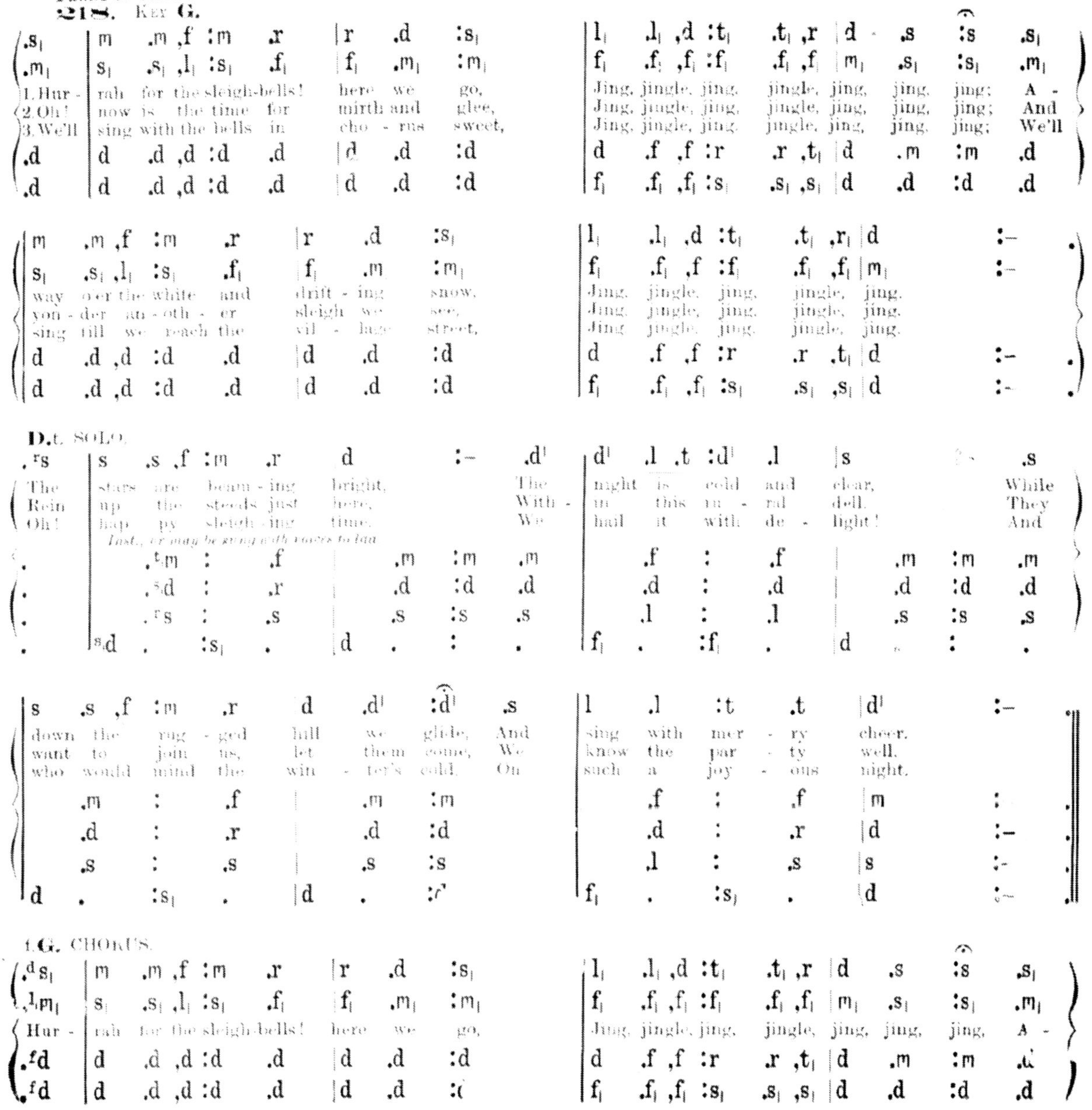

| m .m,f :m .r | r .d :s, | l, .l,,d :t, .t,,r | d :— .r ,r | m,m.r,r :m .s | d :— |
| s, .s,,l, :s, .f, | f, .m, :m, | f, .f,,f, :f, .f,,f, | m, :— .t,,t, | d,d .t,,t, :d .t, | d :— |
way o'er the white and drift-ing snow: Jing, jingle, jing, jingle, jing; Jingle, jingle, jingle, jing, jing, jing.
| d .d,d :d .d | d .d :d | d .f,f :r .r,t, | d :— .s ,s | s,s .s ,s :s .r | m :— |
| d .d,d :d .d | d .d :d | f, .f,,f :s, .s ,s | d :— .s,,s, | d,d .s,,s, :d .s, | d :— |

CHIME AGAIN.

219. Key A♭. H. R. Bishop.

| m :- .r :d | m :- .r :d | f :l, :t, | d :— : | d :- .t, :l, | s, :d :r |
| s, :- .f, :m, | s, :- .s, :s, | l, :f, :f, | m, :— : | l, :- .s, :f, | m, :s, :s, |
1. Chime a-gain, chime a-gain, beau-ti-ful bells, Now your soft mel-o-dy
2. Chime a-gain, chime a-gain, beau-ti-ful bells, Lin-ger a-while o'er the
| d :- .d :d | d :- .t, :d | d :r :r | d :— : | d :- .d :d | d :d :t, |
| d, :- .d, :d, | d, :- .r, :m, | f, :f, :s, | d, :— : | f, :- .f, :f, | d, :m, :s, |

| m :- .r :d | r :— : | 𝄋 m :- .r :d | m :- .r :d | f :l, :t, | d :— : |
| s, :- .s, :fe, | s, :— : | s, :- .f, :m, | s, :- .s, :s, | l, :f, :f, | m, :— : |
floats on the wind, D. S. Burst-ing at in-ter-vals o-ver the sails,
Voi-ces of friend-ship still ring in each sound,
deep dusk-y bay, D. S. Faint-er and faint-er your mel-o-dy swells
Lone-ly I'm left on the wa-ters to weep,
| d :- .r :r | t, :— : | d :- .d :d | d :- .t, :d | d :r :r | d :— : |
| d :- t, :l, | s, :— : | d, :- .d, :d, | d, :- .r, :m, | f, :f, :s, | d, :— : |

FINE. E♭.t.

| d :- .t, :l, | s, :d :r | m :f :- .r | d :— : | ʳs :s :s | l :s :s |
| l, :- .s, :f, | m, :s, :l, | s, :s, :- .f, | m, :— : | ᵗm :m :m | f :m :m |
Leav-ing a train of af-fec-tion be-hind. An-swer-ing ech-oes that
Bid-ding me wel-come that chime with a tear.
Fast fades the land and your sound dies a way. Now the cold lamp of night
Chimes of those beau-ti-ful bells to de-plore.
| d :- .d :d | d :d :d | d :r :- .t, | d :— : | ˢd' :d' :d' | d' :d' :d' |
| f, :- .f, :f, | d, :m, :f, | s, :s, :- .s, | d, :— : | ₛd :d :d | d :d :d |

f f. A♭. D.S.

| s :f :r | d :— : | s :s :s | l :s :s .s | s :- .l :t | ᵈs :— : |
| m :r :t, | d :— : | d :d :d | d :— :d .d | d :- .d :r | ᵐt, :— : |
gath-er a-round, Call from the heart every wish that is dear,
sil-ver the deep, On sails the bark from our own be-loved shore,
| d' :s :f | m :— : | m :m :m | f :m :m .m | m :- .f :f | ˢr :— : |
| s, :s, :s, | d :— : | d :d :d | d :— :d .d | d :- .f :r | ᵈs, :— : |

220. Key D. Chromatic Tones.

|d :t_1 |d :— |r :de |r :— |m :re |m :d |f :— |— : |s :fe |s :— }

|l :se |l :— |t :le |t :s |d^1 :— |— : |d^1 :t |d^1 :— |t :le |t :— }

|l :se |l :d^1 |s :— |— : |f :m |f :— |m :re |m :— |r :de |r :m |d :— |— : ||

221. Key G.

|m :re :m |d :t_1 :d |s_1 :fe_1 :s_1 |l_1 :— :— |r :de :r |f :m :f |t_1 :le_1 :t_1 |d :— :— }

|l_1 :se_1 :l_1 |r :de :r |f :m :f |r :— :— |s :fe :s |m :r :d |t_1 :le_1 :t_1 |d :— :— ||

222. Key C. *Staccato* Round in two parts. T. F. S.

|d^1 :d^1 |t .le :t |l :l |s .fe :s |f :f |m .re :m |r :s |d :— }
Trip, trip, fairies light, Dance-ing all the night, 'Neath the stars so bright, Here and there

* |d :d |r .de :r |f :f |m .re :m |l :l |s .fe :s |t :t |d^1 :— ||
La la la la la, La la la la la, La la la la la, La la la.

223. Key F. Round in three parts T. F. S.

|m :m |re :— |m :m |re :— |m :s |f :r |d :r |m :— |* s :s |fe :— |s :s |fe :— }
Summer flow'rs, past and gone, Show an-oth - er year is done, Autumn winds, sighing low,

|s :m |r :f |m :r |d :— |s_1 :d |l_1 :d |s_1 :d |l_1 :d |s_1 :d |l_1 :f_1 |s_1 :t_1 |d :— ||
Tell us how the time doth flow; Spring and summer, autumn, win-ter, Teach a les - son we should know.

224. Key D.

|d :d |t_1 :d |r :r |de :r |m :m |re :m |f :— |— :— |s :s |fe :s }

|l :l |se :l |t :t |le :t |d^1 :— |— :— |t :t |d^1 :t |l :l |ta :l }

|s :s |la :s |f :— |— :— |m :m |f :m |r :r |ma :r |d :d |ra :ra |d :— |— :— ||

225. KEY D.

|d :t, |d :de |r :de |r :re |m :re |m :m |f :— |— : |s :fe |s :se |

|l :se |l :le |t :le |t :t |d' :— |— : |t :d' |t :ta |l :ta |l :la |

|s :la |s :sa |f :— |— : |m :f |m :ma |r :ma |r :ra |d :ra |d :t, |d :— |— : ||

226. KEY G. Round in two parts.

|d :de |r :t, |d :ta, |l, :t, |d :de |r :re |m :r |d :— |
Sum - mer days are now de - clin - ing, With their pre - cious gold - en hours;

*|m :s |f :r |m :s |f :r |m :m |f :fe |s :f |m :— ||
Dim - ly see the sun is shin - ing Thro' the fad - ing groves and bowers.

227. KEY C. Round in two parts.

|d' :— |t :ta |l :la |s :fe |s :— |fe :f |m : | : |

*|m :d |r :m |f :— |m :re |m :— |ma :r |d :r .m |f .s :l .t ||

NOW THE WINTRY STORMS ARE O'ER.

228. KEY C. T. F. SEWARD.

|m :re :m |s :— :d' |d' :t :d' |l :— :— |r :de :r |f :— :l |s :fe :s |m :— :— |
|d :— :d |m :— :m |f :— :f |f :— :— |t, :le, :t, |r :— :f |m :re :m |d :— :— |
1. Now the win - try storms are o'er, Spring un - locks her ver - dant store;
2. Now re - spon - sive through the grove, Soft - ly tuned to Spring and love;
|s :fe :s |d' :— :s |l :se :l |d' :— :— |s :— :s |s :— :t |d' :— :d' |s :— :— |
|d :— :d |d :— :d |f :— :f |f :— :— |s :— :s |s :— :s |d :— :d |d :— :— |

|m :re :m |s :— :d' |d' :t :d' |l :— :— |t :le :t |m' :— :r' |d' :— :d' |d' :— :— ||
|d :— :d |m :— :m |f :— :f |f :— :— |r :de :r |s :— :f |m :— :f |m :— :— ||
Smil - ing pleas - ure crowns the day, Sweet - ly breathes the May, the May, the May
Ech - o with her sport - ive lay, Sweet - ly sings of May, sweet May, sweet May
|s :fe :s |d' :— :ta |l :se :l |d' :— :— |s :— :s |s :— :s |s :— :l |s :— : ||
|d :— :d |d :— :d |f :— :f |f :— :— |s :— :s |s, :— :s, |d :— :d |d :— :— ||

RISE, CYNTHIA, RISE.

229. Key E♭. M. 100 twice. Hook.

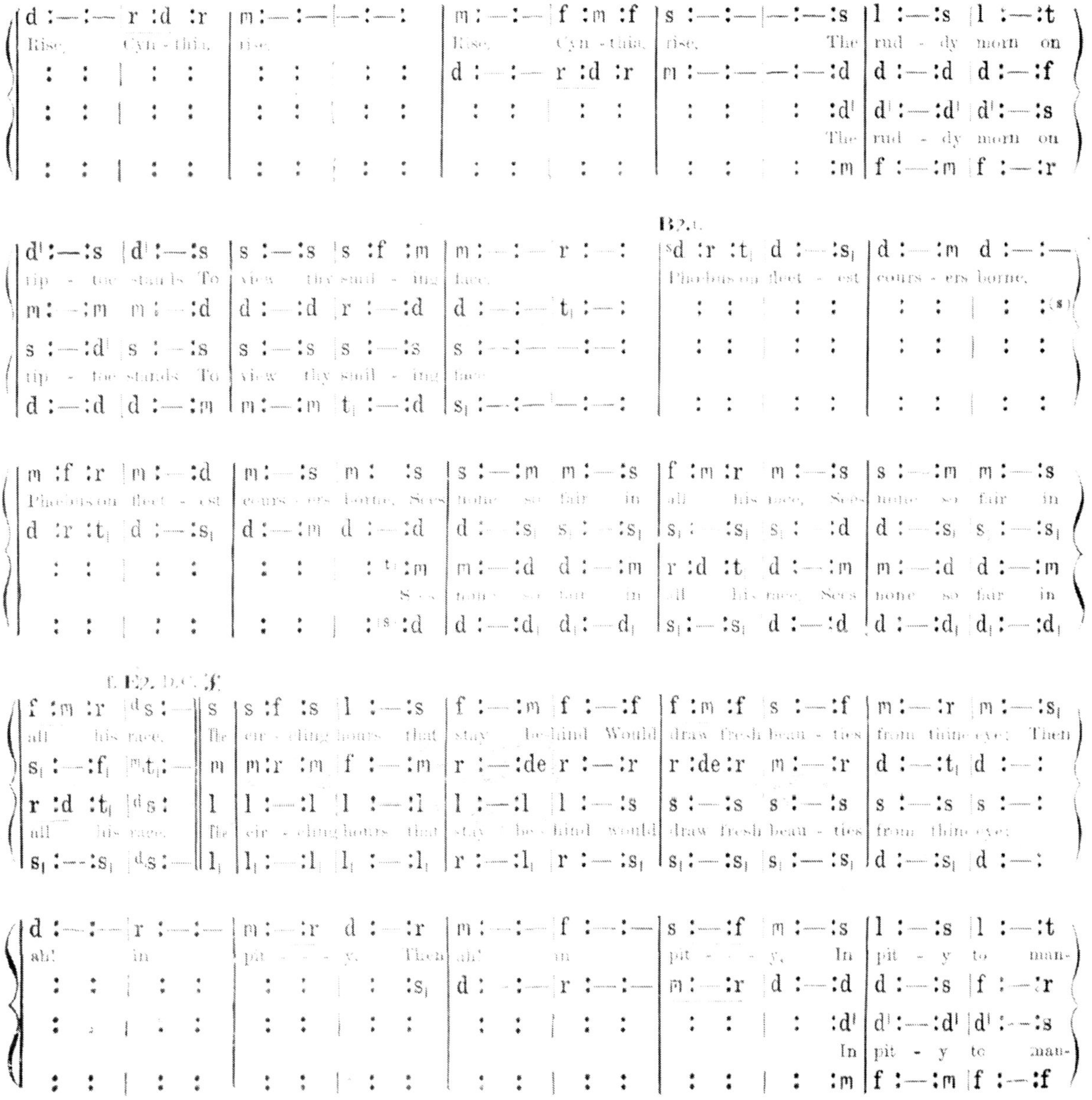
Rise, Cyn - thia, rise, Rise, Cyn - thia, rise, The rud - dy morn on
The rud - dy morn on
tip - toe stands To view thy smil - ing face. Phœbus on fleet - est cours - ers borne,
tip - toe stands To view thy smil - ing face.
B♭.t.
Phœbus on fleet - est cours - ers borne, Sees none so fair in all his race, Sees none so fair in
Sees none so fair in all his race, Sees none so fair in
f. E♭. D.C. ff.
all his race, He cir - cling hours that stay be - hind Would draw fresh beau - ties from thine eye; Then
all his race, He cir - cling hours that stay be - hind would draw fresh beau - ties from thine eye;
ah! in pit - y, Then ah! in pit - y, In pit - y to man-
In pit - y to man-

d':—:—|—:—:d' | d'.—:s |s :—:m | r :m :f |m :—:d' | d':—:s |s :—:m | f :m :r |d :—

kind, No long - er wrapped in vis - ions lie, No long - er wrapped in vis - ions lie,

d :—:—|—:—:d | d :—:m |m :—:d | t₁:d :r |d :—:d | d :—:m |m :—:d | r :d :t₁ |d :—

s :—:—|—:—:s | s :—:d'|d' :—:s | s :—:s |s :—:s | s :—:d'|d' :—:s | s :—:f |m :—

kind, No long - er wrapped in vis - ions lie, No long - er wrapped in vis - ions lie.

m :—:—|—:—:m | m :—:d |d :—:d | s :—:s₁|d :—:m | m :—:d |d :—:d | s :—:s₁ |d :—

WITH THE ROSY LIGHT.

230. Key C. M. 120.

T. F. Seward.

:m .f |s :d' |r' :m' | f' :l |— :l l | l .s :s .l |t :d'.r' | m'.d':d'.r'|m' :m .f

:d .r |m :m |f :s | l :f |— :f .f | f .f :f .f |f :m .f | s .m:m.f |s :d .r

2. With the ros - y light of morn-ing, Where the merry birds awake, And the laughing waters flow, We will
3. By the wood-land streams we'll wan - der, Till the merry bird has gone To its quiet leaf-y nest, And the

:d' .d'|d' :d' |d' :d' | d' :d' |— :d'.d | t .t :t .d'|r' :d' .d'| d' .d':d'.d'|d' :d' .d'

:d .d |d :d |d :d | d :d |— :f .f | s .s :s .s |s :d .d | d .d :d .d |d :d .d

FINE.   G.t.

s :d' |r' :m' | f' :l |— :l l | l .s :s .l |t :d'.r' |d' :— | :t m.m

m :m |f :s | l :f |— :f .f | f .f :f .f |f :m .f |m :— | :s d.d

haste with joy and glad - ness, Singing gayly as we go, as we go. We will
gold - en sun - beams dy - ing, Gently linger in the west, in the west. Then the

d' :d' |d' :d' | d' :d' |— :d'.d | t .t :t .d'|r' :s .s |s :— | :r's .s

d :d |d :d | f :f |— :f .f | s .s :s .s |s :s .s |d :— | :s d.d

f .r :r .m |f :s .f | m :s₁.d |m :f .m | r .t₁:t₁ .d |r :m .r |d :d d.d |d :m .m

r .t₁:t₁ .d |r :m .r | d :s₁.s₁ |s₁ :s₁.s₁ | s₁.s₁:s₁.s₁|s₁ :s₁ .s₁| s₁ :m₁.f₁|s₁ :d .d

carol to the breeze. Where the old for - est trees Wave their branches in the ray Of the bright king of day, And the
fairies tripping light, To the fields say good-night, With a footstep glad and free We will bound o'er the lea In our

s .s :s .s |s :s .s | s :m .m |s :s .s | f .r :r .m|f :s .f |m :d .r |m :s :s

s₁.s₁:s₁.s₁|s₁ :s₁.s₁| d :d .d |d :d .d | s₁.s₁:s₁.s₁|s₁ :s₁ .s₁|d₁ :d₁.d₁|d₁ :d :d

f.C.   D.C.

f .r :r .m |f :s .f | m :s₁.d |m :f .m | r .t₁:t₁ .d |r :m .r |d s :—

r .t₁:t₁ .d |r :m .r | d :s₁.s₁ |s₁ :s₁.s₁ | s₁.s₁:s₁.s₁|s₁ :s₁.s₁|s r :—

music from the dell, Where the young lil - ies dwell, Shall be echoed far a - way, far a - way.
cheerful homes so dear, We will sing sweet and clear, Till the welkin shall resound with our glee.

s .s :s .s |s :s .s | s :m .m |s :s .s | f .r :r .m|f :s .f |m t :—

s₁.s₁:s₁.s₁|s₁ :s₁.s₁| d :d .d |d :d .d | s₁.s₁:s₁:s₁|s₁ :s₁ .s₁|d s₁ :—

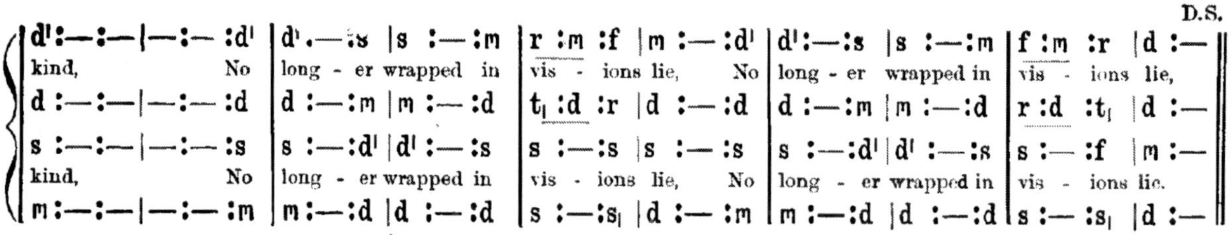

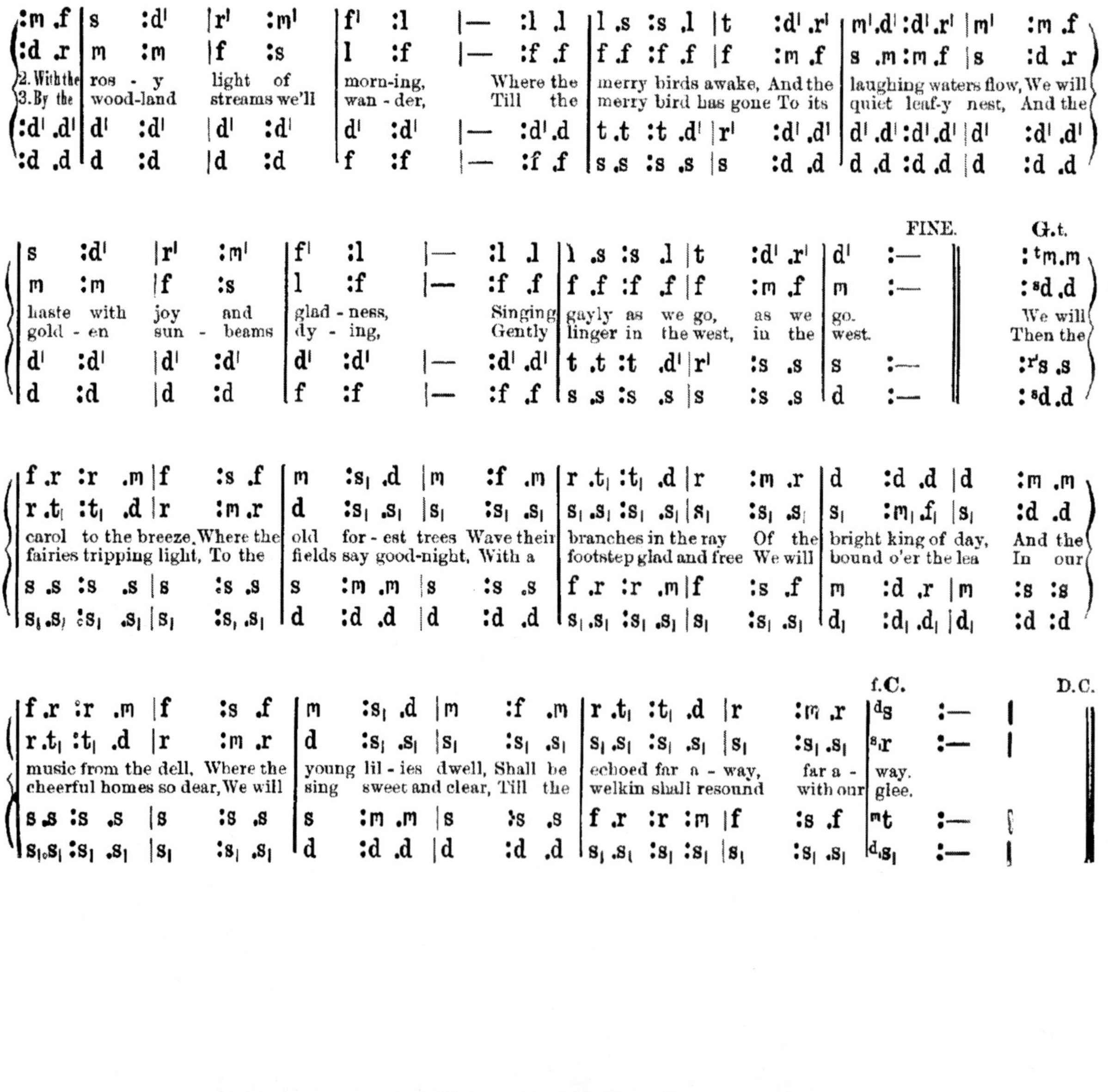

REST, WEARY PILGRIM.

2231. KEY B♭. S. S. C., or T. T. B., or S. C. B. From DONIZETTI

May be sung in key G, by S. C. T., Tenor singing the lowest part an octave higher than written.

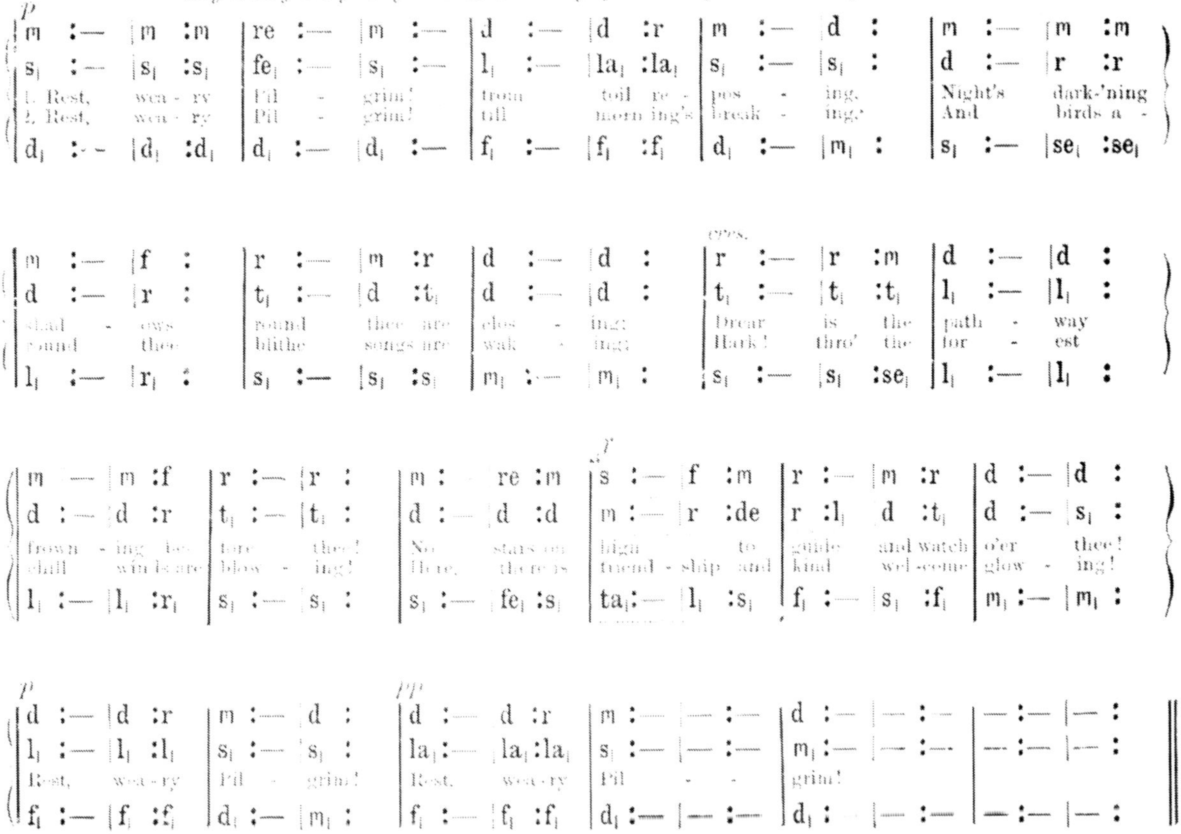

Pitching Tunes. In the third step the pupil was taught to pitch the key tone of a tune by singing down the Standard Scale, stepwise, to the tone required. A shorter way may now be taught. In pitching key G the pupil need not run down to G stepwise, but will fall upon it at once from C'. In pitching key F he will take C' as s, and fall to the key-tone, thus, C'—s m d. Key E may be pitched by falling to m, thus, C' d' s m md. Key A is pitched by falling to l, thus, C'—d' l—ld. Key D, thus, C'—d r'—r d'. The key may be pitched a little-step higher (sharper), or a little-step lower (flatter), than any tone of the Standard Scale. The tones thus required are named "C sharp," "D sharp," "E flat," "D flat," etc., and the sign ♯ is used for "sharp," and ♭ for "flat." A sharp bears no relation to the tone below it, and after which, for convenience, it is named, but its relation is to the tone above it. It is to the tone above it the same that **t** is to **d**, or *fe* to **s**. In order to strike it correctly, sing the tone above, and then smoothly descend a little-step to it. A flat bears no relation to the tone above it, and after which it is named. Its relation is to the tone below it, to which it is the same as **f** to **m**, or *ta* to **l**. To pitch it correctly, in the cases of G♭, A♭ and D♭, we should sing the tone below, and then rise to it a little-step. In the key B♭ take C' as **s**, and sing **s f—fd**. In Key E♭ take C' as **l**, thus, C' **l t d'**.

See *Manual for Teachers School Series*, page 30, for plan for pitching keys.

THE MILLER.

232. KEY G. ZOLLNER.

.s₁	d .,s₁ :m₁ .f₁	s₁ .,l₁ :s₁ .d	m .,r :d .r	m .,f :m .d
.	:	: .d	d .,s₁ :m₁ .f₁	s₁ .,l₁ :s₁ .d
1. To	wan - der is the	mil - ler's joy, To	wan - der is the	mil - ler's joy, To
2. We've	learnt it from the	flow - ing stream, We've	learnt it from the	flow - ing stream, The
3. We	see this al - so	in the wheels, We	see this al - so	in the wheels, The
4. Oh!	wan - d'ring ev - er	is my joy, Oh!	wan - d'ring ev - er	is my joy, Oh!
.	:	:	:	: .m
.	:	:	:	: .d

m :r	d : .s₁	r .r :m ,r .de,r	t₁ .r :s₁ .s₁
d :t₁	d : .s₁	t₁ .t₁ :t₁ .t₁	s₁ .s₁ :s₁ .s₁
wan - - - - -	der. The	mil - lers all do	love to roam, To
flow - - ing	stream. It	neith - er rests by	day nor night Its
bus - - y	wheels, Which	do not turn a -	lone by day. But
wan - der - -	ing. Fare -	well my par - ents,	friends and home. Let
s :f	m : .s	f .s :f .s	f .s :f .s
s₁ :s₁	d₁ : .s₁	s₁ .s₁ :s₁ .s₁	s₁ .s₁ :s₁ .s₁

r .r :m ,r .de,r	t₁ .r :s₁ .s₁	l₁ .t₁ :d .r	m .,r :d .m
t₁ .t₁ :t₁ .t₁	s₁ .s₁ :s₁ .s₁	l₁ .t₁ :d .r	m .,r :d .d
leave their vil - lage,	house and home, To	leave their vil - lage,	house and home, To
course it fol - lows	with de - light, Its	course it fol - lows	with de - light, The
keep it up all	night so gay, But	keep it up all	night so gay, The
me un - to the	wide world roam, Let	me un - to the	wide world roam, And
f .s :f .s	f .s :f .s₁	l₁ .t₁ :d .r	m .,r :d .d
s₁ .s₁ :s₁ .s₁	s₁ .s₁ :s₁ .s₁	l₁ .t₁ :d .r	m .,r :d .d

s :t₁	s :t₁	s :t₁	d :–
t₁ :s₁	t₁ :s₁	t₁ :s₁	s₁ :–
wan - - der,	wan - - der,	wan - - - - - -	der.
flow - - ing,	flow - - ing,	flow - - - ing	stream.
bus - - y,	bus - - y,	bus - - y	wheels.
wan - - der,	wan - - der,	wan - - - - - -	der.
r :s	r :s	r :f	m :–
s₁ :s₁	s₁ :s₁	s₁ :s₁	d₁ :–

233. KEY C. Round in four parts. T. F. S.

s .fe :s	s .fe :s	m .re :m	m .re :m
Soh, fe, soh,	soh, fe, soh,	me, re, me,	me, re, me.

d' .l :s .m	d' .l :s .m	d .d ,d :m .s	d' :
Now be - ware, and	sing with care, And	keep ev - ery voice in	tune.

MURMURING BROOKLET.

MARY C. SEWARD. R. SCHUMANN.

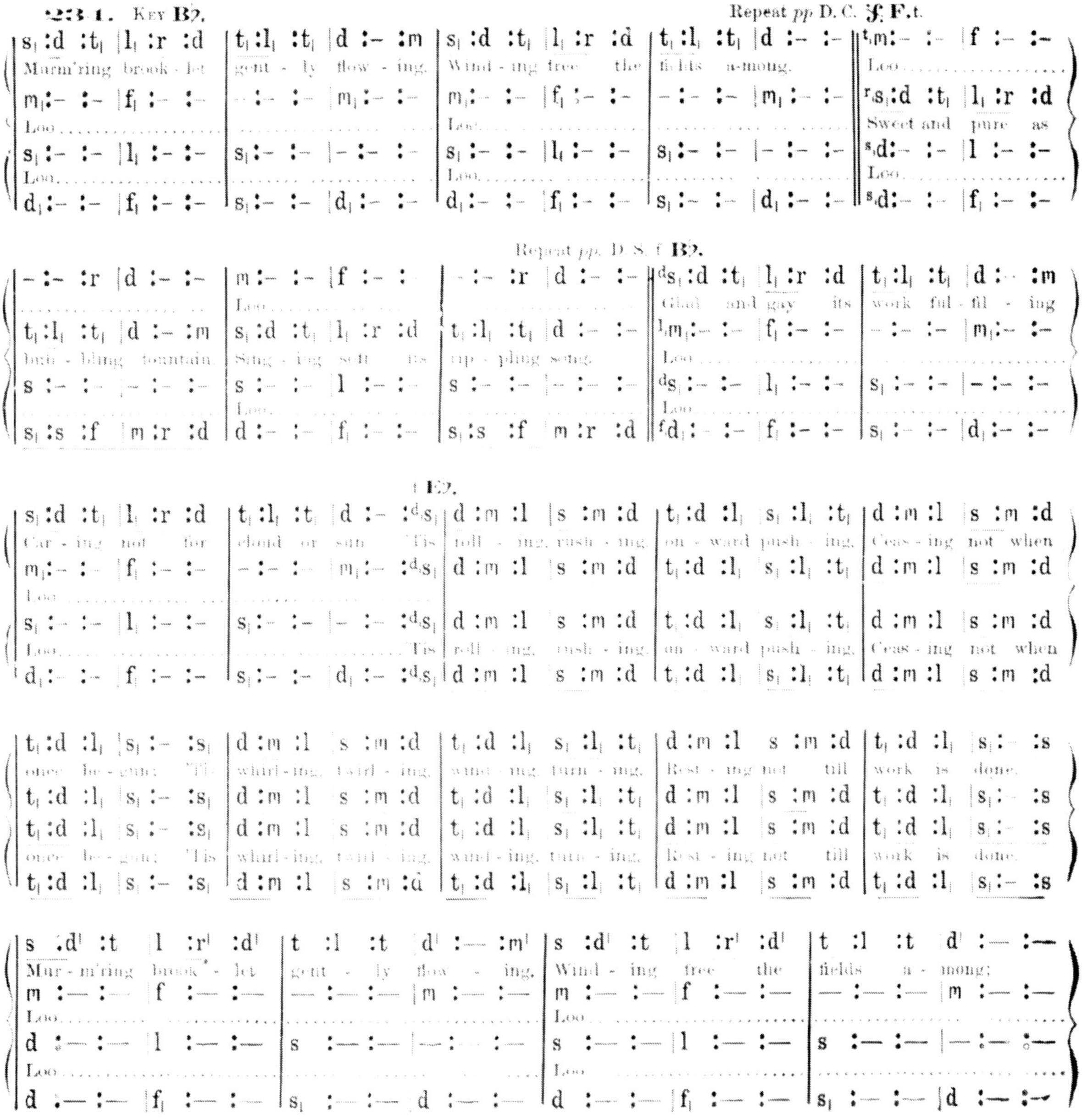
231. KEY B♭.
Repeat pp D. C. ff F.t.
Murm'ring brook-let gent-ly flow-ing, Wind-ing free the fields a-mong.
Loo
Sweet and pure as bub-bling fountain Sing-ing soft its rip-pling song.
Repeat pp. D. S. f B♭.
Glad and gay its work ful-fil-ing
t E♭.
Car-ing not for cloud or sun. 'Tis roll-ing, rush-ing on-ward push-ing, Ceas-ing not when once be-gun; 'Tis whirl-ing, twirl-ing, wind-ing, turn-ing, Rest-ing not till work is done.
Mur-m'ring brook-let gent-ly flow-ing, Wind-ing free the fields a-mong;

t m :— :— | f :— :— | —:— :r | d :—:— | m :— :— | f :— :— | —. :r | d :—:s₁
Loo..........				Loo.....			'Tis

| r s₁ :d :t₁ \| l₁ :r :d \| t₁ :l₁ :t₁ \| d :— :m \| s₁ :d :t₁ \| l₁ :r :d \| t₁ :l₁ :t₁ \| d :— :m₁ |
| Sweet and pure as | bub - bling fount - ain, | Sing - ing soft its | rip - pling song. 'Tis |

| s d :— :— \| — :— :— \| s₁ :— :— \| d :— :— \| d :— :— \| — :— :— \| s₁ :— '— \| d :— :d |
| Loo.......... | | | | Loo..... | | | 'Tis |

| s₁ d₁ :— :— \| f₁ :— :— \| s₁ :— :f₁ \| m₁ :r₁ :d₁ \| d₁ :— :— \| f₁ :— :— \| s₁ :— :f₁ \| m₁ :r₁ :d₁ |

| r :m :f \| m :r :d \| t₁ :l₁ :t₁ \| d :— :s₁ \| r :m :f \| m :r :d \| d :l₁ :t₁ \| d :— :d |
| whirl - ing, twirl - ing, | wind - ing, turn - ing, | Rest - ing not till | work is done: O |

| s₁ :— :s₁ \| s₁ :— :m₁ \| f₁ :— :f₁ \| m₁ :— :m₁ \| s₁ :— :s₁ \| s₁ :— :m₁ \| f₁ :— :f₁ \| m₁ :— : |

| t₁ :d :r \| d :— :d \| r :— :r \| d :— :d \| t₁ :d :r \| d :— :d \| r :— :r \| d :— : |
| whirl - ing. twirl - ing, | wind - ing, turn - ing | Rest - ing not till | work is done: |

| s₁ :— :s₁ \| d₁ :— :d₁ \| s₁ :— :s₁ \| ȧ₁ :— :d₁ \| s₁ :— :s₁ \| d₁ :— :d₁ \| s₁ :— :s₁ \| d₁ :— : |

| t₁ :d :r \| d :r :re \| m :f :fe \| s :— :t₁ \| d :— :— \| d :— :— \| d :— :— \| — :— :— |
| flow for - ev - - er, | mur - m'ring brook - let, | with thy | song. |

| : : \| : : \| : : \| : : \| m₁ :— :— \| m₁ :— :— \| m₁ :— :— \| — :— :— |
| | | | | with thy | song. |

| : : \| : : \| : : \| : : \| d :— :— \| s₁ :— :— \| s₁ :— :— \| — :— :— |
| | | | | with thy | song. |

| : : \| : : \| : : \| : : \| d₁ :— :— \| d₁ :— :— \| d₁ :— :— \| — :— :— |

OH, WIPE AWAY THAT TEAR.

235. Key C. M. 108.

:s | s :— :s | l :t :d¹ | s :—:— | m :— :s | s :— :f | f :— :m | f :— :— | — :— :f | m :r :s | l :t :d¹
:m | m :— :m | re :— :re | m :— :— | d :— :m | m :— :r | r :— :de | r :— :— | — :— :r | m :— :m | re :— :re
1.Oh,	wipe a - way that	tear, love,	The	pearl - y drop	I see;			Let	hope thy bo - som
2.Yes,	when a - way from	thee, love.	Sweet	hope shall be	my star;			We	do not part for
3.At	close of part - ing	day, love,	When	yon bright star	is set;			Still	meet me while a -
4.I'll	watch the set - ting	star, love,	And	think I look	on thee;			And	thus, tho' sun - d'red

| :s \| s :—:s \| fe :— :fe \| s :—:— \| s :— :s \| s :— :s \| s :— :— \| s :— :— :s \| s :— :s \| fe :— :fe |
| :d \| d :—:d \| d :— :d \| d :—:— \| d :— :d \| s₁ :— :s₁ \| s₁ :— :s₁ \| s₁ :— :— :s₁ \| d :— :d \| d :— :d |

s :— :— | d¹ :— :d¹ | m¹ :— :m¹ | f¹ :m¹ :re¹ | m¹ :— :— | d¹ :— :d¹ | r¹ :— :do¹ | r¹ :— :m¹ | d¹ :— :— :—
m :— :— | m :— :m | s :— :s | l :s :fe | s :— :— | m :— :m | f :— :m | f :— :s | m :— :— :—
cheer, love,	Let	hope thy bo - som	cheer, love,	As	yon bright star	we see.
aye, love,	We	do not part for	aye, love,	I'll	wel - come thee	a - far.
way, love,	Still	meet me while a -	way, love,	'Mid	scenes we'll ne'er	for - get.
far, love,	And	thus, tho' sun - d'red	far, love,	How	near our hearts	may be.

| s :— :— \| s :— :s \| d¹ :— :d¹ \| d¹ :— :d¹ \| d¹ :— :— \| s :— :s \| s :— :s \| s :— :s \| s :— :— :— |
| d :— :— \| d :— :d \| d¹ :— :d¹ \| d¹ :— :d¹ \| d¹ :— :— \| d :— :s \| s :— :s \| s :— :s \| d :— :— :— |

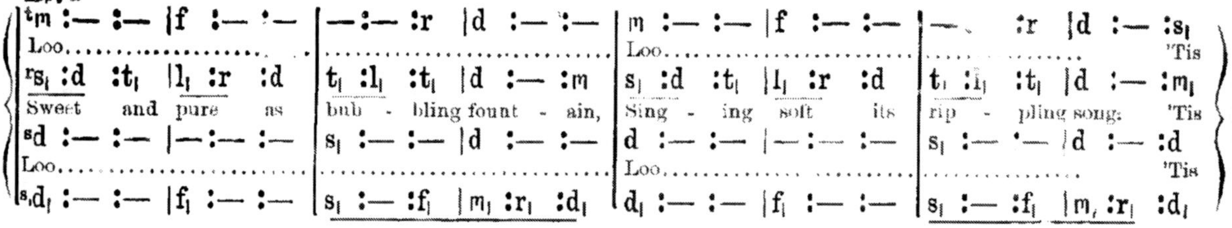

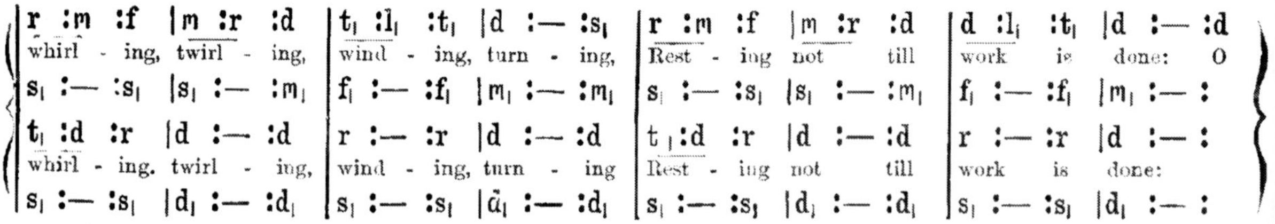

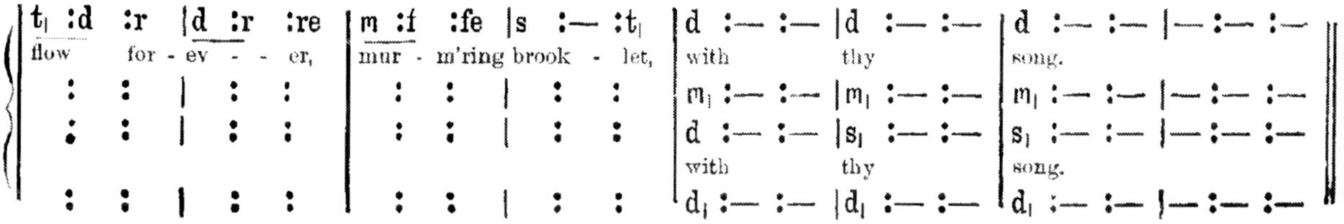

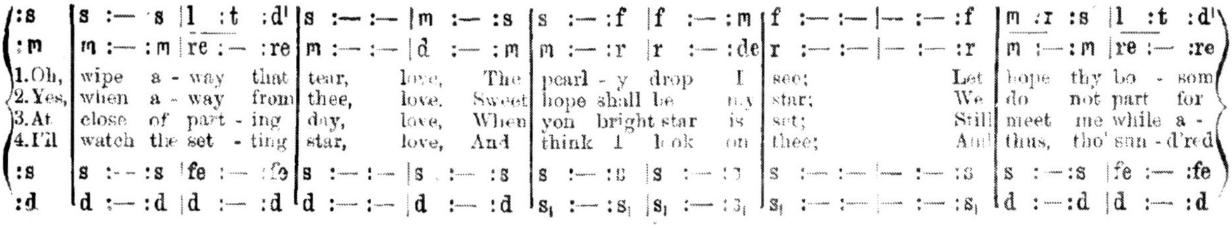

OUT IN THE SHADY BOWERS.

T. F. S. — T. F. Seward.

236. Key A♭.

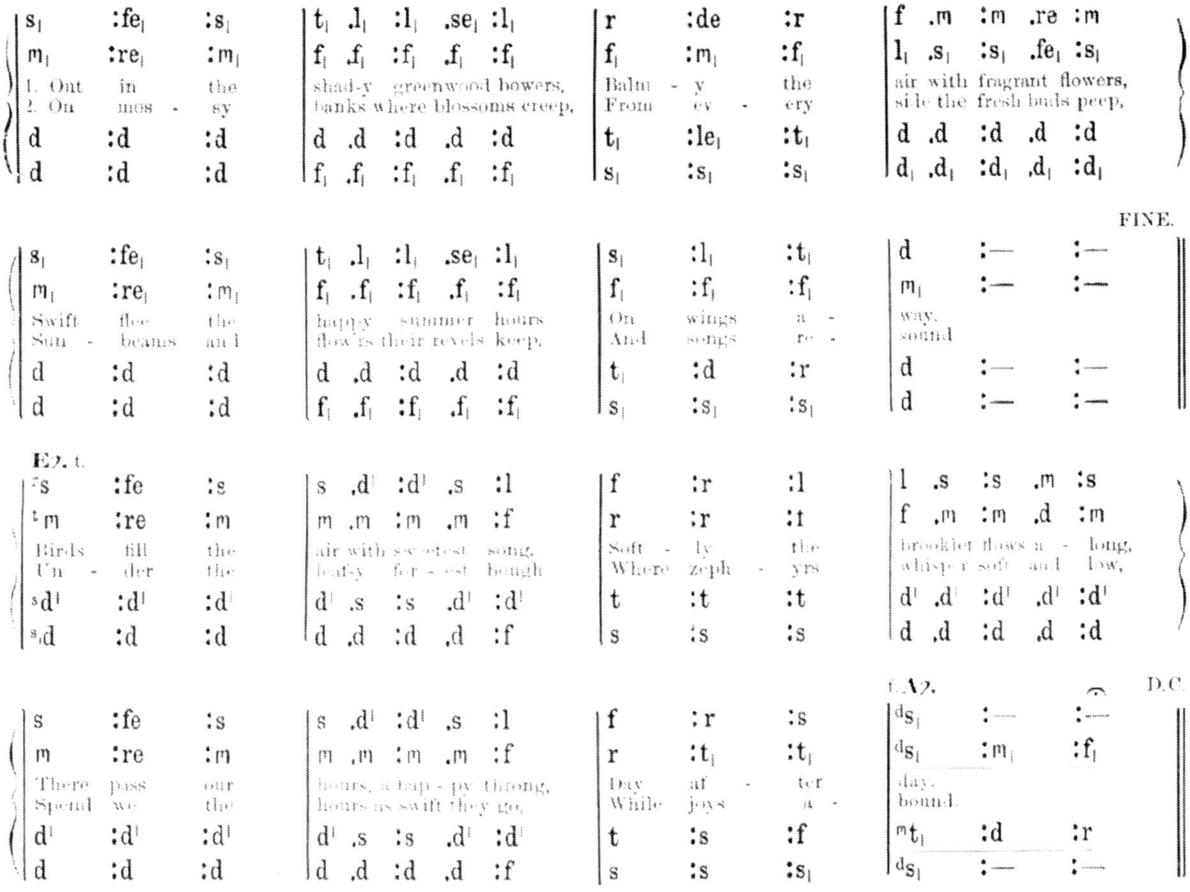
FINE.
1. Out in the shady greenwood bowers, Balmy the air with fragrant flowers,
2. On mossy banks where blossoms creep, From every side the fresh buds peep,
Swift flee the happy summer hours On wings away.
Sunbeams and flowers their revels keep, And songs resound.
E♭. t.
Birds fill the air with sweetest song, Softly the brooklet flows along,
Under the leafy forest bough Where zephyrs whisper soft and low,
f. A♭.
D.C.
There pass our hours, a happy throng, Day after day.
Spend we the hours as swift they go, While joys abound.

SINGING CHEERILY.

237. Key B♭. — Words and Music by W. F. Sherwin.

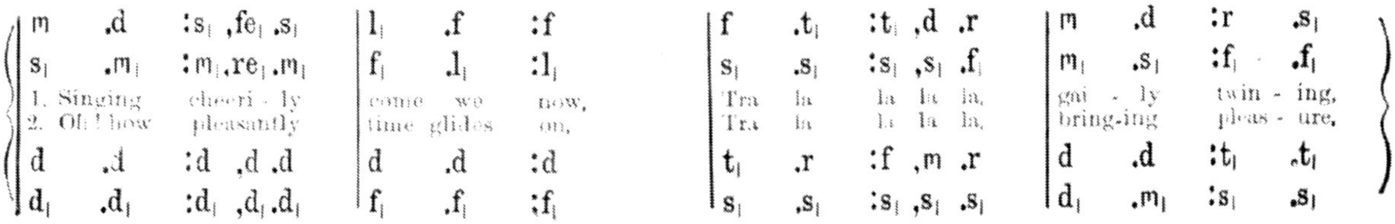
1. Singing cheerily come we now, Tra la la la la, gaily twining,
2. Oh! how pleasantly time glides on, Tra la la la la, bringing pleasure,

FINE.
Wreaths of mel - o-dy for each brow, Tra la la la la la la.
When in harmony sings each one, Tra la la la la la la.
F.t.
Eyes that sparkle with a pure de - light, So bright-ly gleam-ing. On us beam-ing,
All life's trials are a - while for - got, Its troubled dream ing, I - - dle scheming,
f. B♭. D. C.
Bring with beauty in their glance to night, A cheery welcome to our song. So—
Care and wea-ri-ness can harm us not, If we can sing a mer - ry glee. Then—

HOW SWEET TO GO STRAYING.

238. Key B♭. T. F. Seward.

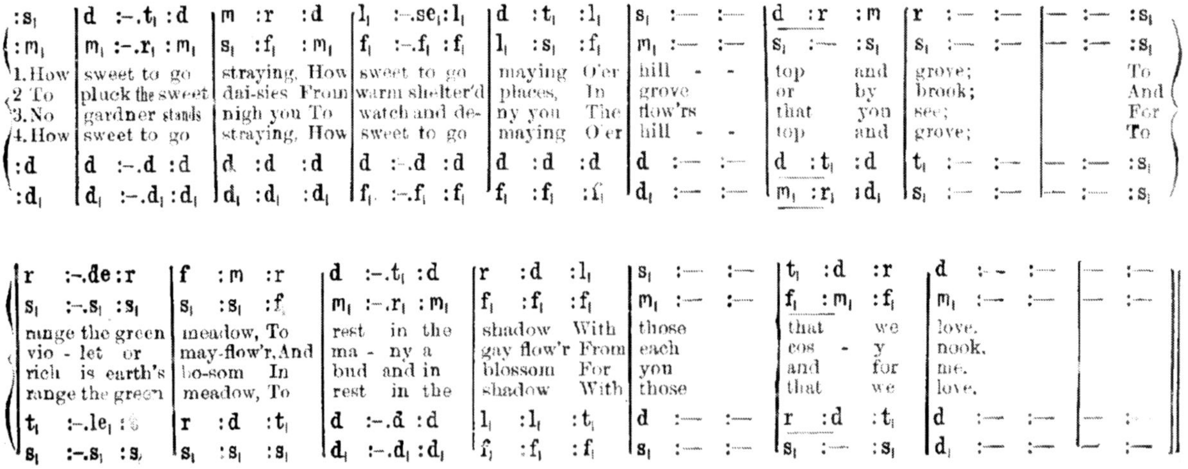
1. How sweet to go straying, How sweet to go maying O'er hill - - top and grove; To range the green meadow, To rest in the shadow With those that we love.
2 To pluck the sweet dai-sies From warm shelter'd places, In grove or by brook; And vio - let or may-flow'r, And ma - ny a gay flow'r From each cos - y nook.
3. No gardner stands nigh you To watch and de-ny you The flow'rs that you see; For rich is earth's bo-som In bud and in blossom For you and for me.
4. How sweet to go straying, How sweet to go maying O'er hill - - top and grove; To range the green meadow, To rest in the shadow With those that we love.

SWEET EVENING HOUR.

T. F. SEWARD.

Arr. from KULLAK, by THEO. F. SEWARD.

239. KEY B♭.

							:.s₁	s₁	:l₁ .d	s₁	:— .m
:	:	:	:	:	:	:		O	sweet ev'n-ing	hour,	O
:	:	:	:	:	:	:.m₁	m₁	:f₁ .r₁	m₁	:— .s₁	
s₁	:—	s₁	:—	s₁	:—	s₁	:—	s₁	:—	s₁	:—
	Sweet		ev'n - - -		ing		hour,		Sweet		ev'n - - -
d₁	:—	d₁	:—	d₁	:—	d₁	:—	d₁	:—	d₁	:—

r .t₁	:d .l₁	t₁	:s₁ .s₁	s₁	:l₁ .d	s₁	:— .m	r .t₁	:s₁ .l₁
calm and quiet	ev'n - - ing. How	gen - - tle thy	power;	1. From care each heart re -
f₁ .s₁	:m₁ .f₁	r₁	:f₁ .f₁	m₁	:f₁ .r₁	m₁	:— .s₁	s₁ .s₁	:s₁ .s₁
s₁	:—	s₁	:—	s₁	:—	s₁	:— .d	r .r	:m .m
ing		hour.		Sweet		hour;		2. From care each heart re -
d₁	:—	d₁	:—	d₁	:—	d₁	:— .d	t₁ .t₁	:d .d

t₁	:s₁ .s₁	f	:m .d	t₁	:d	s₁ .s₁	:s₁ .s₁	l₁	:s₁ .s₁
s₁	:s₁ .s₁	s₁	:s₁ .s₁	s₁	:s₁	f₁ .f₁	:f₁ .f₁	f₁	:f₁ .s₁
hev - - ing. The	birds to their	nests with	cheerful songs to -	ti - - ing. All
hev - - ing. The	stars, one by	one, in	heav'ns blue vault ap -	pear - - ing, The
r	:t₁ .t₁	t₁	:d .m	f	:m .d	t₁ .t₁	:t₁ .t₁	d	:t₁ .t₁
s₁	:s₁ .s₁	s₁	:s₁ .s₁	s₁	:s₁	s₁ .s₁	:s₁ .s₁	s₁	:s₁ .s₁

f	:m .d	t₁	:d	r .r	:r .r	r	:m .r	r	:m .r
s₁	:s₁ .s₁	s₁	:s₁	s₁ .s₁	:fe₁ .fe₁	s₁	:s₁	fe₁	:fe₁
na - - ture's glad	voic - es	come with sound in -	spir - - ing,	Come till
light zeph-yrs	play where	ros - es are in -	twin - - ing,	Fra - grance
t₁	:d .m	f	:m	r .r	:d :d	t₁	:d .t₁	d	:d
s₁	:s₁ .s₁	s₁	:d	t₁ .t₁	:l₁ :l₁	s₁	:s₁	l₁	:l₁

r	:d	t₁	:l₁	s₁	:— .s₁	s₁	:l₁ .d	s₁	:— .m
all	is	hushed	to	rest.	O	sweet	ev'n - ing	hour,	O
s₁	:s₁	f₁	:f₁	f₁	:— .f₁	m₁	:f₁ .r₁	m₁	:— .s
t₁	:m	r	:d	t₁	:— .	s₁	:—	s₁	:—
fling - - ing		ev - - ery - -		where.		Sweet		ev'n - - -
s₁	:s₁	s₁	:s₁	s₁	:— .	d₁	:—	d₁	:—

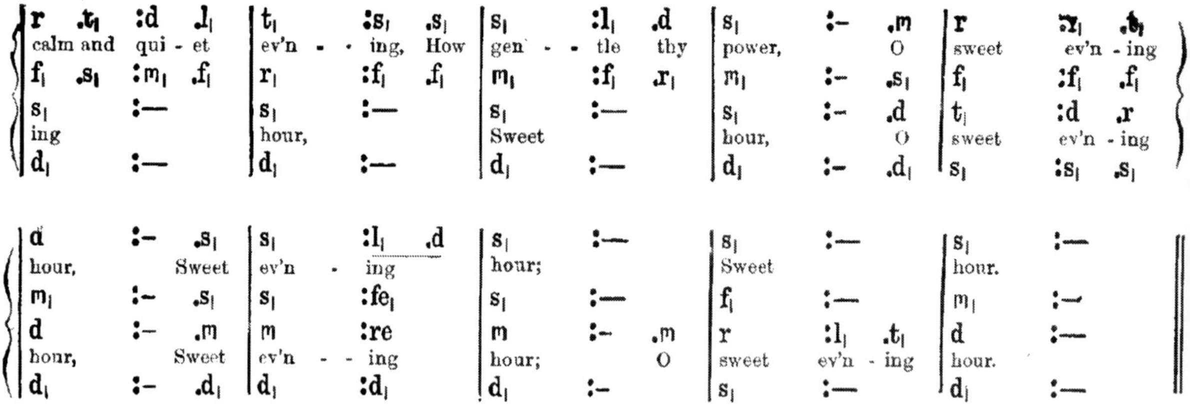
calm and qui - et ev'n - - ing, How gen - - tle thy power, O sweet ev'n - ing
ing hour, Sweet hour, O sweet ev'n - ing
hour, Sweet ev'n - ing hour; Sweet hour.
hour, Sweet ev'n - - ing hour; O sweet ev'n - ing hour.

IN THE VINEYARD.

Eliza M. Sherman.

B. C. Unseld, by per.

240. Key F.

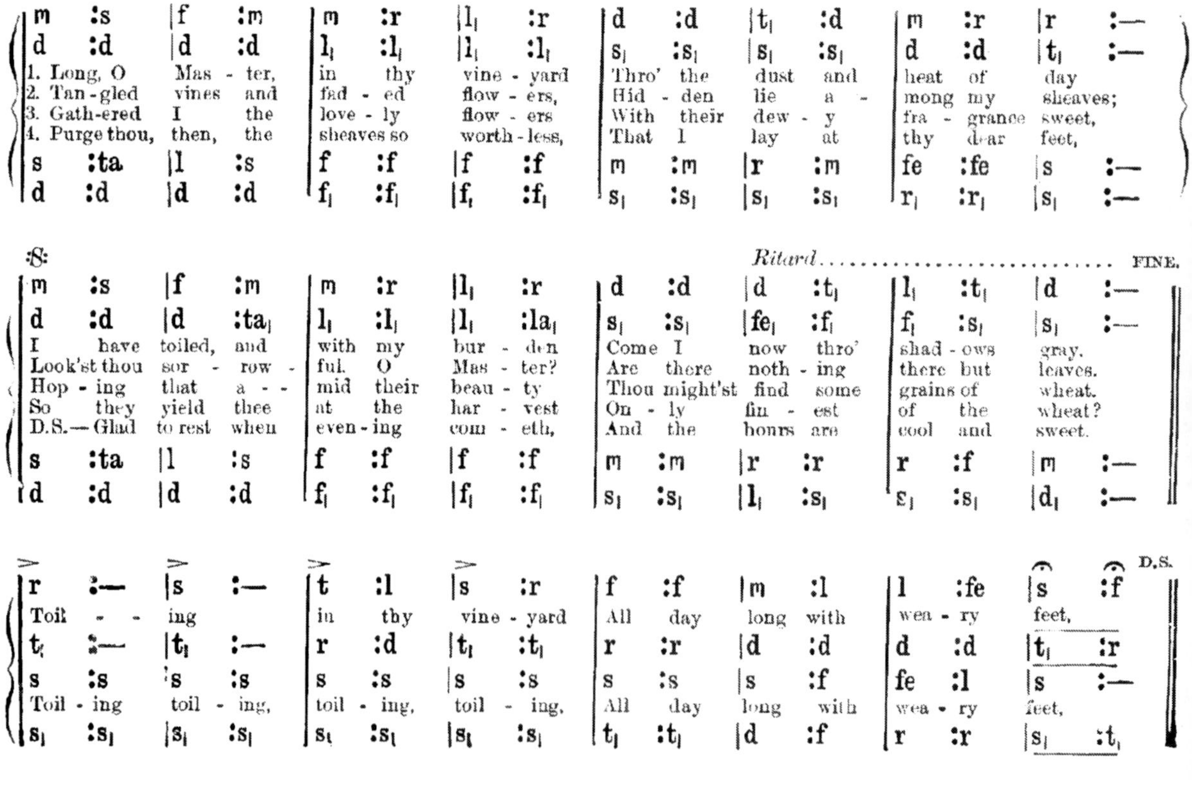
1. Long, O Mas - ter, in thy vine - yard Thro' the dust and heat of day
2. Tan-gled vines and fad - ed flow - ers, Hid - den lie a - mong my sheaves;
3. Gath-ered I the love - ly flow - ers With their dew - y fra - grance sweet,
4. Purge thou, then, the sheaves so worth - less, That I lay at thy dear feet,
𝄋
Ritard.
FINE.
I have toiled, and with my bur - den Come I now thro' shad - ows gray.
Look'st thou sor - row - ful, O Mas - ter? Are there noth - ing there but leaves.
Hop - ing that a - - mid their beau - ty Thou might'st find some grains of wheat.
So they yield thee at the har - vest On - ly fin - est of the wheat?
D.S.—Glad to rest when even - ing com - eth, And the hours are cool and sweet.
D.S.
Toil - - ing in thy vine - yard All day long with wea - ry feet,
Toil - ing toil - ing, toil - ing, toil - ing, All day long with wea - ry feet,

Beating Time. It was recommended in the first step (see note, page 11) not to allow pupils to beat time until they have gained a sense of time. If the teacher wishes, he may now teach beating time according to the following diagrams. The beating should be done by one hand (palm downwards), chiefly by the motion of the wrist, and with but little motion of the arm. The hand should pass swiftly and decidedly from one *point* of the beating to the next, and it should be held steadily at each point as long as the pulse lasts. The direction of the motion is from the thinner to thicker end of each line. The thicker end shows the "point of rest" for each pulse.

NOTE.—It is better to beat the second pulse of three pulse measure to the right, than (as some do) towards the left, because it thus corresponds with the medium beat of the four-pulse measure, and the second pulse of three pulse measure is *like* a medium pulse. It is commonly treated (both rhythmically and harmonically) as a continuation of the *first* pulse. Similar reasons show a propriety in the mode of beating a six-pulse measure; but when this measure moves *very* quickly, it is beaten like a two pulse measure, giving a beat on each accented pulse.

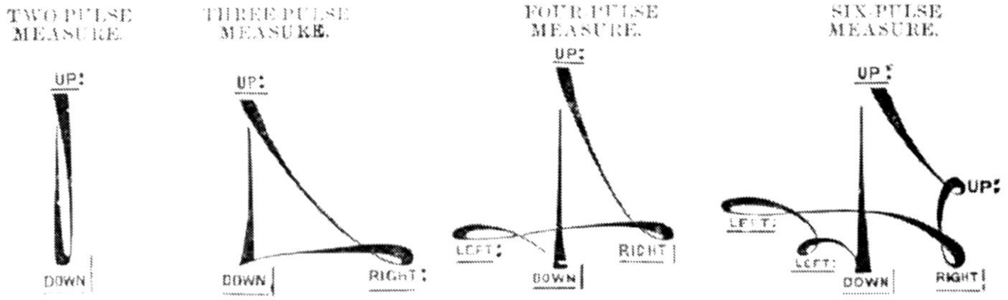

The Silent Quarter-pulse is indicated, like the other silences, by a vacant space among the pulse divisions. It is named *sa* on the accented, and *se* on the unaccented part of a pulse.

211. KEYS C, G.

TAA TAI TAA fe fe	TAA TAI TAA se fe	TAA se fe TAA se fe	TAA TAI TAA
l .l :l .l ,l	l .l :l . ,l	l . ,l :l . ,l	l .l :l
s .s :s .m ,t	s .s :s . ,s	l . ,s :s . ,s	l .t :d^1
m .r :d .r ,m	f .m :r . ,r	m . ,d :r . ,t_1	d .r :d

HURRAH!

212. KEY A. D.C.

.d	d .s_1 :s_1 .d	d .l_1 :l_1 . ,f	m . ,d :r . ,t_1	d :– .
.m_1	m_1 .m_1 :m_1 .m_1	l_1 .f_1 :f_1 . ,l_1	s_1 . ,m_1 :f_1 . ,r_1	m_1 :– .
1. We	shout with joy this	hap - py day, Hur-	rah! hur-rah! hur-	rah!
With	song we drive dull	care a - way, Hur-	rah! hur-rah! hur-	rah!
2. Here	Free - dom's star is	ris - ing high, Hur-	rah! hur-rah! hur-	rah!
It	shines in splen - dor	in the sky, Hur-	rah! hur-rah! hur-	rah!
3. Here	sci - ence fair, and	learn - ing bright, Hur-	rah! hur-rah! hur-	rah!
Have	shed a pure and	bril - liant light, Hur-	rah! hur-rah! hur-	rah!
.d	d .d :d .d	d .d :d . ,d	d . ,d :t_1 . ,r	d :– .
.d_1	d_1 .d_1 :d_1 .d_1	f_1 .f_1 :f_1 . ,f_1	s_1 . ,s_1 :s_1 . ,s_1	d_1 :– .

.d	t_1 .,d :r .t_1	d .,r :m .d	t_1 .,d :r .t_1	d .,r :m .
.m_1	r_1 .,m_1 :f_1 .r_1	m_1 .,f_1 :s_1 .m_1	r_1 .,m_1 :f_1 .r_1	m_1 .,f_1 :s_1 ,
We	love the land that	gave us birth. The	dear - est land of	all the earth;
And	Free - dom's voice will	ev - ev - more In	tri - umph-ring from	shore to shore;
And	know - edge truth and	lib - er - ty, Our	watch - words ev - er -	more shall be.
.d	r .,d :t_1 .r	d .,d :d .d	r .,d :t_1 .r	d .,d :d ,
.d_1	s_1 .,s_1 :s_1 .s_1	d_1 .,d_1 :d_1 .d_1	s_1 .,s_1 :s_1 .s_1	d_1 .,d_1 :d_1 ,

CHORUS.

.d	d .s, :s, .d	d .l, :l, . ,f	m . ,d :r . ,t,	d :– .
.m,	m, .m, :m, .m,	l, .f, :f, . ,l,	s, . ,m, :f, . ,r,	m, :– .
Then	let us shout for	joy, hur - rah! Hur-	rah! hur-rah! hur-	rah!
.d	d .d :d .d	d .d :d . ,d	d . ,d :t, . ,r	d :– .
.d,	d, .d, :d, .d,	f, .f, :f, . ,f,	s, . ,s, :s, . ,s,	d, :– .

Thirds of a pulse are indicated by commas turned to the right, thus, —: ‚ ‚ ‖ The first third of a pulse is named TAA, the second third TAI, the third third TEE; and the silences and continuations are named in the same manner as before.

243. KEYS **C, G.**

TAA TAI TEE TAA	TAA TAI TEE TAA	TAA TAA	TAA TAI TEE TAA
l ‚l ‚l :l	l ‚l ‚l :l	l :l	l ‚l ‚l :l
s ‚l ‚t :d'	d' ‚t ‚l :s	s :d'	t ‚d' ‚r' :d'
d ‚r ‚m :r	r ‚m ‚f :m	m :d	s, ‚l, ‚t, :d

244. KEYS **A, F.**

TAA TAI TEE TAA	TAA-AI TEE TAA	TAA-AI TEE TAA - AI TEE	TAA TAI TEE TAA
l ‚l ‚l :l	l ‚– ‚l :l	l ‚– ‚l :l ‚– ‚l	l ‚l ‚l :l
d ‚t, ‚l, :s,	s, ‚– ‚l, :s,	d ‚– ‚l, :s, ‚– ‚l,	s, ‚l, ‚t, :d
m ‚r ‚d :s	f ‚– ‚m :r	r ‚– ‚m :f ‚– ‚m	f ‚m ‚r :d

245. KEY **G, D.**

TAA TAI TAA	TAA TAI TEE TAA	TAA TAI TEE	
l .l :l	l ‚l ‚l :l	l ‚l ‚l :l ‚l ‚l	l .l :l
d .t, :d	t, ‚d ‚r :d	d ‚r ‚m :f ‚m ‚r	d .t, :d
s .f :m	f ‚s ‚f :m	s ‚l ‚s :f ‚s ‚f	m .r :d

246. KEY **C.** Round in three parts. T. F. S.

d' :d'	d' :t ‚d' ‚r'	d' :s	s :m	*m :m	m :r ‚m ‚f
Ring, ring,	ring, beautiful	chimes are	ring - ing,	Sing, sing,	sing, cheer-i-ly
m :m	m :d	s :s	s :s ‚s ‚s	s :d'	d' :s
birds are	sing - ing,	Per - fumes	sweet flowers a -	broad are	fling - ing.

247 KEY **C.** Round for two parts.

s ‚s ‚s :d' .d'	r' ‚m' ‚r' :d' .s	*m' .d' :s .m	f ‚s ‚f :m
Why should we sigh for	wealth or for pow'r, Since	life is fleet - ing	as an hour?

MERRILY SINGS THE LARK.

248. Key B♭.

```
|s₁ .,s₁ :s₁ .,s₁|d   :s₁ .,s₁|d   :r   |m   :m,m,m|r   :   |   |:r ,r ,r|
|m₁ .,m₁:m₁ .,m₁|m₁  :m₁ .,m₁|s₁  :s₁  |s₁  :s₁,s₁,s₁|s₁  :   |   |:s₁,s₁,s₁|
```
1. Merry sings the lark   at the break   of   day,   Tra la la la,   Tra la la
2. Rouse ye,rouse ye now   at the morn - ing   call,   Tra la la la,   Tra la la
3. Health and strength are found in the morn - ing   air,   Tra la la la,   Tra la la
```
|d .,d :d .,d|d   :d .,d|d   :t₁  |d   :d,d,d|t₁  :   |   |:t₁,t₁,t₁|
|d₁ .,d₁:d₁ .,d₁|d₁  :d₁ .,d₁|m₁ :s₁  |d   :   |   |:s₁,s₁,s₁|s₁  |
```
Tra la la la

```
|d   :   |   :   |s₁ .,s₁ :s₁ .,s₁|d   :s₁ |d   :r   |m   :m,m,m|
|m₁  :   |   :   |m₁ .,m₁:m₁ .,m₁|m₁  :m₁ |s₁  :s₁  |s₁  :s₁,s₁,s₁|
```
la;   Hear her as   she sings   her mer - ry   lay,   Tra la la
la;   Rouse ye - the dream - ers one   and   all,   Tra la la
la;   Beau - ty, youth and life   in   na - ture   fair, Tra la la
```
|d   :   |   :   |d .,d :d .,d|d   :d |d   :t₁  |d   :d,d,d|
|   :d₁,d₁,d₁|   :   |d₁ .,d₁:d₁ .,d₁|d₁  :d₁ |m₁  :s₁  |d   :   |
```
Tra la la la.

```
|r   :   |   :r,r,r|d   :   |   :   |r,r,r:r,.,r|f   :—   |
|s₁  :   |   :s₁,s₁,s₁|m₁  :   |   :   |s₁,s₁,s₁:s₁,.,s₁|s₁  :—   |
```
la,   Tra la la la.   Tra la la la   la la,
```
|t₁  :   |   :t₁,t₁,t₁|d   :   |   :   |t₁  :t₁  |t₁,t₁,t₁:t₁|
```
Tra   la   la la la la,
```
|   :s₁,s₁,s₁|s₁  :   |   :d,d₁,d₁,d₁|   :   |s₁  :s₁  |s₁,s₁,s₁:s₁|
```
Tra la la la,   Tra la la la,

D.S.
```
|d,d,d:d ,d |m   :   |s,s,s:m |f,f,f:r |d,d,d:t₁,t₁,t₁|d   :—   ||
|m₁,m₁,m₁:m₁,m₁,s₁|   :   |s₁,s₁,s₁:s₁|l₁,l₁,l₁:l₁|s₁,s₁,s₁:s₁,s₁,s₁,s₁|   :—   ||
```
Tra la la la   la la,   Tra la la la,   Tra la la la,   Tra la la la la la la.
```
|d   :d  |d,d,d:d |d,d,d:m |r,r,r:f |m,m,m:r,r,r|m   :—   ||
```
Tra   la   la la la   Tra la la la,   Tra la la la.   Tra la la la la la la.
```
|d   :d  |d,d,d:d |d₁,d₁,d₁:d₁|f₁,f₁,f₁:f₁|s₁,s₁,s₁:s₁,s₁,s₁,d₁|   :—   ||
```

249. Key D. Round for four parts.

```
|d   :m  |s   :s .l,t|d¹  :s  .s |r¹,t :s ,f |
```
Too   much   haste   mak - eth   waste: Make haste slow - ly—
```
|m,s,f .m ,d|t₁  :s  :  |s   :—   |r   :—   ||
```
Then you will go   more sure - ly:—   That's   so!

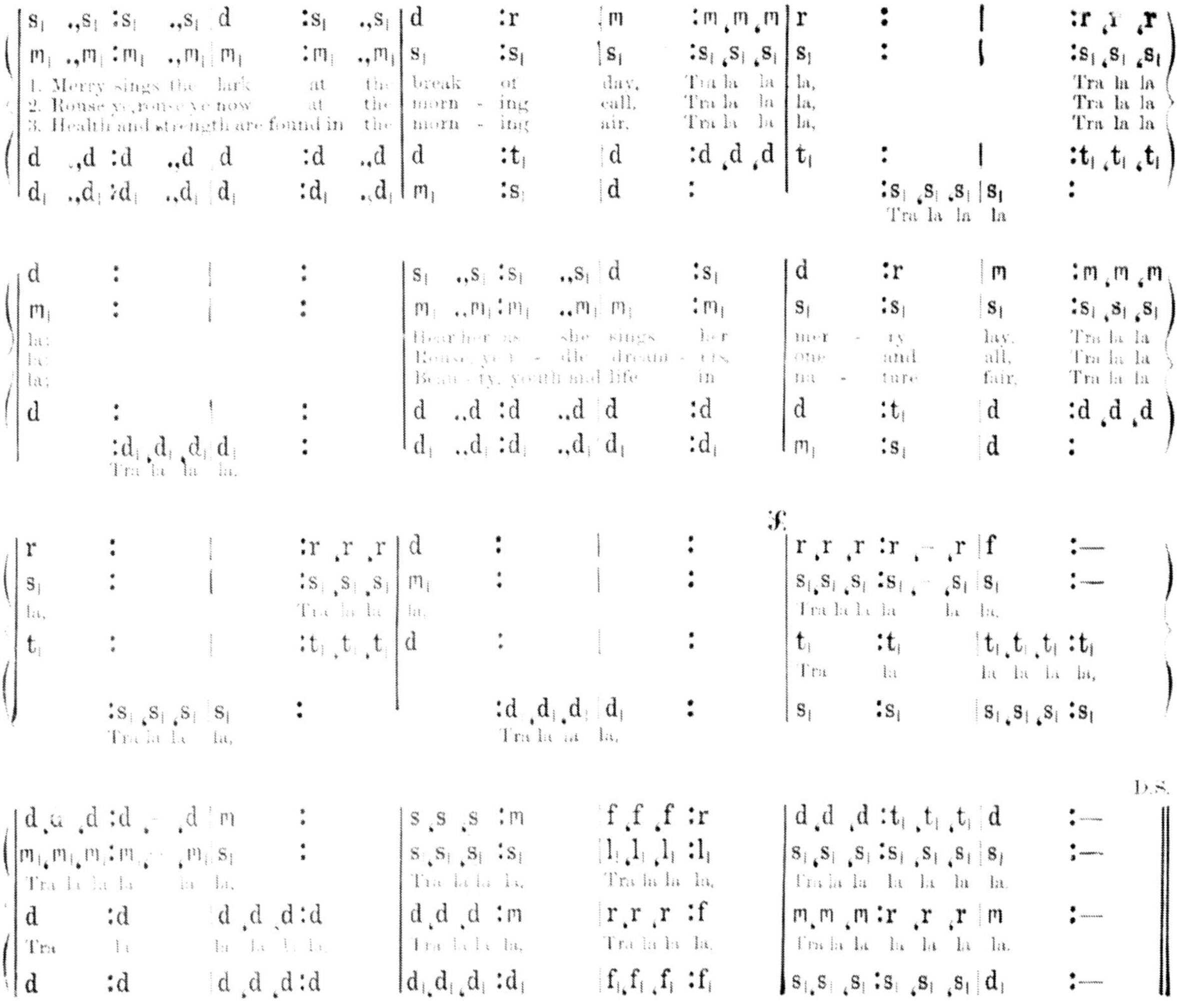

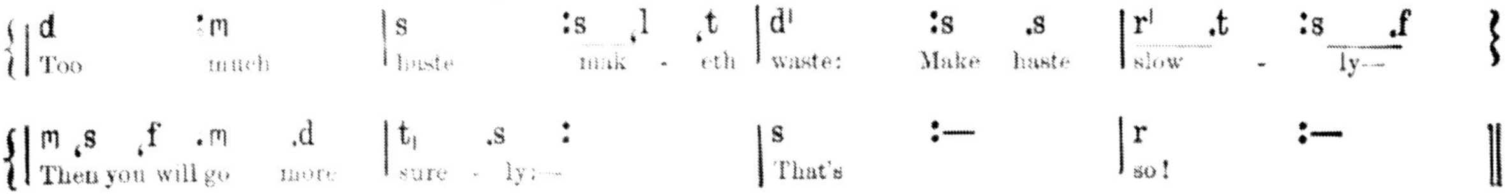

Syncopation is the anticipation of accent. It requires an accent to be struck before its regularly recurring time, changing a *weak* pulse or a weak part of a pulse into a *strong* one, and the immediately *following* strong pulse or part of a pulse into a *weak* one. It must be boldly struck, and the strong accent on the immediately following pulse must be omitted.

250.

|l :l |— :l |l :l |— :l |l :l |— :l |— :l |l :l ||
TAA TAA -AA TAA TAA TAA -AA TAA TAA TAA -AA TAA -AA TAA TAA TAA

251.

|l .l :— .l |l .l :— .l |l .l :l .l |l . :l . ||
TAA TAI - AA TAI TAA TAI - AA TAI TAA TAI TAA TAI TAA *SAI* TAA *SAI*

252. Key C. Round in two parts. T. F. S.

|s :s |— :s |l :l |— :l |t :t |— :t |d' :d' |d' :
Come now, oh, come now, Or we shall be late, I fear.

|m : |m : |f : |f : |s : |s : |d : | : ||
Yes, we're com - ing right a - - long.

253. Key C. Round in two parts.

|d :— |r :— |m :— |f :— |r :— |m :— |f :— |m :—
No, no, no, no, no, no, no, no!

| :d' |— :t |— :ta |— :l |— :r' |— :d' |— :t |d' :— ||
Yes, yes, yes, yes, yes, yes, yes, yes!

254. Key C. Round in two parts.

|d' .d' :— .t |l .l :— .s |f .m :r .f |m :
Come now, O come now, Or we shall be too late;

|m .m :m |f .f :f .m |r .d' :— .t |d' : ||
No, no, no, no, no, no, And you, too, must wait.

255. Key F. Round in three parts.

|m :m .,f |s :d |m :r .,d |r :— .d |m :s .l |s :m .d
Call John the boat - man, call him a - gain, For loud roars the tem - pest and

|s, :m .,r |d : | .d :d .d |d :— .d |d :t, .l, |s, :— .t,
fast falls the rain. John is a - sleep, he sleeps ver - y sound, His

|d .d .d |d :d .d |m :s .,f |m :s |— .d .,r |m .m : .d
oars are at rest, and his boat is a - ground, Loud roars the riv - er, so

|s .s :— .l |t : .s ,s |s .s :m .f |s : .m |s .s :s, .,s, |d : ||
rap-id and deep; But the louder you call John, the sounder he will sleep.

T. F. S.

HEAR THE WARBLING NOTES.

256. Key G. M. 100. T. F. Seward.

1. Hear the war - - bling notes of spring - time, From the gay and cheer - ful
2. Hear the ech - - oes as they're ring - ing Far and near o'er hill and
La la la la la la. La la la la la
La la la
throng, Ev - ery voice is filled with glad - ness, Let us join their hap-py, hap - py
dale Let us join them with our sing - ing, Send - ing out our songs on ev - ery
La la la la
la, La la la la la la, La la la la
la la la,
song. La la la la la la la la la, Hear the echoes so gai - ly
gale.
la, La la la la la la la la la, Hear the echoes so gai - ly
ring - ing, La la la la la la la la la la la la la la la la la la la.

COME, LET US ALL BE MERRY.

257. Key E. M. 80. Arranged, and new words.

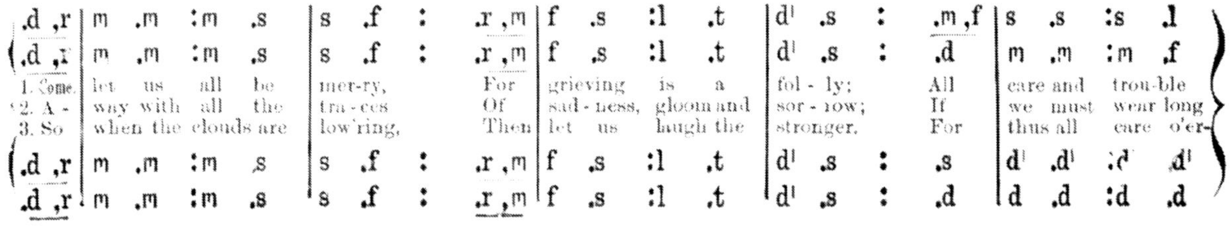
1. Come, let us all be mer-ry, For grieving is a fol - ly; All care and trou-ble
2. A - way with all the tra - ces Of sad - ness, gloom and sor - row; If we must wear long
3. So when the clouds are low'ring, Then let us laugh the stronger, For thus all care o'er-

CHORUS.
With a
bur - y And while we live be jol - ly.
fa - ces, Let's keep them for to - mor row.
pow-'ring, We'll sure - ly last the long-er.
ha ha ha, And a ho ho ho, 'Tis a
ha ha ha, ho ho ho,
jolly old world you know.
ha ha ha ha ho. All be hap-py, all be mer - ry, Let's be jol - ly as we
f
ff
go; All be hap-py, all be mer-ry, Broth-ers all, both friend and foe.

Expression.—The following table shows the names of the different degrees of power; the abbreviations and marks by which they are known, and their definitions. The teacher will explain these topics, as may be required, at convenient points in his course of lessons. *See Manual for Teachers School Series* for method of presenting the subject.

NAME.	PRONOUNCED.	MARKED.	MEANING.
PIANISSIMO	Pe-ah-*nis*simo	*pp*	Very Soft.
PIANO	Pe-*ah*-no	*p*	Soft.
MEZZO	*Met*-zo	*m*	Medium.
FORTE	*Four*-tay	*f*	Loud.
FORTISSIMO	Four-*tis*simo	*ff*	Very Loud.
CRESCENDO	Cre-*shen*-do	*cres.* or <	Increase.
DIMINUENDO	Dim in-oo-*en*-do	*dim.* or >	Diminish.
SWELL		<>	Increase and diminish.
SFORTZANDO	Sfort-*zan*-do	*sf.* or *fz.* or >	Explosive.
LEGATO	Lay-*gah*-to	——	Smooth, Connected.
STACCATO	Stock-*kah*-to	' ' '	Short, Detached.

MOVEMENT WORDS.

LARGO		Very slow.
ADAGIO	A-*daj*-o	Very slow.
LARGHETTO		Slow.
ANDANTE	An-*dahn*-tay	Slow.
ANDANTINO	An-dahn-*tee*-no	Moderately slow.
MODERATO	Mo-day-*rah*-to	Moderately, medium.
ALLEGRETTO		Moderately fast.
ALLEGRO	Al-*lay*-gro	Fast.
RITARDANDO		Gradually slower.
ACCELERANDO	At-chel-e-*rahn*-do	Gradually faster.
A TEMPO	Ah *taim*-po	In Time.

The Hold 𝄐, indicates that the tone is to be prolonged at option of the leader.

Da Capo, or D. C., means repeat from the beginning.

Dal Segno, or D. S., means repeat from the 𝄋.

Fine indicates the place to end after a D. C. or D. S.

NUTTING SONG.

258. Key C. B. C. Unseld.

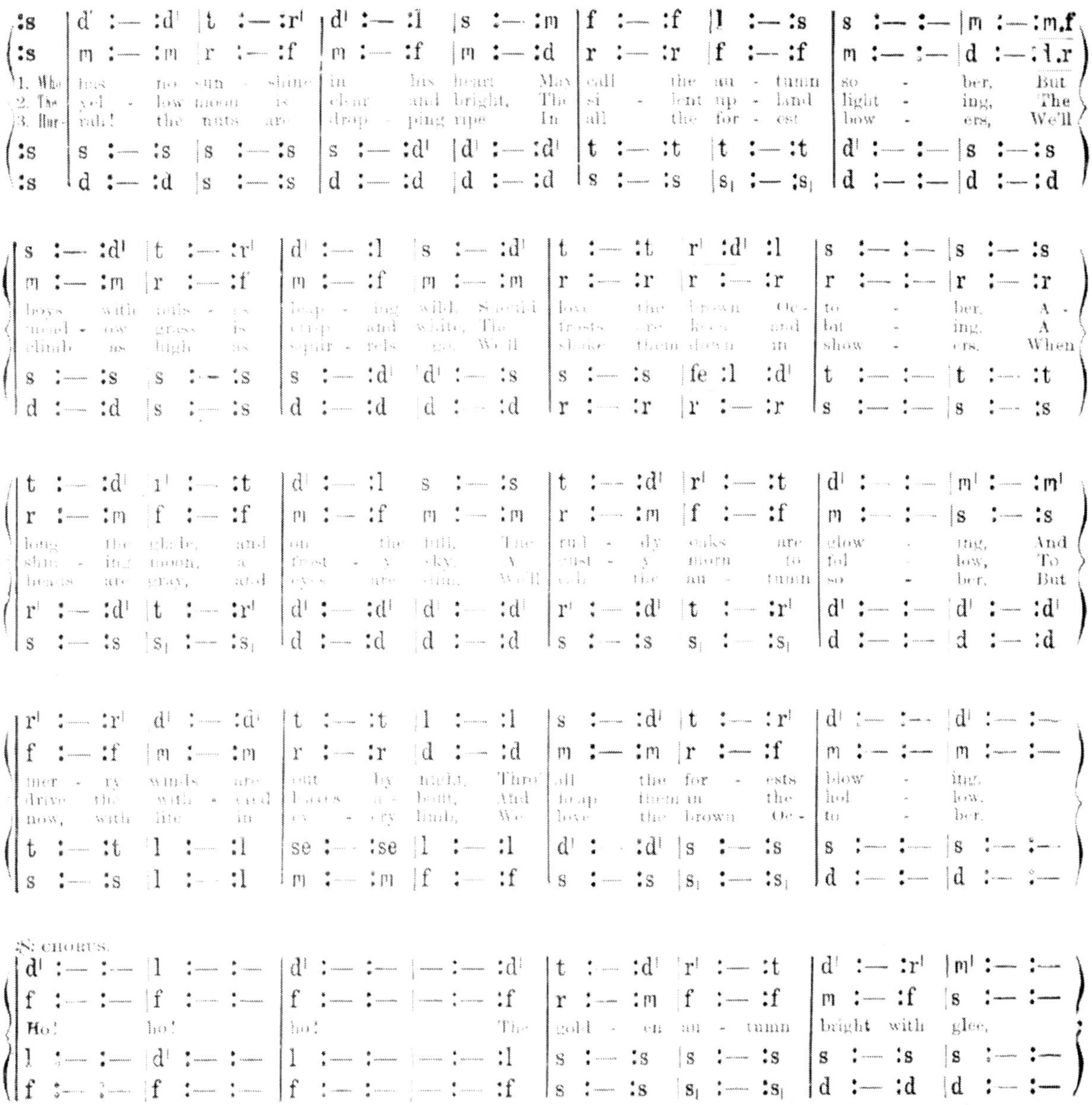
1. Who has no sun - shine in his heart May call the au - tumn so - ber, But
2. The yel - low moon is clear and bright, The si - lent up - land light - ing, The
3. Hur - rah! the nuts are drop - ping ripe In all the for - est bow - ers, We'll
love the brown Oc - to - ber.
CHORUS.
Ho! ho! ho! The gold - en au - tumn bright with glee,

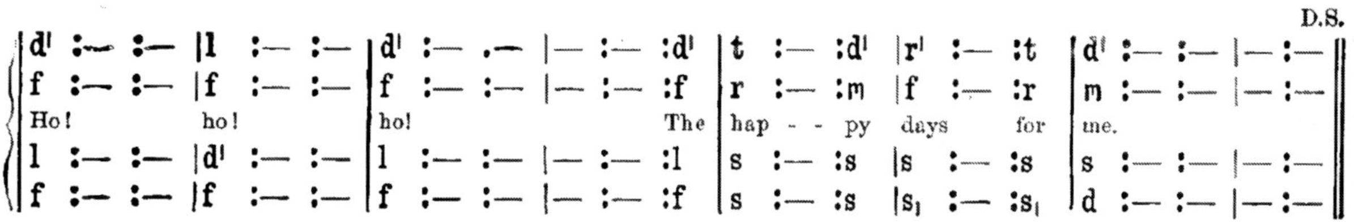
D.S.
Ho! ho! ho! The hap - - py days for me.

CHRISTMAS CAROL.

259. Key A♭.

T. F. Seward.

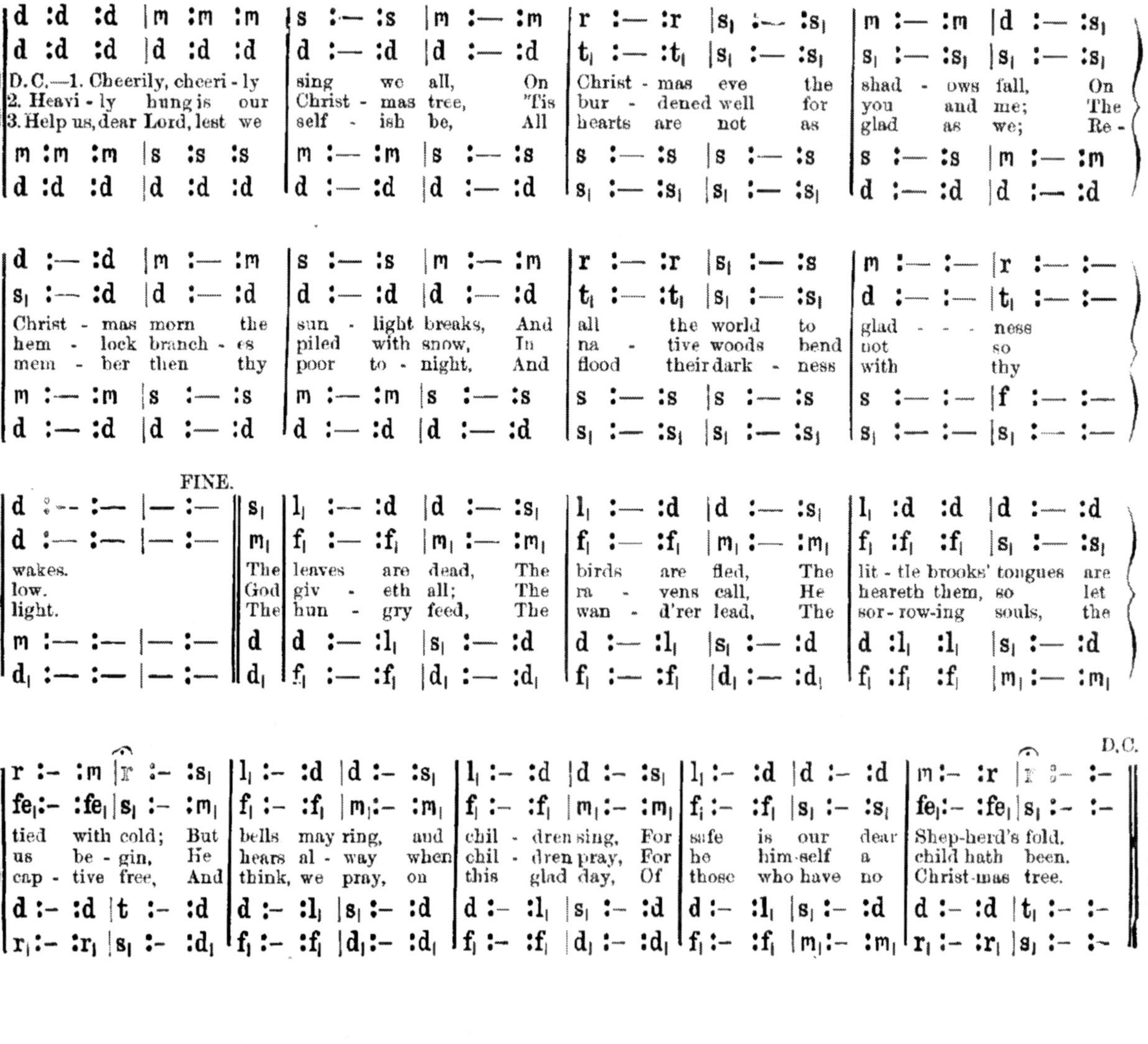
D.C.—1. Cheerily, cheeri - ly sing we all, On Christ - mas eve the shad - ows fall, On Christ - mas morn the sun - light breaks, And all the world to glad - - - ness wakes.
2. Heavi - ly hung is our Christ - mas tree, 'Tis bur - dened well for you and me; The hem - lock branch - es piled with snow, In na - tive woods bend not so low.
3. Help us, dear Lord, lest we self - ish be, All hearts are not as glad as we; Re - mem - ber then thy poor to - night, And flood their dark - ness with thy light.
FINE.
The leaves are dead, The birds are fled, The lit - tle brooks' tongues are tied with cold; But bells may ring, and chil - dren sing, For safe is our dear Shep-herd's fold.
God giv - eth all; The ra - vens call, He heareth them, so let us be - gin, He hears al - way when chil - dren pray, For he him-self a child hath been.
The hun - gry feed, The wan - d'rer lead, The sor - row-ing souls, the cap - tive free, And think, we pray, on this glad day, Of those who have no Christ-mas tree.
D.C.

260. Key Ab.   COME UNTO ME.   T. F. Seward.

```
p
d :— |d :d |d :— |— :— | m :— |— :f :f | m :— |— :d | l₁ :t₁ | d :f
s₁ :— |l₁ :l₁ |s₁ :— |— :— | s₁ :— |— :l₁ :l₁ | s₁ :— |— :s₁ | f₁ :s₁ |— :s₁
Come      un - to   me,          Come      un - to   me,        all   ye          that
m :— |f :f |m :— |— :— | d :— |— :d :d | d :— |— :d | d :1 | d :t₁
d₁ :— |d₁ :d₁ |d₁ :— |— :— | d₁ :— |d₁ :d₁ | d₁ :— |— :m₁ | f₁ :— | m₁ :r₁

m :m |d :m |r :— |d :l₁ | s₁ :s₁ |  :   | s₁ :m |r :d | l₁ :— |d :—
s₁ :s₁ |s₁ :s₁ |s₁ :— |fe₁ :— | s₁ :s₁ |  :   | m₁ :s₁ |s₁ :s₁ | f₁ :— |re₁ :—
ye-bor and are  heav - y       la - den;    Come   un - to   me,      and
l :d |m :d |t₁ :— |l₁ :d | t₁ :t₁ |  :   | d :— |t₁ :d | d :— |d :—
d₁ :d₁ |d₁ :d₁ |r₁ :— |r₁ :— | s₁ :s₁ |  :   | d₁ :— |r₁ :m₁ | f₁ :— |fe₁ :—

p
d :d |r :t₁ |d :— |— :— |   :   |  :   | s :s |f :f | m :— |d :d
m :m₁ |f₁ :f₁ |m₁ :— |— :— |   :   |  :   | t₁ :t₁ |l₁ :s₁ | s₁ :— |s₁ :s₁
I  will  give you  rest,                 Take my  yoke up - on   you  and
d :d |t₁ :r |d :— |— :— | m :— |d :— | r :— |d :r | d :— |d :d
s₁ :s₁ |s₁ :s₁ |d₁ :— |— :— | d :— |m₁ :— | s₁ :— |l₁ :t₁ | d :— |m₁ :m₁

d :— |l₁ :— |s₁ :— |— :s₁ | l :— |l₁ :— |t₁ :— |d :— | f :f |m :— | r :— |— :r
learn   of      me;      For  I   am     meek and   low-ly   of    heart,     And
l₁ :— |f₁ :— |m₁ :— |— :m₁ | f₁ :— |f₁ :— |s₁ :— |s₁ :— | s₁ :s₁ |s₁ :— | s₁ :— |— :s₁
d :— |d :— |d :— |— :— | d :d |d :d |r :— |d :d | t₁ :— |d :— | t₁ :— |— :t₁
learn   of      me;       Take my yoke up - on   you and learn   of    me;      And
f₁ :— |l₁ :— |d :— |— :— | f₁ :f₁ |f₁ :f₁ |f₁ :— |m₁ :m₁ | r₁ :— |d₁ :— | s₁ :— |— :s₁

p                 pp
m :m |d :— |s₁ :— |s₁ :— | s₁ :— |s₁ :— | s₁ :— |m :m | m :d |f :m | s :f |m :r
s₁ :s₁ |m₁ :— |m₁ :— |m₁ :— | r₁ :m₁ |f₁ :r₁ | m₁ :— |s₁ :s₁ | s₁ :m₁ |l₁ :s₁ | ta:l₁ |s₁ :l₁
ye shall find    rest   un - to    your    souls, For my  yoke  is    eas-y  and my
d :d |d :— |d :— |d :— | t₁ :d |r :t₁ | d :— |d :d | d :— |d :— | m :f |s :ſ
d₁ :d₁ |d₁ :— |d₁ :— |m₁ :— | s₁ :— |s₁ :— | d₁ :— |d₁ :d₁ | d₁ :— |d₁ :— | de:r₁ |m₁ :f₁
```

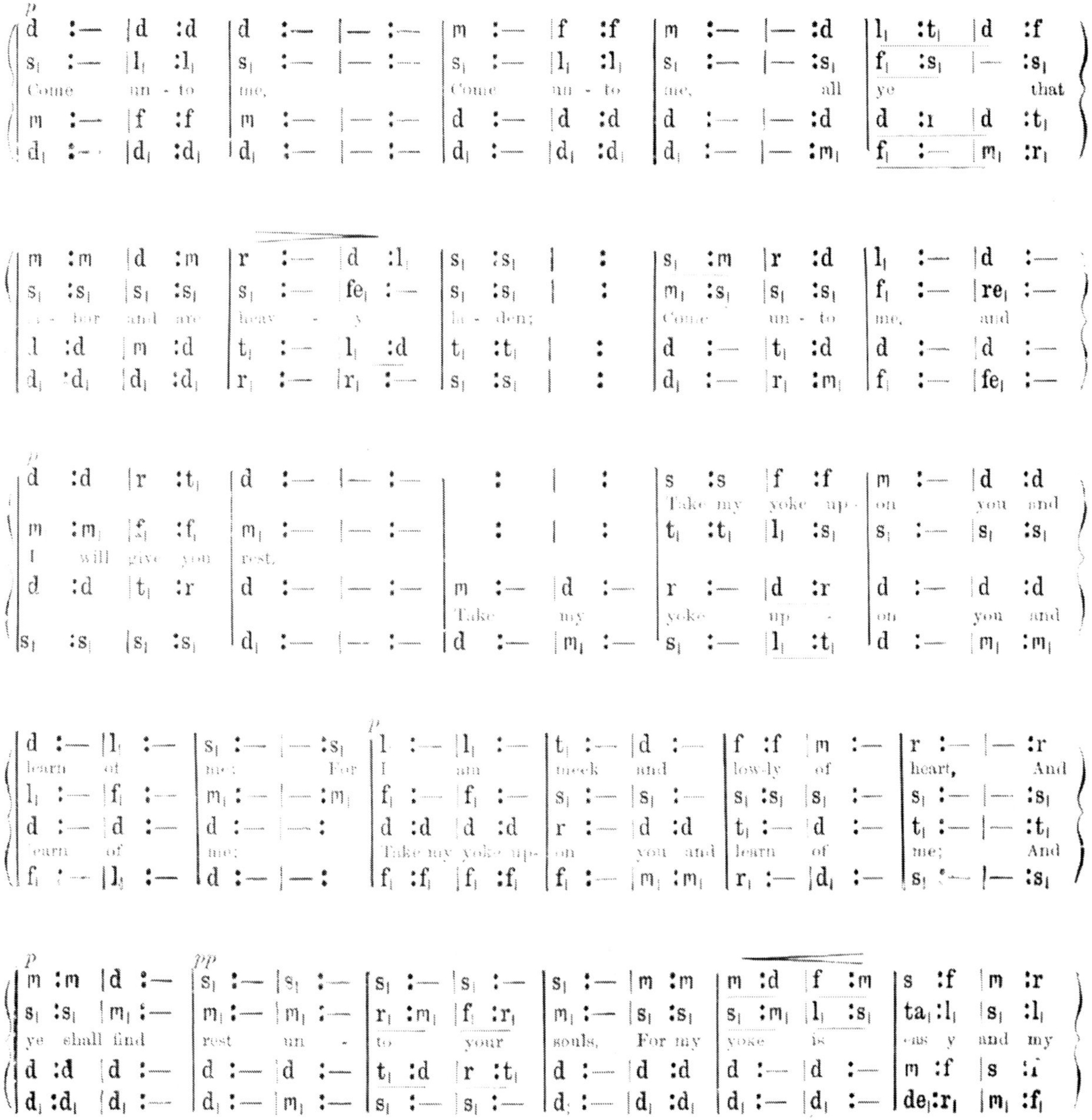

rit. pp

d :m |r :— |d :— |— :— |d :— |r :—.r |m :— |— :— |f :m |r :—.d |d :— |— :— ||
s, :s, |s, :— |s, :— |— :— |m, :s, |s, :—.s, |s, :— |— :— |f, :s, |f, :—.m, |m, :— |— :— ||
burden is | light. | Come un - to | me, | Come un - to | me.
m :s |f :— |m :— |— :— |d :— |t, :—.t, |d :— |— :— |d :— |t, :—.d |d :— |— :— ||
s, :s, |s, :— |d, :— |— :— |d, :m, |s, :—.s, |d :— |— :— |l, :d |s, :—.d, |d, :— |— :— ||

EVERY DAY HATH TOIL AND TROUBLE.

261. KEY A♭. M. 120. BEETHOVEN.

m :m |f :s |s :f |m :r |d :d |r :m |m :— |r :
s, :s, |s, :s, |s, :l,.t, |d :s, |s, :s, |s, :s, |s, :— |— :
1.Ev - ery day hath toil and troub - le, Ev - ery heart hath care;
2.Pa - tient - ly en - dur - ing ev - er Let thy spir - it be
3.La - bor! wait! though mid - night shad - ows Gath - er round thee here,
d :d |r :m |m :r |d :t, |d :d |t, :d |d :— |t, :
d :d |d :d |s, :s, |s, :f, |m, :m, |r, :d, |s, :— |— :

m :m |f :s |s :f |m :r |d :d |r :m |r :— |d :
s, :s, |s, :s, |s, :l,.t, |d :s, |s, :s, |s, :s, |f, :— |m, :
Meek - ly bear thine own full bur - den, And thy broth - er's share..........
Bound, by links that can - not sev - er, To hu - man - i - ty............
And the storm a - bove thee low - 'ring, Fills the heart with fear............
d :d |r :m |m :r |d :t, |d :d |t, :d |t, :— |d :
d :d |d :d |s, :s, |s, :f, |m, :m, |r, :d, |s, :— |d, :

r :r |m :d |r :m.f |m :d |r :m.f |m :r |d :r |s, :—
s, :s, |s, :s, |s, :s, |s, :s, |s, :s, |s, :se, |l,.s, :fe, |s, :—
Fear not, shrink not, though the bur - den Heav - y to thy heart may prove;
La - bor! wait! thy crown is read - y When thy wea - ry task is done;
Wait in hope, the morn - ing dawn - eth, When the gloom - y night is gone;
t, :t, |d :m |t, :d.r |d :m |t, :d.r |d :m |m :r.d |t, :—
s, :s, |d :d |s, :s, |d :d |s, :s, |d :t, |l, :r, |s, :—

m :m |f :s |s :f |m :r |d :d |r :m |r :— |d :
s, :d |t, :ta, |l, :l, |l, :l, |s, :s, |f, :m, |f, :— |m, :
God shall fill thy mouth with glad - ness, And thy heart with love............
Count not lost the fleet - ing mo - ments, Life has but be - gun............
And a peace - ful rest a - waits thee, When thy work is done...........
d :m |r :de |r :r |s :f |m :m |r :d |t, :— |d :
d, :d, |r, :m, |f, :f, |f, :f, |s, :s, |s, :s, |s, :— |d, :

THE SWEET VOICE.

Grace J. Frances.   Hubert P. Main, by per

262. Key D♭.   A♭.t.

```
 :s  | s  :m :f  | s  :d¹ :d¹ | d¹ :— :— | t  :— :l  | s  :r  :m | f  :m :r | m  :— :— |— :— :ᵐl₁ |
(:d  | d  :d :r  | m  :m :m   | f  :— :—  | f  :— :f  | f  :t₁ :d | t₁ :t₁ :t₁ | d :— :— |— :— :ᵈf₁ |
 1. I     dreamed that afar I had  wan - - dered, And  stood on a  des-ert a- lone;     A
 2. The  cares of my life in a  mo - - ment Were  lost in a   thrill of de- light;    The
 3. That  voice in my heart I will  cher - - ish,  And  when I  am  sad and op- pressed,  Its
(:m  | m  :s :s  | d¹ :s :ta  | l  :— :—  | d¹ :— :d¹ | t  :f  :m | r  :s  :s | s :— :— |— :— :ˢd |
 :d  | d  :d :d  | d  :d :d   | f₁ :— :—  | f₁ :— :f₁ | s₁ :s₁ :s₁ | s₁ :s₁ :s₁ | d :— :— |— :— :ᵈf₁ |
```

```
 s₁ :d :r  | m  :f  :m | m  :— :— | r  :— :l₁ | d  :— :d | t₁ :l₁ :t₁ | ᵈs :— :— |— :— :m |
 s₁ :s₁ :s₁ | s₁ :s₁ :s₁ | f₁ :— :— | f₁ :— :f₁ | m₁ :— :m₁ | f₁ :f₁ :f₁ | ᵐt₁ :— :— |— :— :d |
 voice o'er my spir-it came  steal - - ing;  How  soft  its  mag-ic-al  tone.
 desert transform'd to a  gar - - den,  Where  all  was love-ly and  bright.     Sweet
 e - cho, per-haps, in my  slum - - ber  Will  calm  my sor-row to  rest.
 d :d :t₁ | d  :r  :d | l₁ :— :— | l₁ :— :d | d  :— :d | r  :r  :r | ᵈs :— :— |— :— :s |
 m₁ :m₁ :r₁ | d₁ :t₂ :d₁ | f₁ :— :— | f₁ :— :f₁ | s₁ :— :s₁ | s₁ :s₁ :s₁ | ᵈs₁ :— :— |— :— :d |
```

```
 r :— :— |— :— :f | m  :— :— |— :— :  | s  :— :— |— :d¹ :m | s  :— :— |— :— :  |
 t₁ :— :t₁ | t₁ :— :r | d  :— :m | m  :—  | d  :— :— |— :m :d | d  :— :— |— :— :  |
 voice,     sweet voice,  Dear  lov - ing  voice!
 voice,  sweet voice,  sweet voice,  sweet voice,  Dear  lov - ing  voice!
 s :— :s | s  :— :s | s  :— :s | s  :—  | m  :— :— |— :s :s | m  :— :— |— :— :  |
 s₁ :— :— |— :— :s₁ | d  :— :— |— :—  | d  :— :— |— :d :d | d  :— :— |— :— :  |
```

```
 l :— :— |l  :t  :d¹ | m¹ :— :d¹ | s  :— :— | r  :m :f | m  :— :r | d  :— :— |— :— :s |
 d :— :— |f  :f  :f  | m  :— :m  | d  :— :— | d  :d :d | d  :t₁ :— :t₁ | d :— :— |— :— :  |
 Where,  where is the  bliss  it  gave?  Why is the vis - ion  o'er?     Sweet
 f :— :— |l  :se :l  | s  :— :s | m  :— :— | l  :s :l | s  :— :f | m  :— :— |— :— :  |
 f₁ :— :— |f₁ :f₁ :f₁ | d  :— :d | d  :— :— | f  :m :r | s₁ :— :s₁ | d :— :— |— :— :  |
```

```
 r :— :— |— :— :s | m  :— :— |— :— :s | t  :— :l | s  :r :f | m  :d¹ :l | s  :— :— |
 voice,     Sweet voice,     That  made  my  in - - most  soul  re - joice.
 :t₁ :t₁ :t₁ | t₁ :—  | :d :d | d  :— :d | t₁ :— :t₁ | t₁ :— :r | d  :m :re | m  :— :— |
 sil - ver voice,  sil - ver voice,  That  made  my  in - - most  soul  re - joice.
 :s :s | s  :— :  | :m :m | m  :— :m | r  :— :r | r  :s :s | s  :— :fe | s  :— :— |
 :s₁ :s₁ | s₁ :— :  | :d :d | d  :— :d | s₁ :— :s₁ | s₁ :— :s₁ | d  :— :d | d  :— :— |
```

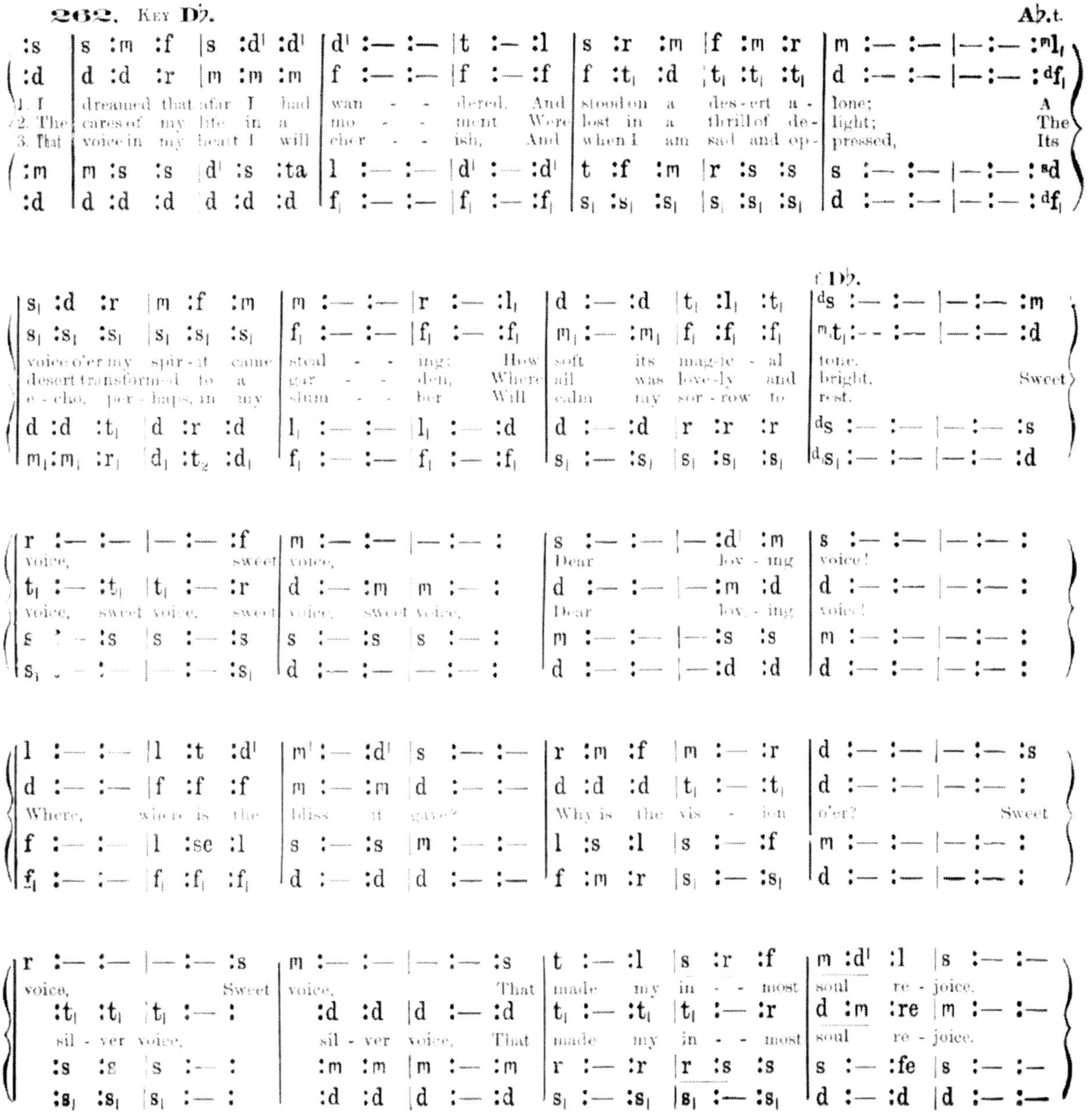

l :— :— |l :t :d' |m' :— :d' |s :— :— |r :m :f |m :— :r |d :— :— |— :—
f :— :— |f :f :f |m :— :m |d :— :— |d :d :d |t, :— :t, |d :— :— |— :—
Oh! say, was it all a dream, Gone to re - turn no more.
d' :— :— |l :se :l |s :— :s |m :— :— |l :s :l |s :— :f |m :— :— |— :—
f, :— :— |f, :f, :f, |d :— :d |d :— :— |f :m :r |s, :— :s, |d :— :— |— :—

SABBATH EVENING.

263. Key B♭. B. C. Unseld.

m, :f, :fe, |s, :— :d |d :— :t, |t, :— :— |t, :l, :s, |f, :— :l, |l, :— :— |s, :— :
d, :r, :re, |m, :— :s, |f, :— :f, |f, :— :— |f, :— :m, |r, :— :f, |f, :— :— |m, :— :
1. Lin - ger still, O bless - ed hours, Slow - ly fade, sweet light,..........
2. Sa - cred songs, O do not cease; Sweet your ech - oes are,............
s, :— :d |d :— :m |r :— :r |r :— :— |t, :— :t, |t, :— :t, |d :— :— |— :— :
d, :— :d, |d, :— :d, |s, :— :s, |s, :— :— |s, :— :s, |s, :— :s, |d, :— :— |— :— :

FINE.

m, :f, :fe, |s, :— :d |m :— :r |d :— :— |d :t, :l, |s, :— :t, |r :— :— |d :— :
d, :r, :re, |m, :— :s, |se, :— :se, |l, :— :— |re, :— :re, |m, :— :f, |f, :— :— |m, :— :
Still de - scend, ye heaven - ly showers. Back - ward roll, O night!.........
Sounds of praise and hymns of peace, Min - gle with my prayer.........
s, :— :d |d :— :d |t, :— :t, |l, :— :— |l, :t, :d |d :— :r |t, :— :— |d :— :
d, :— :d, |d, :— :d, |m, :— :m, |l, :— :— |fe, :— :fe, |s, :— :s, |s, :— :— |d, :— :

F. t.

ᵗm :f :fe |s :— :d' |d' :— :t |t :— :— |r :de :r |l :— :s |fe :— :— |s :— :
ˢd :r :re |m :— :m |m :— :r |r :— :— |t, :le, :t, |r :— :m |re :— :— |m :— :
Tar - ry still, O sa - cred Dove, In this worth - less breast,..........
Bu - sy world, lie still and sleep, Far a - way from me,.............
ʳs :— :s |s :— :s |s :— :s |s :— :— |s :— :s |f :— :m |l :— :— |s :— :
ˢd :— :d |d :— :d |s, :— :s, |s, :— :— |s, :— :s, |t, :— :d |d :— :— |— :— :

D. C. 1st verse.

m :f :fe |s :— :d' |d' :— :t |t :— :— |t :l :s |f :— :t, |r :— :— |ᵈs, :— :
d :r :re |m :— :m |m :— :r |r :— :— |r :d :t, |r :— :s, |t, :— :— |ᵈs, :— :
Come from thine a - bode a - bove, Make with me thy rest..............
Heart of mine, oh, wake - ful keep, Je - - sus calls for thee!............
s :— :s |s :— :s |s :— :s |s :— :— |s :— :s |s :— :f |f :— :— |ᵐt, :— :
d :— :d |d :— :d |s, :— :s, |s, :— :— |s, :— :s, |s, :— :s, |s, :— :— |ᵈs, :— :

HOPE WILL BANISH SORROW.

GEORGE BENNETT. HUBERT MAIN, by per.

264. KEY A♭.

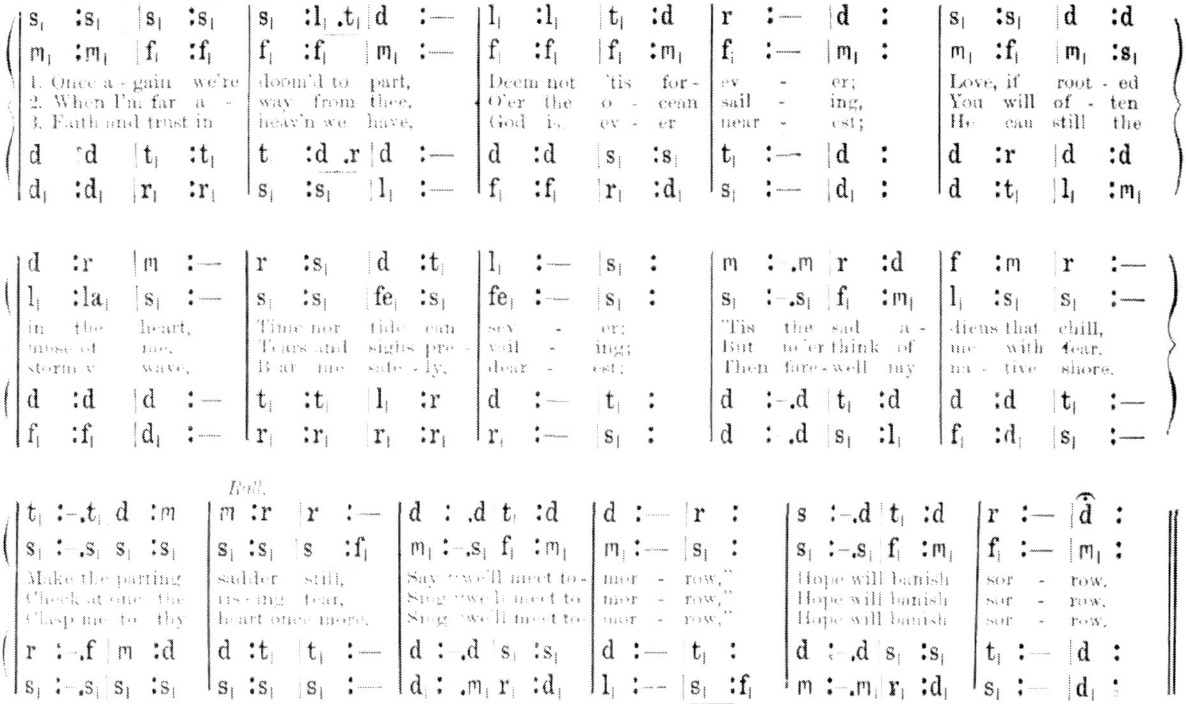
Rall.
1. Once a-gain we're doom'd to part, Deem not 'tis for-ev - er; Love, if root-ed in the heart, Time nor tide can sev - er; 'Tis the sad a-dieus that chill, Make the parting sadder still, Say "we'll meet to-mor - row," Hope will banish sor - row.
2. When I'm far a - way from thee, O'er the o - cean sail - ing, You will of - ten muse of me, Tears and sighs pre - vail - ing; But ne'er think of me with fear, Check at once the ris-ing tear, Sing "we'll meet to mor - row," Hope will banish sor - row.
3. Faith and trust in heav'n we have, God is ev - er near - est; He can still the storm-y wave, Bear me safe-ly, dear - est; Then fare-well my na - tive shore, Clasp me to thy heart once more, Sing "we'll meet to-mor - row," Hope will banish sor - row.

LANGDON. C. M.

265. KEY F. T. F. SEWARD.

1. Fa-ther! I long, I faint, to see The place of thine a - bode; I'd leave thine earth - ly courts, and flee Up to thy seat, my God!
2. There all the heaven - ly hosts are seen, In shin-ing ranks they move, And drink im - mor - tal vig - or in, With won - der and with love.
3. Fa-ther! I long, I faint, to see The place of thine a - bode; I'd leave thine earth - ly courts, and be For - ev - er with my God.

H. H. HAYDEN.

EVENING ON THE LAKE.

266. KEY C. M. 108.

M. L. BARTLETT, by per.

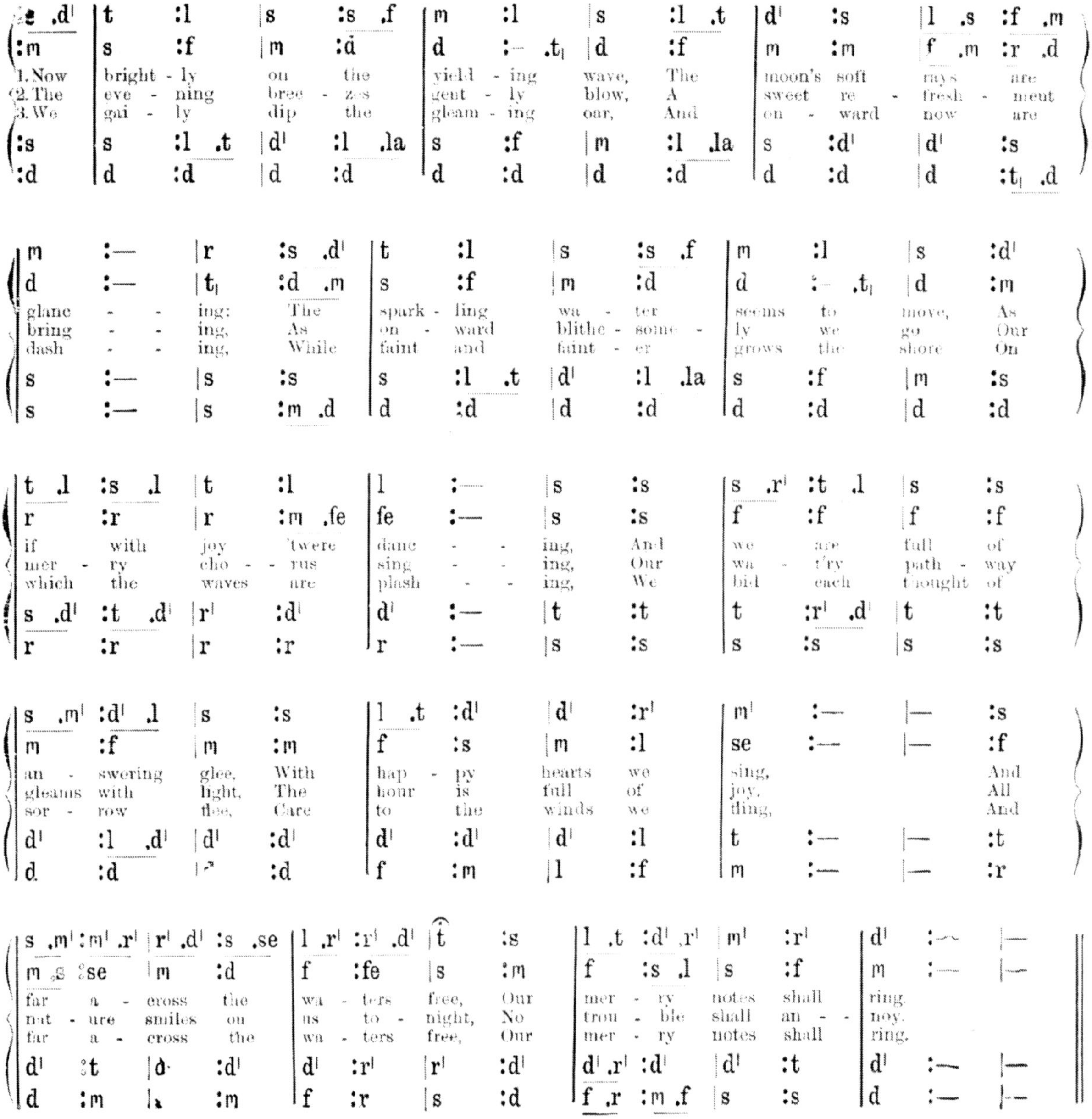
1. Now bright-ly on the yield-ing wave, The moon's soft rays are glanc-ing: The spark-ling wa-ter seems to move, As if with joy 'twere danc-ing, And we are full of an-swering glee, With hap-py hearts we sing, And far a-cross the wa-ters free, Our mer-ry notes shall ring.
2. The eve-ning bree-zes gent-ly blow, A sweet re-fresh-ment bring-ing, As on-ward blithe-some-ly we go Our mer-ry cho-rus sing-ing, Our wa-t'ry path-way gleams with light, The hour is full of joy, All nat-ure smiles on us to-night, No trou-ble shall an-noy.
3. We gai-ly dip the gleam-ing oar, And on-ward now are dash-ing, While faint and faint-er grows the shore On which the waves are plash-ing, We bid each thought of sor-row flee, Care to the winds we fling, And far a-cross the wa-ters free, Our mer-ry notes shall ring.

Mary C. Seward.

SLEEP, BELOVED.

267. Key G.

Theo. F. Seward.

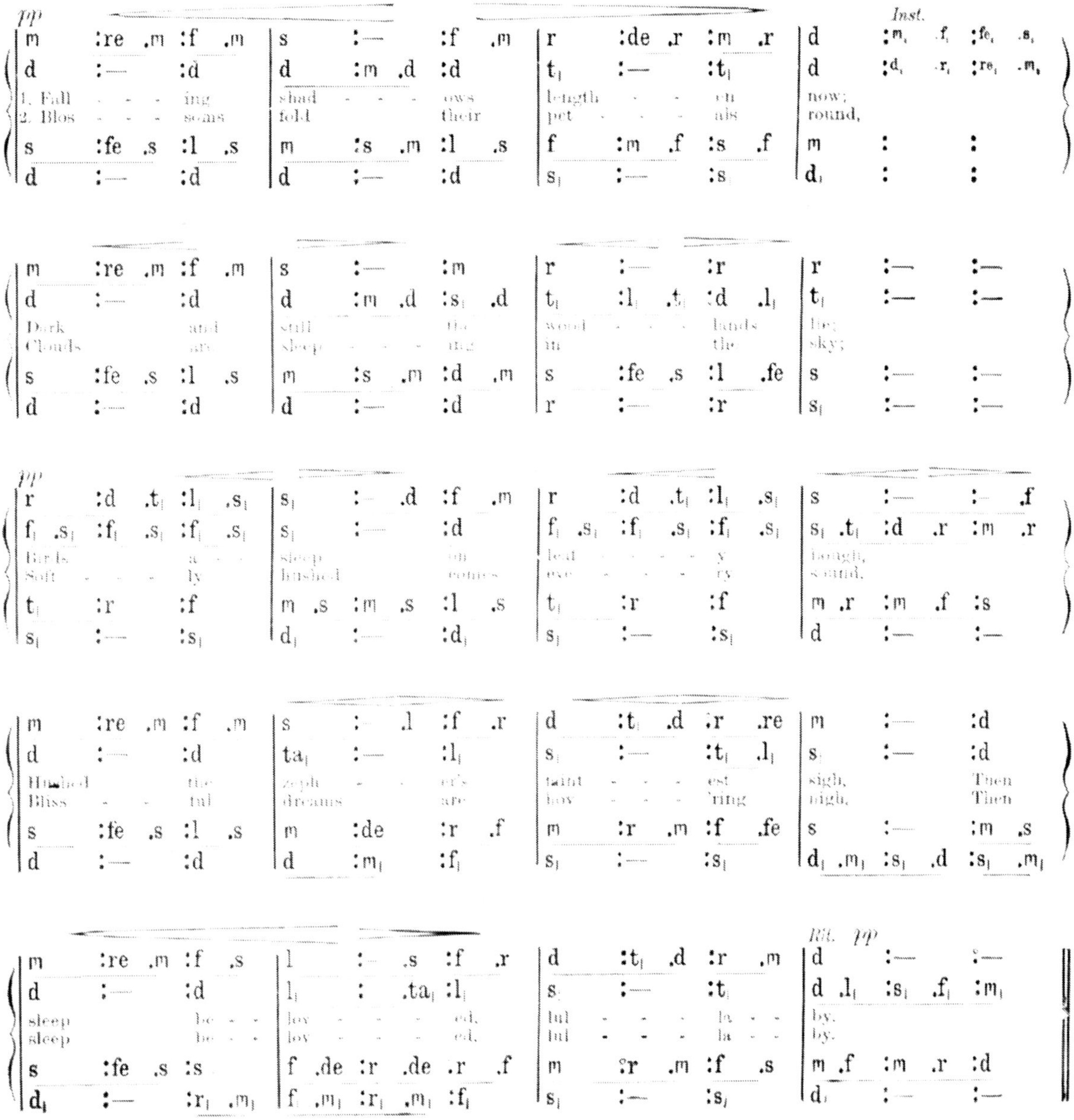
pp
Inst.
1. Fall - - - - ing shad - - - - ows length - - - - en now;
2. Blos - - - - soms fold their pet - - - - als round,
Dark and still the wood - - - - lands lie;
Clouds are sleep - - - - ing in the sky;
pp
Birds a - sleep on leaf - - - - y bough,
Soft - - - - ly hushed comes eve - - - - ry sound,
Hushed the zeph - - - er's faint - - - - est sigh, Then
Bliss - - ful dreams are hov - - - 'ring nigh, Then
Rit. pp
sleep be - - - lov - - - - ed, lul - - - - la - - by.
sleep be - - - lov - - - - ed, lul - - - - la - - by.

ELEMENTARY RHYTHMS.

FOR PUPILS PREPARING FOR THE FIRST AND SECOND GRADE CERTIFICATES.

These Rhythms must be done at the rate indicated by the metronome mark. The pupil must *laa* or *taatai* one complete measure and any portion of a measure which is required, as an introduction to the Exercise—the Exercise itself being taken up without pause or slackening of speed, at the right moment. The exercise must be taatai'd on one tone. For amusement, it may be taatai'd in tune.

The keys are fixed so as to bring the tones within the reach of all voices. The Rhythm may often be learned slower than marked, and when familiar the pupils will take pleasure in largely increasing the speed. J. C.

They are to be taught by pattern. Three or four may be practiced at each lesson until the whole are learned. The pupil is expected to practice them at home until they are thoroughly familiar, so that any one taken by lot can be correctly done.

For the First Grade Certificate, Requirement 2 is, "*Taatai* once, and then *laa* on one tone in perfectly correct time, any of the rhythms (Nos. 1, 3, 4, 5, 7, 9 or 11 which the Examiner may select. [Two attempts allowed; a different test to be given for the second trial.]"

For the Second Grade Certificate, the College (see p. 3) will supply to the Examiner the test to be used. It will not contain any difficulties beyond those in "Elementary Rhythms."

TAATAI.

1. Key **F.** M. 100. *Bugle Call,* "Fall in."

| s_1 .d :d | s_1 .d :d | s .m :s .m | d .d :d | s_1 .d :d | s_1 .d :d | s .m :s .m | d .d :d ‖

2. Key **F.** M. 100. *Bugle Call,* "Close."

:m | d :s_1 .m | d .d :s_1 .m | d :s_1 .m | d .d :s_1 .m | d :— | m ‖

3. Key **A.** M. 100. *Bugle Call,* "Fatigue."

:s_1 | d :m .s_1 | d :m .s_1 | d .s_1 :m .s_1 | d .s_1 :m .s_1 | d :m .s_1 | d :m .s_1 | d .s_1 :m .s_1 | d ‖

4. Key **F.** M. 100. *Bugle Call,* "Guard."

| s .m :d .s_1 | d .m :s_1 | s .m :d .s_1 | d :— | s .m :d .s_1 | d .m :s_1 | s .m :d .s_1 | d :— ‖

5. Key **A.** M. 100. *Bugle Call,* "Advance."

:s_1 | d .d :d .s_1 | d .d :d .s_1 | d .s_1 :d .s_1 | d .d :d | s_1 :— | s_1 :— | s_1 :— | — ‖

6. Key **A.** M. 144. *Bugle Call,* "Extend."

| m :— | d :— | m .d :m .d | s_1 :— | m :— | d :— | m .d :m .d | s_1 :— ‖

7. Key **E.** M. 100. *Bayly,* "In happier hours."

| d :d .r :m .f | s :— :l | s :f .m :f .s | m :d :d |

| d :d .r :m .f | s :s :l | s :f .m :f .s | m :— :— ‖

8. KEY G. M. 100. **-AATAI.** *Hymn Tune,* "Wainwright."

{ :s₁ | d :— :t₁ | l₁ :t₁ :d | r .m :f .m :r .d | d :t₁ :r }

{ | s :— .f :m | l₁ .r :d :t₁ | d :— :— | — : ‖

9. KEY E. M. 100. *Hymn Tune,* "Simeon."

{ | s :s .f | m :— .f | m :r | d :— .d | f :— .m | l :— .s | t₁ :d | r :— .r }

{ | m :r .d | f :m .r | s :l | s :— .s | s :— .l | s .f :m .f | m :r | d :— ‖

SAA.

10. KEY D. M. 100. (The pupils to take each part alternately). J. R. THOMAS, "Picnic."

{ | m .f :r .m | d :s | m .f :r .m | d :s | s .f :m .f | s :d¹ | l .s :f .m | r :— }
{ | d :d | d :t₁ | d :d | d :t₁ | d :d | m :d | t₁ :d | s₁ :— }

{ | :s | :s | :s | :s | f .s :l .t | d¹ :m | r :s | d :— ‖
{ | r : | m : | r : | m : | f :r | m :d | d :t₁ | d :— ‖

11. KEY C. M. 72. **Tafatefe.** *Bugle Call,* "Walk and Drive." Altered.

{ | d ,d .d ,d :d .d | m .d :d | m ,m .m ,m :m .m | s .m :m | d¹ ,d¹ .d¹ ,d¹ :d¹ .d¹ }

{ | s ,s .s ,s :s .m | d ,d .d ,d :m .s | m .d :d | d :d | m .d :d | m :m }

{ | s .m :m | d¹ ,d¹ .d¹ ,d¹ :d¹ | s ,s .s ,s :s | d ,d .d ,d :m .s | m .d :d ‖

12. KEY D. M. 72. **TAAtefe.** *Bugle Call,* "Hay up or Litter down."

{ | d .d ,d :d .d | d .s₁ :d .s₁ | m .m ,m :m .m | m .d :m .d }

{ | s .s ,s :s .s | d¹ .s :d¹ .s | d .d ,d :d .d | d : ‖

13. KEY F. M. 100. **tafaTAI.** *Bugle Call,* "Defaulters."

{ :s₁ .s₁ | d ,s₁ .m :d ,s₁ .m | s .s ,s :s .s₁ | d ,s₁ .m :d ,s₁ .m | d ‖

14. KEY G. M. 100 **TAA-efe.** *Bugle Call,* "Salute for the Guard."

|d :d .,d | s_1 :s_1 .,s_1 | d :d .,d | d : | d .d :m .d | m .s :m .d | s_1 :s_1 .,s_1 | s_1 : ||

15. KEY C. M 100 *Bugle Call,* "Officers"

:s .,s | d^1 :s .,s :s .,s | m :s :s | d^1 :s .,s :s .,s | s :—

:s | d^1 :s .,s :s .,s | m :s :m | d :d .d :d .d | d :— ||

16. KEY F. M 100 *Bugle Call,* "Orders"

:s_1 .,s_1 | d :— | m :s_1 .,s_1 | d :— | m :s_1 .,s_1 | d :s_1 .,s_1 | m :s_1 .,s_1 | d :— | m

:s_1 | d .,s_1 :m .,s_1 | d .,s_1 :m .,s_1 | d .,s_1 :m .,s_1 | d :m | s :— | — :m .,d | s_1 :— .d | m ||

17. KEY C. M 100 *Hymn Tune,* "Truro."

|d :m .,f | s :— .s | l :t | d^1 :— .s | d^1 :s | f .m :r .d | f :m | r : ||

18. KEY F. M 100 *Bugle Call,* "General Salute"

:s_1 | d :d .,d | d .m :s .m | d :d .,d | d :s_1 .,d | m :d .,m | s :s_1 .,s_1 | s_1 :s_1 .,s_1 | s_1

:s_1 | d :d .,d | d .m :s .m | d :d .,d | d :s_1 .,d | m :d .,m | s :s_1 | d :d .,d | d ||

19. KEY F. M 100. **-AA-efe.** *Bugle Call,* "Asembly"

|s :— | — .,m :d .s_1 | d :— | — .,s_1 :d .s_1 | d .,s_1 :d .s_1 | d .,s_1 :d .s_1

|d :m | — :— | s :— | — .,m :d .s_1 | d :— | — : ||

20. KEY F. M 100 *Hymn Tune,* "Serenity"

:d | t_1 .,d :r :s | s :— :fe | s :— :d .,t_1 | l_1 :— .t_1 :d .r | m :— :r | d :— ||

21. KEY F. M 100 *Hymn Tune,* "Arlington."

:d | m .m :m :r | d .,d :d :r | m .s :f :m | m :r

:f | m .,m :m :l | s .,s :s :d^1 | r .f :m :r | d :— ||

22. KEY **F.** M. 100. *Barnett*, "Hark! sweet echo."

| s :– .m :f .l | s .,m :d .d :d | l :– .s :f .m | r .,t_1 :s_1 .s_1 :s_1 ||

23. KEY **F.** M. 72. *Mazzinghi*, "Tom Starboard."

:s | m .,f :r .,m :d .s_1 | d : :r | m .,f :s .,m :l,s .f,m | r : }

:s | m .,f :r .,m :d .s_1 | l_1 : :t_1 | d .r :m .s,f :m .r | d : ||

24. KEY **F.** M. 72. "Home, sweet Home."

:d | m .,f :f .,s | s .,m :m | f .,m :f .,r | m :– .d,d | m .,f :f .,s | s :m .s | f .,m :f .r | d ||

25. KEY **C.** M. 60. J. R. THOMAS, "Picnic."

| s ,f .m ,f :s .l | s .m^1 :d^1 | r^1 .,d^1 :t ,l .s ,f | m :— }

| s ,f .m ,f :s .l | s .m^1 :d^1 | t .d^1,t :l .t ,l | s : ||

26. KEY **F.** M. 100. *Hymn Tune*, "Prestwich."

:s .f | m :— :r.m | f :— :m | m :r :d | d :t_1 :t_1 | d :–.r :m | m.r :d :t_1 | d :— :— | : ||

Modulator Voluntaries now include transition of one remove. These should not be made too difficult by wide and unexpected leaps on to the distinguishing tone; nor too easy by always approaching the distinguishing tone stepwise. While the effects of transition are in process of being learnt, these exercises may be *sol-fa-ed*, but the teacher cannot now be *content* with sol-fa-ing. Every exercise should also be sung to *laa*.

Sight-laa-ing. The laa-voluntaries are really sight-singing exercises, if the teacher does not get into self-repeating habits of pointing. See p. 17. But, at their best, they give no practice in reading *time* at sight. Therefore the absolute necessity of sight-laa-ing from new music from the book or the black-board.

Memorizing the three keys. The pupils should now know from memory, not only what is above any one note on the modulator and what below it, but what is on its right and what on its left. The one key no longer stands alone on the mind's modulator. It has an elder brother on the right and a younger on the left, and each of its tones bears cousinship to the other two families, and may be called to enter them. Therefore, at all the later lessons of this step, exercises should be given in committing to memory this relationship, p. 67. The pupils must learn to say these relations, collectively and each one for himself, *without* the modulator.

Memory Patterns. It is difficult to indicate divisions of time by the motions of the pointer on the modulator with sufficient nicety to *guide* the singers in following a voluntary, and it is important to exercise the memory of tune and rhythm. For these reasons our teachers give *long patterns*—extending to two or more sections—including some of the more delicate rhythms. These patterns are given laa-ing, but pointing on the modulator. The pupils imitate them, *without* the teacher's pointing, first sol-fa-ing and then laa-ing.

Memory Singing. The practice of singing whole pieces to words, from memory—in obedience to the order "Close books: eyes on the baton"—is a very enjoyable one. The singer enjoys the exercise of subordination to his conductor, along with a sense of companionship in that subordination, and delights in the effects which are thus produced. This practice is very needful at the present stage in order to *form a habit*, in the singer, of *looking up* from his book. This should now be his normal position. But, as from necessity, the learner's eyes have hitherto been much engaged with his book, he will have to make a conscious effort to form "the habit of looking up." Occasional "Memory Singing" will make him feel the use and pleasure of this.

Ear Exercises (which will now include *fe* and *ta*, and new difficulties of time), *Dictation, Pointing and Writing from Memory*, should still be practiced. Writing from memory does not at all take the place of pointing from memory. There have been pupils who could write from memory, but could not point the same tunes on the modulator. It is important to establish in the memory that pictorial view of key-relationship which the modulator gives, especially now that the study of Transition is added to that of the scale.

QUESTIONS FOR WRITTEN OR ORAL EXAMINATION.

DOCTRINE.

1. How many greater steps are there in the scale, and between which tones do they occur?

2. How many smaller steps are there and where do they occur?

3. How many little steps are there, and where are they?

4. What is the difference between a greater and a smaller step called?

5. How many kommas has a greater step? A smaller step? A little step?

6. By what other names are intervals called?

7. What is the interval from any tone to the next in the scale called?

8. What is the interval from any tone to the third tone from it called?

9. What is a Second called that is equal to one full step?

10. What is a Second called that is equal to a little step (half-step)?

11. What kind of a Third is equal to two steps?

12. What kind of a Third is equal to one full step and one little step?

13. What is the interval from *fah* to *te* called?

14. Which are the two most marked characteristic tones of the scale?

15. From their mental effects, what are *fah* and *te* called?

16. What is a change of key during the course of a tune called?

17. Which is the sharp distinguishing tone, and what is its mental effect?

18. Which is the flat distinguishing tone, and what is its mental effect?

19. On which side of the modulator is the first sharp key? On which side is the first flat key?

20. In going to the first sharp key what does the *soh* of the old key become in the new? What does the old *lah* become? What does the old *te* become? (The teacher will supply additional questions.)

21. In going to the first flat key what tone of the old key becomes *doh* in the new? What tone becomes *ray*? (The teacher will supply additional questions.)

22. What is that tone called on which the change is made from one key to another?

23. How are bridge-tones indicated in the notation?

24. What is the meaning of the little notes placed on the right or left of the key signature in transition?

25. What are the general mental effects of transition to the first sharp key? To the first flat key?

26. What is a Cadence Transition? Is it written in the "perfect" or "imperfect" way?

27. What is a Passing Transition? How written?

28. What is Extended Transition? How written?

29. What is the name for a silent quarter-pulse on the strong part of a pulse? On the weak part? How is it indicated in the notation?

30. What is the name of a pulse divided into thirds? How indicated in the notation?

31. What is syncopation?

32. What is its effect upon a weak pulse, or weak part of a pulse?

33. What is its effect upon the next following strong pulse?

PRACTICE.

34. Teacher singing to figures, Exercise 175, let the pupil tell to what figure the distinguishing tone of the first sharp key was sung. The same with 176.

35. In the same manner let the pupil name the distinguishing tone of the first flat key, in Exercises 183 and 184.

36. Teacher singing to figures, No. 265 (each line beginning with 1); let the pupil name by its figure, first, the distinguishing tone of the departing transition; and, second, that of the returning transition.

37. Pitch, without a tuning fork, the keys B, B flat, E, E flat and A flat. The pupil has not satisfied this requirement, if, when tested, he is found to be wrong so much as a step.

38. Taatai from memory any one of the Exercises 241, 243, 252, 254, the first pulse being named.

39. Beat a number of two-pulse measures describing the motions of the hand. The same with four-pulse measure. The same with six-pulse measure.

40. Follow the examiner's pointing in a new voluntary containing transition, both to the first sharp and first flat keys, and singing to *laa*.

41. Point and sol-fa on the modulator, from memory, any one of the pieces on pages 73 to 76, chosen by the examiner.

42. Write from memory, any other of these pieces chosen by the examiner.

43. Sing to *laa* at first sight, any exercise not more difficult than these pieces.

44. Tell which is *fe* and which is *ta*, as directed, page 34, question 31.

45. Tell what tone (*fe* or *ta*) is *laa*, as directed, page 34, question 32.

46. Taatai any rhythm of two or three four-pulse measures, belonging to this step, which the examiner shall *laa* to you. See page 34, question 33.

47. Taatai in tune, any rhythm of two or three four-pulse measures, belonging to this step, which the examiner shall *sol-fa* to you.

INDEX.—Part I.

For Index to Part II, see page 221

PART 2

THE

TONIC SOL-FA MUSIC READER

REVISED AND IMPROVED.

A COURSE OF INSTRUCTION AND PRACTICE IN THE

TONIC SOL-FA METHOD OF TEACHING SINGING,

WITH A

CHOICE COLLECTION OF MUSIC SUITABLE FOR DAY SCHOOLS AND SINGING SCHOOLS.

BY THEODORE F. SEWARD AND B. C. UNSELD.

APPROVED BY JOHN CURWEN.

The Biglow & Main Co., Publishers,

135 FIFTH AVENUE, NEW YORK. LAKESIDE BUILDING, CHICAGO.

FOR SALE BY BOOKSELLERS AND MUSIC DEALERS GENERALLY.

PREFACE TO PART II.

The second part of the Tonic Sol-fa Music Reader may be regarded as somewhat unique among books of its class. In the number of the subjects treated, the condensed yet thorough method of their presentation, and the variety of exercises, illustrations and pleasing musical selections, it cannot but prove of great value alike to teachers and to students. Its characteristic features may be classified as follows:

1. The advanced musical work of the fifth and sixth steps clearly elucidated and carefully developed through suitable exercises.
2. A choice set of choruses and part-songs of a corresponding grade.
3. A voice-training department, with helpful suggestions to the teacher and progressive exercises for the pupils.
4. A staff notation department in which the relation of Tonic Sol-fa training to the staff is fully explained and illustrated.

Every great reform, whether it be religious, educational or political, is sure to be misunderstood at first. The great mistake of teachers and the public with regard to Tonic Sol-fa has been in its relation to the staff. It has been supposed to be an enemy of the staff, intended to rival and supplant it. It is no more antagonistic to the staff than arithmetic is to algebra, or a dictionary to Shakespeare. It affords a most important, and, to the average human being, an *indispensable* preparation for the staff. As most of the singing people in America do not yet avail themselves of this preparation, they are very imperfect readers of the staff, while in England thousands are able to join the best vocal societies who are not even known as Tonic Sol-faists.

Yet it should also be understood that Tonic Sol-fa is a complete system in itself. It treats every musical truth philosophically, it symbolizes it educationally, and its literature embraces nearly all the classical vocal music that is printed in the staff notation—English glees, German glees, masses, cantatas and oratorios, from Handel's *Messiah* to Gounod's *Redemption*. Thus it gives music to the masses of the people who have not time to learn the staff. In addition to the thousands of staff readers it has created in England, there are many other thousands who sing oratorios from the Tonic Sol-fa notation.

No greater mistake can be made by teachers or learners than to suppose that the benefits of Tonic Sol-fa can be gained by using its methods and devices without employing the notation. The prevalence of this error is doing vast injury to the musical interests of this country. The use of the notation has placed England far in advance of America in its popular musical culture.

The educational value of the Tonic Sol-fa notation is shown by the fact that the staff department of this book is much more comprehensive than the instruction of ordinary staff books, explaining principles for reading difficult music; modulations, transitions, analysis of the minor, etc., which in staff books usually receive no attention whatever.

THEODORE F. SEWARD.
BENJAMIN C. UNSELD.

Requirements for the Third Grade or Intermediate Certificate.

Questions and answers, to prepare for the Third Grade Musical Theory are supplied by the College at 2 Cents per Copy, plus postage.

Examiners.—Those who hold the Fourth Grade, or a higher certificate, with Theory, and who have been appointed to examine by the College of Music.

Before examination, Candidates must satisfy the Examiner that they hold the Second Grade Certificate.

1. *Memory.*—(a) Bring the names of three tunes, each containing either the sharp fourth (*fe*), the flat seventh (*ta*), or the leading note of the minor mode (*se*), and half pulse notes, and write from memory in time and tune one of these tunes, chosen by lot.

Written or printed copies of the above tunes should be given to the Examiner for comparison with the Written Exercises.

The memory copies are required to be exact as respects name, key, time, tune, etc.

2. *Time.*—*Taatai* at first sight and then *laa* in perfectly correct time, a rhythmic test including any of the following time forms: viz.: triplets, half pulse silences, and syncopations. [Two attempts allowed; a different test to be given for the second trial.]

Candidates may *laa* instead of *taatai-ing* the test.

3. *Modulator.*—(a) Sing *laa* to the Examiner's pointing on the modulator a voluntary including transitions of one remove. (b) *Sol-fa* a voluntary including easy transitions of two and three removes, and phrases in the minor mode.

Candidates may *laa* instead of *sol-faing* 3b.

4. *Tune.*—Pitch the key tone by means of a given C and sing the required tests which shall contain no division of time less than half-pulses: (a) *Sol-fa* once, then *laa* a test including transition of one remove. (b) *Laa* once, then sing to words a test without transition. (c) *Sol-fa* once, then *laa* a test in the minor mode which may contain the tones *ba* and *se*.

Candidates may sing to *laa* instead of *sol-faing* 4 a and 4 c.

5. *Ear Test.*—Write the Sol-fa notes of any two simple phrases of five tones each, the Examiner telling the pitch of the key tone, sounding the Doh chord and singing the tune to *laa* or playing it not more than twice. [Two attempts allowed; a different test to be given for the second trial.]

The College will supply to the Examiner the tests to be used in Nos. 2, 4, and 5.

NOTE.—The registration fee for this Certificate is 30 cents, which is exclusive of Examiner's fee. Registration fee stamp may be purchased from the Examiner.

Persons holding the Third Grade or Intermediate Certificate are Members of The American Tonic Sol-fa Association, but only the members who subscribe the amount of the annual dues, one dollar, shall be entitled to voting privileges, the Official Journal, the College Calendar, and the other prints and pamphlets that may be issued by this organization.

FIFTH STEP.

The Modes, Major and Minor. The Modern Minor. Modulation and Transitional Modulation.

The Modes.—Thus far in our studies *Doh* has been the key-tone, or point of repose. Any tone of the Scale may be made to predominate in a tune so as to bear the character of a key-tone and to give something of its own peculiar mental effects to the music. A mode of using the common Scale which makes *Ray* the most prominent tone is called the *Ray Mode.* A Mode which makes *Lah* predominant is called the *Lah Mode.* Tunes in the *Ray* and *Lah Modes* have a sad, plaintive effect. Tunes in the *Doh Mode* are more or less bright and joyous. The *Doh Mode* on account of its Major Third is called the *Major Mode.* The *Ray* and *Lah Modes* having Minor Thirds are called *Minor Modes.* A Major Mode is distinguished by the Major Third; a Minor Mode by the Minor Third.

The Modern Minor.—Of the Minor Modes the *Lah Mode* is the one most used at the present day. To give *Lah* the importance of a Key-tone, modern harmony requires it to have a *leading* tone (*se*), bearing the same relation to *Lah* that *te* has to *doh.* The introduction of *se* creates an unpleasant melodic interval between *fah* and *se*, to avoid which, Melody occasionally requires a new tone a step below *se*, called *ba*, having the same relation to *se* that *lah* has to *te.* In a *downward* melody *soh* is sometimes used instead of *se.* The *Lah Mode* thus modified by these new tones is called the *Modern Minor.* The essential Seventh of the Modern Minor, that required by Harmony, is *se;* the occasional Seventh, that required by Melody, is *Soh.* The essential Sixth, that required by Harmony, is *fah;* the occasional Sixth, that required by Melody, is *ba.*

Modulation.—A change of mode, during the progress of a tune, is called *Modulation.* A change from the major to the minor mode of the same key is called a Modulation to the Relative Minor. A change from the minor to the major mode of the same key is called a Modulation to the Relative Major. The mental effect of a modulation into the Minor mode is that of passing into shadow and gloom. Modulation into the Major mode has the effect of sunshine and cheerfulness.

The term "modulation" commonly means change of *key*, but in the Tonic Sol-fa method change of *key* is called transition, change of *mode*, modulation.

Transitional Modulation.—A change of both key and mode, during the course of a tune, is called *Transitional Modulation.* The commonest form of this change is that from the Major mode to the Relative Minor of the First Flat key. Another, though less frequent Transitional Modulation, is that to the Relative Minor of the First Sharp key.

Ray Mode.	Doh Mode.	Lah Mode.	Modern with Se.	Minor. with Ba.
Ray'	r'	r'	r'	r'
Doh'	DOH'	d'	d'	d'
Te	*TE*	t	t	t
Lah	*LAH*	*Lah*	*Lah*	*Lah*
			Se	*Se*
Soh	SOH	*Soh*		
				Ba
Fah	*FAH*	*Fah*	*Fah*	
Me	ME	*Me*	*Me*	*Me*
Ray	*RAY*	*Ray*	*Ray*	*Ray*
d	DOH	*Doh*	*Doh*	*Doh*
t,	t,	*Te,*	*Te,*	*Te,*
l,	l,	*Lah,*	*Lah,*	*Lah,*

268. KEY C. *Ray is D.* RAY MODE.

:r	f :r	l :f	m :r	l :l	d' :l	t :r'	l
Their	blood a - -	bout Je - -	ru - sa - -	lem, Like	wa - ter	they have	shed;

:l	d' :s	l :f	m :r	l :d'	t :s	l :m	r
And	there was	none to	bu - ry	them, When	they were	slain and	dead.

269. KEY G. *Ray is A.* RAY MODE.

:l	r :—	f :r	m :—	r :—	l, :r	d :r	m :d	t, :l,
1.'Tis	sweet	to re -	mem -	ber	cher-ished	scenes of	child-hood,	Oh, how
2.But	now	all are	past,	and	dear ones	have gone	with them,	Oh, how

r :—	f :r	m :—	r :l,	l, :r	r :d	r :—	—
pure	is the	fount -	ain of	hap - pi -	ness they	bring.	
sweet,	yet how	sad,	are the	pen - sive	thoughts they	bring.	

270. KEY B♭.   *Lah is A.*   LAH MODE.   This may be sung in the *Modern Minor* by singing se for every s.

```
{ :l₁ | l₁ :t₁ | d :t₁ | l₁ :l₁ | s₁ :d | m :r | d :t₁ | d' }
   My | friends thou | hast put | far from | me, And | him that | did me | love;
```
```
{ :d | m :r | d :t₁ | l₁ :l₁ | s₁ :d | t₁ :l₁ | l₁ :s₁ | l₁ }
   And | those that | my ac- | quaintance | were To | dark - ness | did'st re - | move.
```

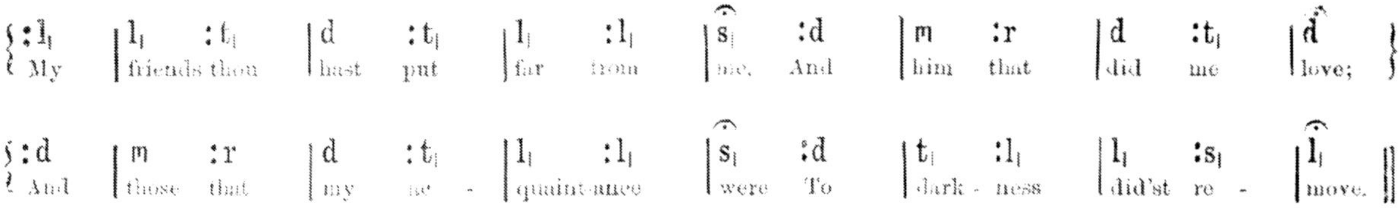

271. KEY E♭.   *Lah is C.*   LAH MODE.   T. F. S.

```
{ :d¹ .t | l :m :f | m :d | :d¹ .t | l :m :f | m :— }
  1 When the | swell of the | o - cean | No | long - er is | seen,
  2 When the | sun fails in | giv - ing | His | lus - tre and | heat,
  3 When the | moon shines no | long - er | On | mount - ain and | glen;
```
```
{ :m .m | r :t₁ :m | d :l₁ | :d | t₁ :m :m | l₁ :— }
  And the | fo - liage of | Sum - mer | Shall | cease to be | green;
  And the | scent of the | rose Be | not | sooth - ing and | sweet;
  O 'tis | then I'll for - | get thee, | But | nev - er till | then.
```

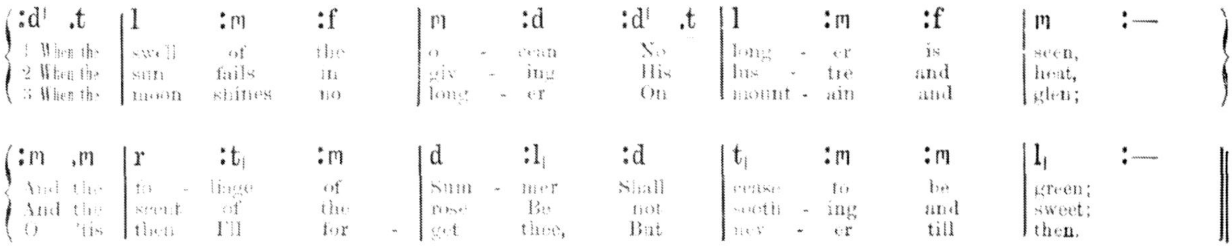

272. KEY C.   *Lah is A.*   MODERN MINOR.

```
{ l :l | se :se | l :— | t :— | d¹ :d¹ | t :t | l :— | :— : }
  Sum - mer | time is | gone and | | sad - ly sighs the | breeze;
```
```
{ m :m | f :f | m :— | l :— | d¹ :t | l :se | l :— | :— : }
  Moan - ing | as it | goes | through | bare and leaf-less | trees.
```

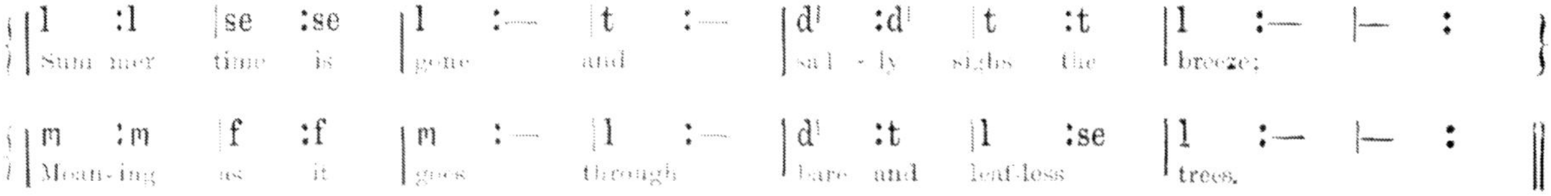

273. KEY G.   *Lah is E.*   T. F. S.

```
{ l₁ :— :l₁ | d :— :d | t₁ :l₁ :t₁ | l₁ :— :m₁ | l₁ :— :t₁ | d :— :r | m :— :f | m :— :— }
  1. Lone - ly | hearts there are | to cher - ish, | While the | days are | go - ing | by;
  2. O! the | world is | full of | sigh - ing, | Full of | sad and | weep - ing | eyes;
```
```
{ f :— :f | t₁ :— :t₁ | m :— :r | d :— :t₁ | l₁ :se₁ :l₁ | d :— :t₁ | l₁ :— :se₁ | l₁ :— :— }
  Wea - ry | souls there | are who | per - ish, | While the | days are | go - ing | by.
  Full of | grief and | bit - ter | cry - ing, | While the | days are | go - ing | by.
```

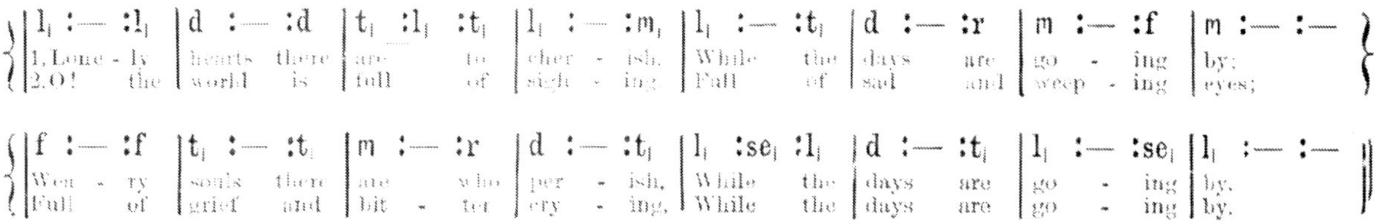

274. KEY F.   *Lah is D.*   Round in four parts.

```
{ l₁ :t₁ | d :— | d :r | m :m | m .l :l .se | l .m :m .r | d :t₁ | l₁ :— }
  Thou, poor | bird, | mourn'st the | tree, Where | sweetly thou dies'd warble in thy | wand'rings | free.
```

275. KEY C.   *Lah is A.*

1st Division.   *2d Division.*

```
{ l | se .l | se :l | se :— | :— :m | f :f | m :r | d :t₁ | l₁ }
```

1st Div.   *2d Div.*   *1st Div.*   *2d Div.*   *Together.*

```
{ l | se :f | m :l | se :f | m :l | se :f | m :se | l :— | :— }
```

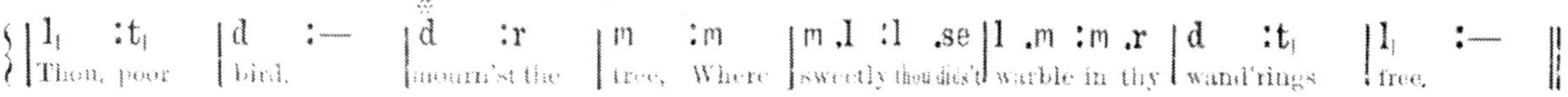

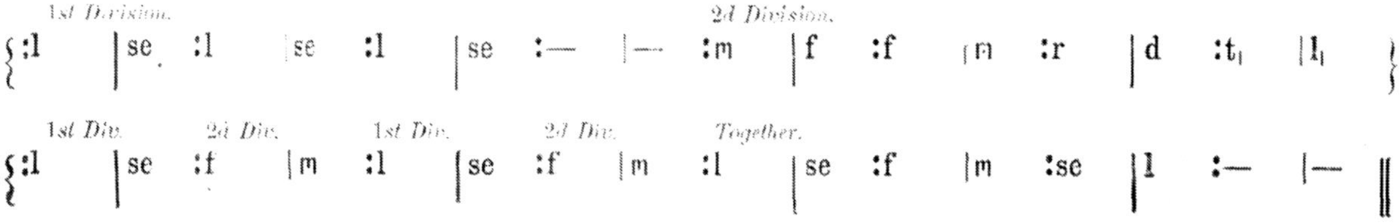

276. Key F. *Lah is D.* Round in two parts.

| l, :l, | t, :t, | d :d | r :— | m :m | f :f | se :se | l :— |

| l :l | se :se | f :f | m :— | r :r | d :d | t, :t, | l, :— ||

277. Key C. *Lah is A.*

d' :—	t :l	se :—	l :—	l :f	m :m	m :—	
m :—	m :m	m :—	m :—	f :r	d :t,	d :—	
:—	t :d'	t :—	l :—	l :l	l :se	l :—	
:—	se :l	m :—	d :—	r :r	m :m	l, :—	

278. Key G. *Lah is E.*

d :—	d :r	m :—	m :—	r :d	t, :t,	l, :—	
l, :—	l, :l,	se :—	l, :—	se :l,	l, :se,	l, :—	
m :—	d :l,	t, :—	d :—	r :m	m :r	d :—	
l, :—	l, :f,	m, :—	d :—	t, :l,	m, :m,	l, :—	

279. Key F. *Lah is D.* Round in two parts.

| l, :l, | t, :t, | d :d | r :— | m :m | ba :ba | se :se | l :— |

| l :l | s :s | f :f | m :— | r :r | d :d | t, :t, | l, :— ||

280. Key C. *Lah is A.*

| l :l | s :s | f :f | m :m | f :m | r :d | t, :l | m :— |
Say, my heart, why art thou swell - ing? Why so heav - y, sad and weak?

| m :m | ba :se | l :se | l :t | d' :t | l :m | ba :se | l :— ||
Tears from out thy depths are well - ing, Say, what would thy fol - ly seek?

281. Key G. *Lah is E.* Round for two parts.

| d :m | d :l, | t, :r | d :— | l, :se, | l, :l, | l, .se, :ba, .se, | l, :— ||
Hark! with - out the storm is loud, See, a - bove the black - en'd cloud.

282. Key E♭. *Lah is C.* Round for four parts.

:l | se :l | t :m | m :ba .se | l :l, | t, :d | r :d .r | m :r | d : |
In dark-ness and in lone - li - ness The watch-man on his way must press:

| m :— | m :— | m :— | — :d .r | m :l | se .ba :m .r | d :t, | l, ||
Twelve o' - - clock! Hear the hol - low sound in the emp - ty street.

283. Key A♭. *Lah is F.* Round for four parts.

| m, :m, | l, :l, | t, :t, | d :— | m :m .r | d :l, | se, :ba, .se, | l, :— ||
Gone is Au - tumn's kind - ly glow, Now the blasts of win - ter blow.

If the teacher prefers, the Minor Mode may be introduced in imitation exercises of **Major with Relative Minor.** **This will show the shadowy, dependent character of the Minor.** The Minor Mode is so much an **artificial imitation of the Major that, perhaps, the easiest way of teaching it is by comparing the Minor with its Relative Major. Let the Major be considered as a substance and the Minor as its shadow.**

284. KEY **G.** *Major.* — *Relative Minor.*

| d :d | r :r | m :r | d :— | l_1 :l_1 | t_1 :t_1 | d :t_1 | l_1 :— ||

285. KEY **E♭.** *Major.* — *Relative Minor.*

| d :r | m :d | s .f :m .r | d :— | l_1 :t_1 | d :l_1 | m .r :d .t_1 | l_1 :— ||

286. KEY **A.** *Major.*

| d :d | t_1 :t_1 | d :r | m :— | m :f | m :r | d :t_1 | d :— |

Relative Minor, with Se.

| l_1 :l_1 | se_1 :se_1 | l_1 :t_1 | d :— | d :r | d :t_1 | l_1 :se_1 | l_1 :— ||

287. KEY **G.** *Major.* — *Relative Minor.*

| d :t_1 | d :r | m .r :d .t_1 | d :d | l_1 :se_1 | l_1 :t_1 | d .t_1 :l_1 .se_1 | l_1 :l_1 ||

288. KEY **F.** *Major.*

| m :r | d :— | r :d | t_1 :— | r :d | t_1 :r | d :t_1 | d :— |

Relative Minor.

| d :t_1 | l_1 :— | t_1 :l_1 | se_1 :— | t_1 :l_1 | se_1 :t_1 | l_1 :se_1 | l_1 :— ||

289. KEY **C.** *Major.* — *Relative Minor.*

| d^1 :s | d^1 :d^1 | t .d^1 :r^1 .t | d^1 :— | l :m | l :l | se .l :t .se | l :— ||

290. KEY **C.** *Major.* — *Relative Minor, with Ba.*

| d^1 :d^1 | t :t | l :t | d^1 :— | l :l | se :se | ba :se | l :— ||

291. KEY **A♭.** *Major.* — *Relative Minor.*

| m :r | d :s_1 | d .t_1 :l_1 .t_1 | d :— | d :t_1 | l_1 :m_1 | l_1 .se_1 :ba_1 .se_1 | l_1 :— ||

292. KEY **C.** *Major.* — *Relative Minor.*

:s | d^1 :t | d^1 :s | l :t | d^1 :m | l :se | l :m | ba :se | l ||

293. KEY **B♭.** *Major.* — *Relative Minor.*

| d :s_1 | l_1 .t_1 :d .r | m :r | d :— | l_1 :m_1 | ba_1 .se_1 :l_1 .t_1 | d :t_1 | l_1 :— ||

AVELIN.

294. Key D. *Lah is B.* Modern Minor.

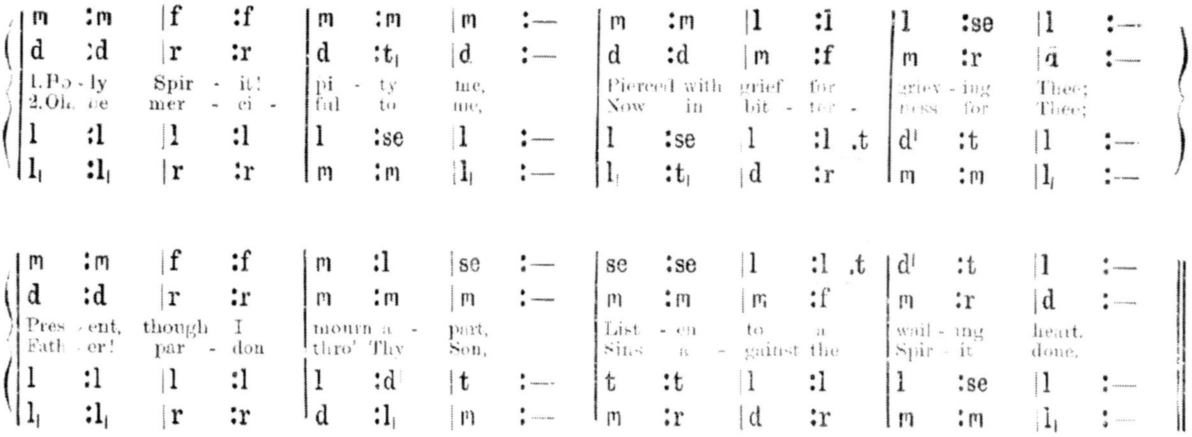
1. Ho - ly Spir - it! pi - ty me, Pierced with grief for griev - ing Thee;
2. Oh, be mer - ci - ful to me, Now in bit - ter - ness for Thee;
Pres - ent, though I mourn a - part, List - en to a wail - ing heart.
Fath - er! par - don thro' Thy Son, Sins a - gainst the Spir - it done.

THE SAD LEAVES ARE DYING.

295. Key B♭. *Lah is G.* Chester G. Allen.

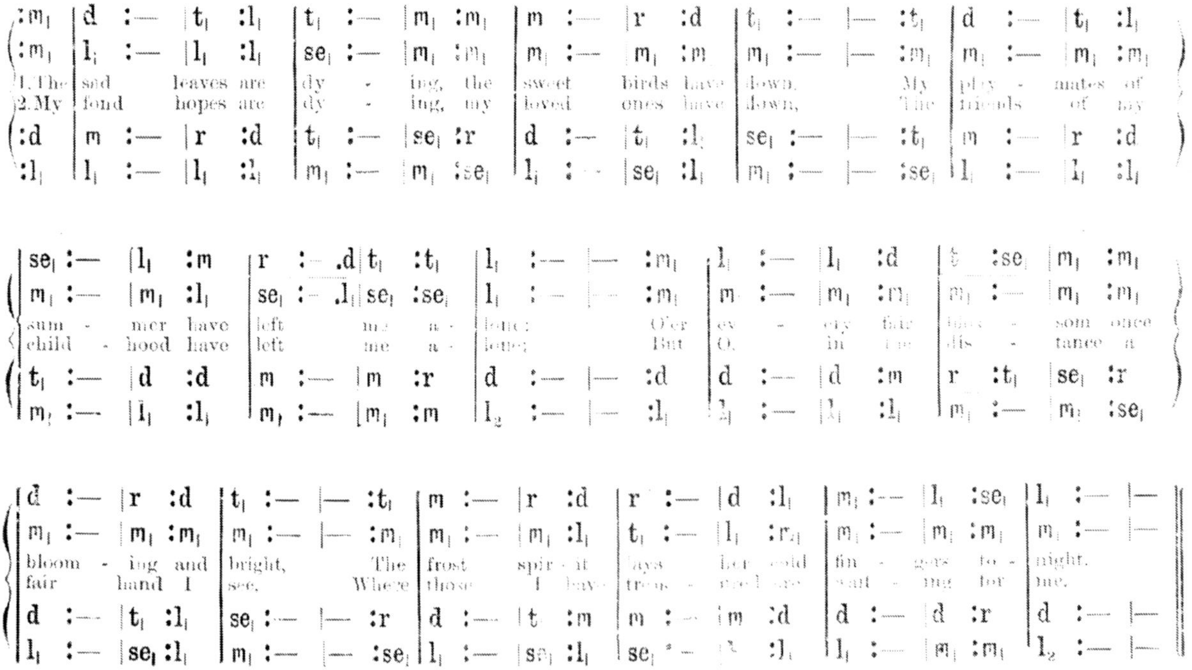
1. The sad leaves are dy - ing, the sweet birds have flown, My play - mates of sum - mer have left me a - lone; O'er ev - ery fair face once bloom - ing and bright, The frost spir - it lays her cold fin - gers to - night.
2. My fond hopes are dy - ing, my loved ones have flown, The friends of my child - hood have left me a - lone; But O, in the dis - tance a fair land I see, Where those I have trea - sured are wait - ing for me.

FREEDOM SPREADS HER DOWNY WINGS.

296. KEY C. *Lah is A.* Extended modulation to Relative Major. Cossack Melody.

1. Free-dom spreads her down-y wings, O - ver all cre - a - ted things, Glo - ry to the King of kings, Bend to Him the knee. Kneel be-fore His ra-diant throne. Bow to Him and Him a - lone, He the on - ly King we own, And He made us free.
2. Happiest spot on which the sun, E'er with ge - nial rays hath shown! Let us hand from sire to son All that makes her great. Sound the clar - ion peals of fame, Breathe Columbia's hal-lowed name, From our fathers freedom came, 'Tis our birth-right here.
3. Hearts a - live with pa - triot fire, Let her fame your deeds in - spire; Weave the strain and wake the lyre, Where your al - tars stand; Far as rolls the swelling sea, Send the song of lib - er - ty, Hon - or thee the brave, the free, And our na - tive land.

HARK! THE PEALING.

297. KEY G. *Lah is E.*

1. Hark! the peal - ing, soft - ly steal - ing, Eve - ning bell, eve - ning bell; Clear - ly ech - o, sweet - ly ech - o, Gen - tly down the dell.
2. Wel-come is the sil - v'ry mu - sic, Sil - v'ry bell, sil - v'ry bell; Sweet-ly tell - ing, gen - tly tell - ing Of the day's fare - well.

LITTLE BY LITTLE.

298. KEY C. *Lah is A.* T. F. SEWARD.

l :l .l |d' :d' |t :t .t |r' :— |d' :d' .d' |m'.r' :d' .t |l :se .se |l :—
d :d .d |m :m |m :m .m |m :— |m :m .m |m :m .f |m :r .r |d :—
1.Lit - tle by lit - tle, sure - ly and slow, Make we our fu - ture of bliss and of woe;
2.Lit - tle by lit - tle creep - eth the tide, Soon like a tor - rent it sweeps far and wide;
l :l .l |l :l |se :se .se |t :— |l :l .l |d' .t :l .r' |d' :t .t |l :—
l, :l, .l, |l, :l, |m :m .m |m :— |l :l .l |l :l .r |m :m .m |l, :—

s :s .f |m.s :d' |s :s .f |m :— |m :m.m |m.r :d |m :— |m :m |l :— |— :
r :r .r |d .m:m |r :r .r |d :— |r :r .r |d .t,:l, |t, :— |d :r |d :— |— :
Ev - er be climb-ing up to the light, Else we must downward go in - to the night.
Guard each begin-ing, turn to the light, Else we must downward go in - to the night.
t :t .t |d' :d' |t :t .t |d' :— |se :se.se |l .l :l |se :— |l :t |l :— |— :
s :s .s |d :d |s :s .s |d :— |t, :t,.t, |l,.l, :l, |m :— |m :m |l, :— |— :

NIGHT! LOVELY NIGHT!

T. F. SEWARD. Arr. from MENDELSSOHN. T. F. SEWARD.

299. KEY B♭. *Lah is G.*

m :t, .,d |l, : .l, |t, .d :r .f |m :l . |m :t, .,d |l, :se,.l, |t, :m, |l, :
m, :f, .,f, |m, : .m, |f, .f, :f, .l, |l, :m, . |m, :f, .,f, |m, :m, .m |m, :m, |m, :
1.Night, lovely night I sing thy wondrous beauty; Stars shining bright Over field and flow'r;
2.Brightly the moon O'er hill and valley shin - ing Robes ev - ery tree With its sil - very light;
d :r .,r |d : .d |r .r :r .r |d :d . |d :r .,r |d :r .d |t, :m |d :
l, :l, .,l, |l, : .l, |l, .l, :l, .l, |l, :l, . |l, :l, .,l, |l, :t, .l, |se, :m, |l, :

FINE.

m :t, .,d |l, : .l, |t, .d :r .f |m :l . |m :t, .,d |l, :se,.l, |t, :m, |l, :
m, :f, .,f, |m, : .m, |f, .f, :f, .l, |l, :m, . |m, :f, .,f, |m, :m, .m, |m, :m, |m :
Perfumes so rare From blossoms sweet ascending, Fill all the air, Like a fra - grant bower.
Soon, ah! too soon Her pearly rays declin - ing, Leave in its dark - ness The si - lent night.
d :r .,r |d : .d |r .r :r .r |d :d . |d :r .,r |d :r .d |t, :m |d :
l, :l, .,l, |l, : .l, |l, .l, :l, .l, |l, :l, . |l, :l, .,l, |l, :t, .l, |se, :m, |l, :

D.C.

.d |r .m :f .r |m.r :d .d |r .m :f .r |m.r :d .m |r .d :t, .r |d .t, :l, .d |t, .l, :se,.t, |m :—
.l, |t, .d :r .t, |d .d :d .d |t, .d :r .t, |d .d :d . | : | : | : |se, :—
No glare of day can equal thee, Thou dark and silent mystery; What marvels are beneath thee hid, O thou mysterious night!
.m |s .s :s .s |s .f :m .m |s .s :s .s |s .f :m .s |f .m :r .f |m .r :d .m |r .d :t, .t, |t, :—
l, |s, .s, :s, .s, |s, .s, :s, .s, |s, .s, :s, .s, |s, .s, :s, . | : | : | : |m, :—

MARIE MASON.

WHEN THE LEAVES ARE FALLING FAST.

300. KEY G. *Lah is E. Tenderly and softly.* M. 96. T. F. SEWARD.

When the leaves are falling fast. 'Mid the forest shadows,
Soft - ly comes the thought of home, Home we prized so dear - ly.
As the years are pass - ing on. Swift - ly, swift - ly pass - ing.
When the Summer
On - ly once in
Mem - 'ry brings the
Dreary are the meadows;
That dear word so nearly.
All our path - way tracing.
Home where sun-shine
Tears may fall, and
on the heart,
comes un-sought,
hearts grow sore.

CHARLES WESLEY.

ASTON. S. M.

301. KEY B♭. *Lah is G.* JOHN HEYWOOD.

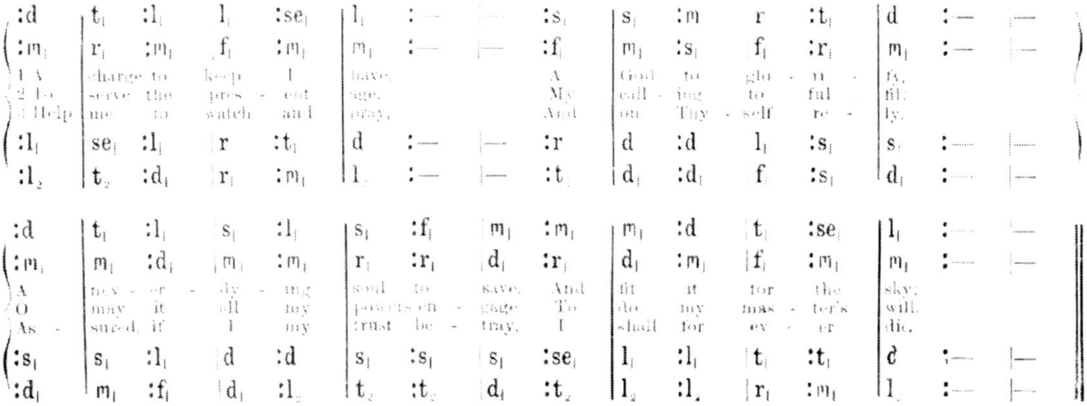

WHY WAILETH THE WIND?

T. F. S.
302. Key B♭. *Lah is G.*

T. F. Seward, by per.

| :m₁ | m :— .r :d | d :— .t₁ :l₁ | se₁.l₁ :t₁ | :m₁ | l₁ .t₁ :d | :m₁ | m :— .r :d |
| :m₁ | m₁ :— .se₁:l₁ | l₁ :— .m₁ :m₁ | m₁ :m₁ | :m₁ | m₁ :m₁ | :m₁ | m₁ :— .se₁:l₁ |

1. Why wail - eth the wind thro' the tree - tops so sad - ly, Why sigh - eth the
2. Why lin - ger the clouds in the sun's part - ing glo - ry, Why rain - gle their
D.C. Why wail - eth the wind thro' the tree - tops so sad - ly, Why sigh - eth the

| :m₁ | d :— .t₁ :l₁ | m :— .r :d | t₁ .d :r | :m .r | d .t₁ :l₁ | :m₁ | d :— .t₁ :l₁ |
| :m₁ | l₂ :— .l₂ :l₂ | l₂ :— .l₂ :l₂ | m₁ :m₁ | :m₁ | l₂ :l₂ | :m₁ | l₂ :— .l₂ :l₂ |

FINE.

| d :— .t₁ :l₁ | se₁.l₁ :t₁ | :m₁ | l₁ :— | s₁ | s :— .f :m | m :— .r :d |
| l₁ :— .m₁ :m₁ | m₁ :m₁ | :m₁ | m₁ :— | s₁ | s₁ :— .t₁ :d | d :— .s₁ :s₁ |

zeph - yr so mourn - ful - ly now? Their mu - sic, though sweet as the
shade with the bright-ness be - low? Their light, though as soft as the
zeph - yr so mourn - ful - ly now?

| m :— .r :d | t₁ .d :r | :m | d :— | s₁ | m :— .r :d | s :— .f :m |
| l₂ :— .l₂ :l₂ | m₁ :m₁ | :m₁ | l₂ :— | s₁ | d₁ :— .d₁ :d₁ | d₁ :— .d₁ :d₁ |

D.C.

| t₁ .d :r | :s₁ | d .r :m | :s₁ | s :— .f :m | m :— .r :d | t₁ .r :d | :t₁ | l₁ :— |
| s₁ :s₁ | :s₁ | s₁ :s₁ | :s₁ | s₁ :— .t₁ :d | d :— .s₁ :s₁ | f₁ :l₁ | :se₁ | l₁ :— |

whis- per of an - gels. Yet tells me the tale of a grief long a - go.
smile of a lov'd one, Yet speaks to my heart of a grief long a - go.

| r .m :f | :s .f | m .r :d | :s₁ | m :— .r :d | s :— .f :m | r .f :m | :r | d :— |
| s₁ :s₁ | :s₁ | d₁ :d₁ | :s₁ | d₁ :— .d₁ :d₁ | d₁ :— .d₁ :d₁ | f₁ .r₁ :m₁ | :m₁ | l₂ :— |

ENNERDALE.

303. Key F. Passing Modulation to Relative Minor.

C. Steggall.

| :s | m :d | l₁ :r | t₁ :— | |— :d | l₁ .t₁ :d | f :m .r | m :— | |— |
| :t₁ | d :s₁ | f₁ :l₁ | s₁ :— | |— :s₁ | f₁ :s₁ | l₁ :t₁ | d :— | |— |

1. Come, we that love the Lord, And let our joys be known;
2. Let those re - fuse to sing That nev - er knew our God;
3. Then let our songs a - bound, And ev - ery tear be dry;

| :s | s :m | d :f | r :— | |— :m | d :m | l :s | s :— | |— |
| :s₁ | d :m₁ | f₁ :r₁ | s₁ :— | |— :m₁ | f₁ :m₁ | r₁ :s₁ | d₁ :— | |— |

| :m | m :— .r :d | :m | l :f | r :s | d .r :m | r :r | d :— | |— |
| :l₁ | se₁ :l₁ .t₁ :d | :t₁ | l₁ :r | t₁ :d | l₁ :d | d :t₁ | d :— | |— |

Join in a song of sweet ac - cord, And thus sur - round the throne.
But fav' - rites of the heavenly King May speak their joys a - broad.
We're march -ing thro' Im - manuel's ground To fair - er worlds on high.

| :d | m :m | m :m | f :l | s :s | m :s | s :— .f | m :— | |— |
| :l₁ | m₁ :ba₁.se₁ l₁ | :s₁ | f₁ :r₁ | s₁ :m₁ | l₁ :m₁.f₁ | s₁ :s₁ | d₁ :— | |— |

SAD MEMORIES.

CARRIE COVINGTON.

304. KEY D.

MARY C. SEWARD, by per.

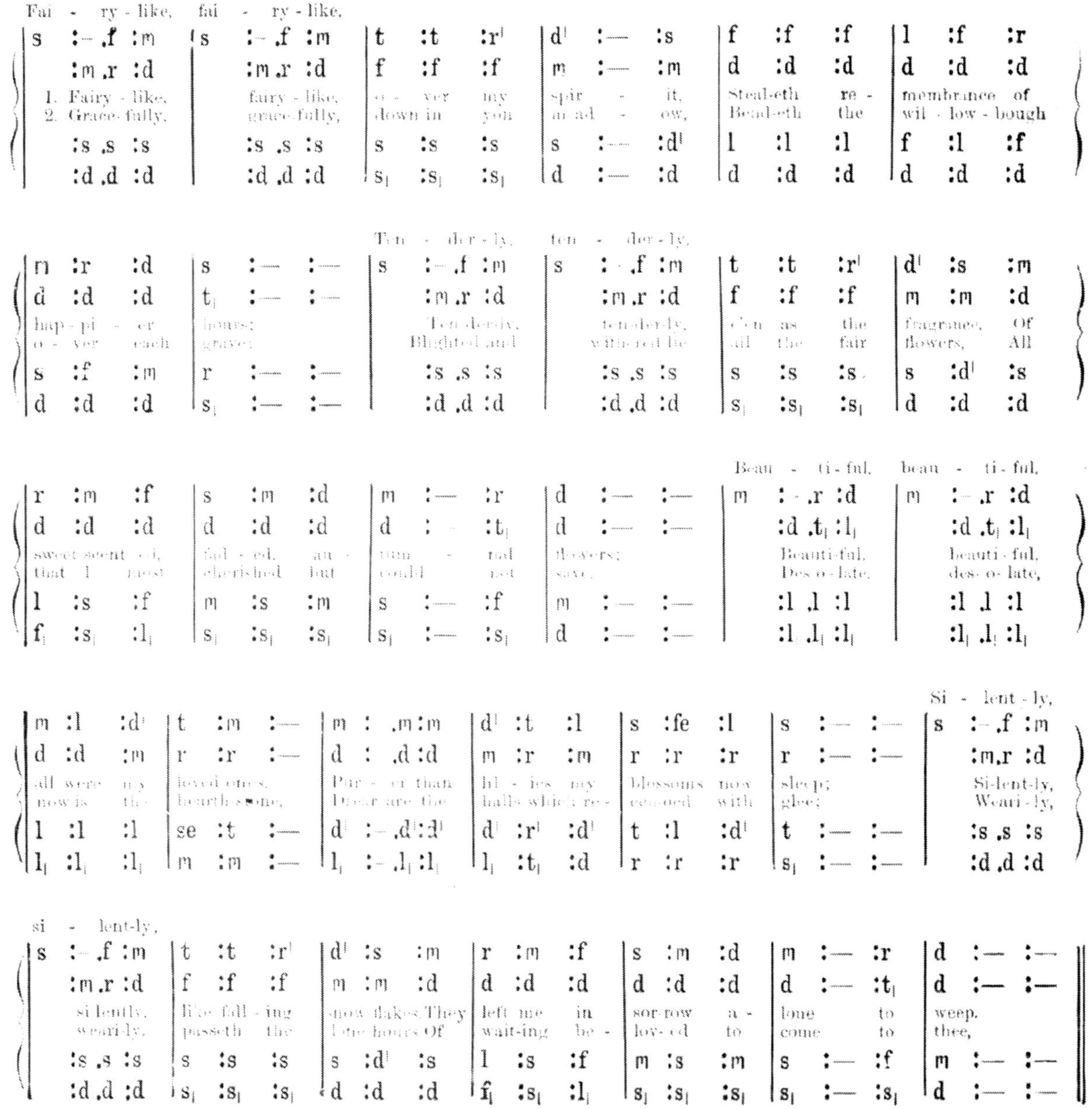
Fai - ry-like, fai - ry-like,
1. Fairy-like, fairy-like, o-ver my spir-it, Steal-eth re-membrance of hap-pi-er hours;
2. Grace-fully, grace-fully, down in yon mead-ow, Bend-eth the wil-low-bough o-ver each grave;
Ten-der-ly, ten-der-ly,
Ten-der-ly, ten-der-ly, e'en as the fragrance, Of sweet-scent-ed, fad-ed, au-tum-nal flowers;
Blighted and withered lie all the fair flowers, All that I most cherished but could not save.
Beau-ti-ful, beau-ti-ful,
Beauti-ful, beauti-ful, all were my loved ones, Pur-er than lil-ies my blossoms now sleep;
Des-o-late, des-o-late, now is the hearth-stone, Dear are the halls which re-echoed with glee;
Si-lent-ly, si-lent-ly,
Si-lent-ly, si-lently, like fall-ing snow-flakes, They left me in sor-row a-lone to weep.
Weari-ly, weari-ly, passeth the lone hours Of wait-ing be-lov-ed to come to thee.

HOME RETURNING.

305. KEY D. *With strong accent.* Extended modulation to Relative Minor. T. F. SEWARD.

1. Home return-ing from a-far, Heart with joy up- lift-ed high, Yonder see the
2. Other lands have treasure vast, Home alone has love to share, Now forget - ting
guiding star, O what pleas - ure draweth nigh; Long I've wandered sad and lone,
all the past, In the joy that waits me there; Ma-ny years have pass'd a-way,
Home and dear ones far a - way, From my heart all hope hath flown, Welcome now this
Weary years they've seen to me, Waiting for this happy day, Home belov - ed
hap-py day;
now I see;
Home return - ing, from a-far, Hearts with joy up - lift-ed high,
Home, &c.
Yonder see the guiding star, O what pleas - ure draweth nigh.
p
cres.
f

HURRAH! WELCOME THE DAY.

308. Key D♭. *With spirit.* M. 112, twice. (Cadence modulation to Relative Minor.) HUBERT P. MAIN, by per.

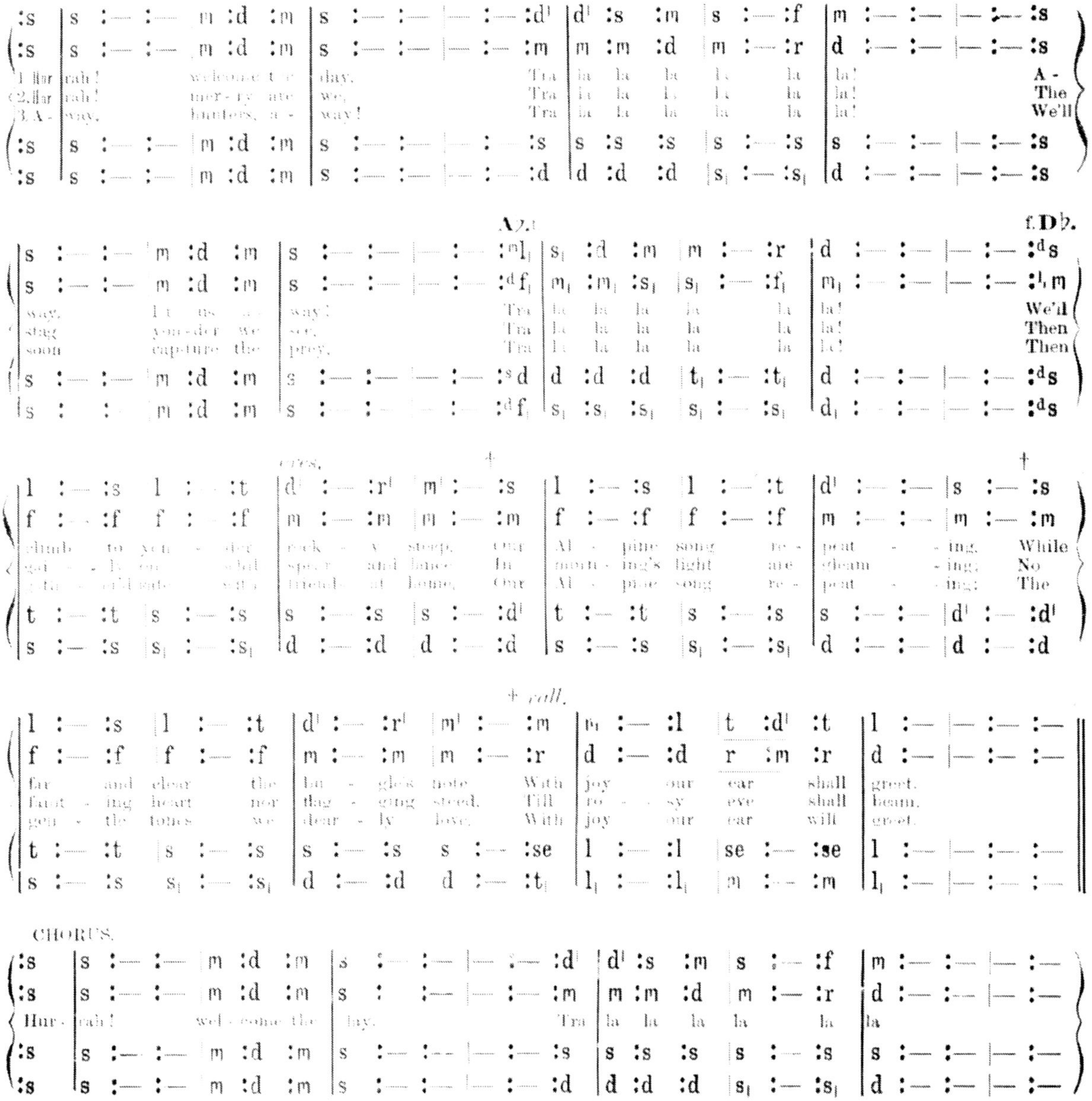
1. Hur - rah! welcome the day, Tra la la la la la la! A - way, let us a - way! Tra la la la la la la! We'll climb to yon - der rock so steep, Our Al - pine song re - peat - ing, While far and clear the bu - gle's note With joy our ear shall greet.
2. Hur - rah! mer - ry are we, Tra la la la la la la! The stag yon - der we see, Tra la la la la la la! Then gai - ly on ... spear and lance In morn - ing's light are gleam - ing; No faint - ing heart nor flag - ging steed, Till ro - sy eve shall beam.
3. A - way, hunters, a - way! Tra la la la la la la! We'll soon capture the prey, Tra la la la la la la! Then ... with friends at home, Our Al - pine song re - peat - ing; The gen - tle tones we dear - ly love, With joy our ear will greet.
A♭. t.
f. D♭.
cres.
rall.
CHORUS.
Hur - rah! wel - come the day, Tra la la la la la la

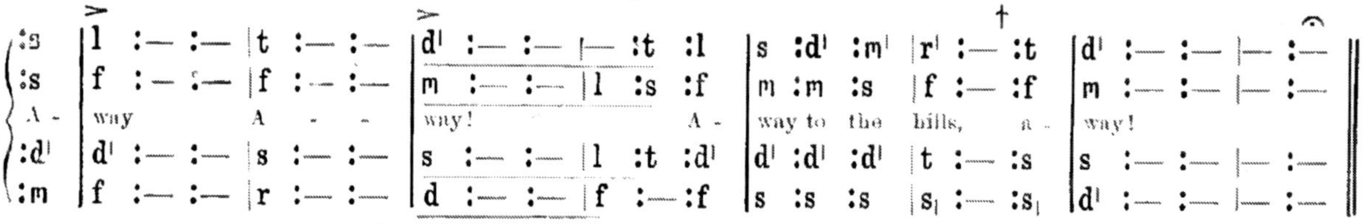
A - way A - - way! A - way to the hills, a - way!

THE SONG OF THE OLD BELL.

307. Key B♭. *With steady movement.*

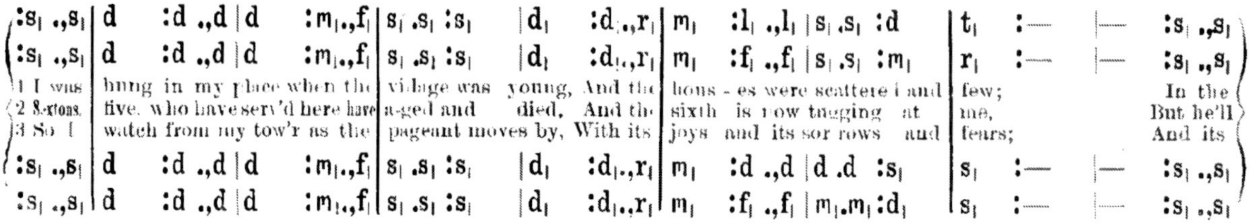
1 I was hung in my place when the village was young, And the hous - es were scattered and few; In the
2 Sextons five, who have serv'd here have a-ged and died, And the sixth is now tugging at me, But he'll
3 So I watch from my tow'r as the pageant moves by, With its joys and its sor rows and tears; And its

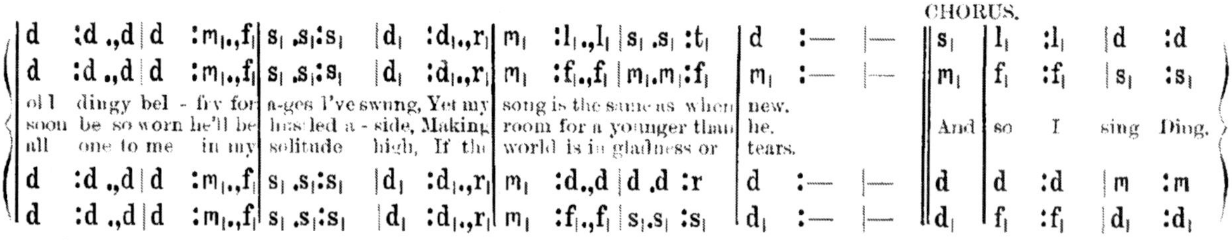
CHORUS.
old dingy bel - fry for a-ges I've swung, Yet my song is the same as when new.
soon be so worn he'll be his led a - side, Making room for a younger than he.
all one to me in my solitude high, If the world is in gladness or tears.
And so I sing Ding,

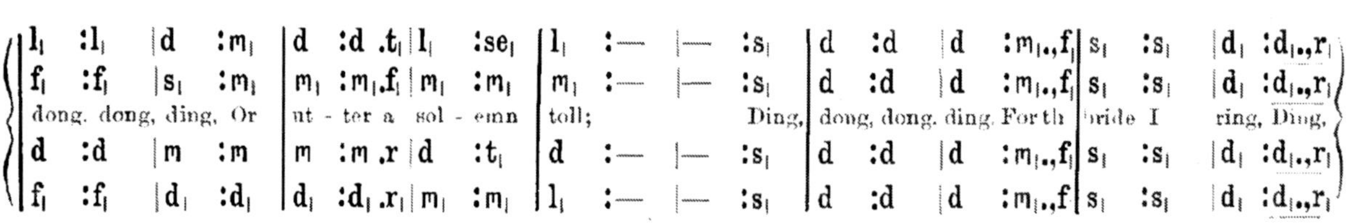
dong, dong, ding, Or ut - ter a sol - emn toll; Ding, dong, dong, ding, For the bride I ring, Ding,

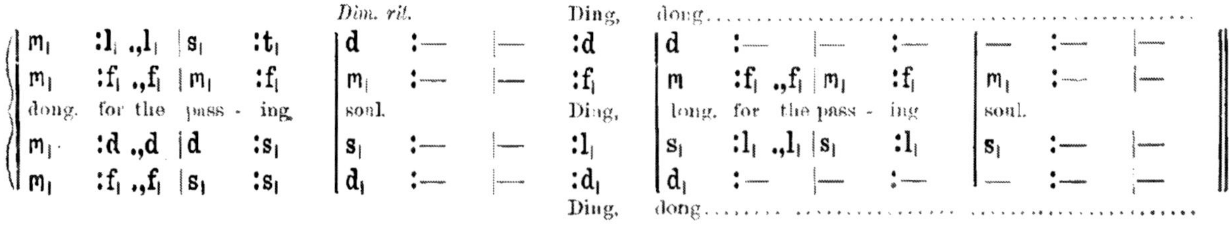
Dim. rit.
Ding, dong
dong, for the pass - ing soul. Ding, long, for the pass - ing soul.
Ding, dong

Transitional Modulation.

308. KEY F. (*First Sharp minor*) **C.t** *Lah is A*   **f F.**

| m :r | d :m | s :f | m :— | ᵐl₁ :se₁ | l₁ :l₁.t₁ | d :t₁ | l₁ :— | ᵗᵐm :m | f :m.r | d :t₁ | d :— |
| | | | | m ·re | m .m.fe | s :fe | m :— | | | | |

309. KEY F. (*First Flat minor.*) f **B♭.** *Lah is G.*   **F.t.**

| m :r | d :m | s :f | m :— | ʳl₁ :se₁ | l₁ :l₁.t₁ | d :t₁ | l₁ :— | ᵗᵐm :m | f :m.r | d :t₁ | d :— |
| | | | | r de | r .r.m | f :m | m :— | | | | |

310. KEY G. (*First Flat minor*)   f **C.** *Lah is A*

| d 's₁ | l₁ :s₁ | d :r | m :— | ʳl :t | d¹ :t | l :se | l :— |
| | | | | r .m | f :m | r :de | l :— |

G.t

| ʳr :r | m :r | d :t₁ | d :s₁ | l₁ :t₁ | d :f | m :r | d :— |

311. KEY G. (*First Sharp minor.*)   **D.t** *Lah is B*

| d :s₁ | l₁ :s₁ | d :r | m :— | ᵐl :t | d¹ :t | l :se | l :— |
| | | | | m :fe | s fe | m :re | m :— |

f G.

| ˢr :r | m :r | d :t₁ | d :s₁ | l₁ :t₁ | d :f | m :r | d :— |

312. KEY G. (*First Flat minor*)

| 'd :— :d | 's₁ :— :d | t₁ :l₁ :t₁ | d :— : | d :— :m | s :— :m | f .:m :r | d :— : |

f C. *Lah is A*

| ʳl :— :t | d¹ :— :l | se :ba :se | l :— : | ·r :— :m | r :— :d | t₁ :l₁ :t₁ | d :— : |
| r :— m | f — r | de .t₁ ·de | r ·— : | | | | |

313. KEY G. (*First Sharp minor*)

| d :— :d | s₁ :— :d | t₁ :l₁ :t₁ | d :— : | d :— :m | s :— :m | f :m :r | d :— : |

D.t *Lah is B*   **f G.**

| ᵐl :— :t | d¹ :— :l | se :ba :se | l :— : | ˢr :— :m | r :— :d | t₁ :l₁ :t₁ | d :— : |
| m :— :fe | s :— :m | re :de :re | m :— : | | | | |

GRACE CHURCH.

314. KEY **G.** Extended Transitional Modulation to First Flat minor.

PLEYEL, arr.

| m :— :r | d :— :t₁ | d :— :r | m :— :— | s :— :f | m :— :r | d :— :t₁ | d :— :— |
| d :— :l₁ | s₁ :— :f₁ | m₁ :fe₁ :s₁ | s₁ :— :— | d :— :t₁ | d :— :l₁ | s₁ :— :s₁ | s₁ :— :— |

1. Depth of mer - cy! can there be grace, Mer - cy still re - served for me?
2. I have long with - stood His grace, Long pro - voked Him to His face;
3. Now in - cline me to re - pent! Let me now my fall la - ment!

| s :— :f | m :— :r | d :— :t₁ | d :— :— | s :— :s | s :— :f | m :— :r | m :— :— |
| d :— :f₁ | s₁ :— :s₁ | l₁ :— :s₁ | d :— :— | m :— :r | d :— :f₁ | s₁ :— :s₁ | d :— :— |

f **C.** *Lah is A.*

| rl :— :t | d¹ :— :t | l :— :se | l :— :— | ᵈf :— :m | l :— :s | f :m :r | d :— :— |
| l₁ m :— :r | m :— :f | m :— :r | d :— :— | ʳs₁ :— :d | d :— :d | r :d :t₁ | d :— :— |

Can my God His wrath for - bear? Me. the chief of sin - ners spare?
Would not heark - en to His calls; Would grieved Him by a thous - and falls.
Now my foul re - volt de - plore! Weep, be - lieve, and sin no more

| rl :— :se | l :m¹ :r¹ | d¹ :— :t | l :— :— | ʳr :— :s | f :— :s | l :s :f | m :— :— |
| f₁d :— :t₁ | l₁ :— :r | m :— :m | l :— :— | ꜰᵉt₁ :— :d | f₁ :— :m₁ | f₁ :s₁ :s₁ | d₁ :— :— |

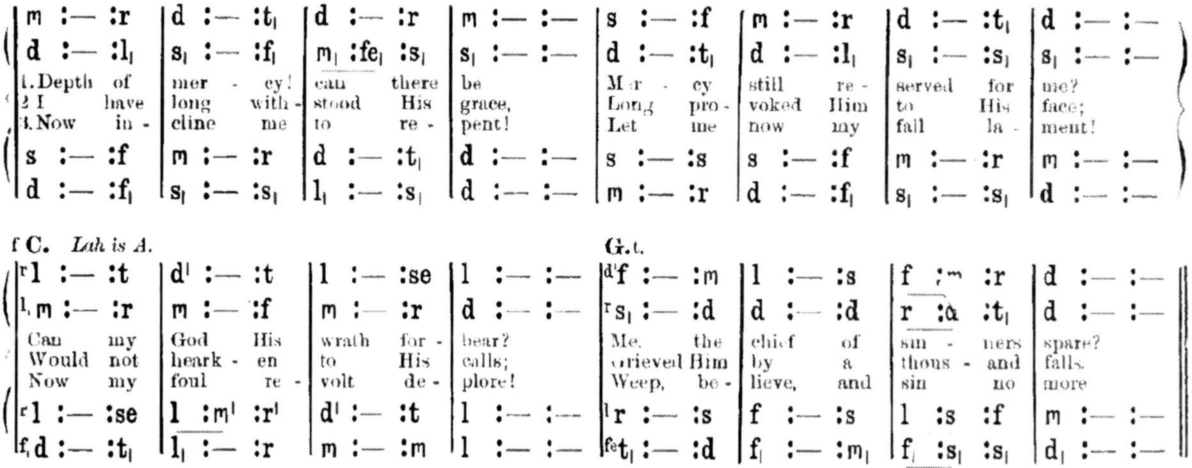

O PARADISE!

315. KEY **E♭.** Extended Transitional Modulation to First Sharp minor.

JOSEPH BARNBY.

| :m | f :—.m|m :m | s :—.f|f :m | r :d |r :f | m :— |— :m|l₁ | l₁ :—.l₁|se₁ :l₁ |
| :d | d :—.d|d :d | d :—.d|d :d | t₁ :d |d :t₁ | d :— |— :l.r₁ | m₁ :—.m₁|m₁ :m₁ |

1. O Par - a - dise! O Par - a - dise! Who dot not crave for rest? Who would not seek the
2. O Par - a - dise! O Par - a - dise! We're look - ing, wait - ing here; We long to be where

| :s | l :—.s|s :d¹ | t :—.l|l :s | f :m |l :s | s :— |— :fet₁ | d :—.d|t₁ :d |
| :d | d :—.d|d :d | d :—.d|d :d | s₁ :l₁ |f₁ :s₁ | d :— |— :df₁ | m₁ :—.m₁|m₁ :l₁ |

f **E♭.** Where loy - al hearts and true, **B♭ t.**

| t₁ :—.t₁|l₁ :d | d :l₁ |t₁ :r | ᵈs :— |— :s | d¹ :s |t :l | s :— |— :ˢd | t₁ :r |
| m₁ :—.m₁|m₁ :fe₁ | s₁ :m₁ |f₁ :f₁ | ᵐt₁ :— |— :t₁ | d :— |t₁ :d | r :t₁ |d :ˢd₁ | f₁ :f₁ |

hap - py land Where they that loved, are b'est? Where loy - al hearts and true Stand ev - er
Je - sus is, To feel, and see Him near.

| r :—.r |d :r | m :d |r :t₁ | ᵈs :— |— :s | s :— |f :— | f :f |m :m₁ | l₁ :l₁ |
| se₁ :—.se₁|l₁ :l₁ | s₁ :s₁ |s₁ :s₁ | ᵈs :— |— :f | m :— |r :d | t₁ :s₁ |d :t.m₁ | r₁ :t₁ |

f **E♭.**

| d :t₁ | ᵈs :— |s :— | d¹ :m |t :l | s :m |d :f | r :— |— :r | d :— |— :— |
| m₁ :m₁ | ᵐt₁ :— |t₁ :— | d :d |d :d | t₁ :t₁ |d :d | d :— |t₁ :— | d :— |— :— |

in the light, All rapt-ure through and thro'. In Gods's most ho - ly sight.

| se₁ :r | ᵈs :— |f :— | m :s |s :f | r :s |m :f | s :r |f :— | m :— |— :— |
| m₁ :m₁ | l.m :— |r :— | d :d |f₁ :f₁ | s₁ :s₁ |l₁ :r | s₁ :— |s₁ :— | d :— |— :— |

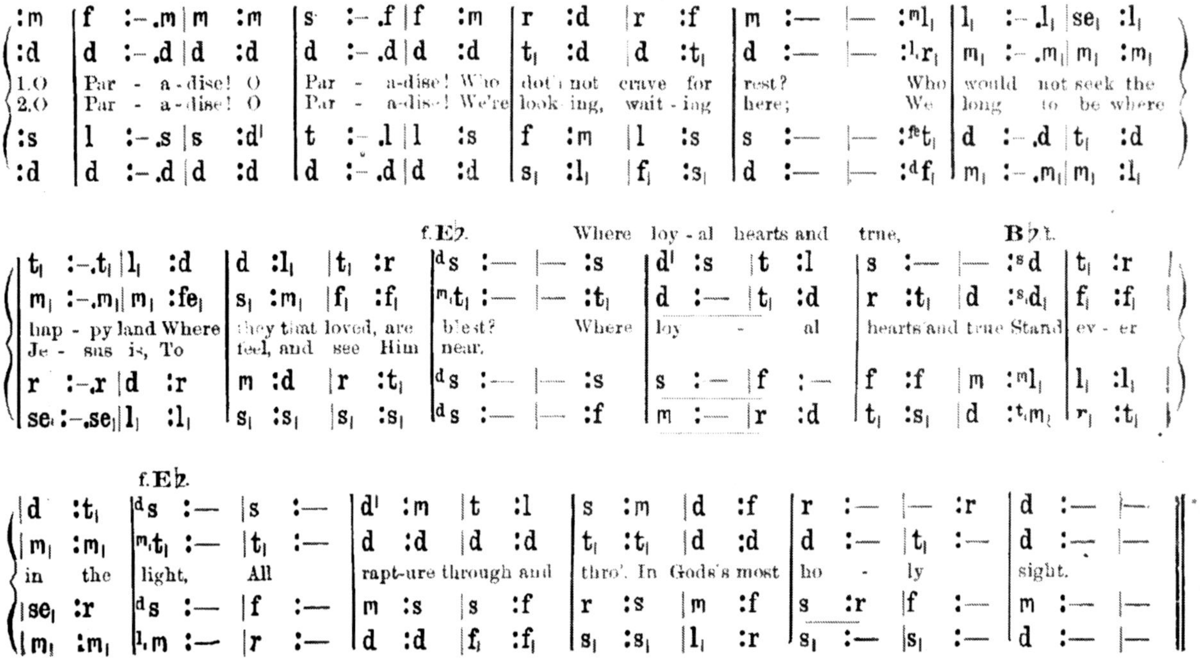

EVENTIDE.

316. KEY E♭. Cadence Transitional Modulation to First Flat minor. W. H. MONK.

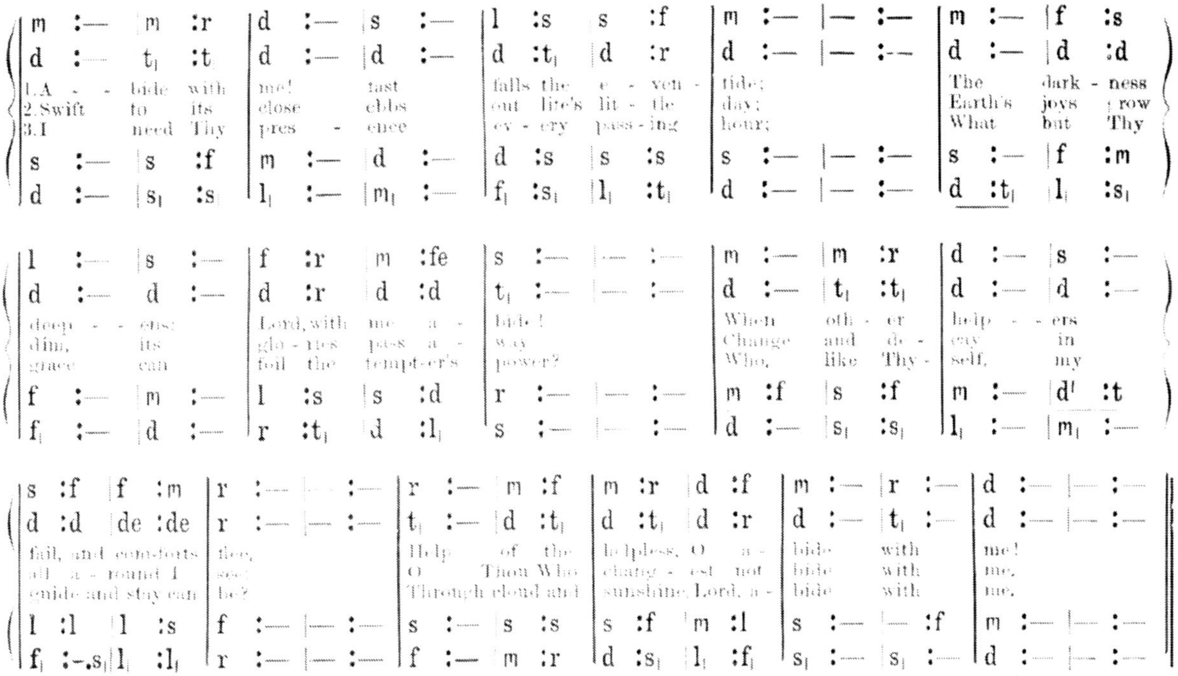
1. Abide with me! fast falls the eventide; The darkness
2. Swift to its close ebbs out life's little day; Earth's joys grow
3. I need Thy presence every passing hour; What but Thy
deepens; Lord, with me abide! When other helpers
dim, its glories pass away; Change and decay in
grace can foil the tempter's power? Who, like Thyself, my
fail, and comforts flee, Help of the helpless, O abide with me!
all around I see; O Thou Who changest not, abide with me.
guide and stay can be? Through cloud and sunshine, Lord, abide with me.

ST. CECILIA.

317. KEY E. Passing Transitional Modulation to First Flat minor. R. R. CHOPE.

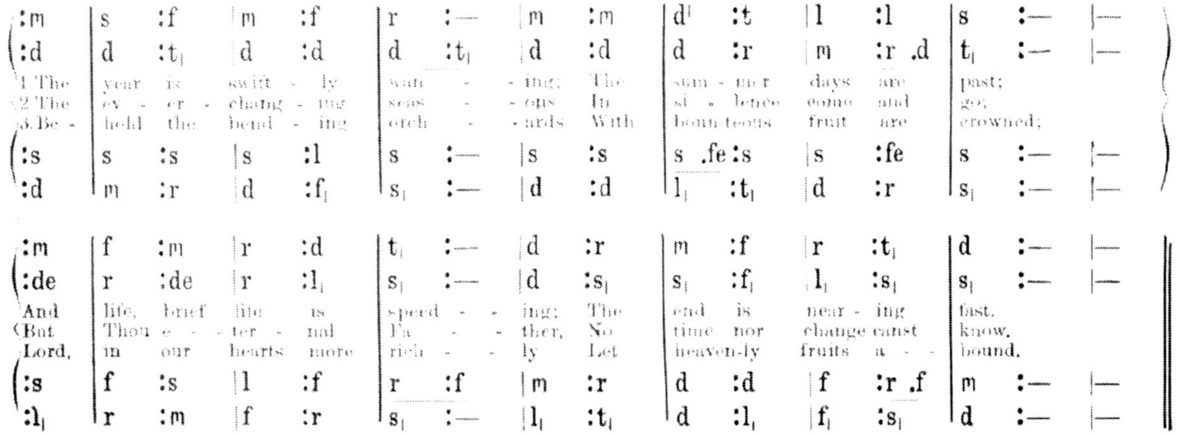
1 The year is swiftly waning; The summer days are past;
2 The ever-changing seasons In silence come and go;
3. Behold the bending orchards With bounteous fruit are crowned;
And life, brief life is speeding; The end is nearing fast.
But Thou eternal Father, No time nor change canst know.
Lord, in our hearts more richly Let heavenly fruits abound.

IN THE HOUR OF TRIAL.

318. KEY F. J. B. DYKES.

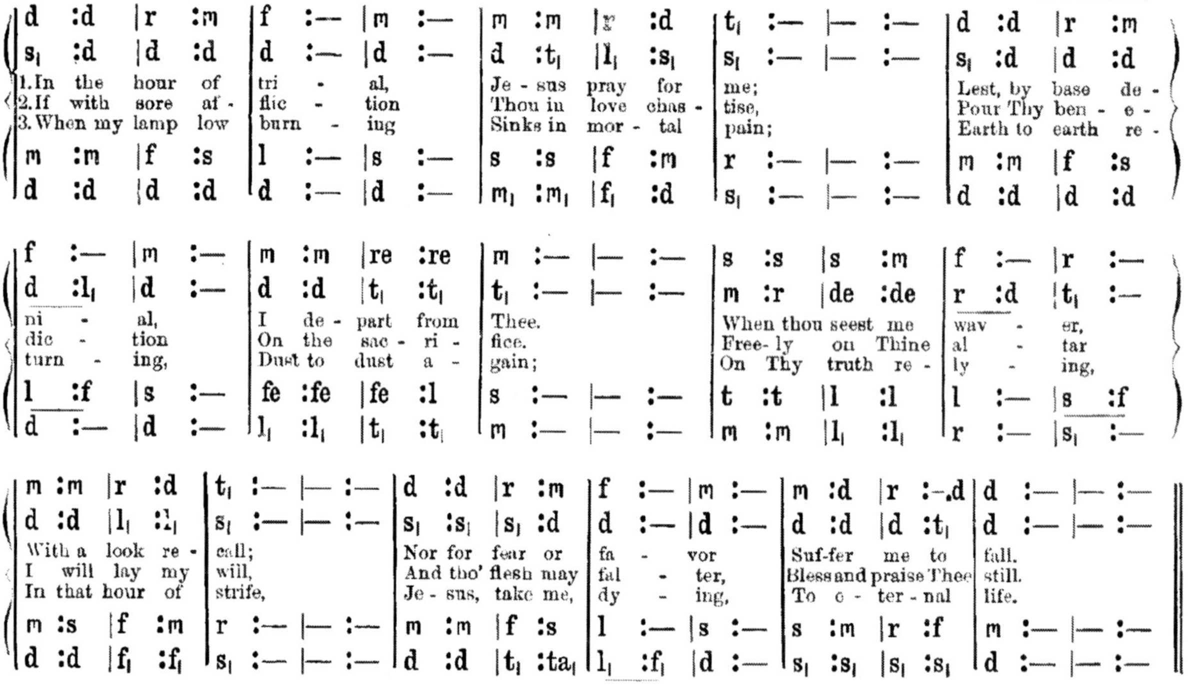
1. In the hour of tri - al, Je - sus pray for me; Lest, by base de - ni - al, I de - part from Thee. When thou seest me wav - er, With a look re - call; Nor for fear or fa - vor Suf-fer me to fall.
2. If with sore af - flic - tion Thou in love chas - tise, Pour Thy ben - e - dic - tion On the sac - ri - fice. Free - ly on Thine al - tar I will lay my will, And tho' flesh may fal - ter, Bless and praise Thee still.
3. When my lamp low burn - ing Sinks in mor - tal pain; Earth to earth re - turn - ing, Dust to dust a - gain; On Thy truth re - ly - ing, In that hour of strife, Je - sus, take me, dy - ing, To e - ter - nal life.

BATTISHILL.

319. KEY G. Cadence Transitional modulation to First Flat minor.

1. Children of the heaven-ly King, As we jour - ney, let us sing: Sing our Sav - iour's wor - thy praise, Glo-rious in His works and ways.
2. We are trav' - ling home to God, In the way our fa - thers trod; They are hap - py now, and we Soon their hap - pi - ness shall see.
3. Lord! o - be - dient - ly we'll go, Glad - ly leav - ing all be - low: On - ly Thou our lead - er be, And we still will fol - low Thee.

DEXTER SMITH.

BROKEN THREADS.

WM. MASON, Mus. Doc., by per.

320. KEY E♭.   B♭. t, *Lah is G.*

```
| d  :d   | d .t₁:l₁ .t₁ | d  :d  | r  :—  | ᵐl₁ :l₁  | l₁ .se₁:ba₁.se₁ | l₁ :l₁ | t₁ :—  |
| s₁ :s₁  | s₁ :s₁      | s₁ :   | :      | ˢd₁ :f₁  | m₁ :m₁          | m₁ :m₁ | m₁ :   |
```

1. As the shut - tle swift - ly flies   Back and forth be - fore our eyes,
2. Weav-ing ev - - er day by day,   As the shut - tles brisk - ly play,
3. Weav-ing in life's bus - y loom,   Ming-ling sun - shine with the gloom.
4. Bro - ken threads in life a - bound,   In each sta - tion they are found;

```
| ᵐ :m | r  :r  | m  :m | f  :—  | ᵐl₁ :r | t₁ :t₁ | d  :d | r  :—          |
| d  :s₁ | r  :s₁ | d  :s₁ | d .t₁:l₁ .t₁ | ᵈf₁ :r₁ | m₁ :m₁ | l₁ :m₁ | l₁ .se₁:ba₁.se₁ |
```

f.E♭.

```
| d :d | d .r :m.f | m :r | d :— | ᵗᵃf :f | f .m :r .d | r :r | s :— | f :f | f .m :r .d |
| m₁ :ta₁ | l₁ :l₁ | s₁ :f₁ | m₁ :— | ˢr :t₁ | d :s₁ | d .t₁:l₁.t₁| d :r .m | r :r | d :s₁ |
```

Blending with its fin-gers light.   Warp and woof, till they u - nite   In a fa - bric
Bro-ken threads how oft an - noy.   And our pre - cious time em - ploy;   Warning us by
Warp and woof of deeds we blend,   Till life's fa - bric has an end;   Bro-ken threads we
May Faith's kind and friend-ly hand,   Help us to ad - just the strand;   That, when life's last

```
| d :r .m | f :d | d .t₁:l₁ .t₁| d :— | ᵈs :s | s :s | s :s | s :— | s :l .t | d¹ :s .d¹|
| l₁ :s₁ | f₁ :f₁ | s₁ :s₂ | d₁ :— | ᵐt₁ :s₁ | d :m | s :f | f .m :r .d | t₁ :s₁ | d :m |
```

```
| r :r | s :l .t | d¹ :—.t l .s :f.m | m.r :m.f | s :l .t | d¹ :—.t l .s :f.m | m :r | d :— |
| s₁ :s₁ | s₁ :f | m.d :r .m f .m:r .d | d.t₁:d r | m :f | m.d:r .m f .m:r .d | d :t₁ | d :— |
```

good and strong,   Let us hear the weav-er's song,   Let us hear the weav-er's song.
warp re - proof,   We must watch the warp and woof,   We must watch the warp and woof.
oft - en bind,   Bur - den - ing the no - ble mind,   Bur - den - ing the no - ble mind.
life shall ebb,   There shall be a per - fect web,   There shall be a per - fect web.

```
| d¹ .t:l .t | d¹ :s | s .m:f .s | l :l | s :s | s :— | s .m:f .s | f :l | s :f | m :— |
| s :f | m :r | d :—.d f :f | s :f | m :r | d :—.d | f₁ :f₁ | s₁ :s₁ | d :— |
```

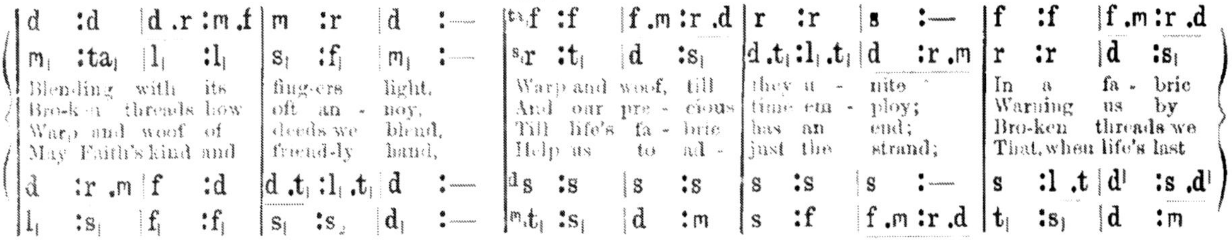

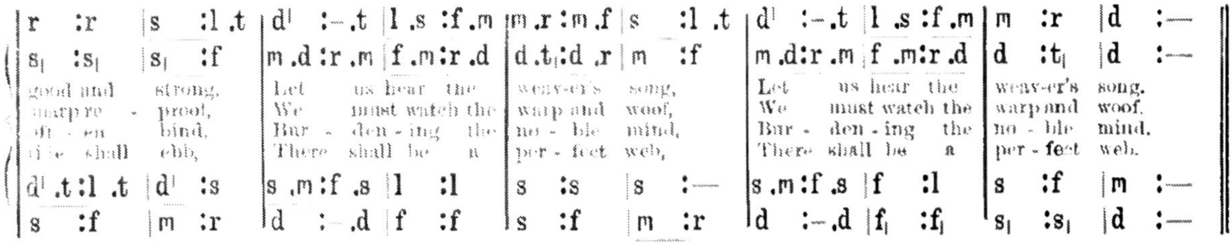

FERNIEHURST. S. M.

321. KEY F. Cadence Transitional modulation to First Sharp minor.

```
| :d | r :m | f :f | m :— | :— | :m | m :m | s :fe | m :— | :— |
| :d | d :d | d :r | d :— | :— | :m | r :d | t₁ :l₁ | s₁ :— | :— |
```

1 Not what these hands have done   Can save this guilt - y soul;
2 Not what I feel or do   Can give me peace with God;
3 Thy work, a - lone, O Christ,   Can ease this weight of sin;

```
| :m | f :s | l :t | d¹ :— | :s | se :l | m :m .re | m :— |
| :d | d :d | d :d | d :— | :d | t₁ :l₁ | t₁ :t₁ | m :— |
```

```
| :m | r :t₁ | d :l | s :f | m :m | m :r | d :r | d :— |
| :t₁ | t₁ :s₁ | s₁ :d | r :t₁ | d :ta₁ | l₁ :l₁ | d :t₁ | d :— |
```

Not what this toil - ing flesh has borne, Can make my spir - it whole.
Not all my pray'rs, and sighs, and tears, Can bear my aw - ful load.
Thy blood a - lone, O Lamb of God, Can give me peace with - in.

```
| :s | s :f | m :m | s :s | s :s | s :f | m :f | m :— |
| :m | f :r | m :l₁ | t₁ :r | d :de | r :r | s₁ :s₁ | d :— |
```

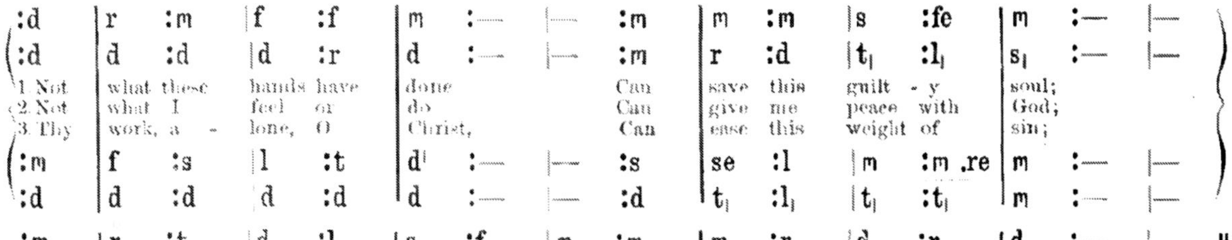

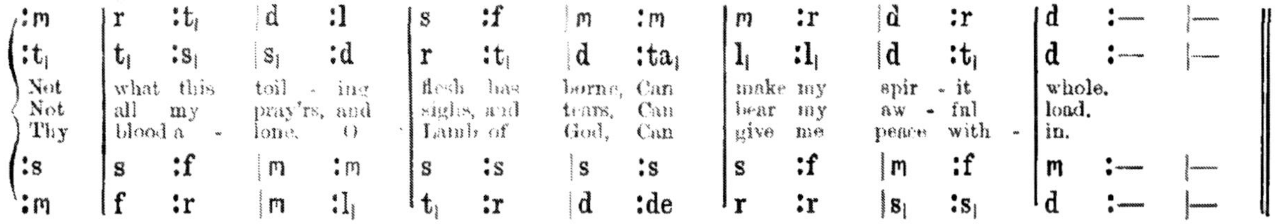

THE HOMELAND.

322. KEY E♭. A. S. SULLIVAN.

1. The Homeland! O the Home - land! The land of souls free - born! No gloomy night is known there, But aye the fade - less morn; I'm sigh - ing for that coun - try, My heart is ach - ing here; There is no pain in the Home - land To which I'm drawing near.
2. My Lord is in the Home - land, With an - gels bright and fair; No sin - ful thing nor e - vil Can ev - er en - ter there; The mu - sic of the ran - somed Is ring - ing in my ears, And when I think of the Home - land My eyes are wet with tears.
3. For loved ones in the Home - land, Are wait-ing to come Where nei-ther death nor sor - row In - vade their ho - ly home: O dear, dear na - tive coun - try! O rest and peace a - bove! Christ bring us all to the Home - land Of His e - tern - al love.

PETROX.

323. KEY E♭. "Passing" Transitional Modulation to First Flat minor. W. BOYD.

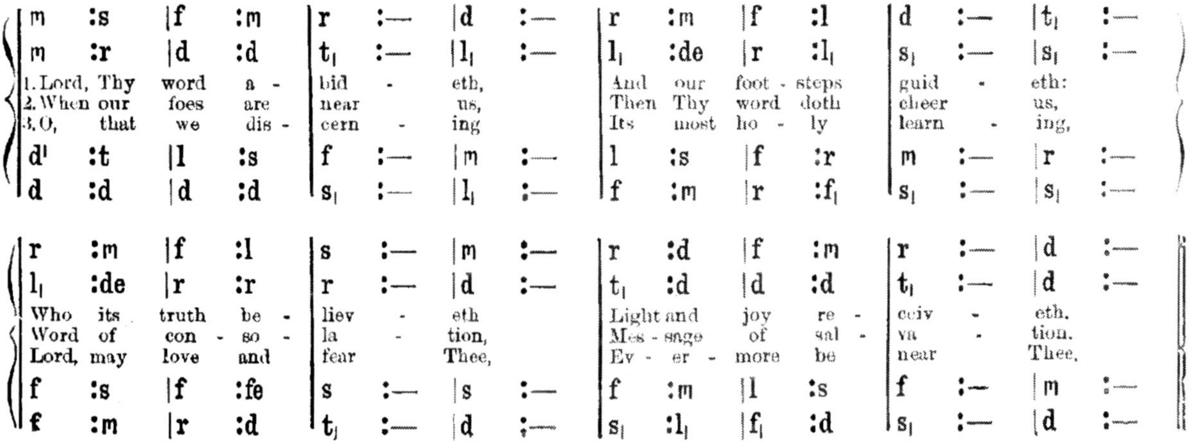
1. Lord, Thy word a - bid - eth, And our foot - steps guid - eth: Who its truth be - liev - eth Light and joy re - ceiv - eth.
2. When our foes are near us, Then Thy word doth cheer us, Word of con - so - la - tion, Mes - sage of sal - va - tion,
3. O, that we dis - cern - ing Its most ho - ly learn - ing, Lord, may love and fear Thee, Ev - er - more be near Thee.

THE LAST SLEEP.

324. KEY D. Transitional Modulation, sharp and flat. J. BARNBY.

1. Sleep thy last sleep, Free from care and sorrow; Rest, where none weep, Till the eternal morrow; Though dark waves roll O'er the silent river, Thy fainting soul Jesus can deliver.
2. Life's dream is past, All its sin, its sadness; Brightly at last Dawns a day of gladness. Under thy sod, Earth receive our treasure, To rest in God, Waiting all His pleasure.
3. Though we may mourn Those in life the dearest, They shall return, Christ, when Thou appearest! Soon shall Thy voice Comfort those now weeping, Bidding rejoice All in Jesus sleeping.

ESTHER.

325. KEY D♭. Transitional Modulation, Sharp Cadence, Flat "passing." J. BARNBY.

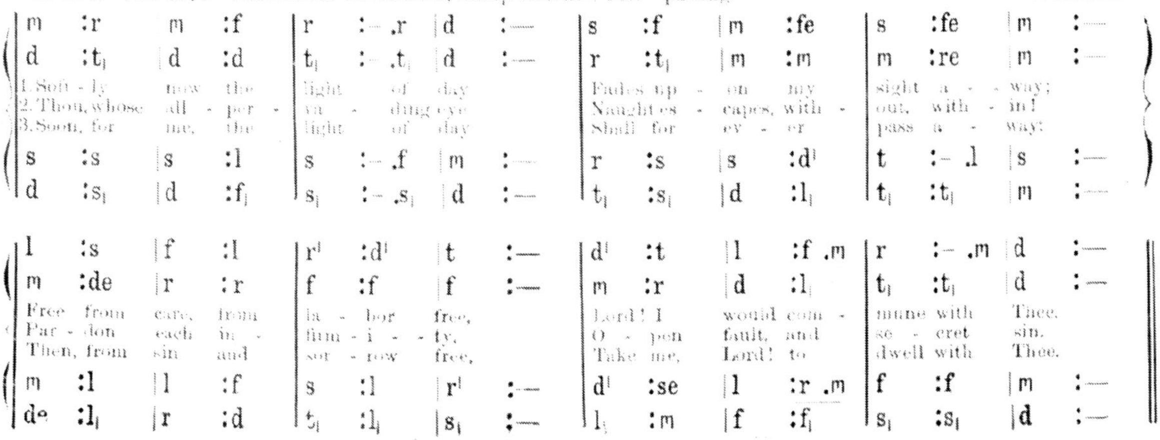
1. Softly now the light of day Fades upon my sight away; Free from care, from labor free, Lord! I would commune with Thee.
2. Thou, whose all-pervading eye Naught escapes, without, within! Pardon each infirmity, Open fault, and secret sin.
3. Soon, for me, the light of day Shall for ever pass away; Then, from sin and sorrow free, Take me, Lord! to dwell with Thee.

SING YE JEHOVAH'S PRAISES.

326. KEY G. *Allegretto.* T. F. SEWARD, by per.

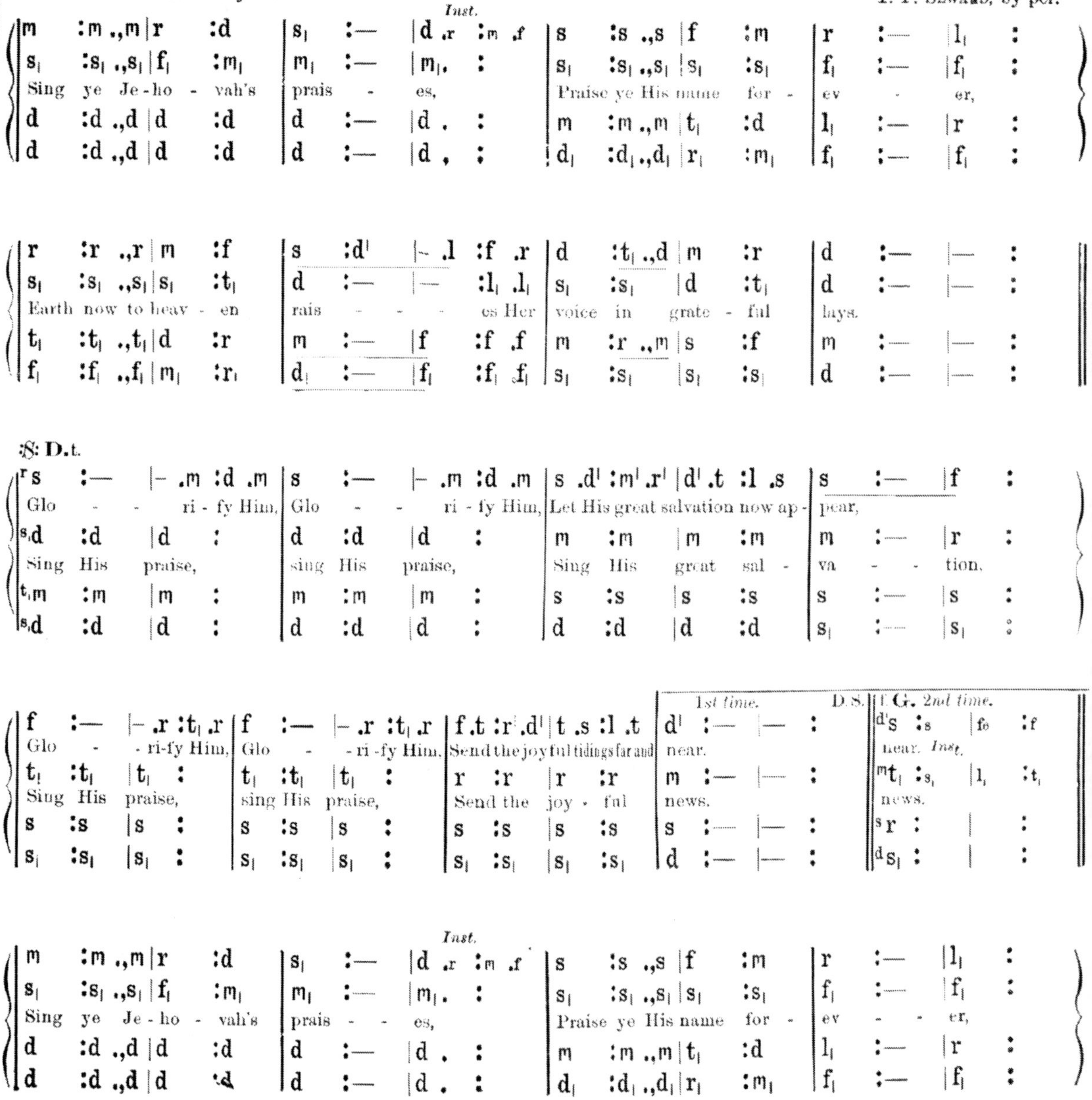
Inst.
Sing ye Je-ho - vah's prais - es,
Praise ye His name for - ev - er,
Earth now to heav - en rais - es Her voice in grate - ful lays.
D.t.
Glo - ri - fy Him, Glo - ri - fy Him, Let His great salvation now ap - pear,
Sing His praise, sing His praise, Sing His great sal - va - tion.
Glo - ri-fy Him, Glo - ri-fy Him, Send the joyful tidings far and near.
Sing His praise, sing His praise, Send the joy - ful news.
1st time. D.S.
f. G. 2nd time.
near. Inst.
news.
Inst.
Sing ye Je - ho - vah's prais - es,
Praise ye His name for - ev - er,

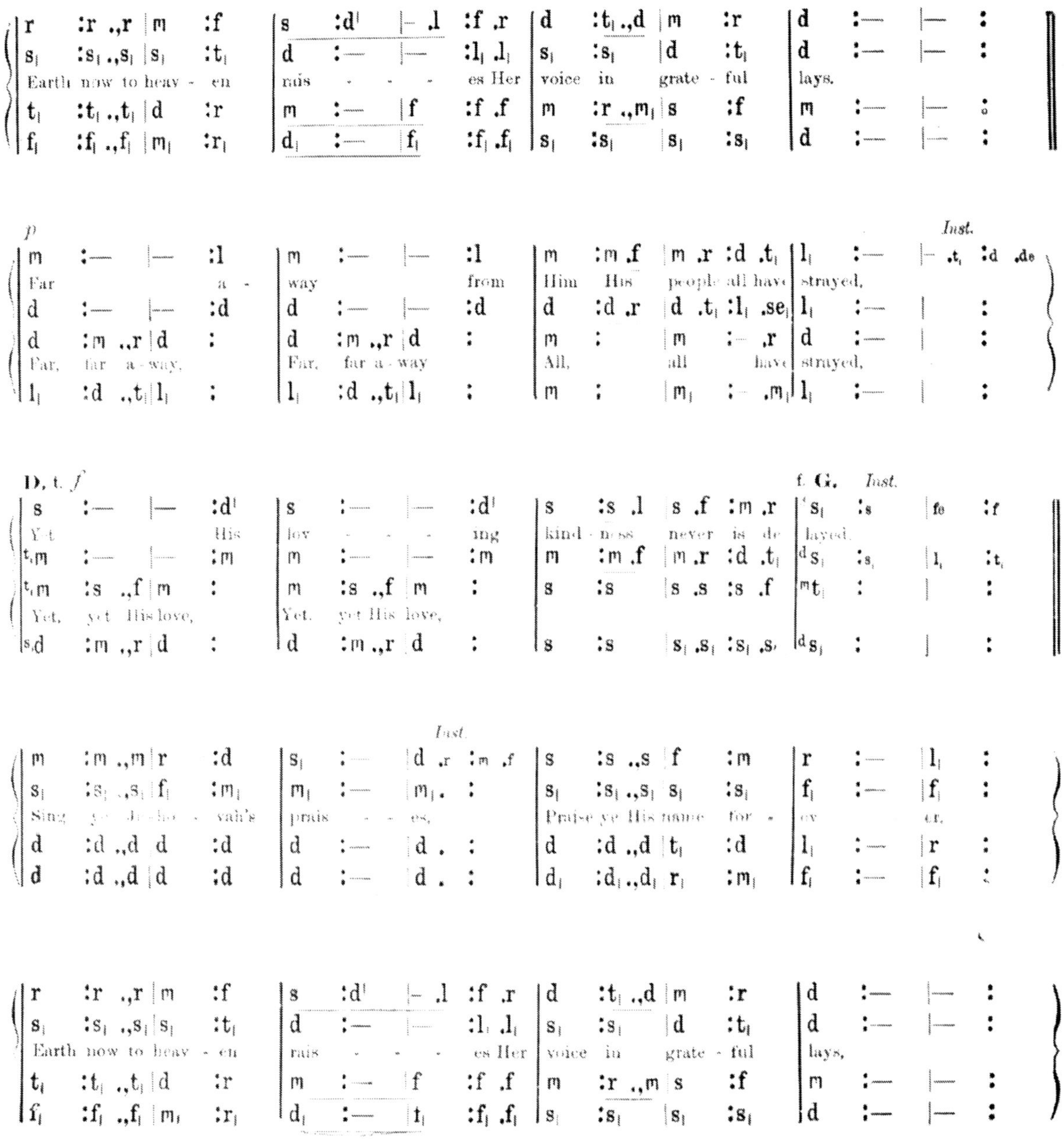
Earth now to heav - en rais - - - es Her voice in grate - ful lays.
Far a - way from Him His people all have strayed,
Far, far a - way, Far, far a - way All, all have strayed,
Yet His lov - - - ing kind - ness never is de - layed.
Yet, yet His love, Yet, yet His love,
Inst.
Sing ye Je - ho - vah's prais - - - es,
Praise ye His name for - ev - er.
Earth now to heav - en rais - - - es Her voice in grate - ful lays,

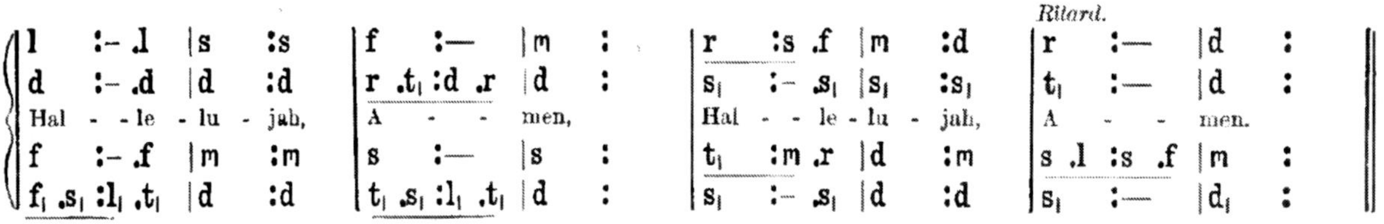
Ritard.
Hal - - le - lu - jah, A - - men, Hal - - le - lu - jah, A - - men.

THE KING AND THE MILLER.

327. KEY C. *Lah is A* U.

1. There dwelt a mil - ler hale and bold, Be - side the riv - - er Dee;
He worked and sang from morn till night, No lark more blithe than he;
And this the bur - - den of his song For ev - er used to be;
"I en - - vy no one— no, not I! And no one en - - vies me!"
2. "Thou'rt wrong, my friend," said old king Hal, "As wrong as wrong can be;
For could my heart be light as thine, I'd glad - ly change with thee.
And tell me now, what makes thee sing With voice so loud and free,
While I am sad, tho' I'm the king, Be - side the riv - - er Dee?
3. The mil - - ler smiled and doffed his cap— "I earn my bread," quoth he;
"I love my wife, I love my friend, I love my chil - dren three.
I owe no one I can - not pay, I thank the riv - er Dee,
That turns the mill that grinds the corn To feed my babes and me!"
4. "Good friend," said Hal, and sighed the while, "Fare-well, and hap - py be;
But say no more, if thou'dst be true, That no one en - - vies thee;
Thy meal - y cap is worth my crown; Thy mill my king - dom's fee,
Such men as thou are Eng - land's boast, O mil - ler of the Dee!"

QUESTIONS FOR WRITTEN OR ORAL EXAMINATION.

DOCTRINE

1. What tone has, thus far, been the key tone, or point of whose?

2. Must *Doh* always be taken as the key tone, or may any other tone be made to predominate in a tune?

3. What is meant by the *Ray Mode*?

4. What is meant by the *Lah Mode*?

5. What are the general mental effects of the *Ray* and *Lah Modes*?

6. What is the mental effect of the *Doh Mode*?

7. What is the *Doh Mode* commonly called?

8. What are the *Ray* and *Lah Modes* called?

9. What is the distinguishing interval of the Major Mode? The Minor Mode?

10. Which of the Minor Modes is the most used at the present day?

11. What is required to give *Lah* the importance of a key tone?

12. What does the introduction of *Se* create?

13. How is this avoided?

14. What is the *Lah Mode* modified by these new tones called?

15. What is the essential Seventh of the Modern Minor? The occasional Seventh?

16. What is the essential Sixth? The occasional Sixth?

17. What is a change of Mode called?

18. What is the change from the Major to the Minor mode of the same key called? From the Minor to the Major?

19. What is the mental effect of a modulation into the Relative Minor? Into the Major?

20. What is a change of both key and mode called?

21. What is the commonest form of this change?

22. What is another, though less frequent Transitional Modulation?

PRACTICE.

23. Draw from memory a modulator illustrating the Minor Mode.

24. Imitate in the Minor Mode any Major phrases sung or played by the Examiner but none more difficult than Nos. 284 to 293.

25. Pitch from the tuning fork the *Lah* of key D, G, E♭, A.

26. Follow the Examiner's pointing in a voluntary containing all the tones of the Modern Minor, including also modulations to the Relative Minor and Transitional modulations to the First Flat and First Sharp Minor.

27. Point and sol fa on the modulator any one of the following four exercises, 272, 274, 280, 281, chosen by the Examiner.

28. Write from memory any other of these four exercises chosen by the Examiner.

29. Sing at sight sol fa or *laa* any exercises in the Minor Mode not more difficult than these pieces.

SIXTH STEP.

Transitions of more than one remove.

Two Removes.—The transitions used thus far have been transitions of *one remove*—to the First Sharp key or First Flat key—requiring the change of but one tone. But the music often passes into the *Second, Third* and *Fourth* Sharp or Flat keys, requiring the change of two, three and four tones. Transitions to the First Sharp or First Flat keys are called transition of One Remove. Transitions to the Second Sharp or Second Flat keys are called transitions of Two Removes. In two-sharp removes the music is placed one step higher; *fah* and *doh* of the old Key are omitted and two new tones, *me* and *te* are taken instead. Of these two distinguishing tones **t** is the more important because it distinguishes the *second* sharp remove from the first. In the signature this new **t** is placed nearest the key-name; thus—**A.**t.m. In two-flat removes the music is placed one step lower; *te* and *me* of the old key are omitted and *doh* and *fah* of the new key take their places. The new **f** is the more important because it distinguishes the *second* flat remove from the first. In the signature this new **f** is placed nearest the key-name, thus—d.f.**A.** Of the mental effects, transition of two sharp removes is expressive of rising emotion, more intense or more excited feeling. Transition of two flat removes is expressive of falling emotion, more intense seriousness and depression. When the music passes over the first sharp key to the first flat key or *vice versa*—swinging across the modulator—we call this form of two removes "oscillating transition." It is of frequent occurrence and is generally quite easy to sing. This "oscillation" across the original key keeps that key in mind, and lessens the violent effect of the two removes. A transition of two removes from a Principal Key (a principal transition) is seldom used except for imitation and sequence. Such transitions are comparatively easy when the music is exactly imitated in the new key.

Three Removes.—Transitions to the Third Sharp or Third Flat keys are called transitions of Three Removes. Three sharp removes place the new key a Minor Third below, and three flat removes a Minor Third above the old key. In other words, *lah* becomes *doh* and *doh*, becomes *lah*. On account of this relation between the *lah* of one key and the *doh* of the other, transitions of three removes are commonly Transitional *Modulations*. The mental effects are obvious—for a transition of three flat removes and a modulation from major to minor together naturally produce a gloomy depression of feeling; and a transition of three sharp removes and a modulation from minor to major combines to produce a strange kind of excitement. In transitions of three removes three tones of the old key are taken out to give place to the three distinguishing tones of the new key. In three-sharp removes *soh*, *doh* and *fah* of the old key are displaced by *lah*, *me* and *te* of the new key. The **t** is the last new tone required and is placed nearest the key-name in the signature, thus—**A.**t.m.l. In three flat removes the *te*, *me* and *lah* of the old key are displaced by *soh*, *doh* and *fah* of the new key. The **f** is the last new distinguishing tone and is placed nearest the key-name in the signature, thus—s.d.f.**A.** In Transitional Modulations of three removes the similarity of the upper part of the two modes (**m ba se l** and **s l t d'**) assists the ear in passing over from one key into the other, especially if that form of the minor mode containing *ba* is used. The third flat remove is the more difficult to sing, simply because the minor mode into which it enters is itself artificial and difficult. The third sharp remove is the less difficult, because the major mode into which it enters is more natural to the ear.

Four Removes.—Transitions into the Fourth Sharp or Fourth Flat keys are called transitions of Four Removes. Four flat removes place the new key a Major Third below, and four sharp removes a Major Third above the previous key. In other words, *doh* becomes *me*, or *me* becomes *doh*. In four-flat removes the tones of the old key displaced are *te*, *me*, *lah* and *ray*; the distinguishing tones of the new key are *ray*, *soh*, *doh* and *fah*. The new **f**, being the last new flat, is placed nearest the key-name in the signature, thus—r.s.d.f.**A.** In four-sharp removes the tones of the old key displaced are *ray*, *soh*, *doh* and *fah*; the distinguishing tones of the new key are *ray*, *lah*, *me* and *te*. The new **t**, being the last new sharp, is placed nearest the key-name in the signature, thus—**A.**t m.l.r.

Difficult Removes.—All removes beyond the first are difficult to sing without the aid of instruments. The greater the number of changes, the greater is the difficulty of adjusting the ear and mind to the new relations. Of 32 or more possible transitions and transitional modulations only nine or ten are much used. Transitions of the third, fourth and other removes are not much used except in connection with instrumental accompaniment.

Relation of Keys in a Tune.—Every tune has its *Principal Key* (that is, commencing, and closing, and prevailing key). The other keys are called *Subordinate Keys.* Transitions from and to the Principal Key are called Principal Transitions. Transitions between Subordinate Keys are called Subordinate Transitions. In speaking of Subordinate Keys we have to bear in mind not merely their relation of one, two, or three removes (flat or sharp) from the last key heard, but also their more important relation to the Principal Key. Subordinate Keys may be three or four removes from each other, but only one or two from the Principal Key.

MODULATOR, Showing Two Removes.	
r'	d'
de'	t
d'	*ta*
t	l
l	s
s	f
fe	m
f	*ma*
m	r
r	d
de	t,
d	*ta,*
t,	l,

328. KEY C. TWO SHARP REMOVES. D.t.m.

|s :f |m :s |d' :t |l :— |ˡs :f |m :s |d' :t |l :— |

f.G. f.C.

|ˡm :f |m :r |d :t, |d :— |ᵈs :f |m :l |s :t |d' :— ||

329. KEY D. E.t.m.

|d :t, |d :m |s .f :m .r |d :— |ʳd :t, |d :m |s .f :m .r |d :— |

f.A. f.D.

|ᵈs, :l, |s, :d |d .t, :l, .t, |d :s, |ˡm :f |m :r |s .f :m .r |d :— ||

330. KEY F. G.t.m.

|m :s |d .r :m |f :m |r :— |s :r |m .f :s |ˡs :r |m .f :s |

f.C. f.F.

|ᶠd' :s |l .t :d' |r' :r' |d' :— |ᵈs :m |r .m :f |m :r |d :— ||

331. KEY G. A.t.m.

|s, :l, .t, |d :t, .d |m .r :d .t, |d :— |ˡs, :l, .t, |d :t, .d |m .r :d .t, |d :— |

f.D. f.G.

|ˡm :s |f .m :r |r :f |m .r :d |ᵈs, :l, .t, |d :t, .d |m .r :d .t, |d :— ||

332. KEY E♭. F.t.m.

|d :m |r :f |m .s :f .m |r :— |ʳd :m |r :f |m .s :f .m |r :— |

f.B♭. f.E♭.

|ʳl, :l, |t, :l, .t, |d :l, |s, :— |ˢd :m |r :m .f |s .f :m .r |d :— ||

333. KEY D. TWO FLAT REMOVES. d.t.C.

| s :l | s .f :m .r | d :r | m :— | ^{f}s :l | s .f :m .r | d :r | m :— |

G.t. D.t.

| ^{m}l$_1$:l$_1$ | s$_1$:d | d .t$_1$:d .r | m :— | ^{m}l :l | s :m | s .f :m .r | d :— ||

334. KEY G. d.f.F.

| m :r | d :s$_1$ | l$_1$ .s$_1$:l$_1$ .t$_1$ | d :— | ^{r}m :r | d :s$_1$ | l$_1$ .s$_1$:l$_1$ .t$_1$ | d :— |

C.t. G.t.

| ^{t_1}m :f | s :m | f .s :l .t | d^1 :— | ^{t}m :f | m :r | d .s$_1$:l$_1$ .t$_1$ | d :— ||

335. KEY C. *Subordinate, sharp.* f.F.

| s :m | d^1 :t | l :d^1 | s :— | ^{s}r :m | f :r | d :r | m :— |

G.t.m. f.C.

| ^{m}r :m | f :r | d :r | m :— | ^{m}t :t | d^1 :s | l :t | d^1 :— ||

336. KEY C. *Subordinate, flat.* G.t.

| s :f | m :s | d^1 :t .,| l :— | ^{l}r :m | f :r | d :t$_1$ | d :— |

d.f.F. f.C.

| ^{d}r :m | f :r | d :t$_1$ | d :— | ^{d}f :f | m :s | l :t | d^1 :— ||

337 KEY B♭. F.t. d.f.E♭.

:s$_1$ | d :t$_1$ | d :s$_1$ | l$_1$:s$_1$ | d :^{t_1}m | s :m | f :r | d :— | — :^{d}r | s :r | m :f |

F.t.m. f.B♭.

| f :m | m :^{m}r | s :r | m :f | f :m | m :^{m}t$_1$ | d :s$_1$ | l$_1$:t$_1$ | d :— | — ||

338. KEY E♭. F.t.m. G.t.m. A.t.m.

| r :f | m :r | d :r | m :— | ^{m}r :f | m :r | d :r | m :— | ^{m}r :f | m :r | d :r | m :— | ^{m}r :f | m :r |

d.f.G. d.f.F. d.f.E♭.

| d :t$_1$ | d :— | ^{d}r :f | m :r | d :t$_1$ | d :— | ^{d}r :f | m :r | d :t$_1$ | d :— | ^{d}r :f | m :r | d :t$_1$ | d :— ||

CORONA.

339. Key F.

C.t.　H. J. GAUNTLETT.

```
:s₁ |m :-.m |r :d |s :— |— :s₁ |f :.f |m :r |m :— |— :m| |s :l |s :d¹
:s₁ |m :-.m |r :d |s :— |— :s₁ |f :.f |m :r |m :— |— :ᵈf |s :r |s :m
```

1.Thou art gone up on high To mans-ions in the skies; And round Thy throne un-
2 Thou art gone up on high: But Thou didst first come down, Through earth's most bit - ter
3 Thou art gone up on high: But Then shalt come a - gain, With all the bright ones

```
:s₁ |m :-.m |r :d |s :— |— :s₁ |f :.f |m :r |m :— |— :s d¹ |d¹ :t |d¹ :d¹
:s₁ |m :-.m |r :d |s :— |— :s₁ |f :.f |m :r |m :— |— :ᵈf |m :f |m :d
```

d.f B♭

```
d¹ :r¹ |r¹ :s |m¹ :-.m¹ |m¹ :r¹ |d¹ :— |— :l t₁ |m :r |d :t₁ |t₁ :— |— :t₁
m :fe |s :s |s :.fe |s :f |m :— |— :s l₁ |se₁ :-.se₁|l₁ :l₁ |se₁ :— |— :m₁
```

ceas-ing - ly The songs of praise a - rise. But we are ling'-ring here With
ng - o - ny To pass un-to Thy crown. And out with griefs and tears Our
of the sky At - tend - ant in Thy train O by Thy sav - ing power So

```
d¹ :d¹ |t :t |d¹ :.d¹ |d¹ :t |d¹ :— |— :ᵈr |r :.t₁ |m :r |m :— |— :r
l :l |s :s |d¹ :.l |s :s₁ |d :— |— :ᵐᵃf₁ |m₁ :-.m₁|m₁ :f₁ |m₁ :— |— :se₁
```

F.t

```
d :.t₁ |l₁ :s₁ |ᶠᵗt₁ :r |t₁ :s₁ |m :-.d |f :r |s :— |— :f |m :-.f |m :r |d :— |—
m₁ :.m₁ |m₁ :m₁ |ʳs₁ :r |t₁ :s₁ |d :-.d |d :t₁ |d :— |— :d |d :-.d |d :t₁ |d :— |—
```

sin and care op-press'd, Lord, send Thy promised Comfort-er, And lead us to Thy rest
onward course must lie, But on - ly dis, That we may make us live and die, That we may stand, in that dread hour, At Thy right hand on high.

```
d :.r |d :d.t₁ |r :r |t₁ :s₁ |s :.l |l :s |s :— |— :l |s :.l |s :f |m :— |—
l₁ :-.se₁|l₁ :d |ʳs₁ :r |t₁ :s₁ |d :-.f |r :f |m :— |— :f |s :-.s₁ |s₁ :s₁ |d :— |—
```

ELLWOOD.

340. Key C.

G. A. MACFARREN.

```
s :m¹ :d¹ |s :— :l |s :— :— m :— : |s :l :t |d¹ :— :t |l :— :— |— :— :
m :s :m |m :— :f |m :— :— d :— : |d :— :d |d :— :s |f :— :— |— :— :
```

1 Je - sus is our Shep - herd Wip - ing ev - ery tear;
2 Je - sus is our Shep - herd, Well we know His voice;
3 Je - sus is our Shep - herd, For the sheep He bled;

```
d¹ :— :d¹ |d :— :d¹ |d¹ :— :— |— :s |s :— :s |s :— :d¹ |d¹ :— : |— |l :— :
d :— :d |d :— :d |d :— :— |— :d |m :— :m |m :— :m |f :— :— |m |r :— :d
```

G.t

```
r¹ :— :s |s :l :t |d¹ :— :— |l :— : |m :l :s |f :— :r |d :— :— |— :— :— |— :— :
f :— :f |f :— :f |m :— : |l :— : |d :— :d |t₁ :— :t₁ |d :— :— |— :— :— |— :— :—
```

Fold - ed in His bo - som, What have we to fear?
How its gen - tlest whis - per Makes our heart re - joice;
Ev - ery lamb is sprin - kled With the blood He shed;

```
s :— :t |t :d¹ :r¹ |d¹ :— :— |m :— : |ʳs :f |m :r :— :f |m :— :— :— |— :— :
t₁ :— :r |s :— :s₁ |l₁ :— :— |d :— : |ʳs₁ :— :s₁ |s₁ :— :s₁ |d :— :— :— |— :— :
```

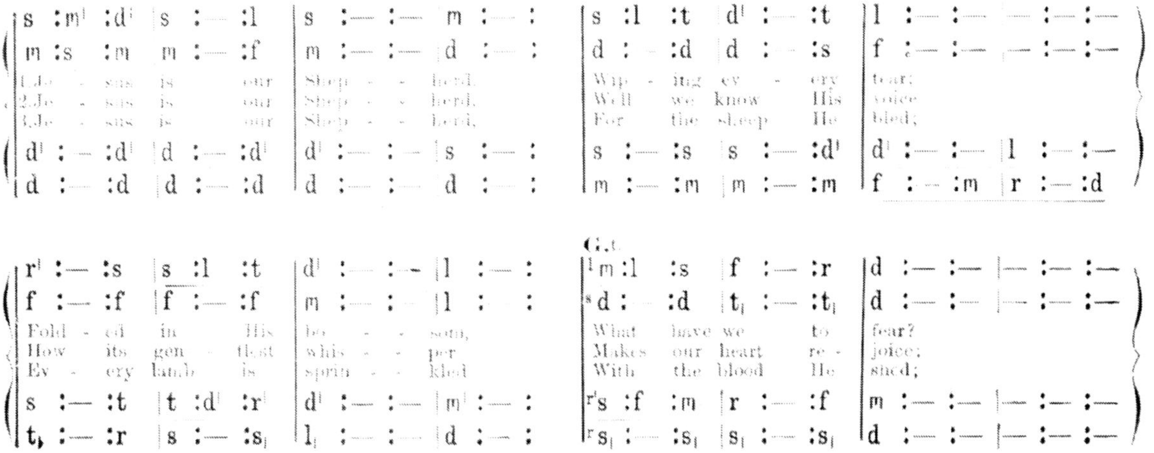

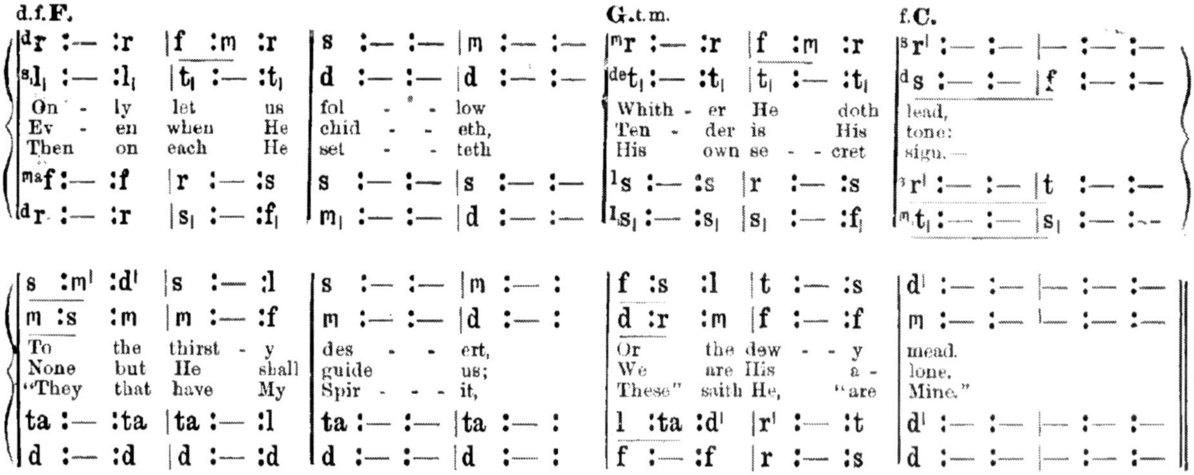
d.f.F.
G.t.m.
f.C.
On - ly let us fol - low Whith - er He doth lead,
Ev - en when He chid - eth, Ten - der is His tone:
Then on each He set - teth His own se - cret sign.
To the thirst - y des - ert, Or the dew - y mead.
None but He shall guide us; We are His a - lone.
"They that have My Spir - it, These" saith He, "are Mine."

CLARK.

341. Key G.

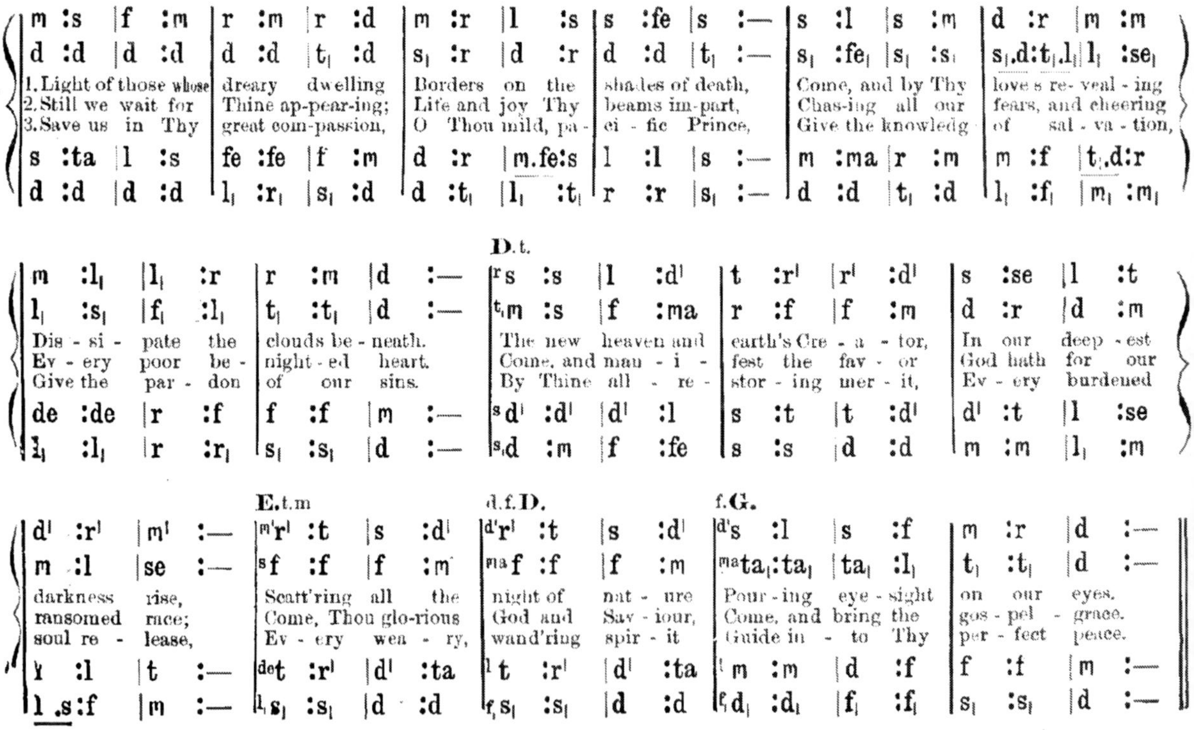
1. Light of those whose dreary dwelling Borders on the shades of death,
2. Still we wait for Thine ap-pear-ing; Life and joy Thy beams im-part,
3. Save us in Thy great com-passion, O Thou mild, pa - ci - fic Prince,
Come, and by Thy love's re - veal - ing Dis - si - pate the clouds be - neath.
Chas-ing all our fears, and cheering Ev - ery poor be - night - ed heart.
Give the knowledg of sal - va - tion, Give the par - don of our sins.
D.t.
The new heaven and earth's Cre - a - tor, In our deep - est darkness rise,
Come, and man - i - fest the fav - or God hath for our ransomed race;
By Thine all - re - stor - ing mer - it, Ev - ery burdened soul re - lease,
E.t.m
d.f.D.
f.G.
Scatt'ring all the night of nat - ure Pour - ing eye - sight on our eyes.
Come, Thou glo-rious God and Sav - iour, Come, and bring the gos - pel - grace.
Ev - ery wea - ry, wand'ring spir - it Guide in - to Thy per - fect peace.

WEST HEATH.

342. Key C.   E. J. HOPKINS.

| :s | m :s | d¹ :s | l :– .t | d¹ :r¹ | m¹ :t | d¹ :l | s :– .f | m |
| :m | d :t͵ | d :s | f :– .s | s :s | s :s | s :f | m :r | d |

1. Fear not, O lit - tle flock, the foe Who mad - ly seeks your o - ver - throw,
2. Be of good cheer: your cause be - longs To Him who can a - venge your wrongs;
3. A - men, Lord Je - sus, grant our pray'r! Great Cap - tain, now Thine arm make bare;

| :s | s :f | s :d¹ | d¹ :– .r¹ | d¹ :t | d¹ :r¹ | d¹ :d¹ | d¹ :t | s |
| :d | d :r | m :m | f :– .f | m :r | d :s | m :f | s :s͵ | d |

G.t.   d.f. F.

| :ᵐl͵ | s͵ :d | r :m | r :— | d :ᵈr | t͵ :r | s :t͵ | d :– .r | m |
| :ᵈf͵ | s͵ :l͵ | l͵ :f͵ | f͵ :— | m͵ | :s͵l͵ | s͵ :fe͵ | s͵ :s͵ | s͵ :– .t͵ | d |

Dread not his rage or power: What tho' your cour - age some - times faints,
Leave it to Him, our Lord Tho' hid - den yet from mor - tal eyes,
Fight for us once a - gain! So shall Thy saints and mar - tyrs raise

| :fet͵ | d :m | r :d | t͵ :— | d :ᵈr | r :d | m :f | m :– .f | s |
| :ˡr͵ | m͵ :l͵ | f͵ :r͵ | s͵ :— | d͵ :ᵐfe͵ | s͵ :l͵ | t͵ :s͵ | m :– .r | d |

G.t.m.   f.C.

| :ᵐr | t͵ :r | s :t͵ | d :– .r | m :ᵈs | d¹ :d¹ | r¹ :m¹ | r¹ :— | d¹ |
| :sefe͵ | s͵ :fe͵ | s͵ :s͵ | s͵ :– .t͵ | d :ᵈs | s :l | l :f | f :— | m |

His seem - ing tri - umph o'er God's saints Lasts but a lit - tle hour.
Sal - va - tion shall for you a - rise! He gird - eth on His sword!
A might - y cho - rus to Thy praise, World with - out end, A - men.

| :ᵐr | r :d | r :f | m :– .f | s :ᵐf | d¹ :m¹ | r¹ :d¹ | t͵ :— | d¹ |
| :t͵l͵ | s͵ :l͵ | t͵ :s͵ | m :– .r | d :taf | m :l | f :r | s :— | d |

PRENTISS.

343. Key E♭.

| m :s | :d¹ | t :l :s | l :s :m | r :— :— | m :ba :se | l :t :d¹ | t :t :l |
| d :d | :d | d :.m :m | re :m :d | t͵ :— :— | t͵ :d :t͵.m | m :– .r :d | r :d :d |

1. More love to Thee, O Christ More love to Thee! Hear Thou the pray'r I make, On bend - ed
2. Let sor - row do its work end grief and pain! Sweet are Thy mes - sen - gers, Sweet their re -
3. Then shall my lat - est breath Whisper Thy praise, This be the part - ing cry My heart shall

| s :m :m | s :.f :m | fe :s :s | s :— :— | se :l :t | l :– .se :l | s :fe :fe |
| d :d :d | d :.d :d | d :d :m | s :— :— | m :m :r | d :.t͵ :l͵ | r :r :r |

f.A.   B.t.m.   f.E♭.

| s :— :— | ˢr :s͵ :f | m :– .r :d | ᵐr :s͵ :f | m :– .r :d | fd¹ :m :r | d :— :— |
| t͵ :— :— | ᵈs͵ :s͵ :t͵ | d :– .t͵ :d | ˡs͵ :s͵ :t͵ | d :.t͵ :d | ᵈs :d :t͵ | d :— :— |

knee; This is my earn - est plea, More love, O Christ, to Thee, More love to Thee!
frain, When they can sing with me, More love, O Christ, to Thee, More love to Thee!
raise, This still its pray'r shall be, More love, O Christ, to Thee, More love to Thee!

| s :— :— | ˢr :r :r | m :– .f :s | ᵐr :r :r | m :– .f :m | fd¹ :s :f | m :— :— |
| s :— :f | ᵐt͵ :t͵ :s͵ | d :– .r :m | det͵ :t͵ :s͵ | d :– .d :d.ta | ˡm :s :s͵ | d :— :— |

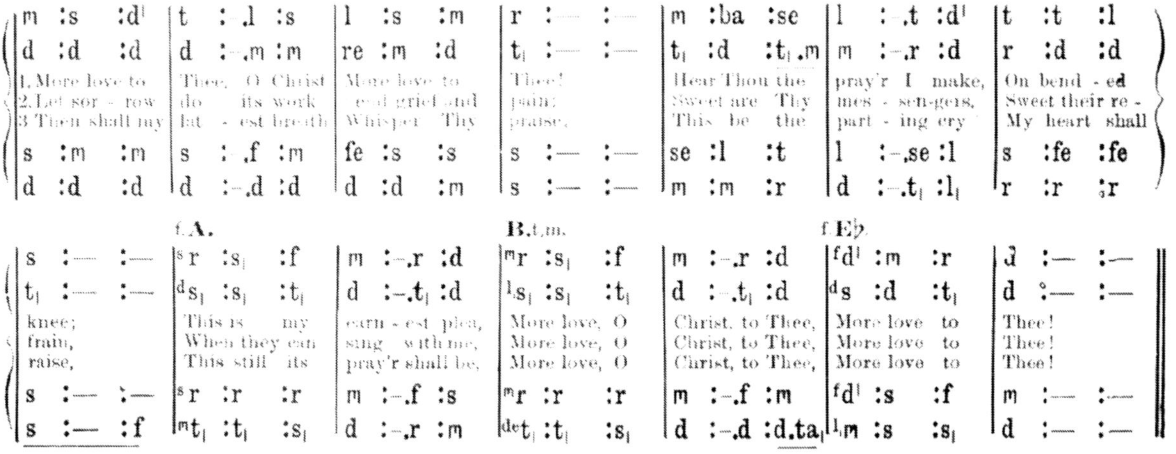

SAUNDERS.

344. Key F.
1. Thine is the pow - er, Lord, Hum - bly we crave, Thou wilt Thy - self re - veal, Might - y to save. Thine is the pow - er, Lord, Help us to win, Hard are we now be - set, Striv - ing with sin.
2. Thine is the pow - er, Lord, Low - ly we bend; Trust - ing Thy gra - cious word, Kins - man and Friend. Thine is the pow - er, Lord, Grant us Thy peace; Now, from the temp - ter, Lord, Grant us re - lease.
3. Thine is the pow - er, Lord, Ours is the need; 'Tis in Thy gra - cious word, Dare we to plead. Thine is the pow - er, Lord, Are we not Thine? Be Thou our watch and word, Sav - iour Di - vine.

GRACIOUS SPIRIT, HOLY GHOST.

CARYL FLORIO.

p 345. Key E♭.
1. Gra-cious Spir - it, Ho - ly Ghost, Taught by Thee, we cov - et most, Of Thy gifts at Pen - te - cost, Ho - ly, Heav'n - ly Love.
2. Love is kind, and suf - fers long; Love is meek, and thinks no wrong; Love than Death it - self more strong; There-fore, give us Love.
3. Faith will van - ish in - to sight; Hope be emp - tied in de - light; Love in Heav'n will shine more bright: There-fore, give us Love.

346. KEY E♭. *Lah is C.* THREE SHARP REMOVES.

|l :l |se :se |l :— |m :— |f :f |d :r |m :— |— :

C.t.l.m.

|ms :s |d' :r' |m' :— |d' :— |m' :r' |d' :t |d' :— |— : ‖

347. KEY C. *Lah is A.*

|l :—.l |se :l |m :m |f :m |l :—.t |d' :d' |t :l |se :—

A.t.m.l.

|ld :—.d |m :r |d :t, |d :s, |l, :—.l, |s, :d |m :r |d :— ‖

348. KEY E. THREE FLAT REMOVES.

|m :r |d :m |s :l |s :m |s :d |t, :d |f :m |r :—

s.d.f.G. *Lah is E.* E.t.m.l.

|md :t, |l, :d |m :f |m :d |ms :m |f :r |d :t, |d :— ‖

349. KEY G. From DYKES.

:s |s, :d |d :m |s :— |— :d |f :m |m :r |d :— |—

s.d.f.B♭. *Lah is G.* G.t.l.m.

:dl, |l, :d |t, :se, |l, :— |— :m |r :d |t, :t, |tr :— |—

:s, |s, :m |r :d |d :f |m :r |d :t,.d |r :—.t, |d :— |— ‖

350. KEY G. s.d.f.B♭. *Lah is G.*

|m :r |d :—.d |f :m |m :r |md :r |m :—.m |f :m |m :—

G.t.m.l.

|m :r |d :—.t, |d :r |m :— |ms :—.f |m :r.d |d :t, |d :— ‖

MODULATOR,
Showing 3 Removes.

d'	*ma'*
t	r'
l	d'
se	t
s	*ta*
ba	l
f	*la*
m	s
r	f
de	m
d	*ma*
t,	r
l,	d

LANDSDOWNE.

351. Key D.

J. B. Dykes.

s.d.f.**F.** *Lah is D.*

| s :—.m | s :d¹ | l :d¹ | s :— | l.t :d¹ | r¹ :s | s :— | — :— | s m :—.d | m :l |
| m :—.d | m :m | f :f | m :— | f :m | r.f :m | m :— | r :— | ma d :—.l | d :d |

1. Ev - ery morn-ing the red sun Ris - es warm and bright; But the eve-ning
2. Ev - ery spring the sweet young flow'rs O - pen fresh and gay, Till the chil - ly
3. Who shall go to that fair land? All who love the right: Ho - ly chil-dren

| d¹ :—.s | d¹ :d¹ | d¹ :d¹ | d¹ :— | d¹ :d¹ | s :s | s :d¹ | t :— | d¹ l :—.m | l :l |
| d :—.d | d :d | f :l | d¹ :— | f :d | t, :d | s :— | — :— | d l, :—.l, | l, :l, |

D.t.m.l.

| f :l | m :d.r | m :— | f :— | m :— | — :— | m s :m | :f | s :— | :d¹ |
| r :r | d :l,.t, | d :— | — :r | d :— | t, :— | de m :d | :r | m :r | :m |

com - eth on And the dark, cold night: There's a bright land
au-tumn hours Wither them a - way! There's a land we
there shall stand, In their robes of white; For that heaven, so

| l :l | l :l.l | m :l | — :t | l :— | :se | d¹ :s | :—.s | s :f | :s |
| r :f | l :m.m | m :— | r :— | m :— | :— | l, d :— | :d | d :— | :d |

| r¹ :— | :d¹ | t :— | :— | d¹ :— | :t.l | l :s | :m | m :— | :r | d :— | :— |
| f :— | :m | f :— | :— | f :m | :re | m :— | :d | t, :— | :t, | d :— | :— |

far a - way Where 'tis nev - er end - ing day.
have not seen, Where the trees are al - ways green.
bright and blest, Is our ev - er - last - ing rest.

| s :t | :d¹ | r¹ :— | :— | d¹ :— | :d¹ | d¹ :— | :s | s :— | :f | m :— | :— |
| s :— | :s | s :— | :se | l :s | :fe | s :— | :s | s, :— | :s, | d :— | :— |

WHEN DAYLIGHT FADES AWAY.

Beethoven.
D.C.

352. Key G.

| :s, | m :r :d | t, :l, :l, | f :m :r | d :t, :t, | l :s :t, | d :m :s | l :s :t, | d :— |
| :s, | s, :— :s, | s, :f, :s, | l, :— :la, | s, :— :s, | t, :— :s, | s, :d :d | d :— :s, | s, :— |

1. When day - light soft - ly fades a - way, In yon - der ma - ny- col - ored west.
   And sol - emn night on si - lent wing, Ap - pears in ob - on man - tle drest.
2. O, ev - er wel - come sa - cred hour, When shep - herds heard the an - gel strain,
   I too by faith can list the song That once re - sound - ed on the plain.

| :s, | d :t, :d | d :— :de | r :de :r | m :r :r | f :— :f | m :s :s | f :m :r | m :— |
| :s, | d, :r, :m, | f, :— :m, | r, :m, :f, | s, :— :s, | s, :— :s, | d :— :m, | f, :s, :s, | d, :— |

:S: s.d.f.**B♭.** *Lah is G.*

G.t.m.l.

D.S.

| :s m | f :m :r | r :d :d | r :d :ta, | ta, :l, :l, | d :t, :l, | m s :m :m | l :s :t, | d :— |
| :d l, | se, :— :se, | m, :— :m, | m, :— :m, | f, :f, :f, | re, :— :—.e, | m s, :d :d | t, :— :s, | s, :— |

'Tis then my thoughts from earth - ly pleasures That ev - er in - suf - fi - cient prove;
Are wont to turn a - way to heaven And might - y love.
O, let my long - ing spir - it ev - er In ho - ly ad - o - ra - tion stray;
To Him who sit - teth in the heavens, When day - light soft - ly fades a - way.

| :ma d | t, :— :t, | l, :— :l, | s, :— :d | d :d :d | l, :t, :d | de m :s :s | f :— :f | m :— |
| :d l, | m, :— :m, | l, :— :l₂ | d, :— :d, | f, :f, :f, | f, :— :f, | m s, :— :s, | s, :— :s, | d, :— |

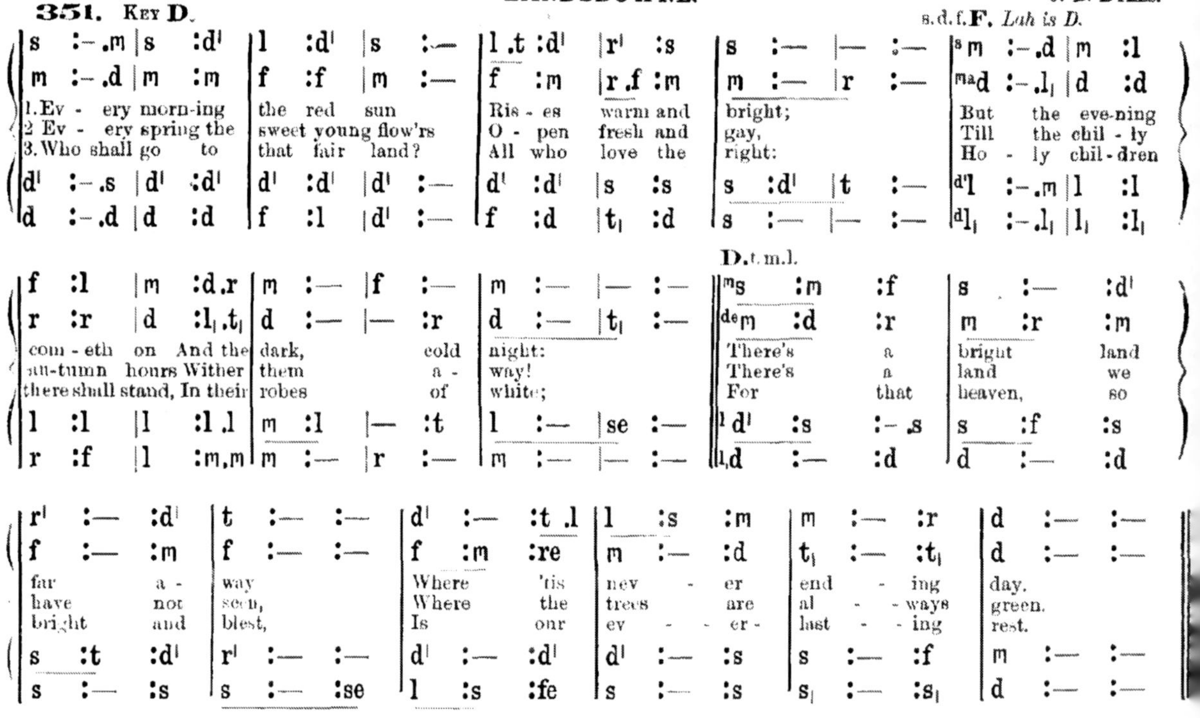

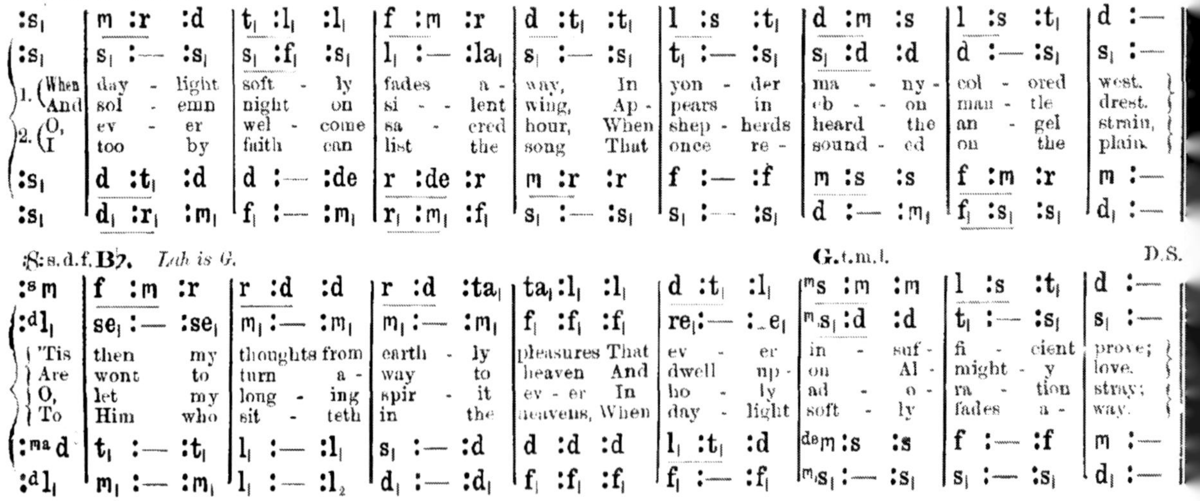

353. Key B♭. *Lah is G.* * **VOX DILECTI.** J. B. Dykes.

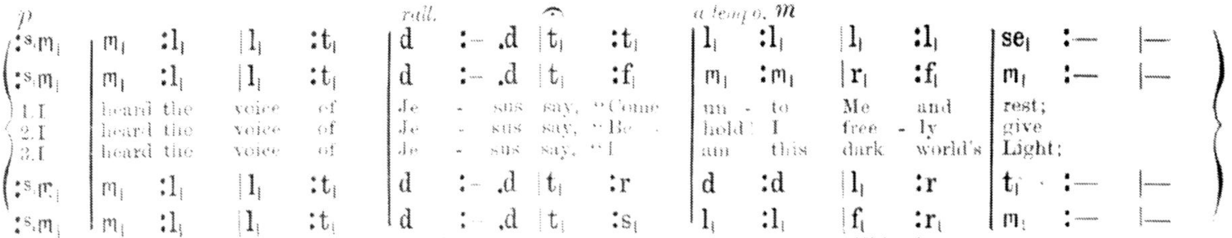
1. I heard the voice of Je - sus say, "Come un - to Me and rest;
2. I heard the voice of Je - sus say, "Be - hold! I free - ly give
3. I heard the voice of Je - sus say, "I am this dark world's Light;

* Bridge notes are sometimes placed at the beginning and sometimes at the end, for the return for additional verses.

Lay down, thou wea - ry one, lay down Thy head up - on My breast;"
The liv - ing wa - ter: thirst - y one! Stoop down, and drink and live:"
Look un - to Me: thy morn shall rise, And all thy day be bright:"
G. t. m. l.
I came to Je - sus as I was, Wea - ry, and worn, and sad;
I came to Je - sus, and I drank Of that life - giv - ing stream;
I looked to Je - sus, and I found In Him, my Star, my Sun;
I found in Him a rest - ing-place, And He has made me glad.
My thirst was quenched, my soul re - vived, And now I live in Him.
And, in that light of life, I'll walk Till trav - 'ling days are done.

THE STORM.

354. Key F. *Lah is D.* *Maestoso.* Bornhardt.

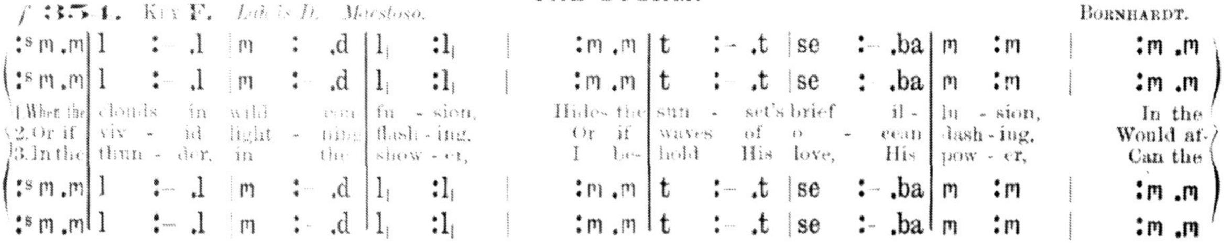
1. When the clouds in wild con fu - sion, Hides the sun - set's brief il - lu - sion, In the
2. Or if viv - id light - ning flash - ing, Or if waves of o - cean dash - ing, Would af-
3. In the thun - der, in the show - er, I be - hold His love, His pow - er, Can the

D.t.m.l. *p Andante.*

| l :m | d :l₁ | m :— | — :ᵈᵉm .f | s :-.s | s¹.l :t .d¹ | r¹ :-.t | s | s .s | s .-.s | s¹.l :t .d¹ |
| l :m | d :l₁ | m :— | — :¹d .r | m :-.m | m :m | f :— | f | :f .f | m :-.m | m :m |

ter - ror of the night, Still my heart is cheer - ful sing - - ing, Un-to Hope's strong an-chor
fright my stead-fast soul, In the Fa - ther's love a - bid - - ing I be-hold the strife sub-
true heart stoop to fear? Lo, the bow of prom - ise cheer - ing, On the eve - ning clouds ap-

| l :m | d :l₁ | m :— | — :ᵐs .s | d¹ :-.d¹ | d¹ :s | s :— | t | :t .t | d¹ :-.d¹ | d¹ :d¹ |
| l :m | d :l₁ | m :— | — :¹d .d | d :-.d | d :d | s :— | s | :s₁.s₁ | d :-.d | d :d |

| r¹ :-.t | s :s .s | m¹ :m¹ | r¹ :r¹ | d¹ :— | d¹ :t .l | s :d¹ | t .d¹:r¹ .t | d¹ :— | — |
| f :— | f :s .s | s :s | f :f | m :— | f :f | m :m | r .m:f .r | m :— | — |

cling - - ing; Or in storm or dusk - y night, I a - wait the cheer - ing light.
sid - - ing; Wave and wind in His con - trol May not harm the trust - ing soul.
pear - - ing! In the west, now doub - ly clear, Doth the beauteous sun ap - pear.

| t :— | r¹ :t .t | d¹ :d¹ | t :t | d¹ :— | l :d¹ | d¹ :s | s :s | s :— |
| s :— | s :s₁.s₁ | d :d | s :s | l :— | f :f | s :s | s₁ :s₁ | d :— |

DAWSON.

355. Key C.   U.

| d :-.d | m :s | f :l | d¹ :s | m¹ :-.m¹ | r¹ :t | d¹ :m¹ | r¹ :— |
| d :-.d | d :d | d :f | s :f | m :-.s | s :s | s :fe | s :f |

1. Now, my soul, thy voice up - rais - ing, Tell, in sweet and mourn-ful strain,
2. Through His heart the spear is pierc - ing, Though His toes have seen Him die;
3. Je - sus, may these pre - cious fount - ains Drink to thirst - ing souls af - ford;

| m :-.m | s :d¹ | l :d¹ | d¹ :t | d¹ :-.d¹ | t :r¹ | d¹ :d¹ | t :— |
| d :-.d | d :m | f :f | m :r | d :-.d | r :f | m :r | s :— |

r.s.d.f. **A♭.**

| ᵈm :-.m | r :t₁ | d :l₁ | s₁ :m₁ | l₁ :-.t₁ | d :d | r :re | m :— |
| ᵐₐs₁ :-.s₁ | s₁ :f₁ | m₁ :f₁ | m₁ :m₁ | f₁ :-.s₁ | s₁ :m₁ | l₁ :l₁ | se₁ :— |

How the Cru - ci - fied, en - dur - ing Grief, and wounds, and dy - ing pain,
Blood and wa - ter thence are stream - ing In a tide of mys - ter - y,
Let them be our cup and heal - ing And at length our full re - ward:

| ᵈᵐ :-.d | t₁ :r | d :d | d :d | d :-.d | d :d | d :t₁ | t₁ :— |
| ˡᵃd :-.d | s₁ :s₁ | l₁ :f₁ | d₁ :d₁ | f₁ :-.f₁ | m₁ :l₁ | f₁ :f₁ | m₁ :— |

C.t.m.l.r.

| ᵐd¹ :-.d¹ | s :d¹ | t :l | s :m | f :-.f | m :d | m :r | d :— |
| se₁m :-.m | f :s | s :f | m :d | d :-.d | d :d | d :t₁ | d :— |

Free - ly of His love was off - ered, Sin - less was for sin - ners slain.
Wa - ter from our guilt to cleanse us, Blood to win us crowns on high.
So a ran - somed world shall ev - er Praise Thee, its re - deem - ing Lord.

| t.s :-.d¹ | t :d | d¹ :d¹ | d¹ :s | d¹ :-.d¹ | d¹ :s | s :f | m :— |
| ᵐd :-.d | r :m | f :f | d :d | l :-.l | s :m | s :s₁ | d :— |

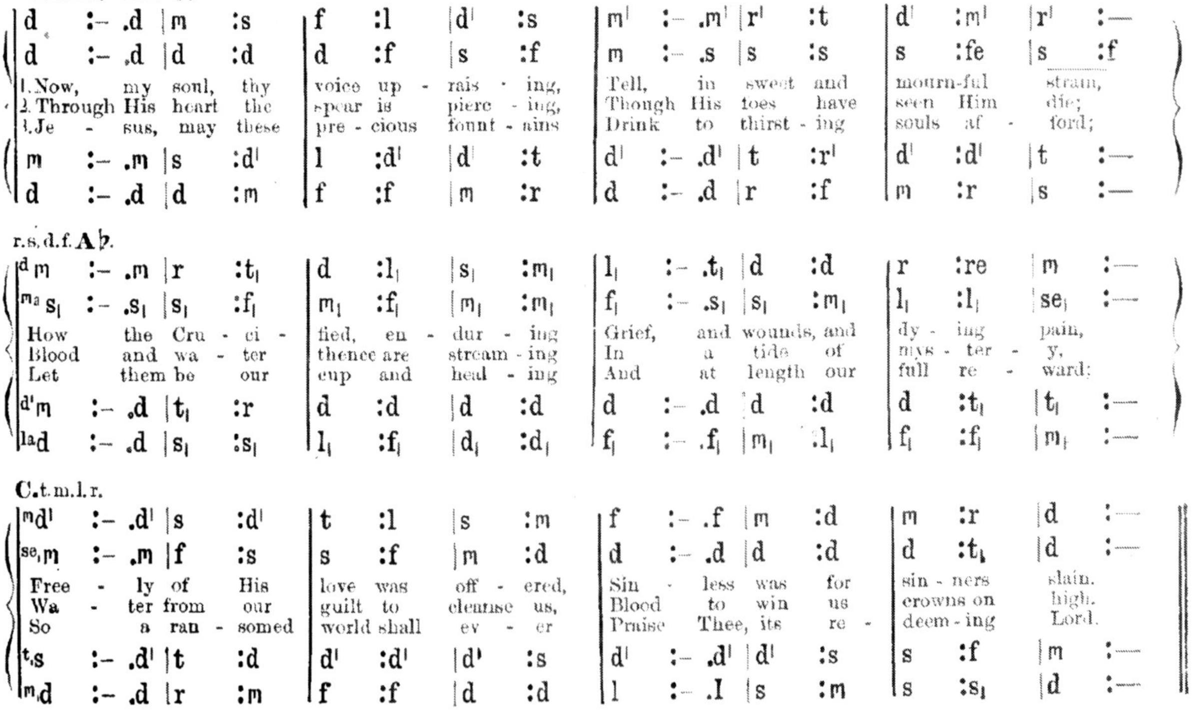

THE LIGHT AT HOME.

WM. MASON, Mus. Doc., by per.

356. Key F. *Moderato.*

| :s₁ | l₁ :-.t₁ | d :r | m :l | s :m | d :d | f :m | r :-.d | r :s₁ |
| .s₁ | s₁ :-.s₁ | s₁ :t₁ | d :d | d :d | d :d | t₁ :d | t₁ :-.l₁ | t₁ :s₁ |

1. The light at home! how bright it beams, When eve - ning shad - ows round us fall! And
2. When through the dark and storm - y night, The way - ward wan - d'rer home - ward hies, How
3. The light at home! how still and sweet, It peeps from yon - der cot - tage door, The

| :m | f :-.r | m :s | s :f | m :s | l :s | s :s | s :-.s | s :t₁ |
| :d | d :-.d | d :s₁ | d :d | d :d | f :m | r :d | s₁ :-.s₁ | s₁ :s₁ |

| l₁ :-.t₁ | d :r | m :l | s :m | r :-.r | l :fe | s :— | :r |
| s₁ :-.f₁ | m₁ :s₁ | s₁ :d | t₁ :le₁ | t₁ :-.t₁ | d :d | t₁ :— | :ta₁ |

from the lat - tice far it gleams, To soothe and com - fort all. When
cheer - ing is that twink - ling light, Which through the gloom he spies! It
wea - ry la - bor - er to greet, When toils of day are o'er! Sad

| d :-.r | d :t₁ | d :m | m :s | s :-.s | fe :l | s :— | :s |
| s₁ :-.s₁ | l₁ :s₁ | d :l₁ | m :de | r :-.r | r :r | s₁ :— | :s |

recit. D₂.

| r :-.m | f :l | r¹ :d¹ | t :tre | m¹ :d¹ | s :f | f :-.m | m :m | ba :se | l :t |
| l₁ :-.de | r :m | r :r | r :fe | s :m | m :r | r :-.d | d :d | m :m | m :m |

wea - ried with the toils of day, And strife for glo - ry, gold or fame, How sweet to seek the
is the light at home he sees That lov - ing hearts will meet him there, And soft - ly through his
is the soul that does not know the blessings that its beams im - part, The cheer - ful joys and

| l :-.s | f :m | f :fe | s :lad¹ | d¹ :s | l :t | t :-.d¹ | d¹ :d¹ | m¹ :r¹ | d¹ :t |
| f :-.m | r :d | t₁ :l | s₁ :l₁ | s₁ :s | s₁ :s₁ | d :-.d | d :d | d¹ :t | l :s |

F. tun'r.

| d¹ :-.t | t :s | d¹ :s | f :m | m :r | d :l₁ | l₁ :s₁ | l₁ :d | d :— | |
| m :-.re | re :t₁ | d :d | d :d | t₁ :t₁ | d :f | m₁ :m₁ | m₁ :l | s₁ :— | |

qui - et way, Where lov - ing lips will lisp our name, A - round the light at home.
o - som steals, The joy and love that leave our care, A - round the light at home.
hopes that flow, And lighten up the heav - iest heart, A - round the light at home.

| l :-.l | l :f | m :s | l :l | s :f | m :r | m :m | d :f | m :— | |
| fe :fe | fe :r | d :m₁ | f₁ :fe₁ | s₁ :s₁ | l :t₁ | d :d | l₁ :f₁ | d₁ :— | |

APRIL.

H. E. NICHOL.

p **357. Key A.** *Allegretto.*

| :s₁ | s₁ :l₁ | t₁ :d | t₁ :l₁ | t₁ :— | t₁ :d | r :m | f :m | r | m :— | :s₁ |
| :s₁ | s₁ :— | s₁ :s₁ | s₁ :s₁ | s₁ :— | s₁ :s₁ | s₁ :s₁ | t₁ :t₁ | | d :— | :s₁ |

1 She comes to us a maid - en, With half a - vert - ed face, Her
2. She loves to hide her blush - es Be - hind a veil of show'r, (Her) But
3. We can - not choose but love her, A maid and still a child; (The) The

| :m | m :— | m :m | m :m | f :— | f :m | r :r | s :— | s :— | :m |
| :d | d :— | d :s₁ | s₁ :s₁ | r :— | s₁ :l₁ | t₁ :t₁ | s₁ :s₁ | d :— | :m |

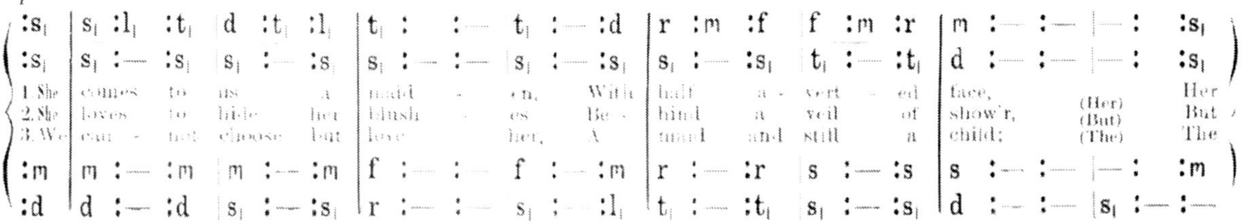

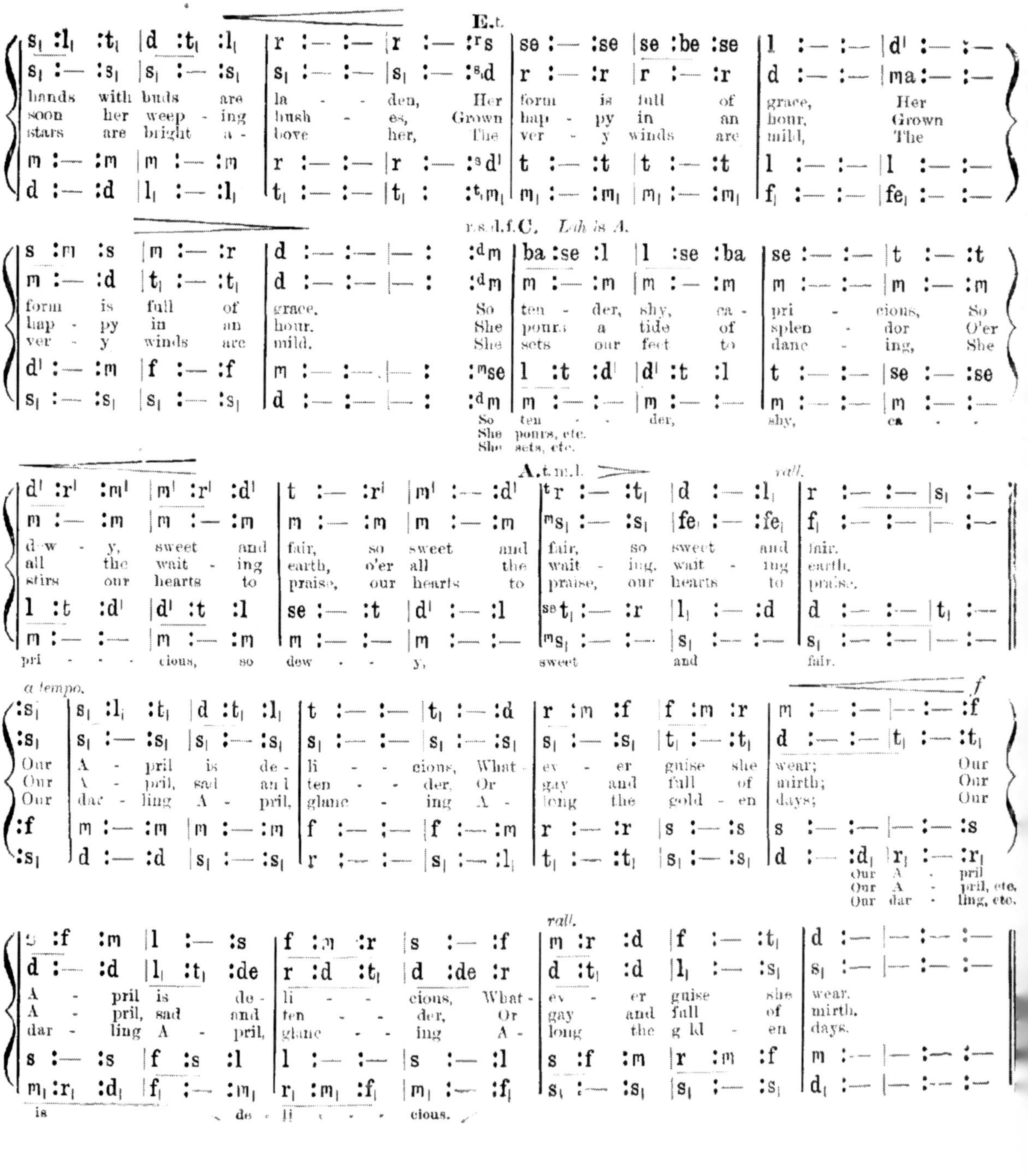
E.t.
hands with buds are la - den, Her form is full of grace, Her
soon her weep - ing blush - es, Grown hap - py in an hour, Grown
stars are bright a - bove her, The ver - y winds are mild, The
r.s.d.f.C. Lah is A.
form is full of grace. So ten - der, shy, ca - pri - cious, So
hap - py in an hour. She pours a tide of splen - dor O'er
ver - y winds are mild. She sets our feet to danc - ing, She
So ten - der, shy, ca - -
She pours, etc.
She sets, etc.
A.t.m.l.
rall.
dew - y, sweet and fair, so sweet and fair, so sweet and fair.
all the wait - ing earth, o'er all the wait - ing, wait - ing earth.
stirs our hearts to praise, our hearts to praise, our hearts to praise.
pri - - - cious, so dew - - y, sweet and fair.
a tempo.
f
Our A - pril is de - li - cious, What - ev - er guise she wear; Our
Our A - pril, sad and ten - der, Or gay and full of mirth; Our
Our dar - ling A - pril, glanc - ing A - long the gold - en days; Our
Our A - pril
Our A - pril, etc.
Our dar - ling, etc.
rall.
A - pril is de - li - cious, What - ev - er guise she wear.
A - pril, sad and ten - der, Or gay and full of mirth.
dar - ling A - pril, glanc - ing A - long the gold - en days.
is de - li - cious.

FAREWELL.

P. David.

f 358. Key D.

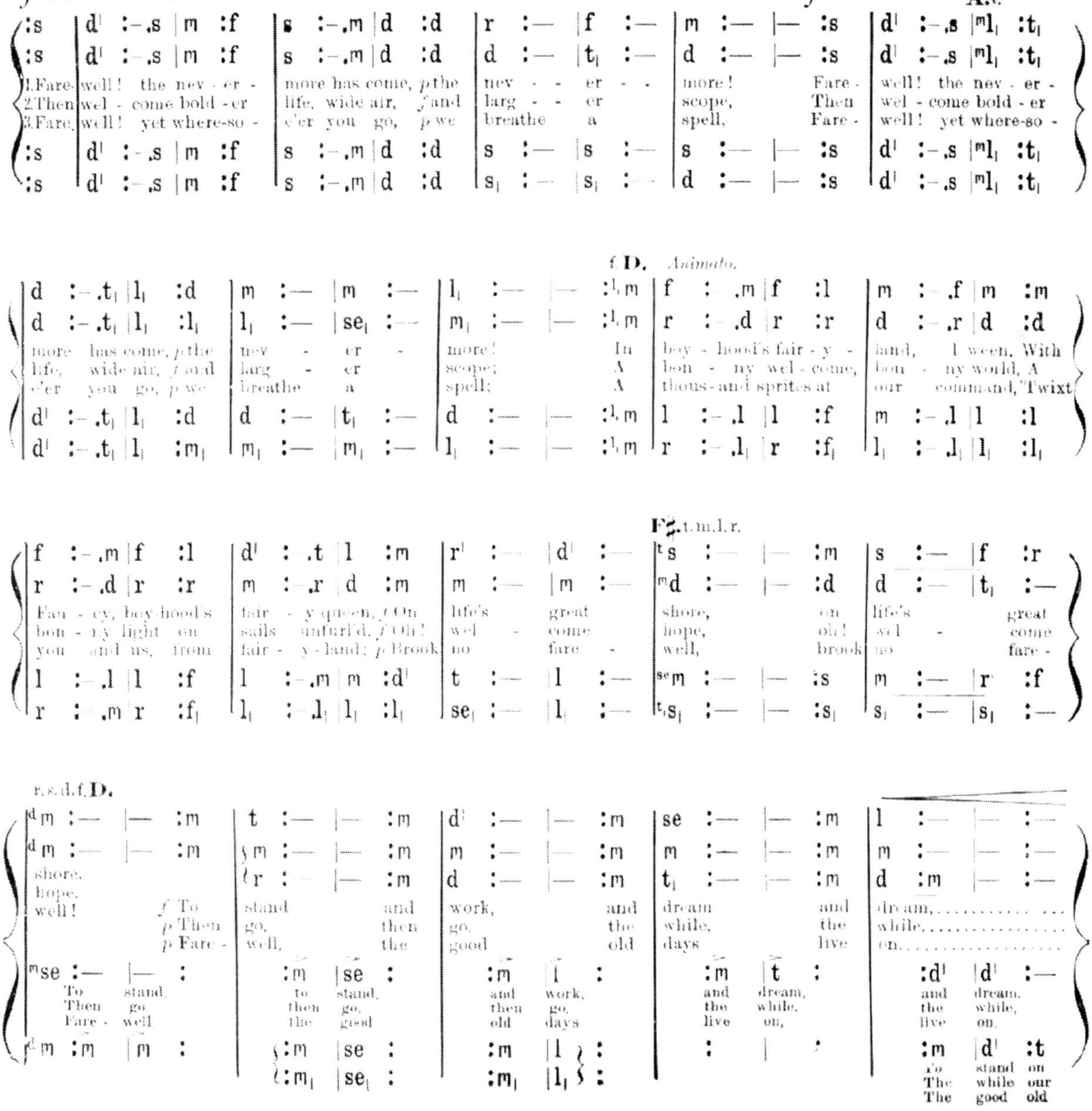
1. Fare-well! the nev - er - more has come, *p* the nev - - er - - more! Fare - well! the nev - er -
2. Then wel - come bold - er life, wide air, *f* and larg - - er scope, Then wel - come bold - er
3. Fare-well! yet where-so - e'er you go, *p* we breathe a spell, Fare - well! yet where-so -
more has come, *p* the nev - er - more! In boy - hood's fair - y - land, I ween, With
life, wide air, *f* and larg - er scope; A bon - ny wel - come, bon - ny world, A
e'er you go, *p* we breathe a spell; A thous - and sprites at our command, 'Twixt
Fan - cy, boy - hood's fair - y queen, *f* On life's great shore, on life's great
bon - ny light on sails unfurl'd, *f* Oh! wel - come hope, oh! wel - come
you and us, from fair - y - land; *p* Brook no fare - well, brook no fare -
shore. *f* To stand and work, and dream and dream,
hope. *p* Then go, then go, the while, the while,
well! *p* Fare - well, the good old days live on,
To stand, to stand, and work, and dream, and dream,
Then go, then go, then go, the while, the while,
Fare - well the good old days live on, live on,
To stand on
The while our
The good old

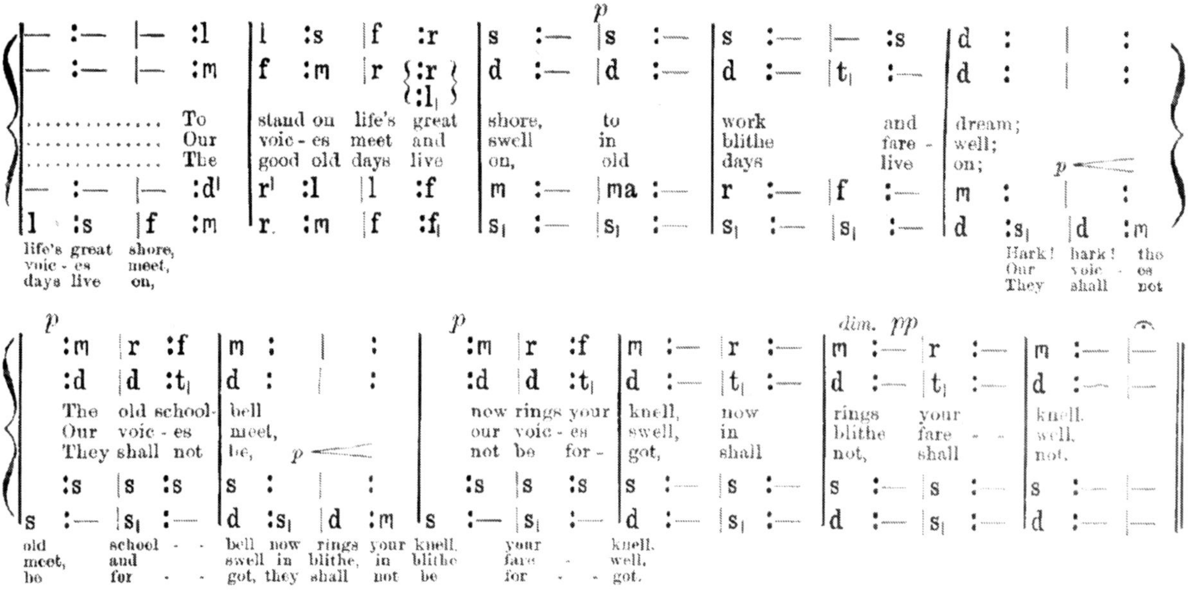
To stand on life's great shore, to work and dream;
Our voic - es meet and swell in blithe fare - well;
The good old days live on, old days live on;
life's great shore,
voic - es meet,
days live on,
Hark! hark! the
Our voic - es
They shall not
The old school-bell
Our voic - es meet,
They shall not be,
now rings your knell, now rings your knell.
our voic - es swell, in blithe fare - - well.
not be for - got, shall not, shall not.
old school - - bell now rings your knell, your knell.
meet, and swell in blithe, in blithe fare - well.
be for - - got, they shall not be for - - got.

MIDNIGHT CRY.

359. Key C. Sir G. A. Macfarren.

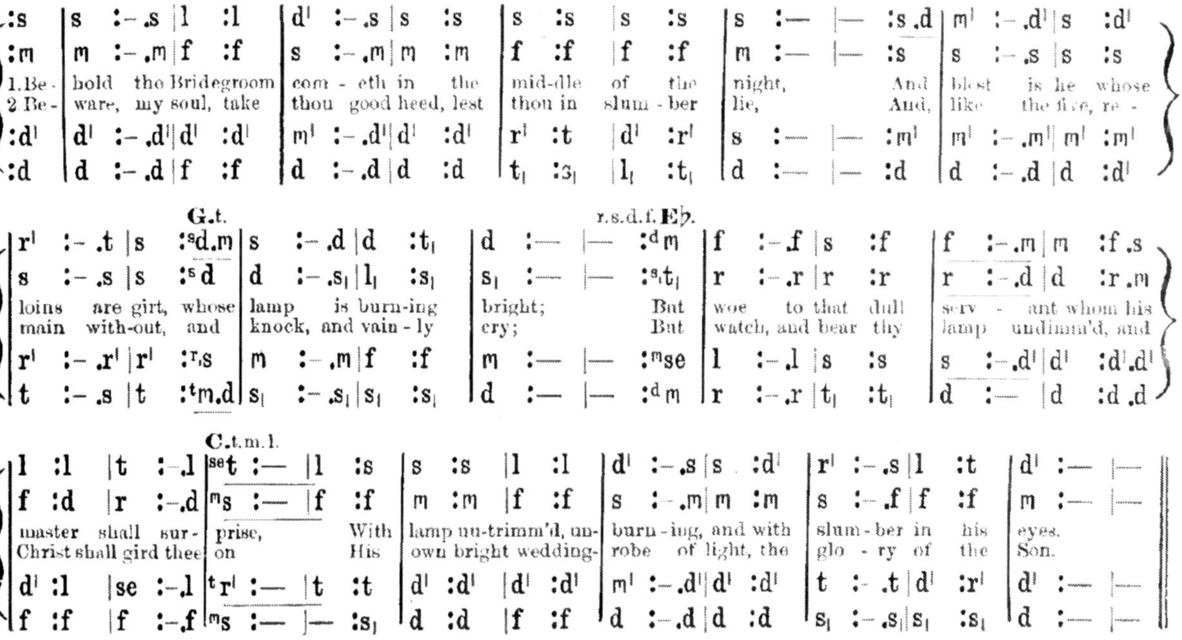
1. Be - hold the Bridegroom com - eth in the mid-dle of the night, And blest is he whose
2. Be - ware, my soul, take thou good heed, lest thou in slum - ber lie, And, like the five, re -
loins are girt, whose lamp is burn-ing bright; But woe to that dull serv - ant whom his
main with-out, and knock, and vain - ly cry; But watch, and bear thy lamp undimm'd, and
master shall sur - prise, With lamp un-trimm'd, un - burn - ing, and with slum - ber in his eyes.
Christ shall gird thee on His own bright wedding- robe of light, the glo - ry of the Son.

JACK AND JILL.

360. KEY F. *Lah is D.*

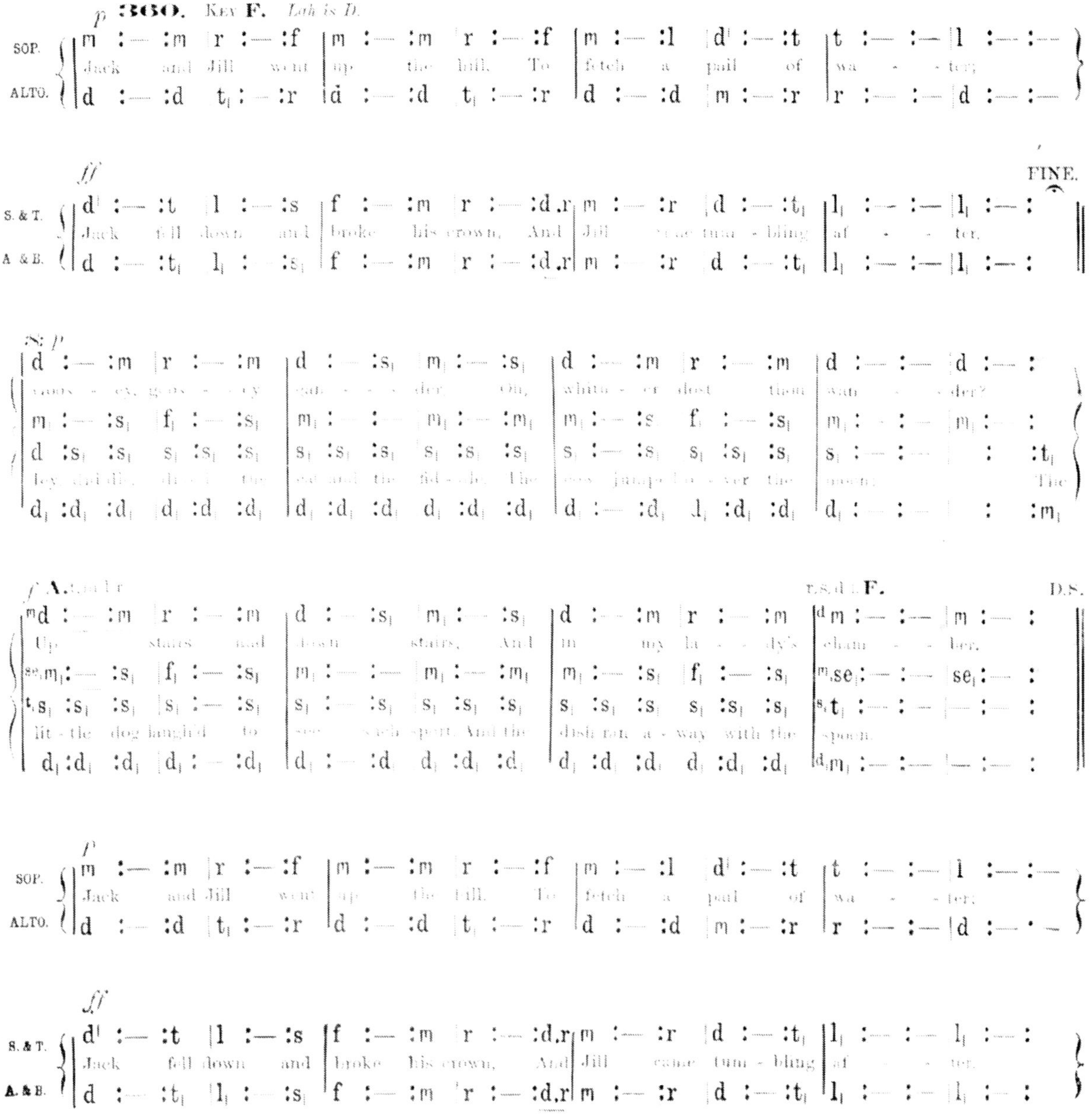

𝄋 D.t.m.l. *p*

de m :m :m	m :— :m	m :m :m	m :— :m	m :m :m	m :— :fe	s :— :—	: :se
l₁ d :d :d	r :— :r	d :d :d	r :— :r	d :d :d	d :— :d	t₁ :— :—	: :d
Lit-tle Jack Hor - ner,	sat in a cor - ner,	Eat-ing his Christ - mas	pie; He
m s :m :s	se :— :se	l :m :l	t :— :t	l :m :l	l :— :r	r :— :—	: :m
l₁ d :d :d	t₁ :— :t₁	l₁ :l₁ :l₁	se₁ :— :se₁	l₁ :l₁ :l₁	l₁ :— :r	s₁ :— :—	: :d

ff — *1st time.* D.S. — *2d time.* s. d.f F. D.C.

l :l :l	l :— :l	l :l :l	l :l :l	l :l :l	l :— :t	d¹ :— :—	: :	d l :— :	: :
d :d :d	de :— :de	r :r :r	m :m :m	f :f :f	f :— :f	m :— :—	: :	m de :— :	: :
put in his thumb, and	pulled out a plum, And said	"what a good boy am	I."	I."
f :f :f	s :— :s	f :f :f	s :s :s	f :r :l	s :— :s	s :— :—	: :	s m :— :	: :
f :f :f	m :— :m	r :r :r	de :de :de	r :r :r	s :— :s₁	d :— :—	: :	d l₁ :— :	: :

ALL MERRILY SINGING.

From "FAUST."

(NOTE.—The first movement is to be sung as a round in four parts, the Soprano, Alto, Tenor and Base following each other consecutively.)

301 KEY A♭.

| m :— :— | f :m :r | d :— :— | s₁ :— :— | d :— :m | r :— :s | s :— :— | — :— :— |
| All mer - ri - ly | sing - - ing, | Fill with mirth the | air; |

FINE

| m :— :— | f :m :r | d :— :— | s₁ :— :— | d :— :m | r :— :s₁ | d :— :— | — :— :— |
| Bells cheer-i - ly | ring - - ing, | Glad - ness ev - - 'ry - | where. |

E♭.t.

s d¹ :— :—	d¹ :t :l	s :— :m	d :— :r	m :— :—	s :m :s	l :— :—	— :— :—
s d :— :—	d :d :d	d :— :d	d :— :d	d :— :—	d :d :d	d :— :—	— :— :—
1. Far o - ver the	fields they come, With	hearts mer - ry and	free,
2. Glad mel - o - dy	fills the breeze, And	glides gai - ly a -	long,
3. O beau-ti - ful	sil - - ver bells, That	ring, cheer-i - ly	ring,
t m :— :—	m :m :m	m :— :s	m :— :f	s :— :—	m :m :m	m :— :—	— :— :—
m l₁ :— :—	l₁ :l₁ :l₁	d :— :d	d :— :d	d :— :—	d :d :d	l₁ :— :—	— :— :—

f A♭. D.C.

d¹ :— :—	d¹ :t :l	s :— :m	d :— :r	m :— :—	s :m :s	l m :— :—	— :— :—
d :— :—	d :d :d	d :— :d	d :— :d	d :— :—	d :d :d	d s₁ :— :—	— :— :—
Birds car - ol wher-	e'er they roam, And	woods ech - o their	glee.
Borne play-ful - ly	o'er the lake Where	waves rip - ple with	song.
Still o - ver the	fair - y dells What	joy ev - er they	bring.
m :— :—	m :m :m	m :— :s	m :— :f	s :— :—	m :m :m	m t₁ :— :—	— :— :—
l₁ :— :—	l₁ :l₁ :l₁	d :— :d	d :— :d	d :— :—	d :d :d	l m₁ :— :—	— :— :—

Questions for Written or Oral Examination.

DOCTRINE.

1 What are transitions to the first sharp or first flat keys called?

2 What are transitions to the second sharp or second flat keys called?

3 What interval, upward or downward, is the music moved in two sharp removes?

4 What tones of the old key are omitted?

5 What new tones are introduced?

6 Which of these is the more important, and why?

7 Where is this new tone placed in the signature?

8 In two flat removes, by what interval upward or downward, is the music moved?

9 What tones of the old key are omitted?

10 What new tones take their places?

11 Which of these is the more important, and why?

12. Where is this new tone placed in the signature?

13 What is the mental effect of two sharp removes? Of two flat removes?

14 What is oscillating transition?

15. What are transitions to third sharp or third flat keys called?

16 In three sharp removes, by what interval, upward or downward, is the new key moved? In three flat removes?

17 In three sharp removes, what does *Lah* become?

18 In three flat removes, what does *Doh* become?

19 On account of the relation between *Lah* and *Doh* of the two keys, transitions of three removes are commonly what?

20 What is the mental effect of a transitional modulation of three flat removes? Of three sharp removes?

21 In three sharp removes, what tones of the old key are displaced?

22. What new tones take their places?

23 Which of these is the last new sharp, and where is it placed in the signature?

24 In three flat removes, what tones are displaced?

25 What new tones take their places?

26. Which is the last new flat and where is it placed in the signature?

27. In transitions of four sharp removes, by what interval, upward or downward, is the new key placed? In four flat removes?

28 In four flat removes, what does *Doh* become?

29 In four sharp removes, what does *Me* become?

30 In four flat removes, what tones are displaced?

31 What new tones take their places?

32 Which of these is the last new flat, and where is it placed in the signature?

33 In four sharp removes, what tones are displaced?

34 What new tones take their places?

35 Which of these is the last new sharp, and where is it placed in the signature?

36 What is the commencing, closing and prevailing key of a tune called?

37 What are the other keys called?

38. What are transitions from and to the Principal key called?

39 What are the transitions between the Subordinate keys called?

PRACTICE.

40 Follow the Examiner's pointing in a voluntary containing transitions of two or three removes.

41 Sing your part in Exs. 340, 342, 344, which the Examiner may select.

42 Sing your part in Exs. 351, 353, 354, which the Examiner may select.

43 Sing your part in Exs 355, 359, which the Examiner may select.

44 Sol fa and point on the modulator from memory an example containing transitions of two and three removes.

45 Write from memory a similar example.

MISCELLANEOUS.

SLUMBER SWEETLY.

(SERENADE.)

Wm. Mason, Mus. Doc., by per.

Key B♭. *Dolce.* *Sempre e legato.*

m₁ :f₁ :fe₁	s₁ :d :m	r :— :d	t₁ :— :l₁	s₁ :— :t₁.l₁	s₁ :f :m	r :— :d	s₁ :— :
d₁ :r₁ :re₁	m₁ :— :s₁	se₁:— :l₁	s₁ :— :f₁	r₁ :re₁ :m₁	f₁ :l₁ :s₁	m₁ :f₁ :m₁	d₁ :r₁ :re₁

Slum - - - ber sweet - ly, dear - est, Close thy wea - ry eyes.

d :t₁ :l₁	s₁ :m :d	t₁ :— :d	f :d :l₁	t₁ :d :de	r :t₁ :s₁	s₁ :l₁ :s₁	m₁ :f₁ :fe₁
d₁ :— :		:— :d₁	f₁ :— :—	f₁ :— :l₁	s₁ :— :	s₂ :— :	d₁ :— :	:— :— :

Slum - - - ber sweet - ly, Close thine eyes.

F. t.

m₁ :f₁ :fe	s₁ :d :m	m l :— :s	s :— :f	m :d :f	m :— :r	d :— :—	:— :— :
m₁ :r₁ :re₁	m₁ :— :s₁	fe₁t₁ :d :de	r :t₁ :s₁	d :— :d	d :l₁ :t₁	d :— :l₁	s₁ :— :

Guard - ian an - gels round thee ho - ver Till the morn - ing rise,

s₁ :t₁ :l₁	s₁ :m :d	l r :re :m	f :r :t₁	d :m :l	s :fe :f	m :— :f	m :— :
d₁ :— :d₁	d₁ :— :d₁	r₁s₁ :— :s₁	s₁ :— :s₁	d₁ :— :d₁	s₁ :— :s₁	d :— :—	:— :

f. B♭.

s r :— :de	r :f :m	r :d :l₁	s₁ :— :d	s₁ :— :s₁	s₁ :fe₁ :s₁
ta f₁ :— :m₁	f₁ :l₁ :s₁	m₁ :— :m₁	m₁ :r₁ :d₁	t₂ :d₁ :de₁	r₁ :— :r₁

Then may love on air - y pin - ions, Bear thy heart in

m t₁ :s₁	:le₁	t₁ :s₁	:t₁	d :— :d	d :s₁ :m₁	s₁ :l₁ :le₁	t₁ :l₁ :s₁
d s₂ :— :s₂	s₂ :— :s₂	d₁ :m₁ :s₁	d₁ :— :d₁	s₂ :— :s₂	s₂ :— :s₂

l₁ :s₁ :fe₁	s₁ :— :	m₁ :f₁ :fe₁	s₁ :d :m	r :— :d	t₁ :d :l₁
re₁ :m₁ :re₁	m₁ :— :	d₁ :r₁ :re₁	m₁ :— :s₁	se₁ :— :l₁	se₁ :l₁ :f₁

trans - port bound. To its own do - min - ions. Where no

fe₁ :s₁ :l₁	s₁ :— :	d :t₁ :l₁	s₁ :m :d	t₁ :— :d	r :d :d
d₁ :— :d₁	d₁ :— :	d₁ :— :d₁	d₁ :— :d₁	f₁ :— :f₁	f₁ :— :f₁

Ritard.

s₁ :d :m	r :— :s₁	d :— :—	s :— :s	s :— :—	s₁ :m₁ :s₁	d :— :—	:— :— :
m₁ :— :s₁	fe₁ :— :f₁	m₁ :— :—	s₁ :l₁ :t₁	d :— :—	m₁ :— :r₁	d₁ :— :—	:— :— :

earth - ly care is found; Maid - en sleep, Maid - en sleep.

d :— :d	l₁ :— :t₁	d :— :—	t₁ :d :r	m :— :—	s₁ :— :f₁	m₁ :— :—	:— :— :
s₁ :— :s₂	s₂ :r₁ :s₁	d₁ :— :—	s₂ :— :s₂	d₁ :— :—	s₂ :— :s₂	d₁ :— :—	:— :— :

MY DREAM.

KEY A♭. (SONG WITH VOCAL ACCOMPANIMENT.) T. F. SEWARD, by per.

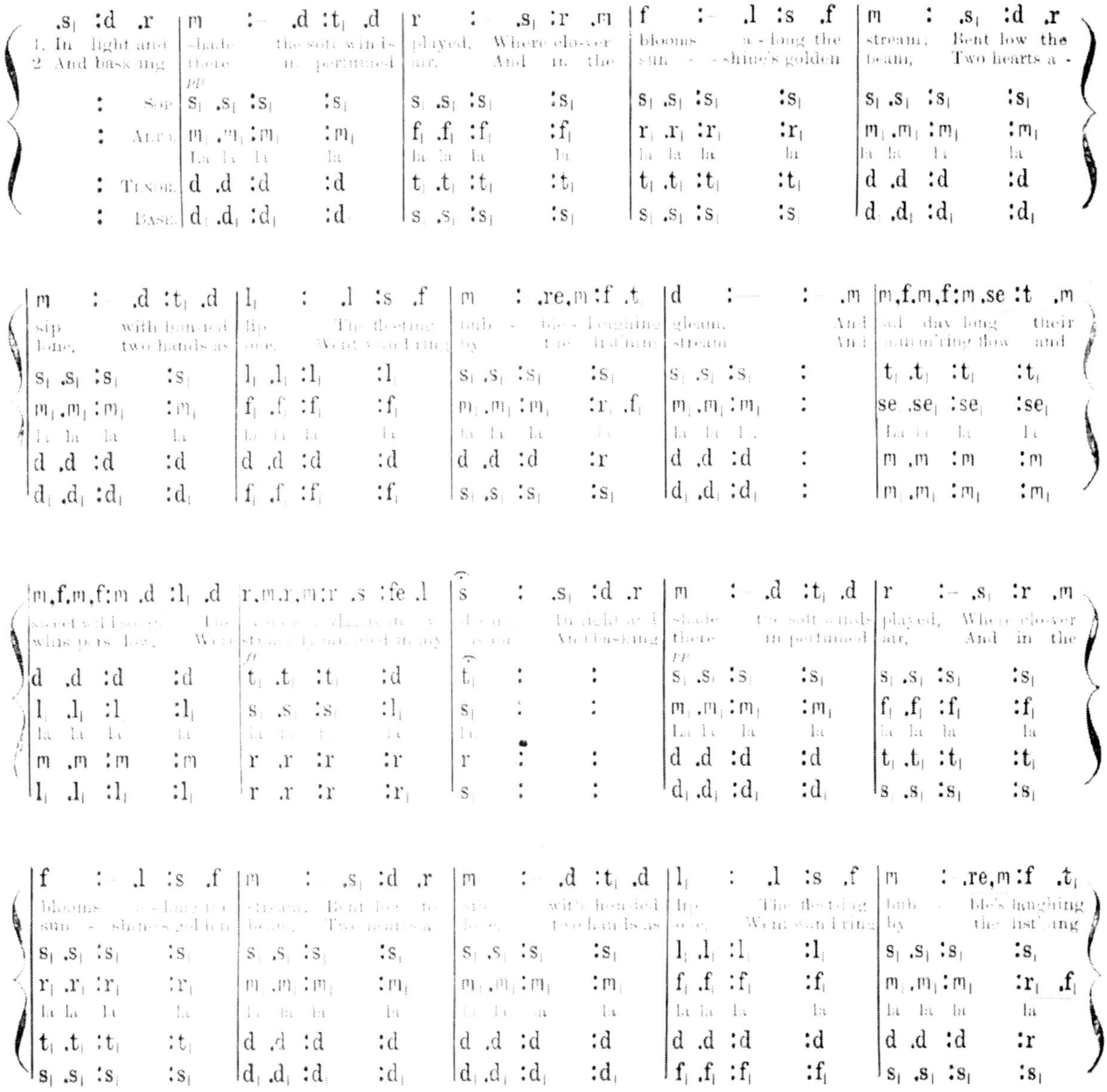
1. In light and shade the soft winds played, Where clover blooms a-long the stream; Bent low the
2. And basking there in perfumed air, And in the sun-shine's golden beam, Two hearts a-
SOP.
ALTO.
TENOR.
BASE.
sip with honied lip The fleeting bubble's laughing gleam. And all day long their
lone, two hands as one, Went wand'ring by the list'ning stream And murm'ring flow and
sweet whispers low,
shade the soft winds played, Where clover
there in perfumed air, And in the
blooms a-long the stream; Bent low to sip with honied lip The fleeting bubble's laughing
sun - shine's golden beam, Two hearts a-lone, two hands as one, Went wand'ring by the list'ning
la la la la

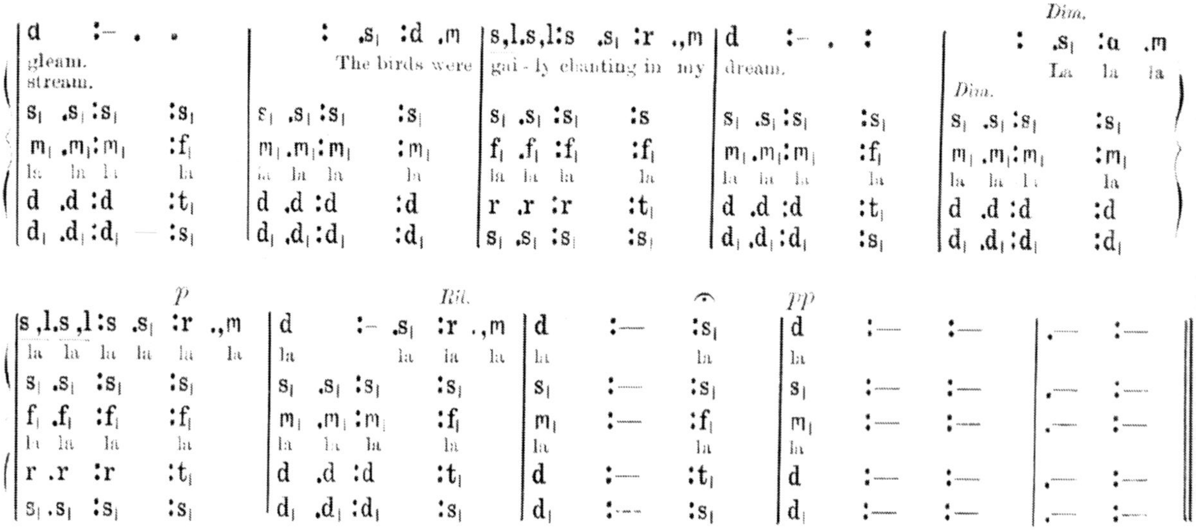
Dim.
gleam.
stream.
The birds were gai - ly chanting in my dream.
La la la
p
Rit.
pp

KEY A♭. **SUPPORT.** E. CORKHILL.

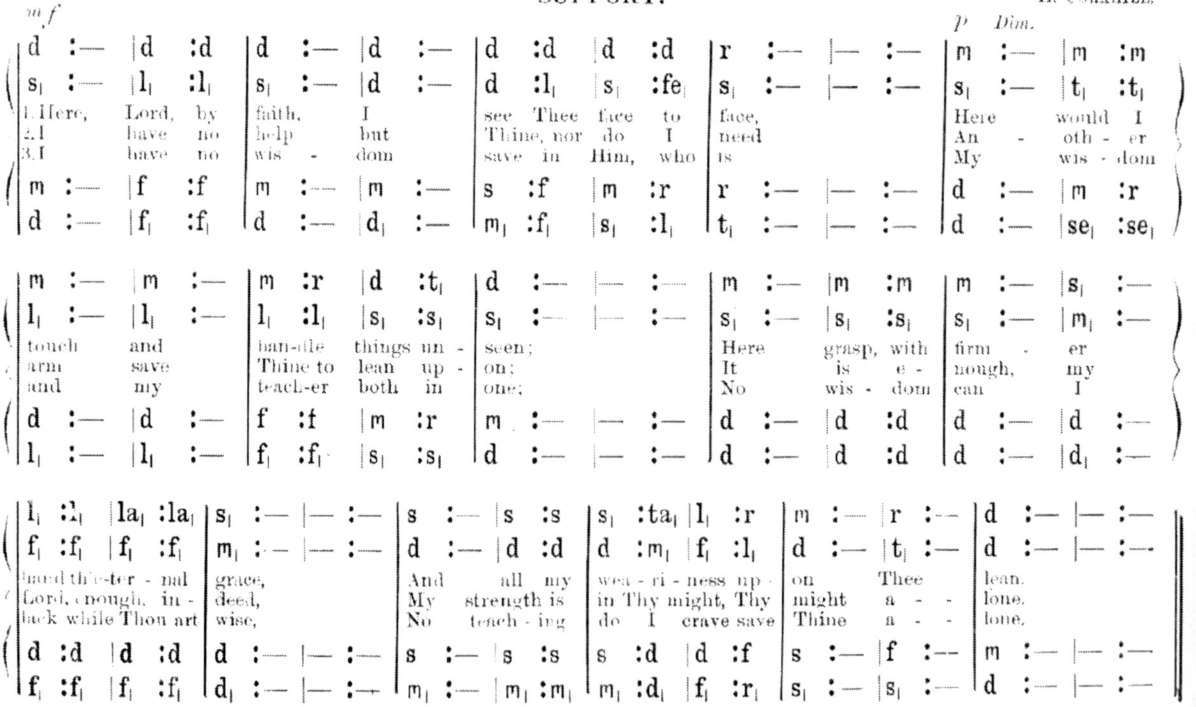
mf
p Dim.
1. Here, Lord, by faith, I see Thee face to face, Here would I touch and han-dle things un - seen; Here grasp, with firm - er hand th'e-ter - nal grace, And all my wea - ri - ness up - on Thee lean.
2. I have no help but Thine, nor do I need An - oth - er arm save Thine to lean up - on; It is e - nough, my Lord, enough, in - deed, My strength is in Thy might, Thy might a - lone.
3. I have no wis - dom save in Him, who is My wis - dom and my teach-er both in one; No wis - dom can I lack while Thou art wise, No teach - ing do I crave save Thine a - lone.

THE FAIRY'S ISLE.

MARY LADD. THEO. F. SEWARD.

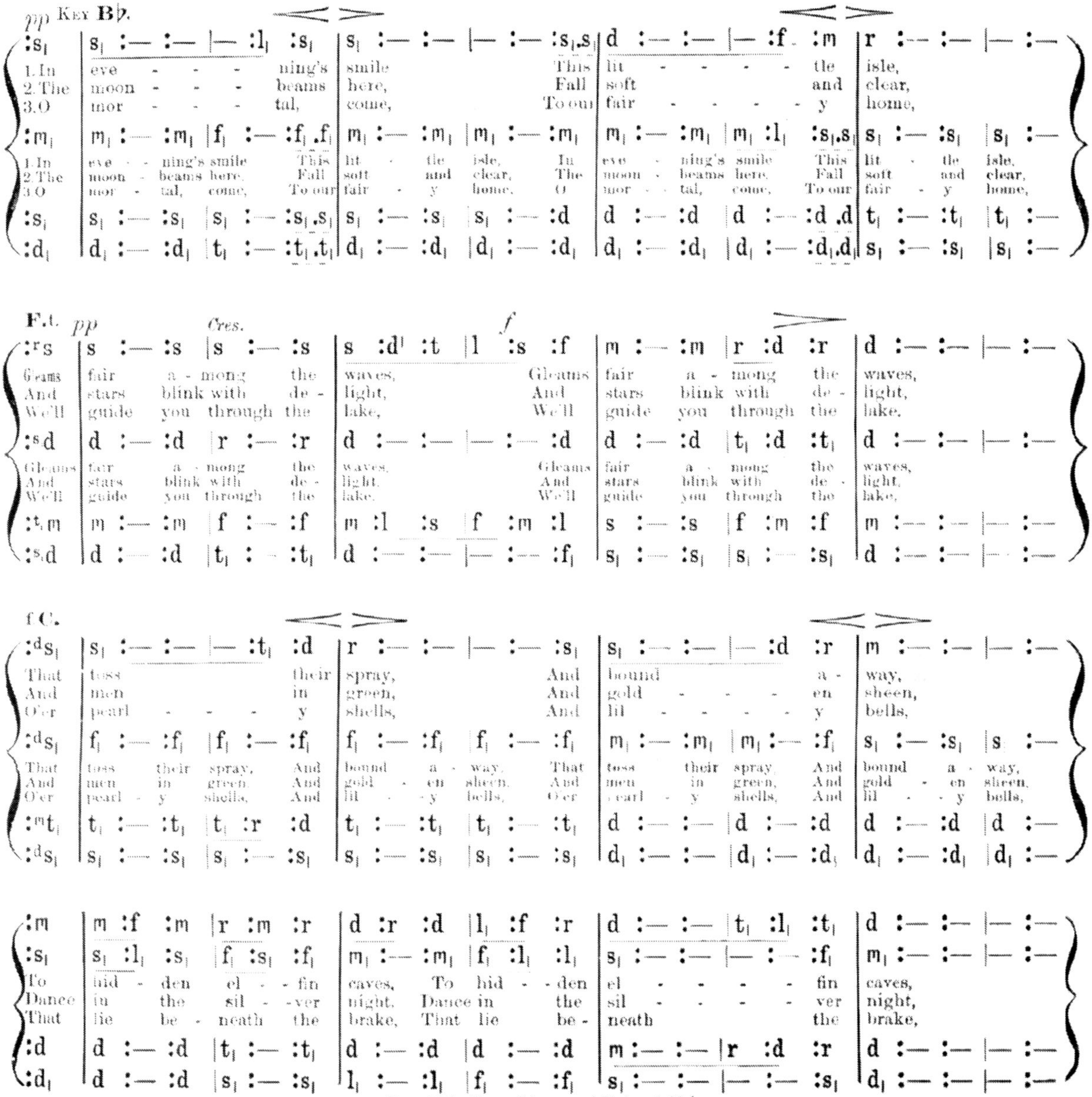
pp KEY B♭.
1. In eve - - - ning's smile This lit - - - - - tle isle,
2. The moon - - - beams here, Fall soft and clear,
3. O mor - - - tal, come, To our fair - - - - - y home,
F.t. pp Cres. f
Gleams fair a - mong the waves, Gleams fair a - mong the waves,
And stars blink with de - light, And stars blink with de - light,
We'll guide you through the lake, We'll guide you through the lake,
f.C.
That toss their spray, And bound a - way,
And men in green, And gold - - - - en sheen,
O'er pearl - - - y shells, And lil - - - - - y bells,
To hid - den el - fin caves, To hid - den el - - - - - fin caves,
Dance in the sil - ver night, Dance in the sil - - - - - ver night,
That lie be - neath the brake, That lie be - neath the brake,

From "The Singer," by per. of Biglow & Main.

vp

:d	t₁ :— :t₁	t₁ :— :t₁	d :— :—	:— :d	d :— :d	d :— :d	d :— :—	:— :—
:s₁	s₁ :— :s₁	s₁ :— :s₁	s₁ :— :m₁	m₁ :— :f₁	m₁ :— :f₁	m₁ :— :f	m₁ :— :—	:— :—
To	hid - den el - fin	caves, to caves, To	hid - den el - fin	caves.
Dance	in the sil - ver	night, the night, Dance	in the sil - ver	night.
That	lie be - neath - the	brake, the brake, That	lie be - neath the	brake.
:m	r :— :r	r :m :f	m :— :s₁	s₁ :— :l₁	s₁ :— :l₁	s₁ :— :l₁	s₁ :— :—	:— :—
:d₁	s₁ :l₁ :s₁	f₁ :m₁ :r₁	d₁ :— :—	:— :d₁	d₁ :— :d₁	d₁ :— :d₁	d₁ :— :—	:— :—

THROUGH THE DAY.

KEY E♭.

B. C. UNSELL.

m :— :f	m :r :d	s :— :l	s :f :m	m :— :r	d :— :d	r :d :r	m :— :
d :— :d	d :— :d	d :— :d	d :— :d	d :— :t₁	d :— :l₁	t₁ :l₁ :t₁	d :— :
1.Through the	day Thy	love hath	spared us;	Now we	lay us	down to	rest,
2.Pil - grims	here, on	earth, and	strang - ers,	Dwell - ing	in the	midst of	foes,
s :— :l	s :f :m	m :— :f	m :l :s	s :— :f	m :— :fe	s :— :s	s :— :
d :— :d	d :— :d	d :— :d	d :— :d	d :— :s₁	l₁ :— :l₁	s₁ :— :s₁	d :— :

m :— :f	m :r :d	s :— :l	s :f :m	m :— :m	m :l :s	fe :m :fe	s :— :
d :— :d	d :— :d	d :— :d	d :— :d	d :— :r	d :— :d	d :— :d	t₁ :— :
Through the	si - lent	watch - es	guard us,	Let no	foe our	peace mo -	lest.
Us and	ours pre -	serve from	dan - gers,	In Thy	love may	we re -	pose.
s :ta :l	s :f :m	m :— :f	m :l :s	s :— :se	l :m :ma	r :s :l	s :— :
d :— :d	d :— :d	d :— :d	d :— :d	d :— :t₁	l₁ :— :d	r :— :r	s₁ :— :

s :— :l	s :f :m	m :— :r	d :— :—	d :— :d	d :l :s	s :r :m	d :— :—
d :— :d	d :— :d	t₁ :— :t₁	d :— :—	d :— :ta₁	l₁ :d :d	t₁ :— :t₁	d :— :—
Je - sus,.	Thou our	guard - ian	be;	Sweet it is	to rest	in Thee.
And when	time's short	day is	past,	Rest with Thee	in heaven	at last.
m :— :f	m :l :s	s :— :f	m :— :—	m :— :m	f :— :m	r :f :s	m :— :—
d :— :d	d :— :d	s₁ :— :s₁	l₁ :— :—	l₁ :— :s₁	f₁ :— :s₁	s₁ :— :s₁	d :— :—

s :— :l	s :d¹ :—	d¹ :— :l	s :m :—	m :— :m	s :f :r	d :— :t₁	d :— :—
d :— :d	d :m :—	f :— :f	m :d :—	d :— :ta₁	l₁ :— :l₁	s₁ :— :s₁	s₁ :— :—
O, 'tis	sweet,	O, 'tis	sweet,	O, 'tis	sweet to	rest in	Thee.
m :— :f	m :s :ta	l :— :d¹	d¹ :s :m	m :— :m	r :— :f	m :— :r	m :— :—
d :— :d	d :— :—	f :— :f	d :— :—	l₁ :— :s₁	f₁ :— :f₁	s₁ :— :s₁	d :— :—

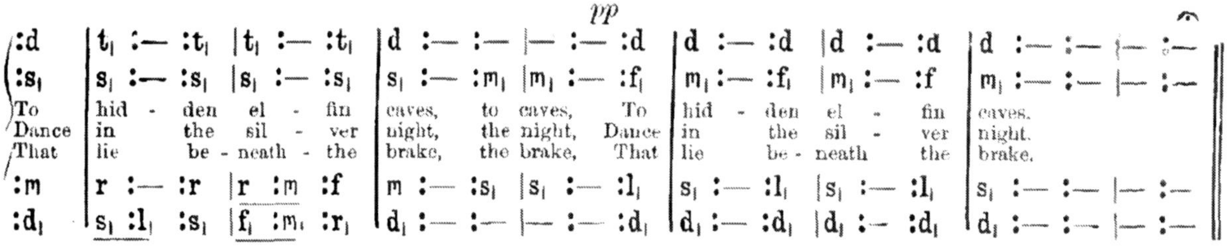

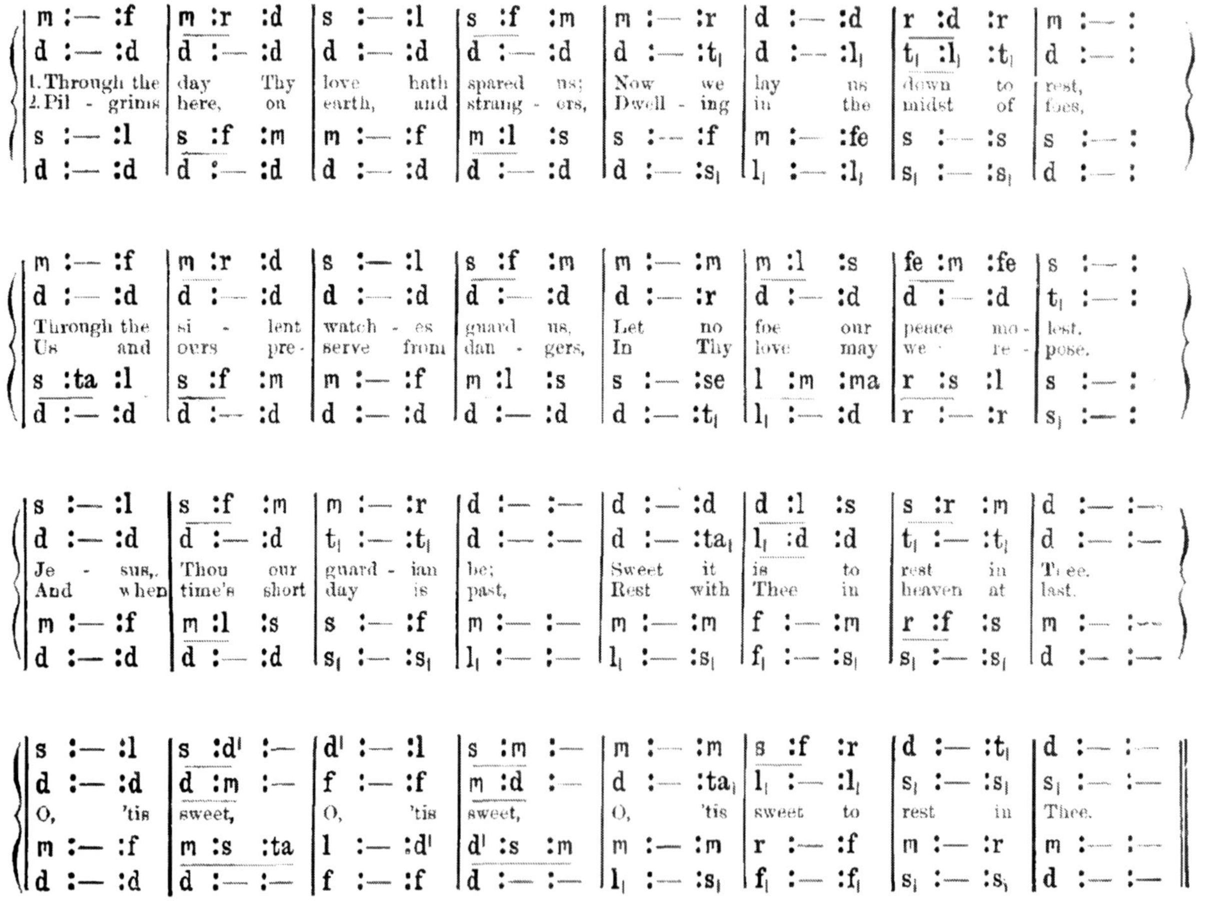

O LOVE DIVINE.

O. W. Holmes.

Mendelssohn, arr. by T. F. S.

Key F. *Andante.*

:s₁	d	:— .s₁	:d .r	r	:m	:s	f	:m	:r	s	:—	:m	d	:t₁	:d
:s₁	s₁	:—	:s₁ .t₁	t₁	:d	:d	d	:—	:d	d	:—	:s₁	l₁	:—	:l₁
O	Love		Di -	vine,		that	stooped	to		share		Our	sharp -	-	est
:m	m	:—	:m .f	f	:s	:ta	l	:s	:f	m	:—	:m	m	:r	:m
:d	d	:—	:d	d	:—	:d	d	:—	:d	d	:—	:d	l₁	:—	:l₁

d	:r	:m	f	:— .m	:r .d	d	:t₁	:s₁	d	:— .s₁	:d .r	r	:m	:s
l₁	:—	:d	r	:.d	:l₁	s₁	:—	:s₁	s₁	:—	:s₁ .t₁	t₁	:d	:d
pang,		our	but	-	thest	tear,		On	Thee		we	cast		each
f	:—	:s	l	:— .s	:f .m	m	:r	:f	m	:—	:m .f	f	:s	:ta
f₁	:—	:m₁	r₁	:— .m₁	:f₁ .fe₁	s₁	:—	:	d	:d	:d	d	:—	:d

On Thee

f	:m	:r	s	:—	:m	d	:t₁	:d	d	:r	:m	f	:— .r	:d .t₁
d	:—	:d	d	:—	:	fe₁	:fe₁	:fe₁	s₁	:t₁	:ta₁	l₁	:—	:s₁
earth	-	born	care,		We	smile		at	pain		while	Thou		art
l	:s	:f	m	:—	:	r	:r	:r	r	:s	:s	f	:—	:m .r
d	:—	:d	d	:—	:	r₁	:r₁	:r₁	s₁	:—	:d	f₁	:—	:s₁

We smile at pain

d	:—	:s₁	s	:— .m	:r .m	f	:— .m	:r .d	t₁	:d	:l₁	fe₁	:s₁	:s₁
s₁	:—	:s₁	m	:— .d	:t₁ .d	d	:—	:s₁	s₁	:—	:l₁	fe₁	:s₁	:s₁
near.	Though	long			the	wea	-	ry	way		we	tread,		And
m	:—	:		:.s	:s .s	l	:— .s	:f .m	r	:m	:d	d	:t₁	:
d	:—	:		:	:	:	:	:	:	:	:	:	:	:

Tho' long the

s	:— .m	:r .m	s .f	:— .m	:r .d	t₁	:d	:m	m	:r	:	.s₁	:t₁	:d
m	:— .d	:t₁ .d	d	:—	:s₁	s₁	:—	:d	d	:t₁	:	.s₁	:s₁	:—
sor	-	-	row	crown	each	ling	-	'ring	year,		(*Inst.*)
	:.s	:s .s	l	:— .s	:f .m	r	:m	:m .fe	s	:—	:		:f	:m
	:	:	:	:	:	:	:	:	:	:	:	s₁	:—	:—

And sor-row

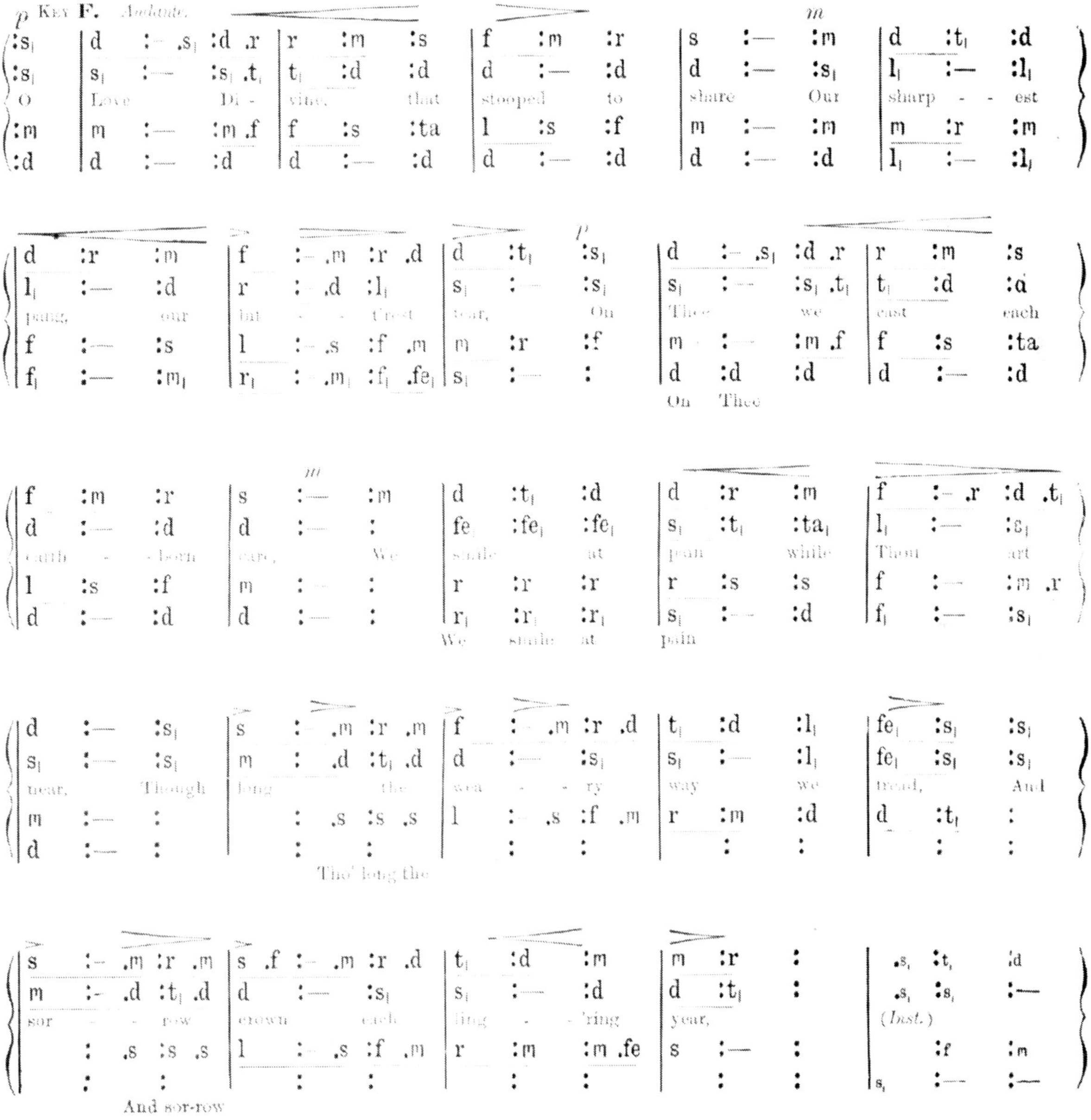

f
No path we shun, no dark - ness dread, O Love Di -
No path
O Love

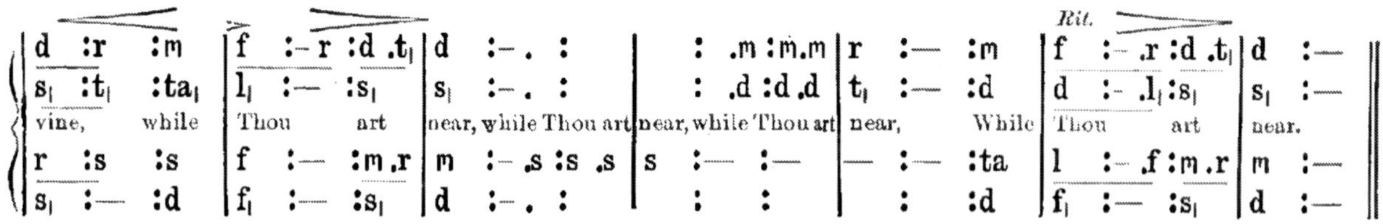
Rit.
vine, while Thou art near, while Thou art near, while Thou art near, While Thou art near.

FOREST SONG. EVENING.

MARY A. LATHBURY. T. F. SEWARD.

KEY B♭.

1.Soft thro' the fad - ing light, Falls the twi - light's pur-ple veil! Far o'er the
2.Arms of the for - est trees, Rock the rest - less winds to sleep; Si - lent the
3.Fold, then, your wea - ry wings, Troubled heart and bus - y brain, "Rest, rest," the

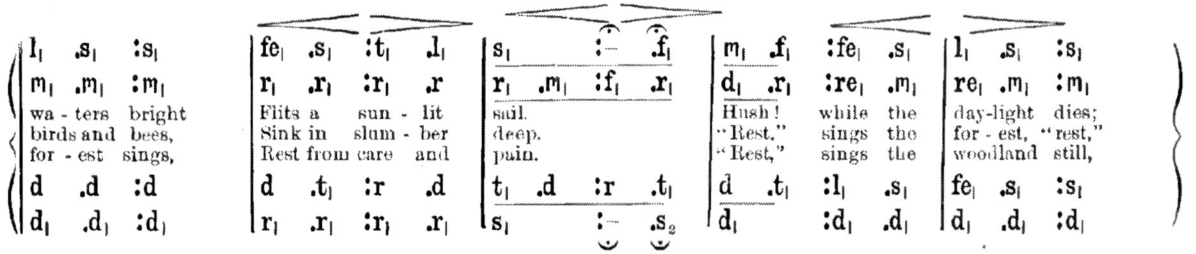
wa - ters bright Flits a sun - lit sail. Hush! while the day-light dies;
birds and bees, Sink in slum - ber deep. "Rest," sings the for - est, "rest,"
for - est sings, Rest from care and pain. "Rest," sings the woodland still,

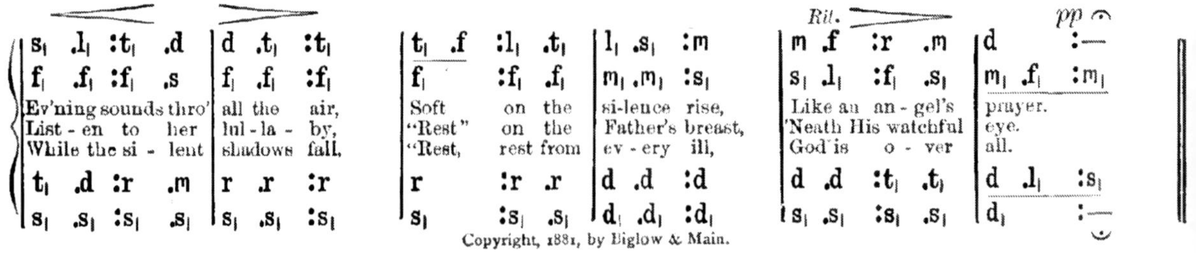
Rit. pp
Ev'ning sounds thro' all the air, Soft on the si-lence rise, Like an an - gel's prayer.
List - en to her lul - la - by, "Rest" on the Father's breast, 'Neath His watchful eye.
While the si - lent shadows fall, "Rest, rest from ev - ery ill, God is o - ver all.

AUTUMN SONG.

Emma S. Stillwell.

Key A♭.

T. F. Seward, by per.

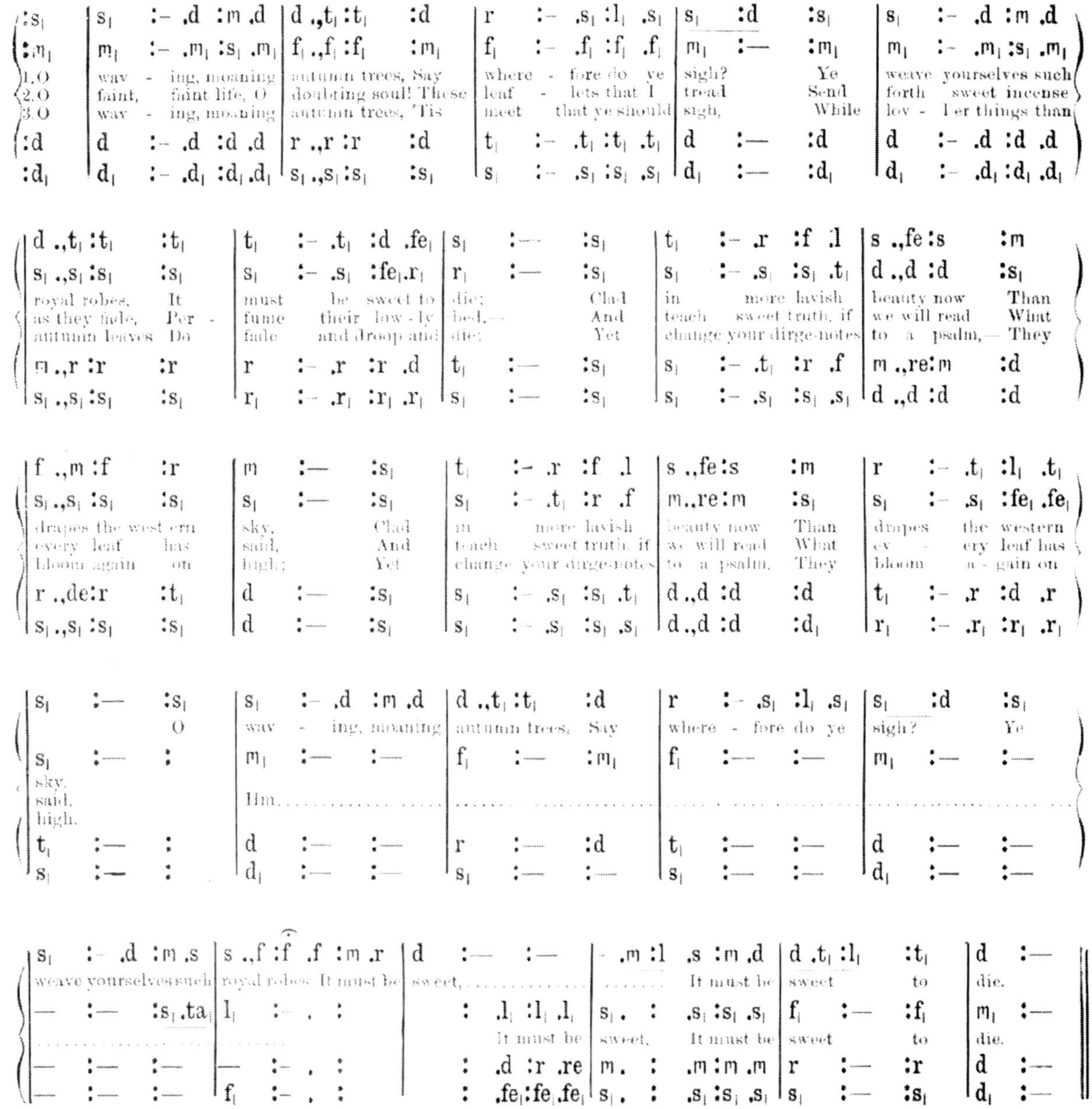

SWEET AND LOW.

Tennyson.   J. Barnby.

pp Key C. *Larghetto.* M. 100.

| m :— :m | l :— :— | s :— :s | d¹ :— :— | d¹ :t :l | s :— .s :fe |
| m :— :m | re :— :— | m :— :m | f :— :— | m :m :m | r :— .r :r |

1. Sweet   and   low,   Sweet   and   low,   Wind of   the   west - - ern
2. Sleep   and   rest,   Sleep   and   rest,   Fa - ther   will   come   to thee

| s :— :s | fe :— :— | s :— :s | l :— :— | s :r¹ :d¹ | t :— .t :l |
| d :— :d | d :— :— | d :— :d | d :— :— | d :d :d | r :— .r :r |

| l :— .— :— | s :— :— | m :— :— | l :— :l | s :— :ᵐl₁ | r :— :— |
| r :— :— | l :— :— | m :— :— | re :— :re | m :— :ᵐl₁ | t₁ :— :— |

sea,   Low,   low,   breathe   and   blow,
soon;   Rest,   rest   on   moth - - er's   breast,

| d¹ :— :— | t :— :— | s :— :— | fe :— :fe | s :— :ᵐl | s :— :— |
| s :— :— | — :— :— | d :— :— | d :— :d | d :— :ᵈf₁ | f :— :— |

p

| s :m :f | r :— .r :m | r :— :— | d :— :— | ᵈs :t :l | s :l :s | s :d¹ :l | s :— :— |
| d :d :d | d :— .d :t₁ | t₁ :— :— | d :— :— | ᵗᵃf :— :— | f :— :f | m :m :re | m :— :— |

Wind the   west - - ern   sea.   O - ver the   roll - ing   wa - ters go,
Fa-ther will   come to thee   soon.   O - - ver   the   wa - ters   go,
                                       Fa - - - ther   will   come to his   babe,

| s :s :f | l :— .l :s | f :— :— | m :— :— | ˢr¹ :t :d¹ | r¹ :d¹ :r¹ | d¹ :d¹ :d¹ | d¹ :— :— |
| m :d :l₁ | f₁ :— .f₁ :s₁ | d :— :— | — :— :— | ᵐt :s :l | t :l :t | d¹ :m :fe | s :— :— |

                                       Fa - ther will come to   his   babe in the   nest,

pp

| s :t :l | s :l :s | s :d¹ :fe | s :— :— | d¹ :d¹ :d¹ | d¹ :— :t | l :— :— | la :— :— |
| f :— :f | f :— :f | m :— :re | m :— :— | d :m :l | se :— :se | l :— :— | d :— :— |

Come from the   dy - - ing   moon   and blow,   Blow him a - gain   to   me,
Come   from   the   moon   and blow,   Un-der the   sil - - ver   moon,
Sil - ver   sails   out   of   the west,

| t :s :l | t :l :t | d¹ :s :l | s :— :— | l :d¹ :m¹ | m¹ :— :r¹ | d¹ :— :— | ma¹ :— :— |
| s₁ :— :s₁ | s₁ :— :s₁ | d :— :d | d :— :— | l₁ :l₁ :d | m :— :m | f :— :— | fe :— :— |

Sil - - ver   sails   all   out of   the west,

p   *rall. e dim.*   *pp*

| s :— :s | s :— .l :s | s :— :s | s :— .l :s | d¹ :— :— | — :— :— | — :— :— | — :— :— |
| d :— :m | r :— .r :r | d :— :d | d :— .f :f | m :— :— | f :— :— | m :— :— | — :— :— |

While   my   lit - tle one,   while   my   pret - ty one,   sleeps.
Sleep,   my   lit - tle one,   sleep,   my   pret - ty one,   sleep.......................

| m¹ :— :d¹ | t :— .t :t | d¹ :— :d¹ | t :— .t :ta | ta :— :— | l :— :la | s :— :— | — :— :— |
| s :— :s | f :— .f :f | m :— :ma | r :— .r :ra | d :— :— | — :— :— | — :— :— | — :— :— |

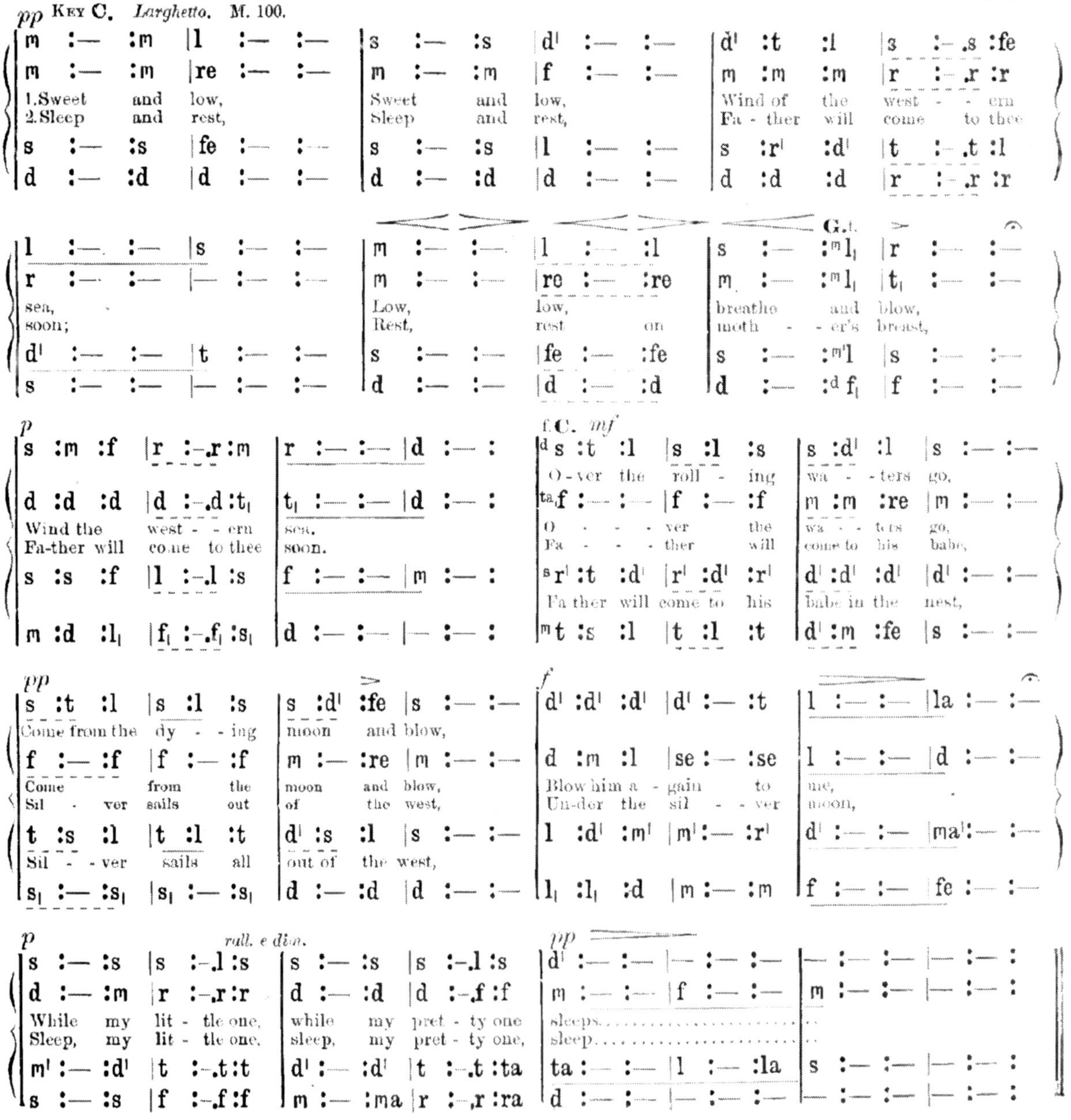

GRANDEUR.

KEY E♭. *With the utmost dignity and firmness.* Arr. from WAGNER.

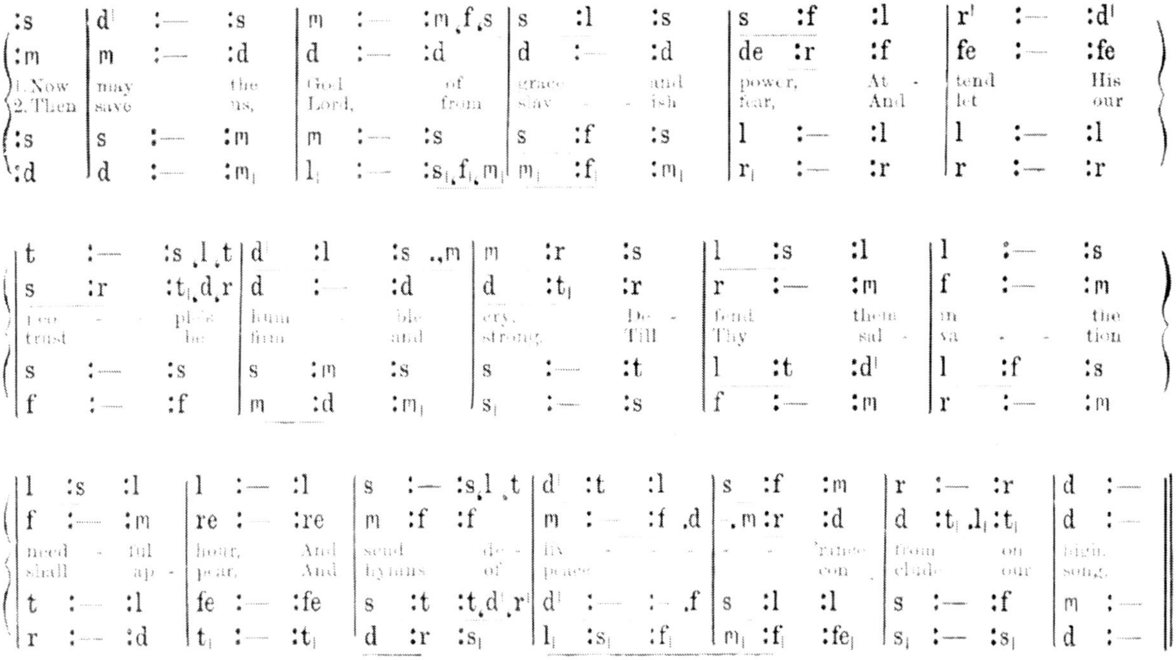
1. Now may the God of grace and power, At - tend His
2. Then save us, Lord, from slav - ish fear, And let our

TRUST.

KEY B♭. T. F. SEWARD, by per.

1. O Love Di - vine! that stooped to share Our sharp - est pang, our bit - t'rest tear, On
Thee we cast each earth - born care, We smile at pain, while Thou art near.

BOAT SONG.

MARY A. LATHBURY.

KEY F.

THEO. F. SEWARD.

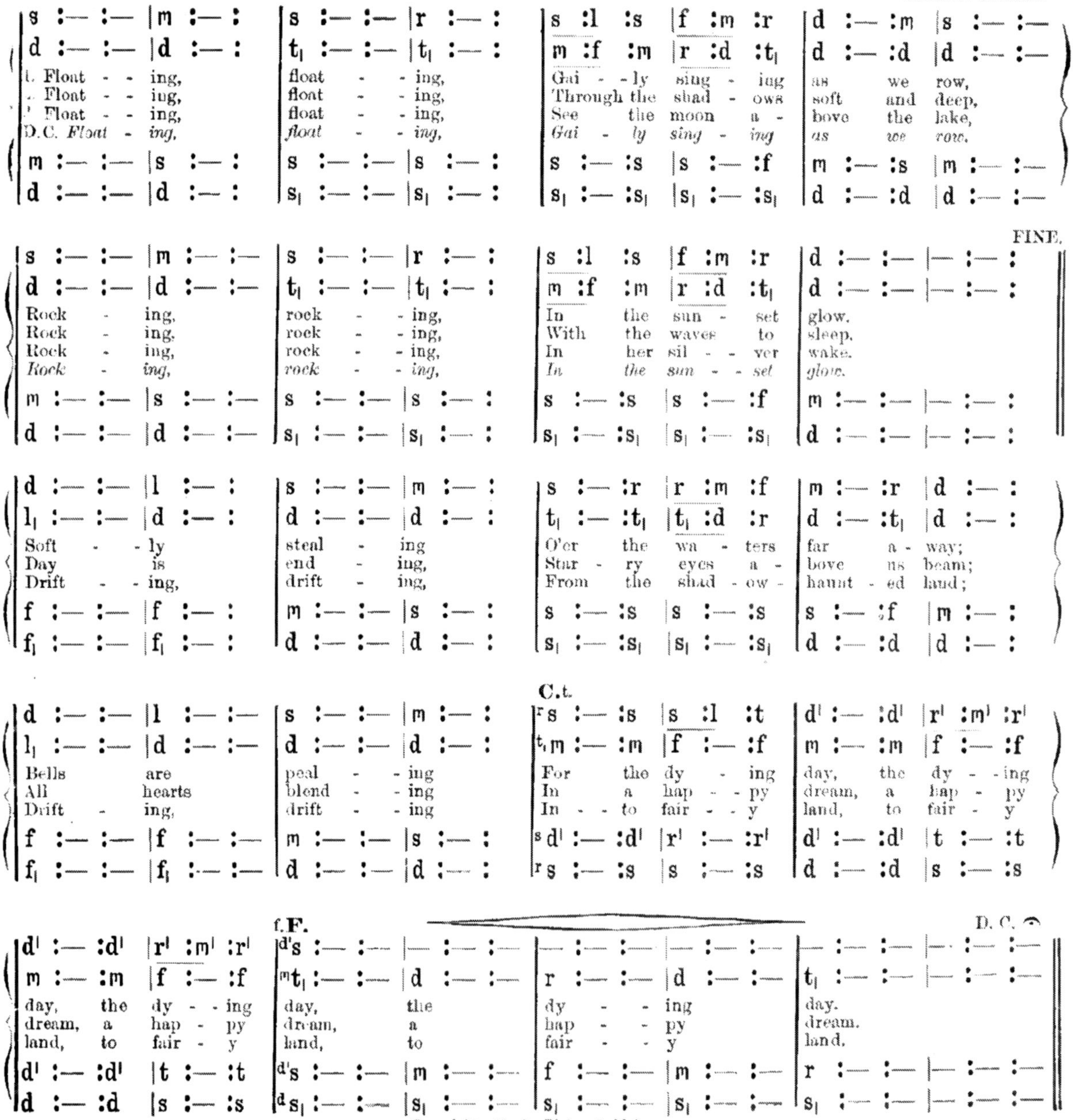
1. Float - - ing, float - - ing, Gai - - ly sing - ing as we row,
2. Float - - ing, float - - ing, Through the shad - ows soft and deep,
3. Float - - ing, float - - ing, See the moon a - bove the lake,
D.C. Float - ing, float - - ing, Gai - ly sing - ing as we row,
Rock - ing, rock - - ing, In the sun - set glow.
Rock - ing, rock - - ing, With the waves to sleep.
Rock - ing, rock - - ing, In her sil - - ver wake.
Rock - ing, rock - - ing, In the sun - - set glow.
FINE.
Soft - - ly steal - ing O'er the wa - ters far a - way;
Day is end - ing, Star - ry eyes a - bove us beam;
Drift - - ing, drift - ing, From the shad - ow - haunt - ed land;
Bells are peal - - ing For the dy - ing day, the dy - - ing
All hearts blend - - ing In a hap - - py dream, a hap - py
Drift - ing, drift - - ing In - - to fair - - y land, to fair - y
C.t.
day, the dy - - ing day, the dy - - ing day.
dream, a hap - py dream, a hap - - py dream.
land, to fair - y land, to fair - - y land.
f.F.
D.C.

EVENING HYMN.

Key D. DANIEL BATCHELLOR.

1. Day - light from the sky has fad - ed, Shad - ows fall on land and sea;
2. Flow'rs a - mid the calm of e - ven, Lift their heads refreshed with dew;
3. Babes their trusting eyelids clos - ing, Slum - ber on their mother's breast;
Ere in sleep our eyes are sha - ded, Lord, we raise our hearts to Thee!
Wea - ry hearts look up to heav - en, There to find our strength a- new.
Lit - tle birds in peace re- pos - ing, Un - der parent wings find rest.
Take not Thou Thy light a- way, Fair - er than the light of day;
Thus we thirst for Thee, O Lord! Let Thy grace on us be poured;
Whith - er shall Thy children flee, Heav'n - ly Father, but to Thee?
Fa - ther, let thy presence cheer us, Dark-ness flies when thou art near us.
Cleanse and pardon and re - store us, Shed the dew of blessing o'er us.
Thou wilt watch while in thy keep - ing, Calm and peaceful we are sleep - ing.

FABEN.

Key C. J. H. WILLCOX.

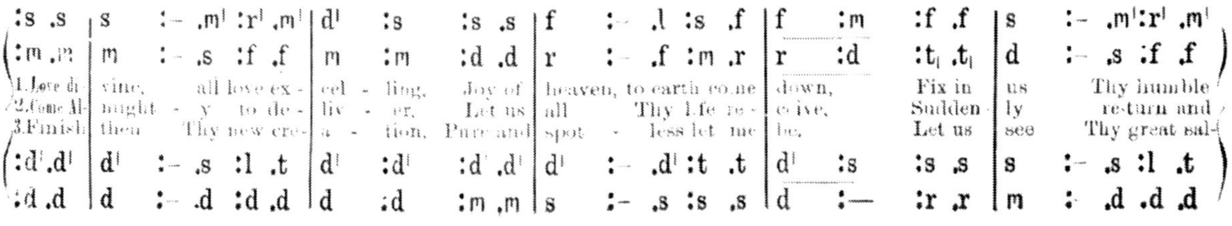
1. Love di- vine, all love ex - cel - ling, Joy of heaven, to earth come down, Fix in us Thy humble
2. Come Al- might - y to de - liv - er, Let us all Thy life re - ceive, Sudden - ly re-turn and
3. Finish then Thy new cre- a - tion, Pure and spot - less let me be, Let us see Thy great sal-

dwell - ing, All Thy faith - ful mer-cies crown: Je - sus, Thou art all com- pas - sion, Pure, un-
nev - er, Nev - er more Thy temples leave. Thee we would be al-ways bless - ing, Serve Thee
va - tion Per-fect-ly se cured in Thee: Changed from glo - - ry in - to glo - ry, Till in
bound - ed love Thou art, Vis - it us with Thy sal- va - tion, En-ter every trem-bling heart.
as Thy hosts a - bove, Pray and praise Thee without ceas -ing, Glo-ry in Thy per - fect love.
heav'n we take our place, Till we cast our crowns be- fore Thee, Lost in wonder, love and praise.

H. P. M. & Grace J. Frances.

GOOD-NIGHT, MY DARLING.

(FOR MALE VOICES.)

Key D. Hubert P. Main.

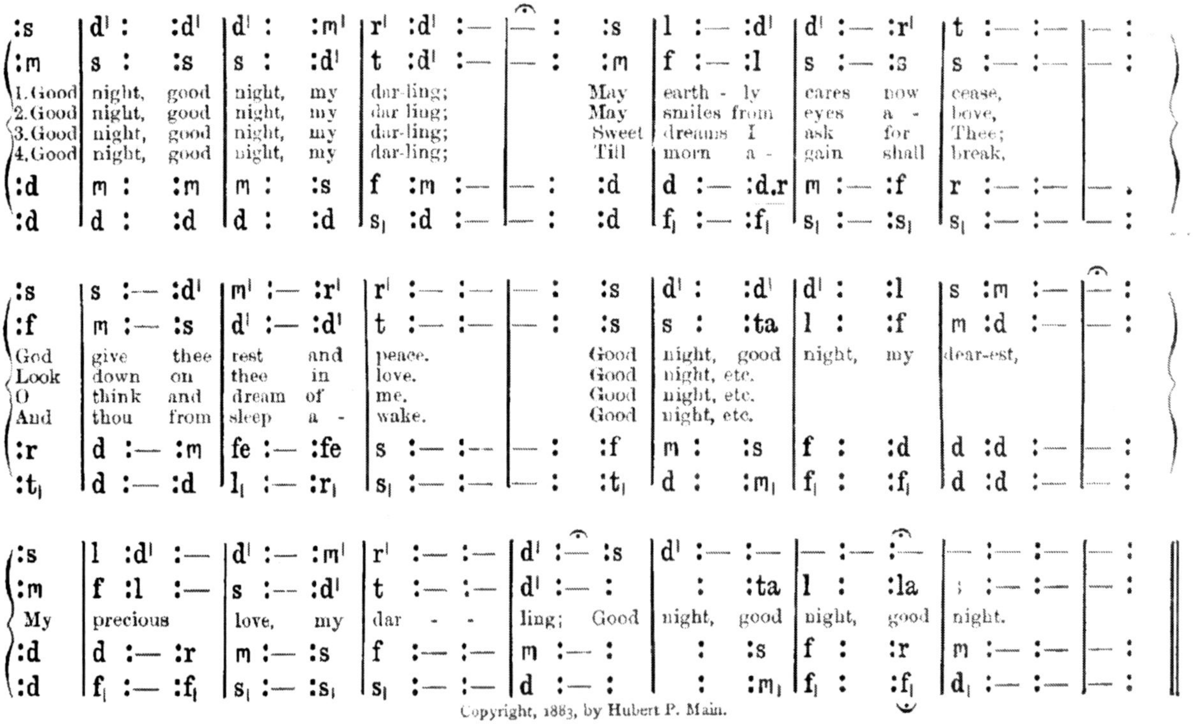
1. Good night, good night, my dar-ling; May earth - ly cares now cease, God give thee rest and peace. Good night, good night, my dear-est, My precious love, my dar - - ling; Good night, good night, good night.
2. Good night, good night, my dar-ling; May smiles from eyes a - bove, Look down on thee in love. Good night, etc.
3. Good night, good night, my dar-ling; Sweet dreams I ask for Thee; O think and dream of me. Good night, etc.
4. Good night, good night, my dar-ling; Till morn a - gain shall break, And thou from sleep a - wake. Good night, etc.

JESUS, I COME TO THEE.

Key **C.**

T. F. Seward, by per.

m	:m	:m	s	:– .f :m	f	:f	:f	f	:—	:—	t	:t	:t
d	:d	:d	m	:– .r :d	r	:r	:r	r	:—	:—	r	:r	:r

1. Je - sus, I come to Thee, no one be - side Cares for the
2. Far from the nar - row way long have I strayed, Dark clouds have
3. Back to Thy dear love for shel - ter and rest, Flee I, O

| s | :s | :s | s | :– .s :s | s | :s | :s | s | :— | :— | s | :s | :s |
| d | :d | :d | d | :– .d :d | s₁ | :s₁ | :s₁ | s₁ | :— | :— | s₁ | :s₁ | :s₁ |

r¹	:– .d¹ :t	d¹	:m	:l	s	:—	:—	m	:m	:m	s	:– .f :m
f	:– .m :r	m	:d	:f	m	:—	:—	d	:d	:d	m	:– .r :d

sor - row I'm try - ing to hide; Help - less and des - o - late,
row - ed me where I have prayed; Now to Thy mer - cy I
Lord, like a bird to its nest: Noth - ing I bring Thee, but

| s | :– .s :s | s | :d¹ | :d¹ | d¹ | :— | :— | s | :s | :s | d¹ | :– .d¹ :d¹ |
| s₁ | :– .s₁ :s₁ | d | :d | :d | d | :— | :— | d | :d | :d | d | :– .d :d |

d¹	:d¹	:d¹	l	:—	:—	l	:r¹ .d¹ :t .l	s	:l .t :d¹	s .f	:m	:r
m	:m	:m	f	:—	:—	f	:t .l :s .f	m	:f	:m	m .r	:d	:t₁

tired with my sin, O - pen Thine arms to me, Lord, take me
come with my sin, Pit - y and Thine com - fort me, Lord, take me
sor - row and sin, O - pen Thine arms for me, Lord, take me

| d¹ | :d¹ | :d¹ | d¹ | :— | :— | d¹ | :l | :t .d¹ | d¹ | :s | :s | s .l | :s | :f |
| l | :l | :l | f | :— | :— | f | :f | :f | m | :r | :d | m .f | :s | :s₁ |

d	:—	:—	s .s :s .s :s .s	s	:—	:—	l .l :l .l :r¹ .d¹	t	:—	:—
d	:—	:—	m .m :m .m :r .f	m	:—	:—	f .f :f .f :fe .fe	s	:—	:—

in.
in. Open now Thine arms to me, Pity, Lord, and comfort me;
in.

| m | :— | :— | d¹ .d¹ :d¹ .d¹ :t .r¹ | d¹ | :— | :— | d¹ .d¹ :l .l :l .l | s | :— | :— |
| d | :— | :— | d .d :d .d :s₁ .s₁ | d | :— | :— | f .f :f .f :r .r | s | :— | :— |

d¹ .d :r¹ .d¹ :t .l	s	:l .t :d¹	s .f :m	:r	d	:—	:—
m .m :f .m :s .f	m	:f	:m	m .r :d	:t₁	d	:—	:—

O - pen now Thine arms for me, for me, Lord, take me in.

| s .s :s .s :s .s | s | :d¹ | :d¹ | d¹ .l :s | :s .f | m | :— | :— |
| d .d :d .d :d .d | d | :d | :d | m .f :s | :s₁ | d | :— | :— |

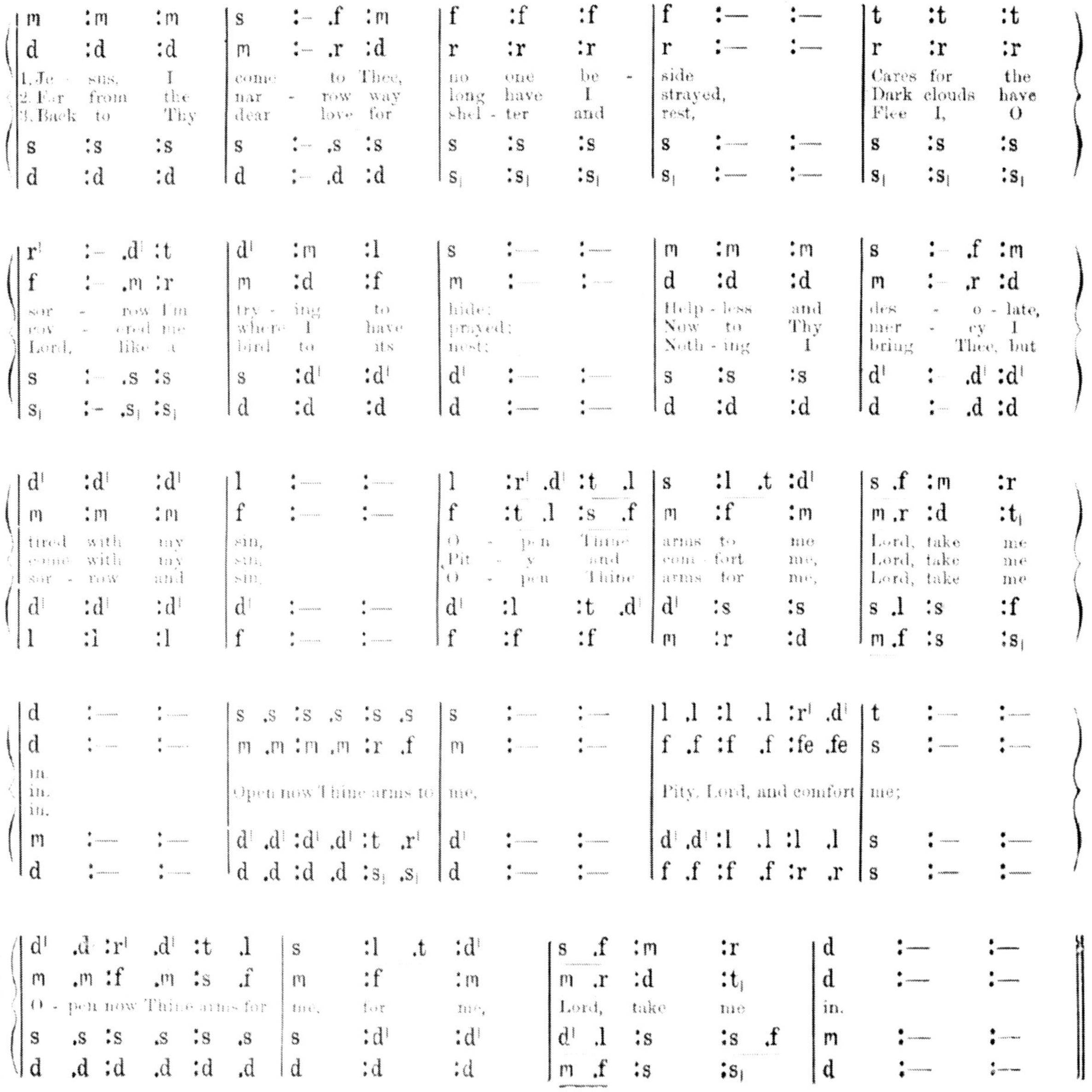

STAND BY THE FLAG.

KEY D. *Maestoso e marcato.* HENRY TUCKER.

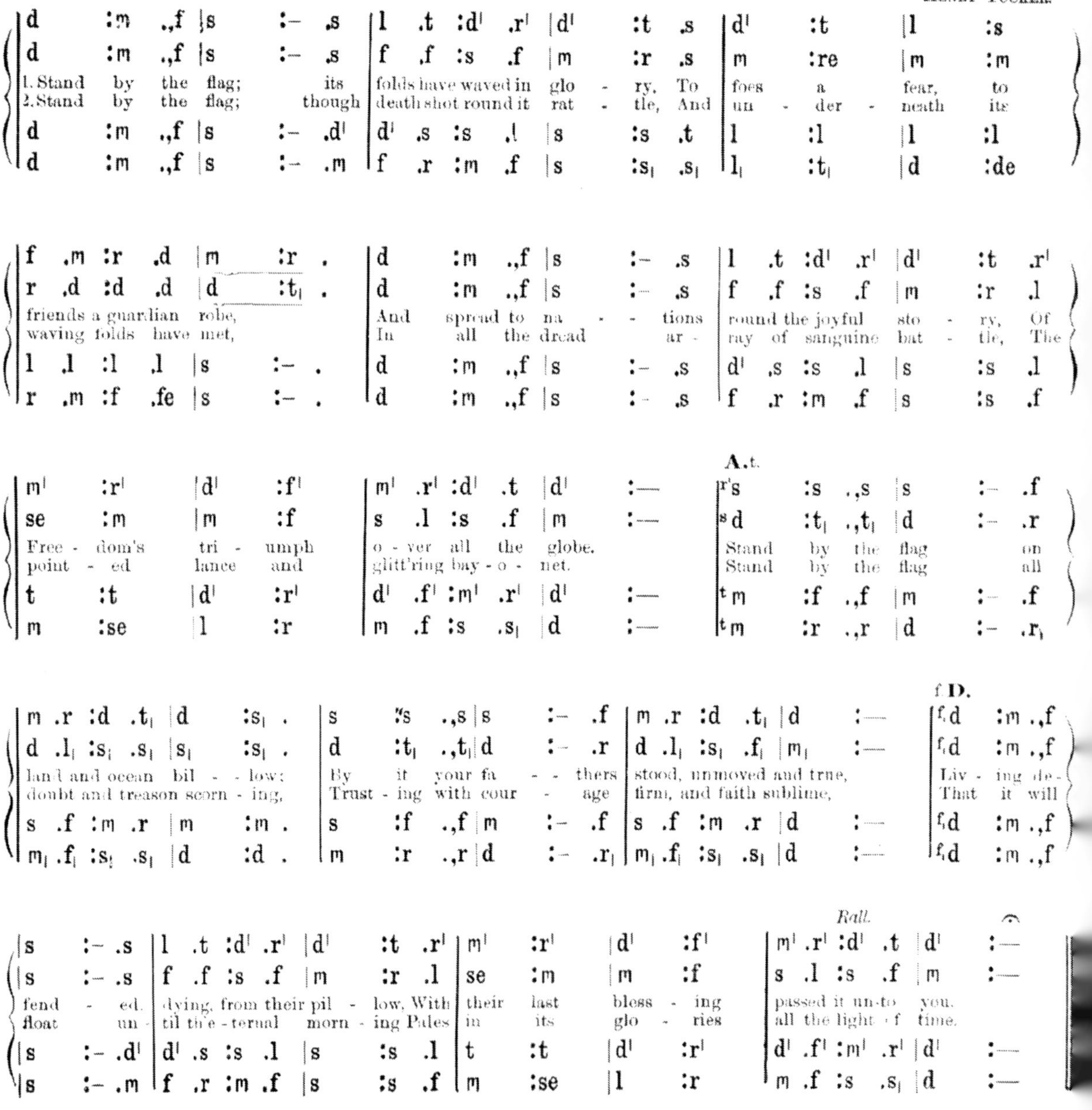
1. Stand by the flag; its folds have waved in glo - ry, To foes a fear, to
2. Stand by the flag; though death shot round it rat - tle, And un - der - neath its
friends a guardian robe, And spread to na - - tions round the joyful sto - ry, Of
waving folds have met, In all the dread ar - ray of sanguine bat - tle, The
Free - dom's tri - umph o - ver all the globe. Stand by the flag on
point - ed lance and glitt'ring bay - o - net. Stand by the flag all
land and ocean bil - - low; By it your fa - - thers stood, unmoved and true, Liv - ing de -
doubt and treason scorn - ing, Trust - ing with cour - age firm, and faith sublime, That it will
fend - ed, dying, from their pil - low, With their last bless - ing passed it un-to you.
float un - til th'e - ternal morn - ing Pales in its glo - ries all the light of time.
A.t.
f. D.
Rall.

FAITHFUL AND TRUE.

RICHARD WAGNER.

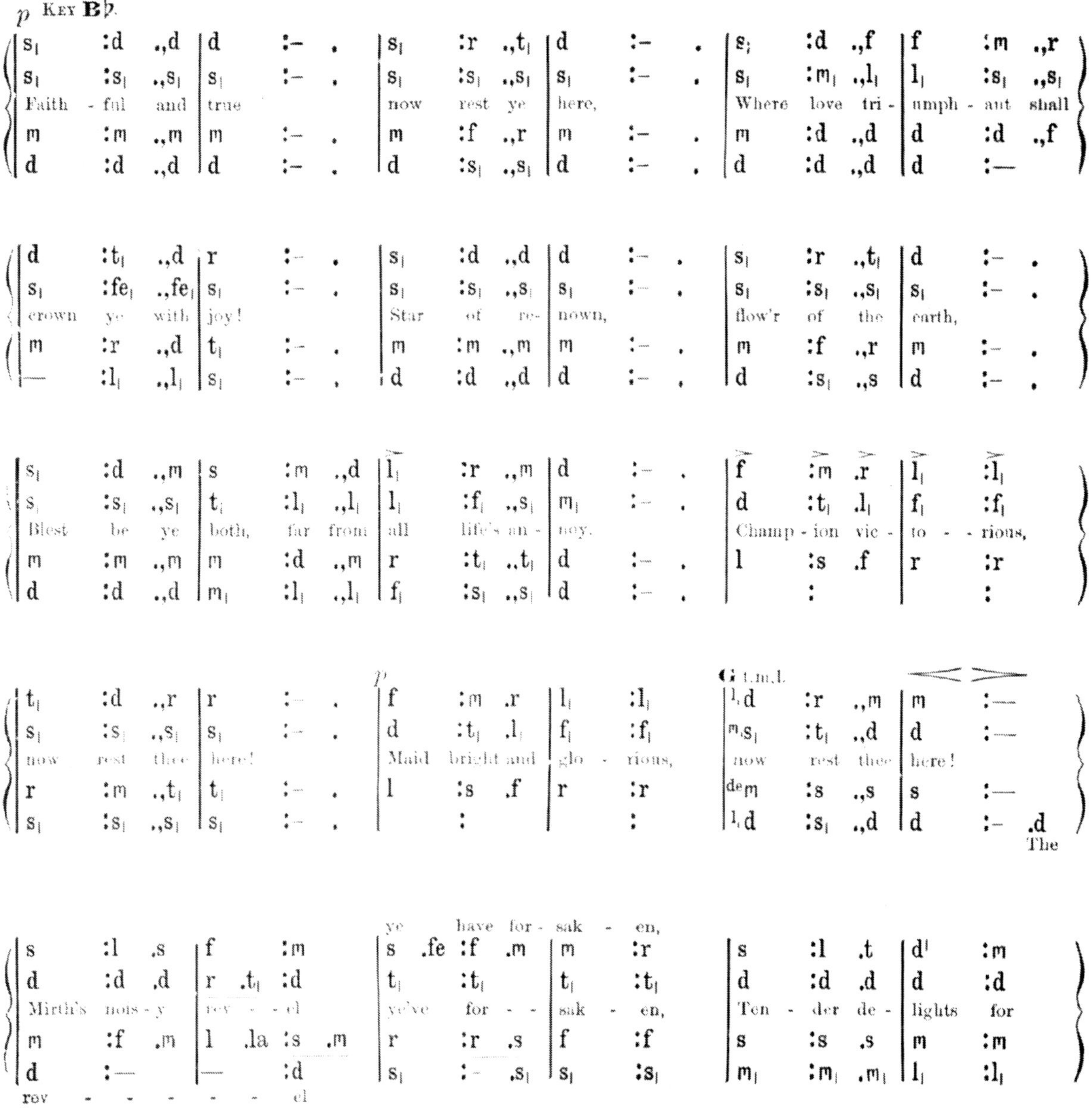

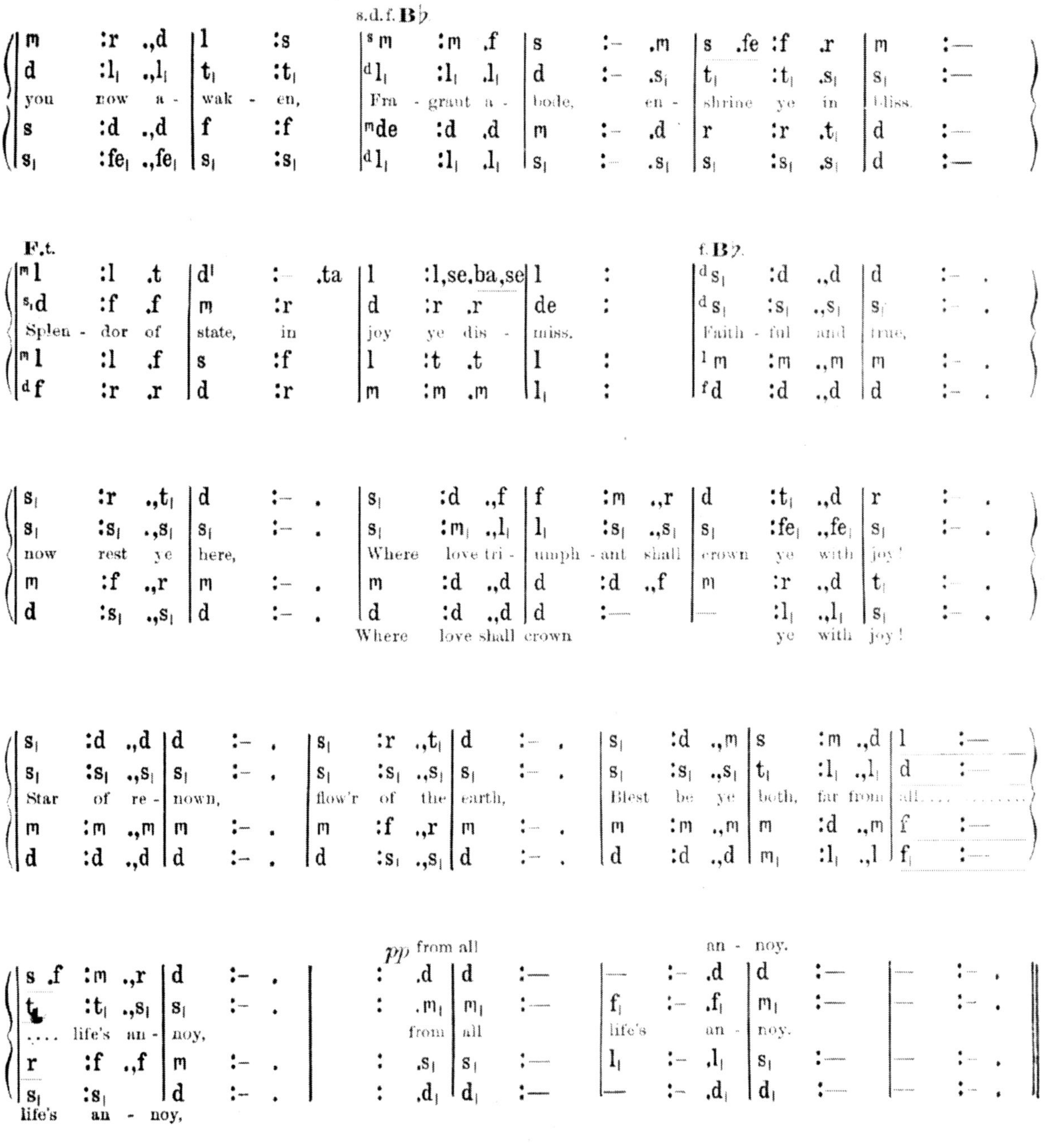

s.d.f.B♭

m	:r .,d	l	:s	ˢm	:m .f	s	:– .m	s .fe:f .r	m	:—
d	:l₁ .,l₁	t₁	:t₁	ᵈl₁	:l₁ .l₁	d	:– .s₁	t₁ :t₁ .s₁	s₁	:—
you	now a -	wak -	en,	Fra -	grant a -	bode,	en -	shrine ye in	bliss.	
s	:d .,d	f	:f	ᵐde	:d .d	m	:– .d	r :r .t₁	d	:—
s₁	:fe₁ .,fe₁	s₁	:s₁	ᵈl₁	:l₁ .l₁	s₁	:– .s₁	s₁ :s₁ .s₁	d	:—

F.t.   f.B♭.

ᵐl	:l .t	dˡ	:– .ta	l	:l,se,ba,se	l	:	ᵈs₁	:d .,d	d	:– .
ˢ₁d	:f .f	m	:r	d	:r .r	de	:	ᵈs₁	:s₁ .,s₁	s₁	:– .
Splen -	dor of	state,	in	joy	ye dis -	miss.		Faith -	ful and	true,	
ᵐl	:l .f	s	:f	l	:t .t	l	:	ˡm	:m .,m	m	:– .
ᵈf	:r .r	d	:r	m	:m .m	l₁	:	ᶠd	:d .,d	d	:– .

s₁	:r .,t₁	d	:– .	s₁	:d .,f	f	:m .,r	d	:t₁ .,d	r	:– .
s₁	:s₁ .,s₁	s₁	:– .	s₁	:m₁ .,l₁	l₁	:s₁ .,s₁	s₁	:fe₁ .,fe₁	s₁	:– .
now	rest ye	here,		Where	love tri -	umph - ant shall	crown	ye	with	joy!	
m	:f .,r	m	:– .	m	:d .,d	d	:d .,f	m	:r .,d	t₁	:– .
d	:s₁ .,s₁	d	:– .	d	:d .,d	d	:—		:l₁ .,l₁	s₁	:– .
				Where	love shall crown			ye	with	joy!	

s₁	:d .,d	d	:– .	s₁	:r .,t₁	d	:– .	s₁	:d .,m	s	:m .,d	l	:—
s₁	:s₁ .,s₁	s₁	:– .	s₁	:s₁ .,s₁	s₁	:– .	s₁	:s₁ .,s₁	t₁	:l₁ .,l₁	d	:
Star	of re -	nown,		flow'r	of the	earth,		Blest	be ye	both,	far from	all......	
m	:m .,m	m	:– .	m	:f .,r	m	:– .	m	:m .,m	m	:d .,m	f	:—
d	:d .,d	d	:– .	d	:s₁ .,s₁	d	:– .	d	:d .,d	m₁	:l₁ .,l	f₁	:—

pp from all   an - noy.

s .f	:m .,r	d	:– .	: .d	d	:—	:	:– .d	d	:—	:	: .
t₁	:t₁ .,s₁	s₁	:– .	: .m₁	m₁	:—	f₁	:– .f₁	m₁	:—	:	: .
.... life's an -	noy,			from all			life's	an -	noy.			
r	:f .,f	m	:– .	: .s₁	s₁	:—	l₁	:– .l₁	s₁	:—	:	: .
s₁	:s₁	d	:– .	: .d₁	d₁	:—	:	:– .d₁	d₁	:—	:	: .
life's	an - noy,											

MINOR MODE PHRASES,

SELECTED FROM WELL-KNOWN COMPOSERS

For the 5th requirement of the Intermediate Certificate, any one of Nos 11 to 22, taken by lot, must be Sol-faed in correct tune and time. Two attempts allowed. The key may be changed when necessary

No. 1 KEY G. *Lah is E* — From "'Tis when to sleep." SIR H. BISHOP.

| l, :l, .t, | d :r | m :f | t, :m | l .l :d | r :m | l, :— | :l, |
Still as un - daunt - ed on we stray, Through many a tan - gled brake, We

| m :— .r | d .r :d .t | l, :d | t, :m, | l, :t, | d :r | m, :— | — :— ||
pause to mark the si - lent way The cau - tious trav - 'lers take.

No 2 KEY B♭ *Lah is G* — From the "Turkish Drinking Song" MENDELSSOHN.

| l, :m, .,m, | l, :m, | t, :m, | t, :m, .,m, | d :l, .,t, | d :l, .,d | m :— | d : ||
Bump not the flask, thou churl - ish clown, On the board as tho' you would break it!

No 3 KEY A. *Lah is F♯* — From a Part-Song. W. BOYD.

:m .r | d :l, | t, :m, | l, :— .t, | d :d | r :r | f :f | m :— | — |
At Christmas - time, when frost is out, The year is grow - ing old,

:m, | l, :— .t, | d :r | m :f | m :r | d :t, .l, | t, :se, | l, :— | — ||
But sure - ly, soon as A - pril comes, 'Twill wake and bloom a - gain.

No 4. KEY C. *Lah is A* — From "The Dawn of Day" WELSH AIR.

:l | l :m | m :d' | d' :— | t :t | l :d' | t :l | l :— | se |
Sweet Spring a - gain re - turn - ing, Makes ev - 'ry bo - som glad,

:l | m :f | r :m | d :r | t, :— .d | l :l | d' .t :l .se | l :— | — ||
The birds are sing - ing from each spray, 'Tis I a - lone am sad

No 5 KEY A. *Lah is F* — From "There are good fish in the sea" J R THOMAS.

:m .r | d :d | t, .l, :t, .d | l, :— | :l, .t, | d .t, :l, .t, | m, :se, | l, :— |

:m | m .f :m .f | m :l, | m :— | :m | m :r .d | t, :m | l, :— ||

No 6 KEY D♭ *Lah is B♭* — From "Of noble race was Shenkin" WELSH AIR.

:l .t | d' :t .l | se .l :t .se | l :l, | :l, .t, | d .l, :r .t, | m :m | d :l, |
From his cave in Snow - don's mountains, Hath the pro - phet min - strel spo - ken,

:l .t | d' .m' :r' .d' | t .r' :d' .t | l .d' :t .l | se :— .m | f .m :f .r | m :se | l :l, ||
It o - mens great suc - cess in war, Of con - quest the sure to - ken.

No. 7. KEY C. *Lah is A.* From a Part-Song. H. LAHEE.

:m |l :m |f :m .r |l :m |f :m .r |l :l .se |l :l .t |d' :— |—
We | all must work, it | is our lot, Each | one must take his | part;

:m .r' |d' :d' |d' :d' .t |l :l |l :l .se |l :l .se |l :— |— ||
There's | no - thing done, There's | no - thing won, With - | out the earn - est | heart.

No. 8 KEY A. *Lah is F♯.* From a Part-Song C G ALLEN

:m, |d :— |t, :l, |t, :— |m, :m, |m :— |r :d |t, :— |—
The | sad leaves are | dy - ing, the | sweet birds have | flown,

:m, |l, :— |t, :d |t, :se, |m, :m, |d :— |r :d |t, :— |—
O'er | ev - 'ry fair | blos - som once | bloom - ing and | bright,

:t, |m :— |r :d |r :— |d :l, |m, :— |l, :se, |l, :— |—
The | frost spi - rit | lays her cold | fin - - gers to - | night

No 9 KEY B♭ From "Judas" HANDEL.

:d .r |m :se, |l, :t, .d |r :d .t, |d :r .m |f :m .r |m :r .d |t, :l, |m :— |— ||
Where war - like | Ju - - - - das | wields his | right - - eous | sword

No. 10. KEY F. *Lah is D.* From "The Owl" J R. THOMAS

:m |l :m .,m |d :m .,m |t, :m |l, : .,t, |d :d .,r |m :m |l, : |
Mourn | not for the owl, nor his | gloom-y plight, The | owl hath his share of | good,

:m |m :t, .,d |l, :m .,m |m :t, .d |l, :t, |d :m .,m |l :— .r |m :— |
Nor | lone - ly the bird, nor his | ghast - ly mate, They're | each un- to each a | pride,

:se |l :s .s |f :m .m |r :d |f :— .m |l :f .r |m :m |l, :— |
Thrice | fond - er, per-haps, since a | strange dark fate Has | rent them from all be - | side.

No. 11. KEY B♭. *Lah is G* From "Good night, thou glorious sun" HENRY SMART

:m, |m, :— .m, |ba, :se, |l, :l, |t, :t, |d :m |r :l, |d :— |t, ||
Veil'd | by thy cloak of | crim- son gold, Thy | day's high du - ty | done

No 12 KEY C. *Lah is A* From the tune "Hereford" P LA TROBE

:l |se :l |se :m |m :re |m :m |ba :se |l :t |d' :t |l ||
On | thee a - lone our | spi - rits stay, While | held in life's un - | e - ven way.

No. 13. KEY D. *Lah is B.* From "Jephtha." HANDEL.

:m |l :m |ba :se |l :— | :t |d' :se |l :t
Or | heav'n, earth, seas and | sky In | one con fu - sion

|d' :— | :f |m :r |d :t |l, :— |— ||
lie, Ere | in a daugh - ter's | blood.

No. 14 KEY D. *Lah is B* From "The Lady of the Lea." HENRY SMART.

| m :m | ba :se | l :t | d^1 :— | d :d | r :— .d | d :— | — :— ‖
Cold with - in the grave lies she, Sleep - ing peace - ful - ly.

No 15 KEY D. *Lah is B* From "Black-eyed Susan." LEVERIDGE.

.m :l .t | d^1 :t .l :se .l | m :— .f :m .r | d :t_1 .l_1 :d .,r | m :—
All in the downs the fleet was moor'd, The streamers wav - ing in the wind,

.d :m .ba | se :m .m :l .t | d^1 :m^1 . : | m .,l :d^1 .t :l .,se | l :— ‖
Does my sweet Wil - liam, Does my sweet Wil - liam Sail a - mong your crew?

No 16 KEY C. *Lah is A.* From "Now May is here" HENRY SMART

:l .se | l :t | se.ba :se.l | t :se | m :l .se | l :se | t :m | d^1 :— | — ‖

No 17. KEY A. *Lah is F♯* From the same.

:l_1 | m :— | t_1 :se_1 | m_1 :— | — :m_1 | ba_1 :se_1 | l_1 :t_1 | d :— | — ‖

No 18 KEY C. *Lah is A* From "Achieved is the glorious work." HAYDN.

| m :m | ba :m | ba :se | l : | l :se | l :s | f :— | m :

| l :t | d^1 :d^1 | l :t | se : | se :se | l :l | m :— | m : ‖

No 19 KEY C. *Lah is A* From "Esther" HANDEL.

:m | se :m | l :— | se :m | ba :se | l :— | se :l | t :se | d^1 :— | t ‖
For ev - er bless - ed, For ev - er bless - ed, For ev - er bless - ed.

No 20 KEY B♭ *Lah is G* From "Jack Frost" J L HATTON

| d :t_1 | se_1 :m_1 | ba_1 :se_1 | l_1 :t_1 | d :r | t_1 :se_1 | l_1 :t_1 | se_1 :—

| m_1 :se_1 | l_1 :l_1 | d :t_1 | t_1 :l_1 | m :se_1 | l_1 :d | t_1 :se_1 | l_1 :— ‖

No 21 KEY C. *Lah is A* From "The Three Fishers" G. A. MACFARREN.

| m :ba | m :ba | se :l | se :l | t :d^1 | t :d^1 | r^1 :d^1 | r^1 :t | l :— | — :— ‖

No. 22 KEY E♭ *Lah is C* Phrases from "Israel in Egypt." HANDEL.

:se | l :m | ba :se | l :f | m :— | l :— | — :se | ba :se | l

:se | l .t :d^1 .l | se :— | m :— | :d^1 | l :se | m :m | ba :ba | se

:se | l :— | :m | se :ba | m :ba | se :l .t | d^1 :l | se :— | ‖

Voice training naturally divides itself into three departments—the training of the chest, the training of the larynx and the training of the mouth; in other words, the control of the breath, the proper use of the registers and the production of good tone. There must be exercises for training and strengthening the muscles of the chest, to obtain control over the slow emission of the breath; exercises for developing and strengthening the registers, and exercises for placing and purifying or beautifying the tone. Only the general principles of voice training are given here. More complete instructions will be found in the Standard Course and Teachers' Manual. Behnke's "Mechanism of the Human Voice" and Webb and Allen's "Voice Culture" are also recommended, especially the latter for exercises and studies.

The vocal organ is a wind instrument, the machinery of which consists of—

THE BELLOWS.—The *Chest* and *Lungs*—which supplies the motive-power—breath.

THE TONE-PRODUCER.—The *Larynx*—which creates the tone.

THE RESONATOR.—The *Throat* and *Mouth*—which gives color or quality to the tone.

The Bellows.—The apparatus of breathing may be thought of as a wind-chest, having at the back the back-bone, at the sides and in front the ribs and breast-bone, and at the bottom a movable floor called the diaphram. This diaphram is a muscular membrane placed across the body, forming a flexible partition between the chest and abdomen. It is arched upward like an inverted basin. During inhalation it flattens and descends, thus increasing the capacity of the chest. The lungs, which fill the greater part of this wind-chest, are like two great sponges, full of cells, containing air. Respiration consists of two acts—namely, inspiration, taking in the air, and expiration, giving it out. The forces by which these acts are carried on are the natural elasticity of the lungs and the muscular action of the ribs and diaphram. It is not necessary for our present purpose to describe all the actions of the muscles used in breathing, it is enough for the singer to know that such muscles exist and that they need to be trained and strengthened. *The Wind-pipe* is a tube or passage-way for the air to and from the lungs. On the top of the wind-pipe is placed

The Tone-Producer—The instrument of voice, which is in every persons throat, is called the *Larynx* or *Voice-box*. It is a very complex structure, consisting of various cartilages and ligaments, and may be described as resembling a funnel, the bowl of which has been bent into a triangular shape. The most prominent angle forms the protuberance, which may be seen and felt on the outside of the throat, commonly known as Adam's apple. Inside the larynx are—

The Vibrators or real producers of the voice. They are two elastic cushions, or lips, with sharp edges, called rather inappropriately the "vocal cords." They are attached to the walls of the larynx, one on each side, and in ordinary breathing are drawn apart, thus allowing the air to pass up and down freely. When the voice is to be produced they are brought together in the middle of the larynx, thus closing the passage, so that the air from the the lungs being forced past the vocal cords, sets them in vibration and thus produces a tone. The *pitch* of the tone produced is according to the *thickness*, the *tightness*, and the *length* of the vocal cords set in vibration. The thicker, looser and longer the cords are the lower is the tone produced; and the thinner, tighter and shorter they are the higher is the pitch of the tone. Let it be clearly understood that the voice *originates* in the larynx, its pitch is varied there, its quality, good or bad, it gets in the mouth.

The Registers are caused by the *quantity*, that is, the thickness and length, of the vibrating membranes put in use. A register is a series of tones produced by the same mechanism—by the same adjustment or action of the vocal cords. In the lowest or *Thick* register the tones are produced by the vibration of the vocal cords through their whole length and *thickness*. The sensation is as though the tones were produced in the chest, and for this reason this series of tones is called by many teachers the "Chest" register. In the middle or *Thin* register the tones are produced by the *thin* edges of the vocal cords alone vibrating. The sensation is that of a vibration in the throat, for this reason this series is called by many teachers the "Medium" or "Falsetto" register. For the tones of the highest or *Small* register the vocal cords are *shortened*, leaving only about one third of their length to vibrate. The sensation is as though the tones were produced in the head, hence the term "Head" register. The physical cause of the change of register is this: as the voice ascends in the Thick register the cords are stretched more and more tightly for each higher tone. When this process of tightening has been carried as far as the cartilages will bear the strain, the register is changed, and the thin edges of the cords vibrate, producing a higher sound with less effort. As the voice ascends, the process of tightening once more commences, and goes on until again the cartilages have reached the utmost point of tension. Beyond this point the voices of men do not go, but women have a still higher register, which is produced by shortening the cords. These doctrines of the registers are not founded upon mere conjecture, but are based upon facts obtained by actual observation, by means of the laryngoscope,* of the action of the vocal cords in the living throat.

The point at which the vocal cords naturally change from the *Thick* to the *Thin* register is just below the pitch G, most commonly the break occurs at E or F. This break is at the same point of absolute pitch in all voices, whether of men or women. It is in the higher part of the male voice and lower part of the female voice. The change from the Thin to the Small register occurs only in the upper part of the female voice, about the pitch of g', top of the treble staff. The change from the Lower Thick into the Upper Thick, and from the Lower Thin into the Upper Thin are changes of quality more than changes of mechanism or action of the larynx.

* The laryngoscope (*larynx-seer*) is a small mirror with a slender handle. By placing it in the back of the mouth, over the throat, and with a properly adjusted light, the whole machinery of the larynx may be plainly seen.

The diagram shows the ordinary range of the human voice, the compass of the different voices and the divisions of the registers. It will be noticed that the Tenors and Basses use the Thick register almost exclusively. Men naturally use this register in speaking. Very rarely a man may be heard speaking in his Thin register, with a thin, squeaking quality. The constant use of the Thick register in speech is the reason why men are tempted to strain their voices upward, and to neglect the cultivation of their Thin register. Tenors should carefully train the upper tones of the Thick and Lower tones of the Thin register. Women commonly speak in their Thin register—occasionally a woman is heard to speak in the rough Lower Thick. It is this common habit of using the Thin register in speech which tempts them, in singing, to employ it downward more than is necessary, and so to neglect and ignore the better tones of the Thick register. In women's voices it is the Thick register which is commonly found to be uncultivated. Many soprano singers do not know what it is, and even contraltos are afraid to employ what they think is a man's voice. In men it is the Thin register which is usually untrained, and Tenors hesitate to use what they think is a woman's voice.

It is never safe to force a lower register higher than the limit here given. The upper register may and should be carried downward over or through several tones of the lower register. It is in this way that a blending or equalization of the registers is accomplished. A good singer should be able to pass from one register to another without allowing the difference to be noticed. The three tones of the Upper Thick register, D E F, which may be sung in either the Thick or the Thin register, are called optional tones, and the pupil is advised to exercise both registers on these three tones in order to equalize their quality and power and to use either register interchangeably.

We now come to the third and last part of our instrument, namely—

The Resonator—The throat and mouth. *Quality of Voice* (that which makes the difference between a hard, wiry voice, a soft, clear voice, a muffled, hollow voice, a full, rich voice, etc.), depends chiefly upon the mouth, though to some extent on the management of the breath and the natural peculiarity of the larynx. The mouth can be put into a great variety of positions, so as to enlarge, lessen, or alter its cavity. The different positions produce the different vowels—"oo," "ah," "ee," etc. It is the shaping of the mouth more than all that determines the quality of the tone produced; and the physical part of voice training, besides strengthening the lungs and bringing the vocal cords under the will of the singer, consists in learning to strengthen the good and suppress the bad elements of which every sound is made up.

The direction of the breath is an important point. The cardinal rule is "throw the breath forward." Do not let it strike at the back of the mouth, or pass up through the nostrils, but try to direct it upon the *roots* of the upper front teeth. Think of the tone as being produced, apparently, between the lips, rather than in the throat. The quality of the tone depends greatly upon the *habit* of throwing the air stream *forward* in the mouth. Certain vowels naturally favor this habit more than others. In English, "*ee*," "*ai*," "*o*" and "*oo*" (as in "*peel*," "*pail*," "*pole*" and "*pool*"), are all "forward" vowels. These vowels, however, do not promote the proper opening of the mouth. The most useful vowel in vocal practice, that which opens the mouth properly and places the tongue most favorably, is the open vowel "*ah*" (as in *father, bar, far*, etc.). But this vowel is commonly formed by most persons far back in the mouth. To bring it forward, begin the tone with "*oo*" placed well forward, upon the lips, then change the "*oo*" to "*o*," keeping the tone forward, and finally change the "*o*" to "ah," keeping the "*ah*" forward. It is better to precede these "*oo, oh, ah*" exercises with staccato exercises upon the syllable "*koo*" to secure a *clear attack*; they also throw the tone forward and make the throat supple.

Voice Training in Class.—It is only to a small extent that voice training can be carried out in class, but the experience gained in a well trained class will encourage many pupils to seek additional practice in private lessons under a competent teacher. Only when the pupils themselves are intelligent and observant students of their own voices can voice training in class be profitable. In ignorant and careless hands it may destroy voices by forcing them up into unnatural registers. No teacher should attempt to carry his pupils far into these studies, who has not himself studied and been trained in them. It is well for the student to know at once that the secret of success will not be in the particular form of his exercises, or in the multitude of them, or in their being written by this man or the other,—but in their being frequently used and perfectly worked through. Every one should seek to have a *cultivated* voice. The cultivated voice is known from another by its first sound. There is no mistaking the master of his instrument.

a.—The double horizontal lines at *a* shows the places of the great break between the Thick and Thin registers.

b.—The single lines at *b*, *c* and *d* show the places of the lesser breaks.

e.—The dotted lines show the average places of the breaks.

Only the ordinary compass of voices is given in the above diagram. Many voices are capable of carrying the tones several degrees higher or lower than the limit here assigned. In practice, however, it is best never to force the extreme tones. The pupil should confine his practice to those tones that can be reached with comparative ease.

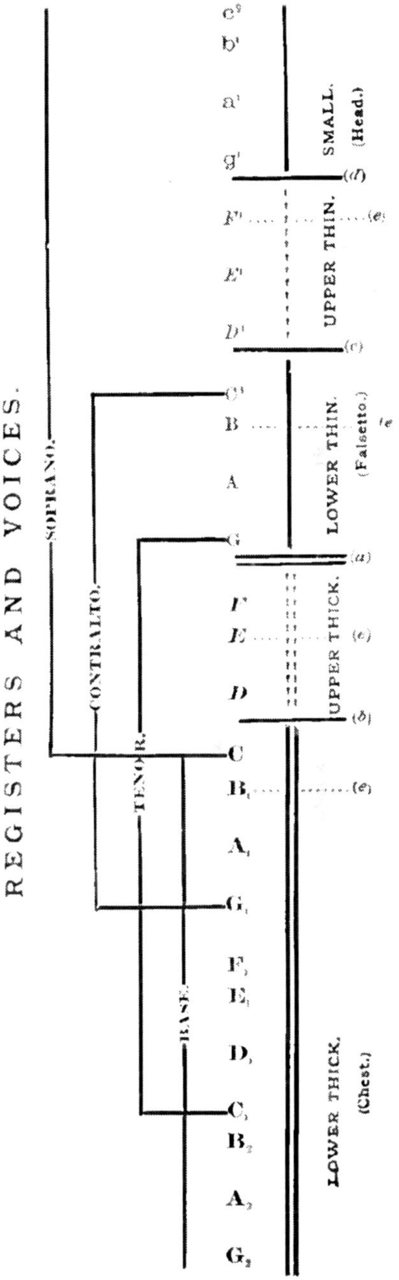

Breathing Exercises.—Position Pupils standing, arms akimbo, hands upon the waist, fingers in front

I *Inhale* slowly as the teacher raises his hand

Draw in the breath through a small opening in the nearly closed lips, as though sipping hot soup Expand the waist and lower part of the chest bu to not raise the shoulders

Exhale suddenly as the teacher drops his hand

Expel the air through the wide open mouth, as in a heavy sigh

Repeat a number of times.

II *Inhale* as above Hold the breath while the teacher's hand remains up, about four seconds.

The breath must be held, not by closing the throat, but by keeping the chest distended—the mouth and throat open

Exhale as above Several repetitions

III. *Inhale* rapidly and deeply, through the nostrils, as the teacher raises his hand with a quick movement

Exhale slowly and steadily as the teacher gradually lowers his hand

Expel the air through a small orifice in the lips, as though "blowing the fire" or cooling the hot soup. The air must not ooze out, as it were, of it own weight, but should be forced out with more or less pressure from the chest Repetitions

IV *Inhale* quickly as in III

Exhale slowly through the closed teeth forming the sound of *s* (as in *hiss*) This may also be done with *f*, *th*, *sh*, also changin from *s* to *f*, etc, without stopping the flow of breath

Repetitions

V *Inhale* as in III

Exhale sustaining the tone G, vowel *Ah*, while the teacher slowly counts eight; again ten, and again twelve, etc Increase th length of tone at each lesson until it reaches twenty or more counts

It is not intended that *all* of the above exercises are to be done at each lesson, only one or two should be done at a time They should be introduced in the order given, and when all of them have been practiced the teacher will vary the exercises so as t avoid sameness and mere routine

1 Keys **D, E, F.** May be used in First Step To be taught by pattern

| d : | d : | d .d :d .d | d : | d :— | — :— | — :— | — : |
| Koo, † | koo † | koo, koo, koo, koo, koo, † | Oo | Oh | Ah . . † |

| m : | m : | m .m :m .m | m : | m :— | — :— | — :— | — : |
| Koo, | koo | koo, koo, koo, koo, koo, | Oo | Oh . | Ah |

| s : | s : | s .s :s .s | s : | s :— | — :— | — :— | — : |
| Koo, | koo | koo, koo, koo, koo, koo, | Oo | Oh | Ah . . . |

| s : | m : | d .d :d .d | d : | d :— | — :— | — :— | — : |
| Koo | koo | koo, koo, koo, koo, koo, | Oo | Oh | Ah . . |

2 Keys **C, D.**

| d :— | m :s | d' :— | — :— | — :— | — : | d' :— | s :m | d :— | — :— | — :— | — : |
| Koo | koo koo | koo | Oh | Ah † | koo, | koo, koo, | koo | Oh | Ah . . |

1. KEYS **E, F, G.** *May be used in Second Step.*

d :—	—̂ : †	r :—	—̂ : †	m :—	—̂ : ‖
Koo......oh........ah		Koo.....oh........ah		Koo......oh........ah	

2. KEYS **E, F, G.**

d :—	—̂ :	d :r	m :r	d :r	m :r	d :r	m :r	d :—	— : ‖

Oo.................. † Oo..

Oo,...oh............ † Oh..

Oo,...oh....ah...... † Ah..

Koo................. † Oo.......................oh.......................ah..........................

3. KEYS **E, F, G.**

d :—	—̂ :	d.r :d.r	m.r :m.r	d.r :d.r	m.r :m.r	d.r :m.r	m.r :m.r	d :—	— : ‖

Oo.................. † Oo..

Oo....oh............ † Oh..

Oo....oh....ah...... † Ah..

Oo.................. † Oo.......................Oh.......................Ah..........................

4. KEYS **D, E♭.** For Third Step.

d :—̂ †	r :—̂ †	m :—̂ †	f :—̂ †	s :—̂ †	l :—̂ ‖
Koo-oh-ah,	Koo-oh-ah,	Koo-oh-ah,	Koo-oh-ah,	Koo-oh-ah,	Koo-oh-ah,

† If a piano or organ is available the following exercise may be used instead of No. 1 and 2, page, 179, and Nos. 1 and 4, page, 180. May also be used with the time-form of No. 1, page, 179.

Koo-oh-ah, etc.
May be carried up to E at the discretion of the teacher.

At first the practice to be confined to the limit here given. Later on, at the discretion of the teacher, the compass to be extended up to G[1] and down to, G_2 in the proper registers.

1. KEYS E, F, F♯, G.

| d :— . | d .r :m .f | s .f :m .r | d .r :m .f | s .f :m .r | d .r :m .f | s .f :m .r | d :— | — : ||

Koo....... † Oo..
Koo, .oh... † Oh..
Koo-oh-ah.. † Ah..
Koo....... † Oo......................Oh......................Ah..............................

2. KEYS E, F, F♯, G.

| d :— . | d .m :r .t | m .s :f .r | d .m :r .f | m .s :f .r | d .m :r .f | m .s :f .r | d :— | — : ||

Koo....... † Oo..
Koo, .oh... † Oh..
Koo oh-ah.. † Ah..
Koo....... † Oo......................Oh......................Ah..............................

3. KEYS D, E♭, E, F.

| d :— . | 𝄋 d :r .m :f .s | l :s .f :m .r D.S. | d :— :— | : : ||

Koo, etc. | Oo, etc.

4. KEYS C, D♭, D, and higher at the discretion of the teacher.

| d :— | 𝄋 d :r .m | f .s :l .t | d' :t .l | s .f :m .r D.S. | d :— | — : ||

Koo, etc. † | Oo, etc.

5. KEY A, A♭, G down to D. For Thin register, male voice.

Thick........................ *Thin* *Thin*

| d :— | m :s | d' :— | — : | d' :d' | d' : | t :t | t : |

Koo koo koo | *Koo* | *Koo koo koo* | *Koo koo koo*

| d' :t | l :s | l :t | d' :— | d' :— | t :— | d' :— | — : ||

Koo koo koo koo | *Koo koo koo* | *Koo koo* | *Koo.*

6. KEYS E♭, E, F, F♯, G. For Thin register, male voice.

| d :— | m :s | d' :— | — : | d' :t | l :s | d' :t | l :s | d' :r' | m' :r' | d' :t | d' :— ||

Koo koo, koo, | *Koo.......* † | *Koo koo koo koo* | etc.

7. KEYS E♭, D, D♭, C. For Thin register, male voice. May be sung by ladies and gentlemen together, ladies singing an octave lower than written.

| m' :f' | m' :r' | m' :f' | m' :r' | m' :f' | s' :f' | m' :r' | d' :— ||

Koo, koo koo koo, | etc.

KEYS D, E♭, E, F. For blending the registers.

1 LADIES.

Thick | d :— |— : † *Thin* | d :— |— : ||
Koo - oh - ah † *Koo - oh - ah*

2 GENTLEMEN

Thick | d' :— |— : † *Thin* | d' :— |— : ||
Koo - oh - ah † *Koo - oh - ah*

3 KEYS D to F. For blending registers, female voice

Thick | d' :— *Thin* |m :— *Thick* | d :— |— : † *Thick* | d :— *Thin* |s :— *Thick* | d :— |— : † *Thick* | d :— *Thin* |d' :— *Thick* | d :— |— : ||
Ah . † Ah . † Ah . . . .

4 KEYS C, C♯, D, E♭. For blending registers, male voice

Thick | d' :— *Thin* |r' :— *Thick* | d' :— |— : † *Thick* | d' :— *Thin* |m' :— *Thick* | d' :— |— : † *Thick* | d' :— *Thin* |s' :— *Thick* | d' :— |— : ||
Ah † Ah † Ah . . . ...

5. KEYS C to E, for female voice. KEYS A to D♭, for male voice

Thick | d :— *Thin* |m :— | s :— |— : | *Thick* d :— *Thin* |f :— | l :— |— :
Ah . Ah .

Thin | s :— |f :— | m :— |— : | *Thin* m :— |r :— | d :— |— : ||
Ah Ah

6 KEYS D to F.

| d :- . |m :- . | s :- . |d' :- . | d' :- . |s :- . | m :- . |d :- . ||
Oo oh ah ai ai ah oh oo.
Oh ah ai ee ee ai ah oh.

7. KEYS C to E♭.

| d :-. |m :-. | s :-. |d' :-. | m' :— |— : | m' :-. |d' :-. | s :-. |m :-. | d :— |— : ||
Oo oh ah ai ee ee ai ah oh oo.

pp 8. KEYS F. E, E♭ D.

| d .t, :d .r | m : | *pp* m .r :m .f | s :
Oo oh ah ai ee oo oh ah ai ee

| s .s :s .f | m : | s .s :l .t | d' :— ||
Oo ah ah ai ee oo oh ah ai ee

1. Keys **B♭, A, A♭** and **G.** For the *Thick* register. Sing slowly, with full, deep, resonant tones.

| m, :f, | m, :r, | m, :f, | m, :r, | m, :f, | m, :r, | d, :— | — : ||
Ah..........

2. Keys **G, A♭, A** and **B♭.**

| s, :f, | m, :f, | s, :f, | m, :f, | m, :— | r, :— | d, :— | — : ||
Ah..........

3. Keys **G, A♭** and **A.** *Small* register only. Sing softly, use very little breath.

| d' :t | l :s | d' :t | l :s | d' :t | l :t | d' :— | — : ||
Ah..........

4. Keys **G, A♭** and **A.**

Thin..........
| d :— | m :f | s :— | — : | *Small*.......... d' :— | t :l | s : | — : | *Thin*.......... f :— | m :r | d :— | — : ||

5. Keys **D, E♭, E** and **F.**

Thin.......... | d :m | s :d' | *pp* *Small*.......... m' :— | — :d' | *Thin*.......... s :m | d :— ||
Ah..........
Oo, oh, ah, ai, ee,.......... ai, ah, oh, oo.

6. Different keys for different voices.

| d :m | s :— | s .l :s .f | m :— | m .f :m .r | d :— | d .t :l, .t, | d :— ||
Oo oh ah.......... Ah.......... Ah.......... Ah..........
Ah oh oo.......... Oo.......... Oo.......... Oo..........
Ah ai ee.......... Ee.......... Ee.......... Ee..........

pp 7. Keys **C, C♯, D.**

| d .m :s .m | d .m :s .m † | f .l :d' .l | f .l :d' .l † | *m* s .t :r' .t | s .t :r' .t | *f* d' :— | — :— ||
Ah..........
| d :— | — :— | f :— | — :— | s :— | — :— | d' .s :m .s | d :— ||

8. Keys **F** to **A** for female voices. Keys **B♭** to **E♭** for male voices.

p | s, :— | — :d | m :— | — :r | d :— | — : | *m* s, :— | — :r | f :— | — :m |
Ah..........

| r :— | — : | *f* s, :— | — :m | s :— | — :f | m :— | — : | *m* s, :— | — :r |
Ah..........

| f :— | — :m | r :— | — : | *p* s, :— | — :d | m :— | — :r | d :— | — : ||
Ah..........

1. KEYS C to G. Sing the first measure three times.

D.C. twice.

| d ,r .m ,f :s ,l .f ,r | d : ||
Ah........................|...

2. KEYS C to G.

D.C. twice.

| d ,r .m ,s :l ,s .f ,r | d : ||
Ah....................|...

4. KEY C to G. Basses and Altos not higher than E♭.

D.C. twice.

| d ,d' .t ,l :s ,f .m ,r | d : ||
Ah........................|..

3. KEYS C to G.

D.C. twice.

| d',d .r ,m :f ,s .l ,t | d' : ||
Ah........................|..

5. KEYS C to G.

D.C. Sing the first and fourth measures twice. :S: D.S.

| d .r,m:f .m,r | d .r,m:f ,s.l ,t | d' : | d' .t ,l :s .l ,t | d' .t ,l :s ,f .m ,r | d : ||
Ah........

6. KEYS C to G. D.C. twice.

| d .m :s .d' :s .m | d :— : ||
Ah............................|..

7. KEYS C to G. D.C. twice.

| d ,m .s ,d' :t ,s .f ,r | d : ||
Ah............................|..

8. KEY D.

| d .m :r .f | m .s :f .l | s .t :l .d' | t .r' :d' † | d' .l :t .s | l .f :s .m | f .r :m .d | r .t, :d ||
Ah........ | ... Ah............ | ...

9. KEY D.

| d .r :m .d | r .m :f .r | m .f :s .m | f : | s .l :t .s | l .t :d' .l | t .d' :r' .t | d' : }
La la | la la | la la | la, | La........... | la........... | la........... | la,

| d' .r' :m' .d' | t .d' :r' .t | l .t :d' .l | s : | f .s :l .f | m .f :s .m | r .m :f .r | d : ||
La........... | .... | .... | ... | La........... | .... | .... | ...

10. KEYS B♭, up to F. M. 60 to 132.

:d ,r ,m | r ,m ,f :m ,f ,s | f ,s ,l :s ,l ,t | l ,t ,d' :t ,d' ,r' | d' || m' ,r' ,d' | r' ,d' ,t :d' ,t ,l | t ,l ,s :l ,s ,f | s ,f ,m :f ,m ,r | d ||
Ah.....|......

11. KEYS B up to E. M. 60 to 132.

:d ,t, ,d | r ,d ,r :m ,r ,m | f ,m ,f :s ,f ,s | l ,s ,l :t ,l ,t | d' || d' ,r' ,d' | t ,d' ,t :l ,t ,l | s ,l ,s :f ,s ,f | m ,f ,m :r ,m ,r | d ||
Ah.... |......

12. KEYS B up to E. M. 60 to 160.

| d .m :r .d | r .f :m .r | m .s :f .m | f .l :s .f | s .t :l .s | l .d' :t .l | t .r' :d' .t | d' :— }
Ah..............

| d' .m' :r' .d' | t .r' :d' .t | l .d' :t .l | s .t :l .s | f .l :s .f | m .s :f .m | r .f :m .r | d :— ||
Ah..............

1. KEYS C to E, changing registers.

{| d .r,m:f,s .l,t | d' :r' | m' :— | r',d'.t,l :s ,f.m,r | d :d' | d :— ||

2 KEYS F down to B♭.

{| d' .t ,l :s ,f.m,r | d :t, | l, :— | t,,d.r,m :f ,s.l ,t | d' :d | d' :— ||

3. KEYS G, A♭ and A. To be sung *legato* to "ah". The parts may afterwards sing simultaneously, making three octaves

SOPRANOS. CONTRALTOS and TENORS

{| d' :t .l | s .f :m .r | d :— | t, :— || d :t, .l, | s, .f, :m, .r | d :— | t,, :— ||
{| : | : | : | : || d' :t .l | s .f :m .r | d :— | t, :— ||

BASSES

{| d :t, .l, | s, .f, :m, .r, | d, :— | t,, :— | d, : | — :— ||

4 KEYS C to E, changing registers

{| d .t, .d :m .r .d | r .d .r :f .m .r | m .r .m :s .f .m | f f .m .f :l .s .f | s .f .s :t .l .s }

{| l .s .l :d' .t .l | t .l .t :r' .d' .t | d' :— | d' .t .d' :m' .r' .d' | t .l .t :r' .d' .t }

{| l .s .l :d' .t .l | s s .f .s :t .l .s | f .m .f :l .s .f | m .r .m :s .f .m | r .d .r :f .m .r | d :— ||

5. KEYS G to B♭, changing registers

BASSES D.t. TENORS.

{| d, :r, .m, | f, .s, :l, .t, | d :— | t, :l, | s d :r .m | f .s :l .t | d' :— | t :l }

A.t. ALTOS. E.t. SOPRANOS

{| s d, :r, .m, | f, .s, :l, .t, | d :— | t, :l, | s d :r .m | f .s :l .t | d' :— | — : }

SOPRANOS f A. ALTOS

{| d' :t .l | s .f :m .r | d :— | r :m | f d :t, .l, | s, .f, :m, .r, | d, :— | r, :m, }

f D. TENORS f G. BASSES

{| f d' :t .l | s .f :m .r | d :— | r :m | f d :t, .l, | s, .f, :m, .r, | d, :— | — : ||

SOLFEGGIOS.

1. KEY **G.**

| d :— | m :s | l, :— | f :r | d :t, | l, :s, | d :— | :ʳs (D t.) | l :— | t :— |

| d' :— | — :l | s :— | f :r | d :— | : | ˢr :— (f.G.) | m :— | f :— | — :s |

| m :d | l, :r | s, :— | : | d :— | r :— | m :s | l, :r | s, :— | t, :— | d :— | — : ||

2. KEY **C.**

| d :— | m :.f | s :— | d : | d' :— | t :.l | s :— | m : | ˢd :— (G.t.) | s, :— |

| l, :— | d :— | t, :.d | r :.m | d :— | — : | ᶠd :— (f.C.) | m :.f | s :— | d : |

| d' :— | t :.l | s :— | m : | d' :m | f :s | l :— | d' :— | s :m | f :r | d :— | — : ||

3. KEY **E♭.** *Lah is C.*

:m | l : :d' | t :— :se | l :— :— | m :— :d | r :— :m | d :— :m | t, :— :— | m :— |

:se | l :— :d' | t :— :se | l :— :— | m :— :d | f :— :r | m :— :— | l, :— :— | — :— || *pp* D.C.

𝄋 :m | t :— :se | m :— :se | l :— :— | m :— :d | f :— :— | t, :— :— | t, :— :— | — :— |

:m | l :— :d' | t :— :se | l :— :— | r :— :re | m :— :— | — :— :— | l, :— :— | — :— || *pp* D.S.

ETUDES.

KEY F. From WEBB & ALLEN'S VOICE CULTURE,* by per.

```
  m               p                 m                p                  m
|d,r.d,r:m  .  |d,r.d,r:m  .  |r,m.r,m:f  .  |r,m.r,m:f  .  |m,f.m,f:s  .  |f,m.f,m:r  .
 Ah.................. (and other vowels.)

                                D.C. :S:
|d,r.d,r:m,r.m,r|d  :  |r,m.r,m:r,m.r,m|r  .  :  |m,f.m,f:m,f.m,f|m  .  :

                                                                                 D.S.
|f ,s .f ,m:r  .  |m ,f .m ,r :d  .  |r  .m ,r :m ,r .m ,r |d  :  ||
```

2. KEY F. From WEBB & ALLEN'S VOICE CULTURE, by per.

```
|d ,r .d ,r:m ,f .m,f |s  :m  .  |f ,s .f ,m:r  .  |m,f .m ,r :d  .  |d,r .m,r :d ,r .m ,f
 Ah.... etc.

                                       D.C. :S:
|s  :m  .  |r  .s  :- ,fe.m,fe|s  :  |f ,s .f ,m :f ,s .f ,m|f  :r  .

                                                       †                                 D.S.
|m,f.m,r:m,f.m,r|m  :d  .  |r,m.f,m:s ,f .m,r|d  .m,r :f ,m.r ,d|s  :f,m.f ,r|d  :  ||
```

3. KEY D. From WEBB & ALLEN'S VOICE CULTURE, by per.

```
|d ,r .d ,r :d ,r .d ,r|d  :m  .  |s ,l .s ,l :s ,l .s ,l |s  :d'  .  |t ,d'.t ,d':t ,d'.t ,d'

|l ,t .l ,t :l ,t .l ,t|s  :t  .,l  |s  :  |s ,l .s ,l :s ,l .s ,l |s  :r'  .

|s ,l .s ,l :s ,l .s ,l |s  :d'  .  |l ,t.l ,t :l ,t .l ,d'|t,d'.t ,d':t,d' .t,r'|d',r' .d',r':d',r'.d',r'|d'  :
```

4. KEY D. From WEBB & ALLEN'S VOICE CULTURE, by per.

```
|d ,r .m ,f :s  .d'  |d ,r .m ,f :s  .d'  |r',d'.t ,l :s  .  |r',d'.t ,l :s  .  |d,r .m ,f :s  .d'

                                              D.C. FINE. A.t.
|r ,m .f ,s :l  .r'  |s ,d'.r',d':t ,s .f ,r |d  :d'  .  ||s d,r .m ,f :s  .l  |s ,f .m ,r :d  .

                                                                              f.D.      D.C.
|l₁,t₁.d ,r :m  .f  |m,r.d,t₁:l₁  .  |r,m.f ,s :l  .  |d,r.m,f:s  .  |s₁,l₁.t₁,d:r  .m  |d s  :  .
```

* "Voice Culture."—A complete method of theory and practice for the cultivation and development of the voice by George James Webb and Chester G. Allen. Published by The Biglow & Main Co., 76 East Ninth St., New York. In this work, which contains nearly 200 large pages, the laws governing the use and development of the human voice are fully and carefully explained. The position of the vocal organs in using the different registers of the voice is illustrated by means of diagrams. The book contains also the largest and best variety of Exercises and Etudes of any now in use.

Pronunciation.—A pure and exact enunciation, making every word stand out clear and distinct, is an essential feature of good singing. This can only be secured by special practice upon the vowels and consonants. Vowels are ways of emitting the breath; consonants are ways of interrupting it. Both require *definite* positions and movements of the lips and tongue. Musical tones cannot be prolonged upon consonants, the vowels are therefore the more important to the singer in the production of a good tone. But distinctness of utterance depends upon a sharp, clean delivery of the consonants. Some of the vowels have already been practiced in connection with the voice exercises, and will be studied more fully presently. In first attracting the attention of the pupil to the action of the articulating organs it is easier to begin with the consonants. *An articulation* is a joint. A joint implies in this case both a separation and a connection of spoken sounds. The lips may come into contact with one another, or the lip touch the upper teeth, or the tongue touch teeth or palate. There may be thus an absolute or nearly absolute stopping of the vowel sounds. And these points of separation are also made points of junction. They are joints or articulations. The muscles of articulation are chiefly in the lips and tongue, for the teeth are comparatively stationary.

The work has to be done by the *Lips*, and by *Tip*, *Middle* and *Back* of the tongue. Properly devised exercises in articulation are intended to give special practice to these muscles. Thus the teacher will arrange a group of consonants to give exercise to the lips, another group to exercise the lips and teeth, and so on.

The teacher will arrange groups for Tip-tongue, such as. *To*, *No*, *Lo*, *Do*. For the Mid-and Back tongue, *Jo*, *Go*, *Yo*, *Ko*. Various groupings may be made, as *Bo*, *Co*, *Fo*, *Lo*; *Mo*, *No*, *Po*, *To*, etc. Various forms of melody may be used instead of the scale. The consonants may also be arranged as *finals* instead of *initials*, thus, *ōp*, *ōm*, *ōb*, *ōv*, etc (long sound of ō, *ope*, *ome*, etc.) Again as both initial and finals thus, *Pōp*, *Mōm*, *Bōb*, *Vōv*, etc. And again as double articulations, thus, *op-po*, *om-mo*, *ob-bo*, *ov-vo*, etc. Consonantal diphthongs should also be practiced, such as *Blo*, *Clo*, *Flo*, *Glo*, etc. The limits of this book will not admit of a full list of such combinations. The teacher will construct such as he may think useful in his work. In these exercises the movements of the articulating muscles should be decided and energetic, considerably exaggerating the consonant element.

Vowels are produced by giving certain fixed forms to the cavity between the larynx and the lips. When the tongue, palate and lips are properly adjusted, the shape of the cavity thus formed becomes a mold into which the vowel is cast. Any change in the shape of the cavity will modify the character of the vowel. For the *Simple vowels*—those in which there is no change from beginning to end—the mouth remains fixed in one position. For the *Compound vowels*—those which end with a glide into another vowel—the mouth changes from one position to another. A common fault is to make the change too soon—thus, for "day" is heard "*da-ee*;" "great" becomes "*gra-eet*;" "high," "*hi-ee*;" "how," "*how-oo*," etc. In singing a compound vowel the position taken for the first element must be steadily held until just at the close, and then an easy glide made into the vanishing sound. The teacher will arrange different successions of vowels, as *oh*, *ah*, *ai*, *ee*, or *oo*, *aw*, *a* (at) *e* (let), and others, and sing them to the scale, ascending and descending, as suggested in the exercise below.

LONG VOWELS.

aa	(ah)	in	*bah*,	*far*.
au	(aw)	"	*Paul*,	*law*.
oa	(oh)	"	*load*,	*pole*.
oo	....	"	*cool*,	*pool*.
ai	(ay)	"	*paid*,	*pay*.
ee	....	"	*bee*,	*fee*.

SHORT VOWELS.

u	....	in	*but*,	*cut*.
a	....	"	*bat*,	*cat*.
e	....	"	*bet*,	*get*.
i	....	"	*bit*,	*sit*.
uo	(u)	"	*full*,	*pull*.

DIPHTHONGS.

ei	(I)	in	*height*,	*pine*.
oi	(oy)	"	*boil*,	*boy*.
ou	(ow)	"	*out*,	*how*.
eu	(ew)	"	*feud*,	*few*.

CONSONANTS.

LIPS.

P	in	*pine*,	*pipe*.
B	"	*bay*,	*babe*.
Wh	"	*wheel*,	*when*.
W	"	*weal*,	*way*.
M	"	*may*,	*maim*.

LIPS and TEETH.

F	in	*file*,	*fife*.
V	"	*vile*,	*revive*.

TONGUE and TEETH.

Th	in	*thin*,	*teeth*.
Dh	"	*then*,	*bathe*.

TIP-TONGUE.

T	in	*tin*,	*tint*.
D	"	*deal*,	*deed*.
L	"	*lean*,	*leal*.
N	"	*nut*,	*nun*.
R	"	*roll*,	*roar*.

MID-TONGUE.

S	in	*sell*,	*less*.
Z	"	*zone*,	*nose*.
Sh	"	*shine*,	*dash*.
Zh	"	*azure*,	*treasure*.
Ch	"	*churn*	*church*.
J	"	*just*	*judge*.
Y	"	*you*,	*due*.

BACK-TONGUE.

K	in	*keen*,	*kick*.
G	"	*game*,	*gag*.
N	"	*sing*,	*song*.

ASPIRATE.

H	in	*hail*,	*ha-ha*.

KEY **C**. The scale, ascending and descending.

d	:d	d	:d	r	:r	r	:r	m	:m	m	:m	f	:f	f	:f, etc.
Po,	Mo,	Bo,	Wo,	Po,	Mo,	Bo,	Wo, etc.								
Oh,	ah,	ai,	ee,	oh,	ah,	ai,	ee, etc.								

Make different groupings—ascending with one series and descending with another. Various forms of melody and different groups of vowels will suggest themselves to the teacher. Prefix a consonant to each vowel, thus, *Boh*, *Bah*, *Bai*, *Bee*, etc. Suffix a consonant, thus, *ohb*, *ahb*, *aib*, *eeb*, etc. Then both prefix and suffix—thus, *bohb*, *bahb*, *baib*, *beeb*, etc.

THE STAFF NOTATION.

It is recomended that instruction in the Staff Notation be defered until the Third, or better still, the Fourth Step of Tonic Sol-fa has been passed. But for the sake of those teachers who may find it expedient or who may be *compelled* to introduce the staff early in their lessons, the exercises are arranged to correspond with the steps of the method, so that the staff *may be* taught concurrently with the Tonic Sol fa. Nothing in the staff notation should be taught until the corresponding matter in Tonic Sol fa has been learned. Music is a thing apart from Notation, and the more thoroughly pupils understand the principles of *music*, the more easily will they master the staff notation.

FIRST STEP.

1. The Staff.

2. Degrees.

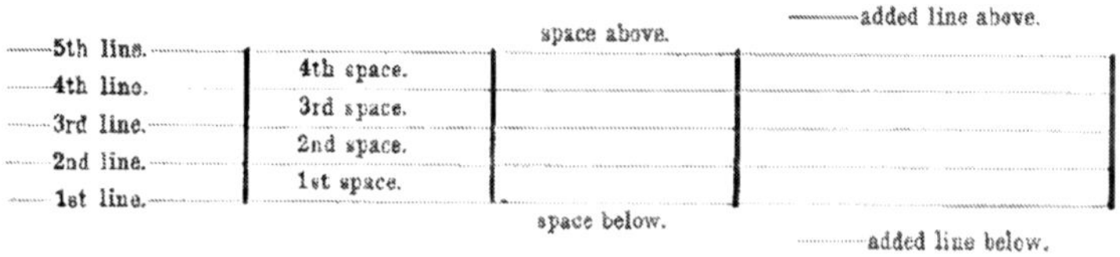

The teacher may have the pupils name the degrees as he points, thus—"First line," "Third space," "Second line," etc.

First Rule.—When *Doh* is on a line, *Me* and *Soh* are on the next two lines above. When *Doh* is in a space, *Me* and *Soh* are in the next two spaces above. *Doh, Me* and *Soh* are *similarly* placed—all on lines, or all in spaces.

The place of *Doh* is shown by the square character (■) at the beginning of each exercise. The staff *without the clef*, as in the following exercises, does not represent absolute pitch, therefore, any pitch suitable for the voices may be taken for the key-tone. The letters in parenthesis suggest the pitch which may be taken for *Doh*.

As a preliminary exercise the pupils may name the degrees in the order in which the notes are placed, thus in No. 3, the pupils will say, "First line, second line, third line, second line," and so on. The pupils may next "read the notes," that is, name the Sol-fa syllables in the speaking voice. After this the exercise is to be sung—sol-faed.

The bars are used in these exercises mainly to help the eye to keep the place in reading. The measures are numbered as a convenience in calling attention to certain notes, correcting errors, etc.

3. (E)

4. (G or B)

5. (F)

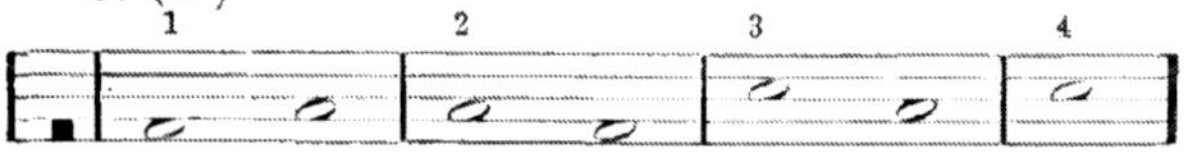

6. (A or C)

7. (D)

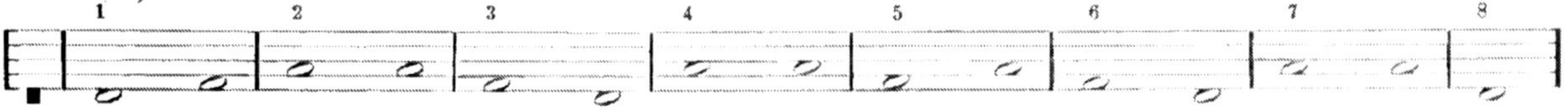

8. (D or B♭.)

1 (E)

2 (C)

3 (G)

4. (F)

5 (C)

6. (B♭ or D)

7 (G)

8 (D)

Writing Exercises.—Copy into the staff notation any of the exercises from Nos 9 to 26, pages 9 and 10, selected by the ...cher, or similar ones supplied by him They should also be sung from the staff copies

Copy into the Sol-fa notation any of the foregoing staff exercises, and then rewrite them on the staff from the sol-fa copy, plac... *Doh* differently from the printed copy

The place of *Doh* for key D space below or third line, key C, added line below, or second space; key E, first line or third ...ace, key F, first space or fourth line, key G, second line or fourth space, key A, second space

Time.—In the Staff Notation the relative length of tones is represented by notes of different shapes for the different length. The notes in common use are:

WHOLE. HALF. QUARTER. EIGHTH. SIXTEENTH.

Notes have two uses: 1. To indicate by their position on the staff, which tones are to be sung. 2. By their shape, the length of each tone. Notes have no fixed or absolute value, they represent relative length only. The names of the notes indicate their relative values. A Whole note represents a tone twice as long as a Half note, or four times as long as a Quarter note, and so on.

Any note may be taken to represent the time of a pulse. The notes commonly used as pulse-notes, are the Half, the Quarter and the Eighth. The different kinds of measures and the kind of note taken as the pulse-note are indicated by the *Measure Signature*, consisting of two figures in the form of a Fraction. The upper figure denotes the number of pulses in the measure, and the lower figure the kind of note that goes to a pulse.

Measure Signatures.

2/4 *Two-pulse measure. Quarter note to the pulse.* 2/2 *Two-pulse measure, Half note to the pulse.* 3/4 *Three-pulse measure, Quarter note to the pulse.* 3/2 *Three-pulse measure, Half note to the pulse.*

The bar indicates the strong accent, but there are no marks for the weak and medium accents.

1. TAA TAA TAA - AA

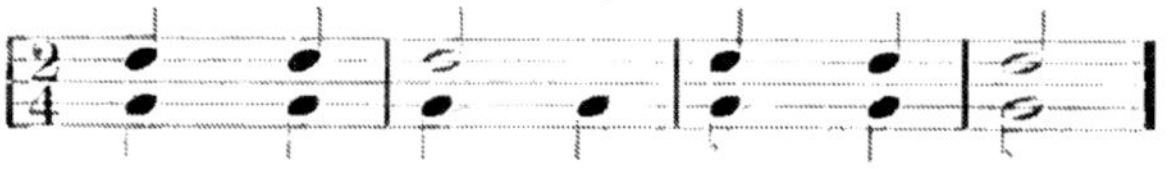

2. TAA TAA TAA TAA TAA - AA

Each part to be taataied as a separate exercise, then the two continuously as one.

The **Tie** indicates the continuation of the tone for the time of both notes. The **Dot** increases the value of any note one half.

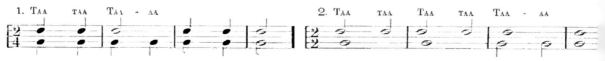

The Tie.

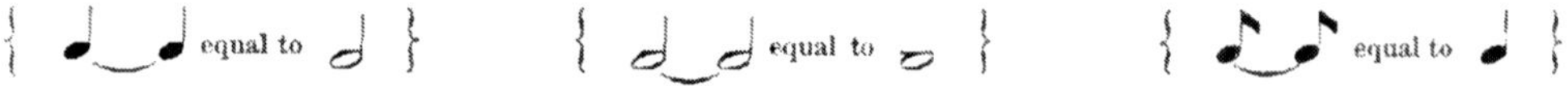

The Dot.

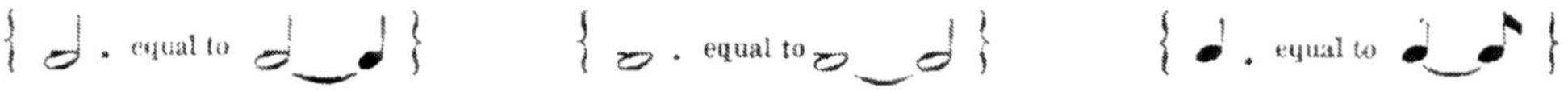

3.

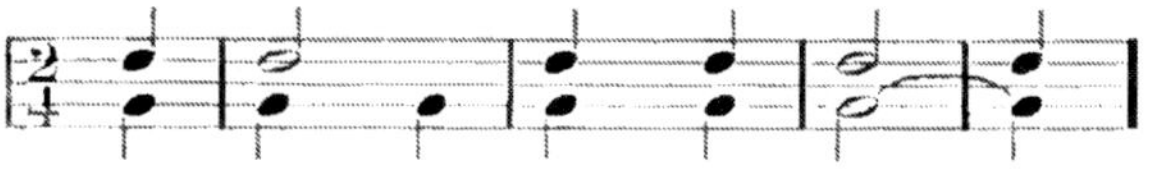

4.

5.

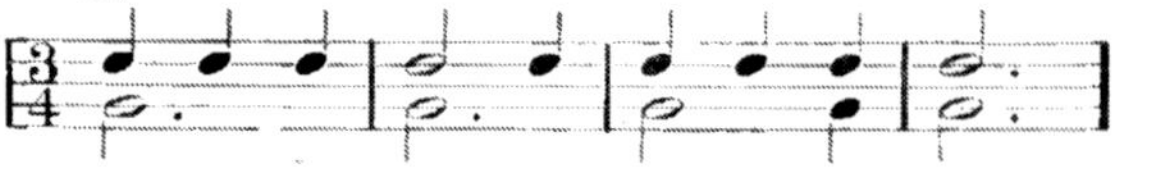

6.

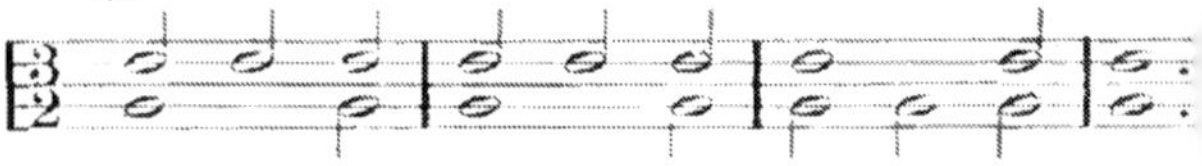

7.

8. *Three-pulse measure. Eighth note to the pulse.*

1. (C)

2. (G)

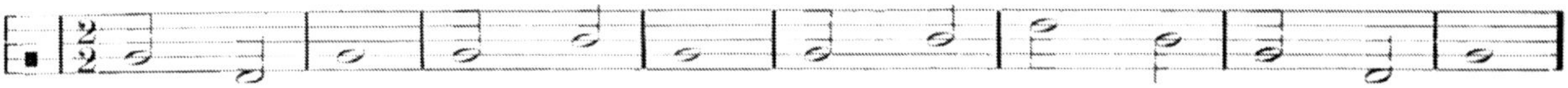

3. (D)

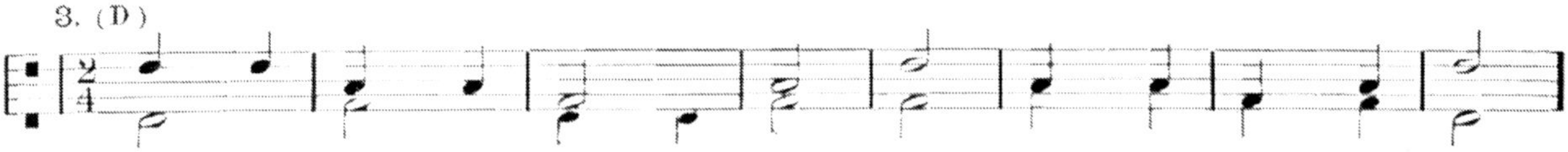

4. (F)

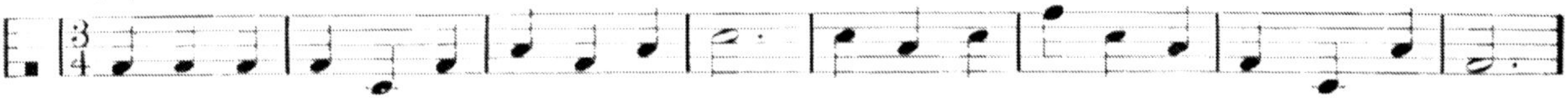

5. (A)

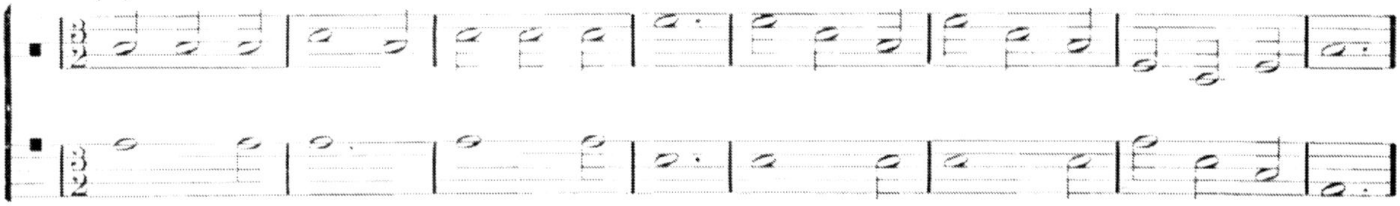

6. (E♭)

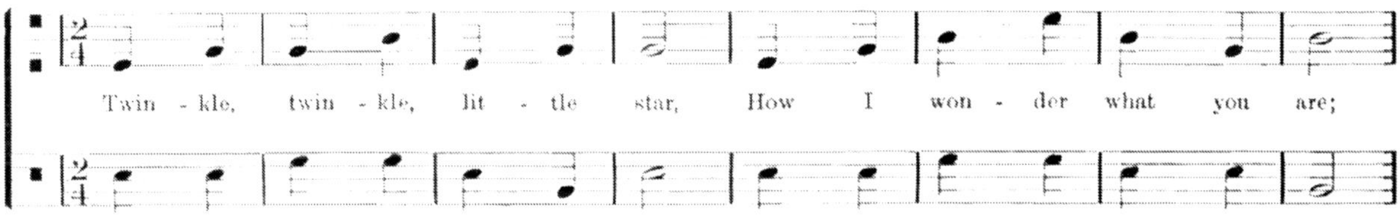

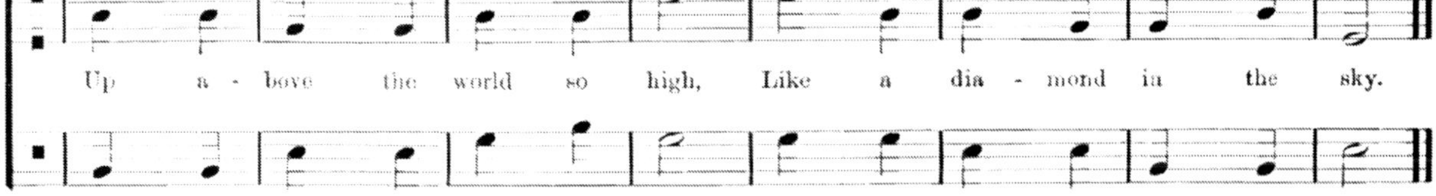

Writing Exercises.—Copy into Staff notation, quarter note to the pulse, **Exercises 38, 39, 43; half note to the pulse, Exs. 40, 44,** pages, 14 and 15. Copy into Sol-fa notation, **Exs. 1, 2, 4, 5, page, 192.**

Half-pulses.

1. *Quarter-note to the pulse.*

TAA taa TAA - tai taa

2. *Half-note to the pulse.*

TAA taa - tai TAA taa

Each part to be tantaied as a separate exercise, then the two continuously as one.

3. TAA taa TAA - - tai taa

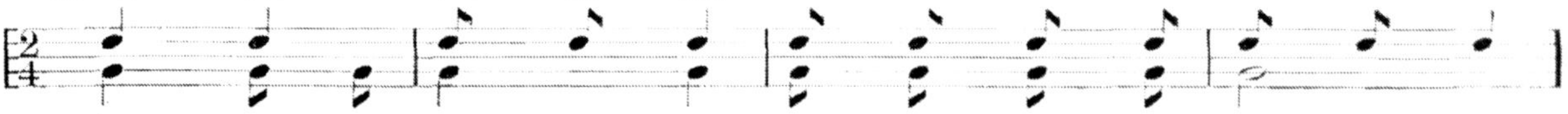

4. TAA - tai taa TAA - tai taa

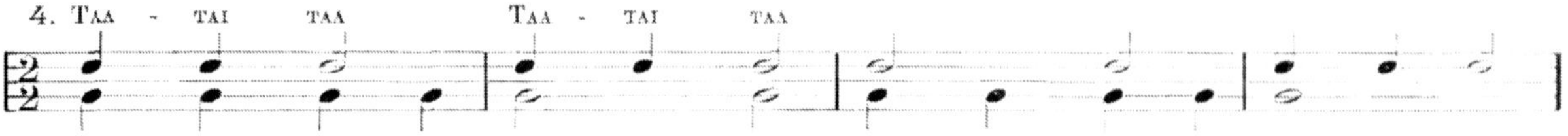

5. (C)

6. (G)

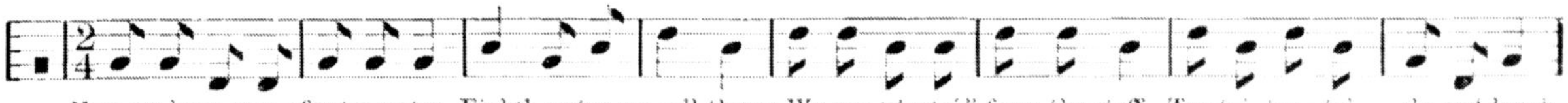

Now we have some fas-ter notes, Eighth notes we call them; We can "taatai" from the staff. Taa-tai, taa - tai, do not laugh.

7. (F)

8. (C)

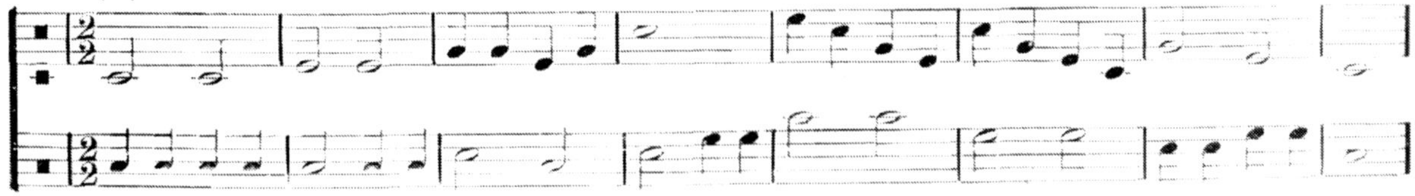

Writing Exercises.—Copy into the Staff notation, quarter note to the pulse, Exs. 48 and 50; half note to pulse, Ex. 49, page, 16. Copy into Sol-fa notation, Exs. 5, 6 and 8, page, 193.

SECOND STEP.

Third Rule.—*Ray* is placed next above *Doh*, and *Te* next below *Doh*.

1. (C)

2. (G)

3. (D)

4. (A or C)

5. (E♭)

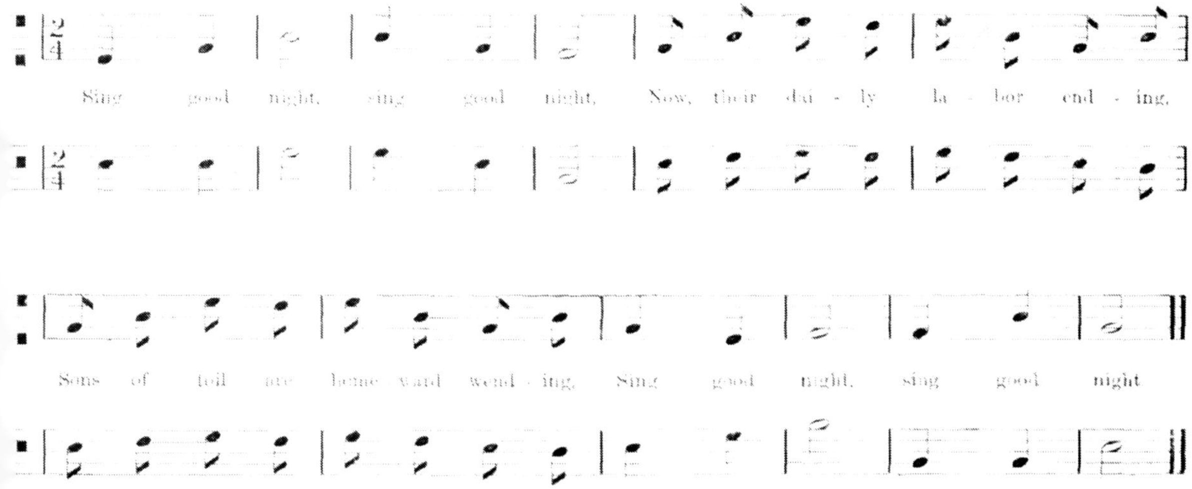
Sing good night, sing good night, Now, their dai - ly la - bor end - ing,
Sons of toil are home ward wend - ing, Sing good night, sing good night.

Writing Exercises.—Copy into the Staff notation, quarter note to the pulse, Exs. 59, 60, 61; half note to the pulse, **Ex. 2**, page, 20. Copy into Sol-fa Exs. 1, 2, 3 and 4, page, 194.

Four-pulse and Six-pulse Measures.

MEASURE SIGNATURES.

4/4 *Four-pulse measure, Quarter note to the pulse.*

4/8 *Four-pulse measure, Eighth note to the pulse.*

6/4 *Six-pulse measure, Quarter note to the pulse.*

6/8 *Six-pulse measure, Eighth note to the pulse.*

Each part to be taataied as a separate exercise; then the two continuously as one.

1. TAA TAA

2. TAA TAA

3. TAA TAA

4. TAA TAA

5. (C)

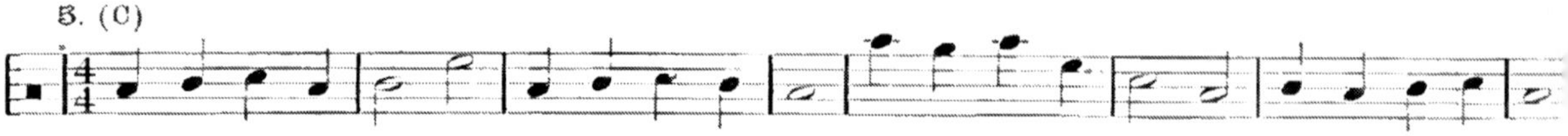

6. (G)

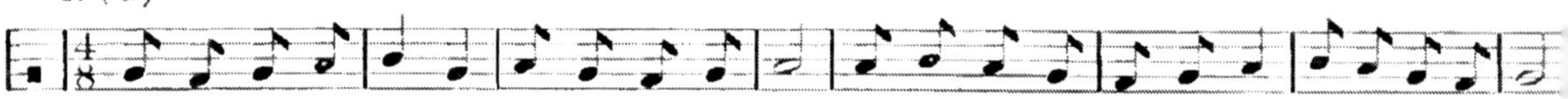

7. (F)

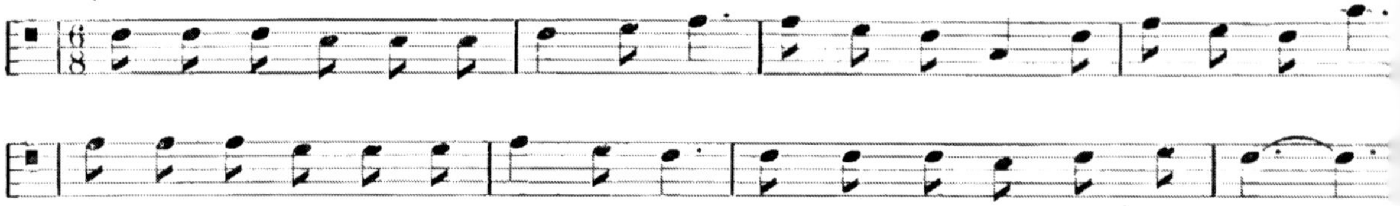

8. (B♭ or D)

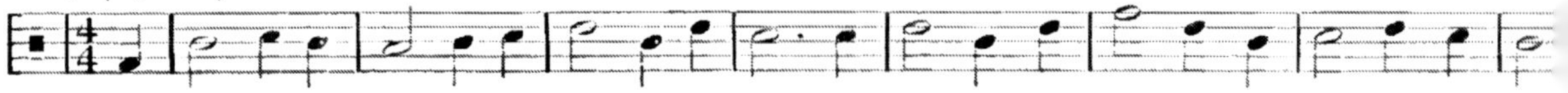

9. (C)

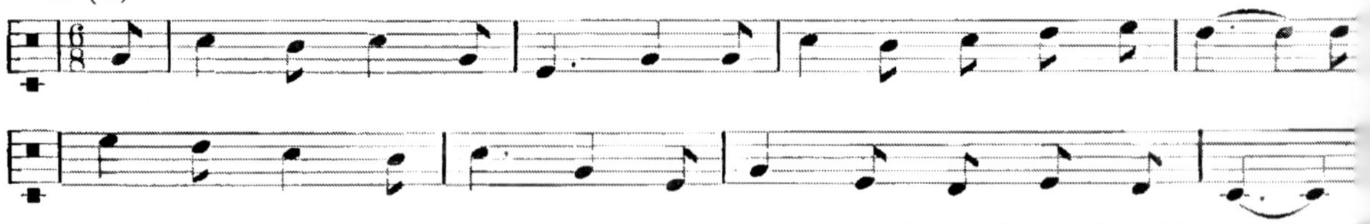

Writing Exercises.—Copy into Staff notation, quarter note to the pulse, Exs. 76, 79, page, 25; eighth note to the pu
Ex. 83, page, 26. Copy into Sol-fa, Exs. 5, 6, 7, page, 195.

The Clefs and Key Signatures are explained on page 200. At present no notice need be taken of them, unless the pupils have passed the Third Step in Tonic Sol fa, in which case the teacher may explain as much of the subject as will answer present purposes.

CHORAL SONG.

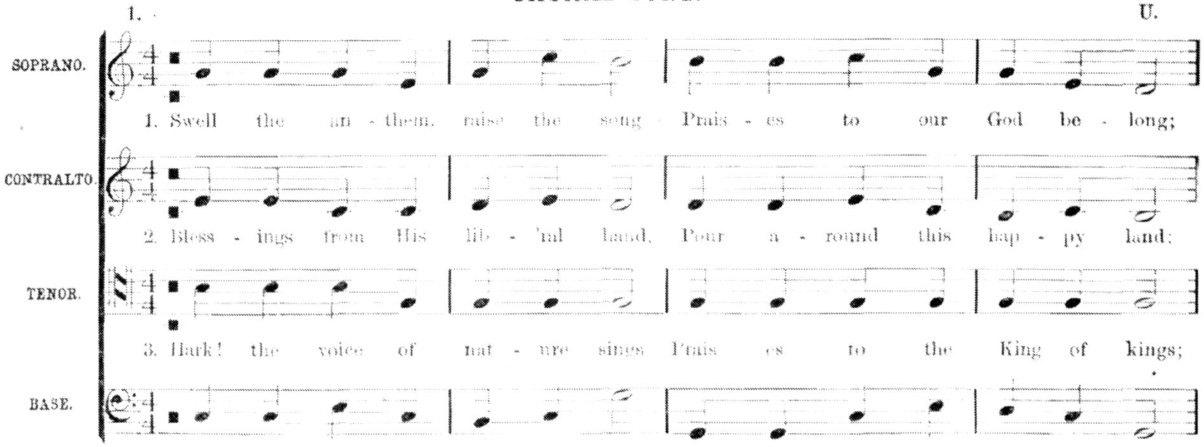

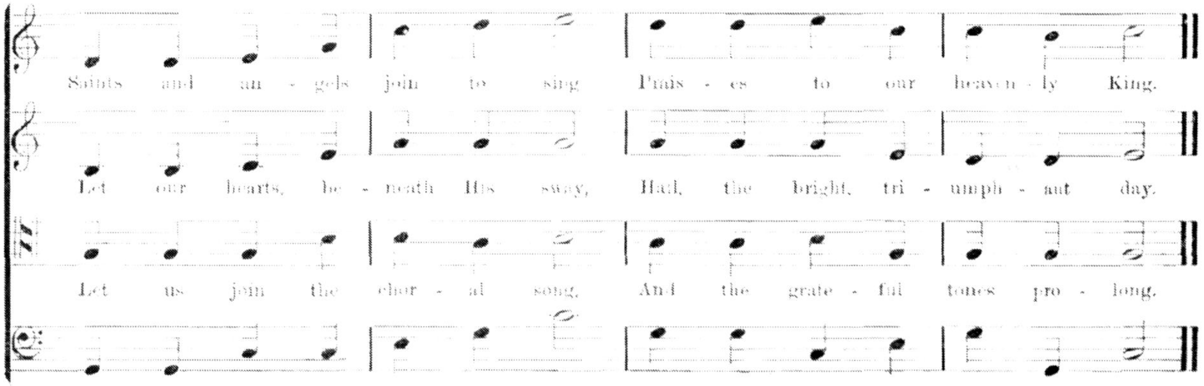

2. Round for four parts. *

3. Round for four parts. *

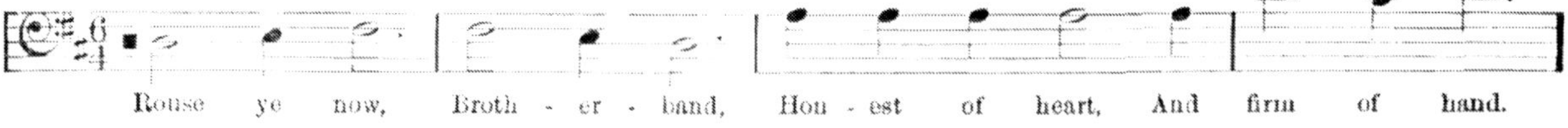

1. GOD IS LOVE.

U.

1. God is love; His mer - cy bright-ens All the path in which we rove;
2. Chance and change are bu - sy ev - er; Man de - cays and a - ges move;
3. E'en the hour that dark - est seem - eth, Will His change - less good - ness prove;
Bliss He wakes, and woe He light - ens; God is wis - dom, God is love.
But His mer - cy wan - eth nev - er: God is wis - dom, God is love.
From the gloom His bright - ness stream - eth, God is wis - dom, God is love.

2. THE MORN OF LIFE.

1. The morn of life, how fair and gay! How cheer - ing and how new!
2. Youth's ar - dent mind, with joy e - late, E - las - tic and sin - cere,
What hope il - lumes each ope - ning day, And bright - ens ev - ery view.
Sus - pects no ills that may a - wait, Nor yields a thought to fear.

THIRD STEP.

Fourth Rule.—The place of *Fah* is next above *Me*; *Lah* next above *Soh*. Or, *Lah* is one degree above *Soh*, and *Fah* one degree below.

1.

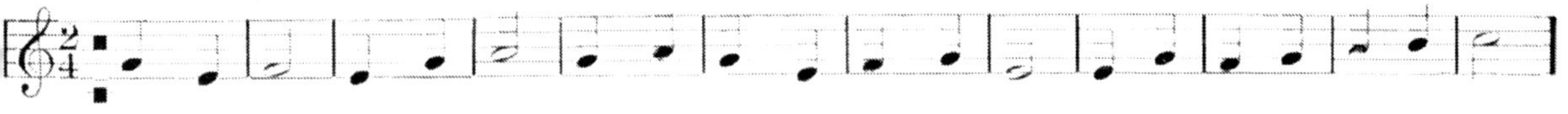

2. Round for two parts.

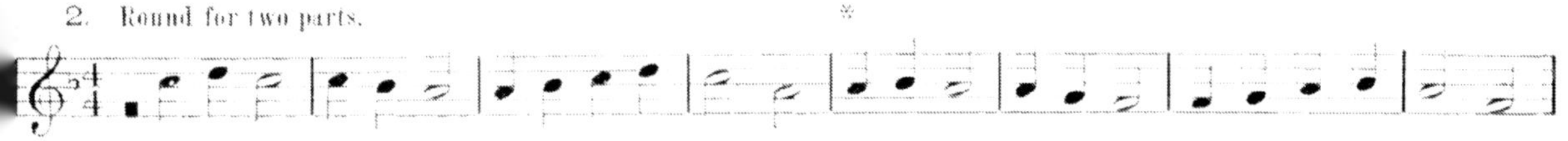

3.

4.

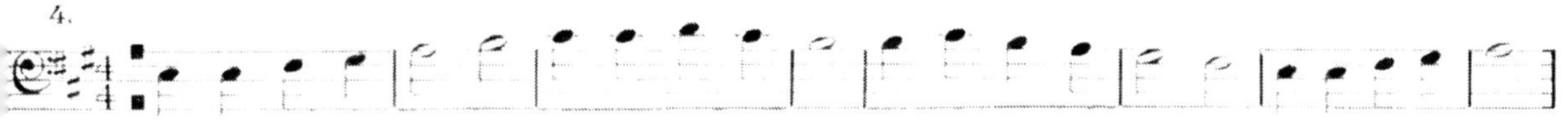

5.

6. Round for three parts.

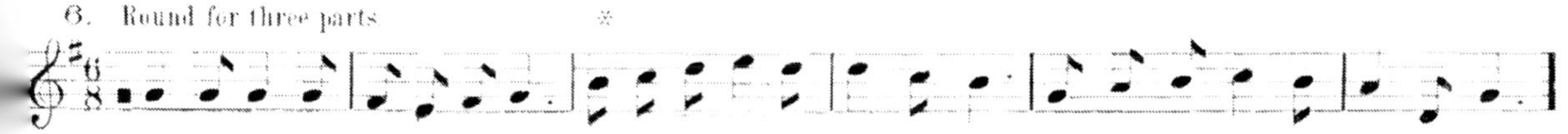

7.

Come and roam the wild-wood, Thro' the ver - dant plain, O - ver hill and mead - ow, Spring is come a - gain.

Fifth Rule.—Alternate tones of the scale are *similarly* placed. *Doh, Me, Soh* and *Te* are placed alike; *Ray, Fah, Lah* and *Doh*ˡ are placed alike. When **d, m, s** and **t** are on lines, **r, f, l** and **d**ˡ are in spaces. When **d, m, s** and **t** are in spaces, **r, f, l** and **d**ˡ are on lines.

1.

2.

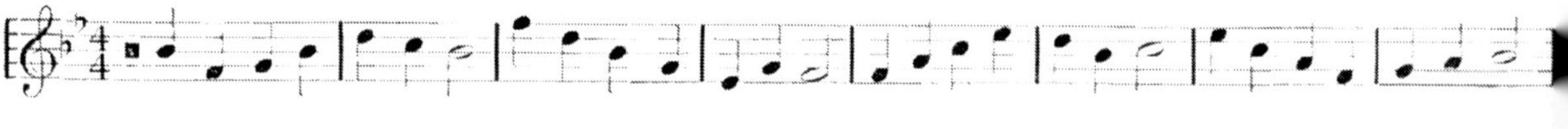

3.

4.

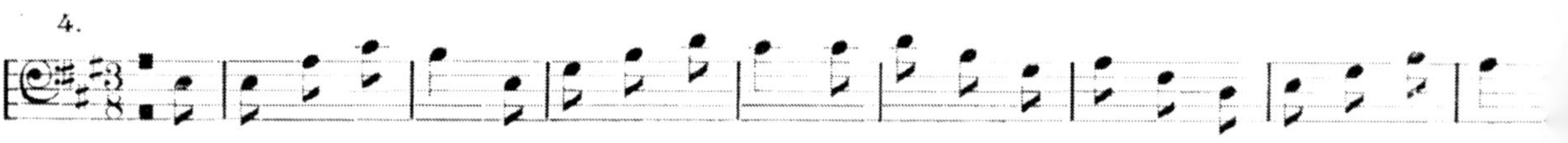

5. Round for four parts.

Sweet-ly sounds the roun-de - lay, Mu - sic charm-ing care a - way; Sing we then, sing we then.

6.

7. Round for four parts.

Writing Exercises.—Copy into Staff notation, quarter note to the pulse, exs. 111, 112, 116; eighth note to the pulse, exs. 113, 117. Copy into Sol-fa notation, exs. 1, 2, 4, p. 198; 2, 3, 4, p. 199.

The Clefs.

The Treble, or G clef. The Base, or F clef. The Tenor, or C clef.

THE POSITION OF THE LETTERS AS FIXED BY THE CLEFS.

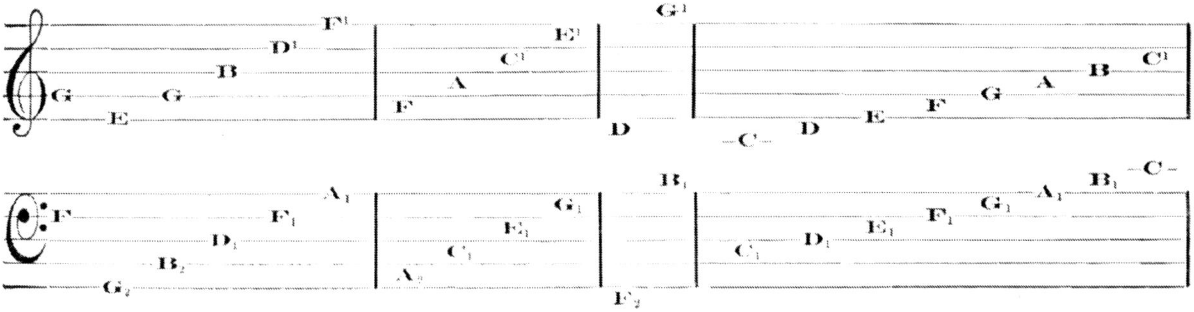

THE STANDARD SCALE AND PITCH OF VOICES.

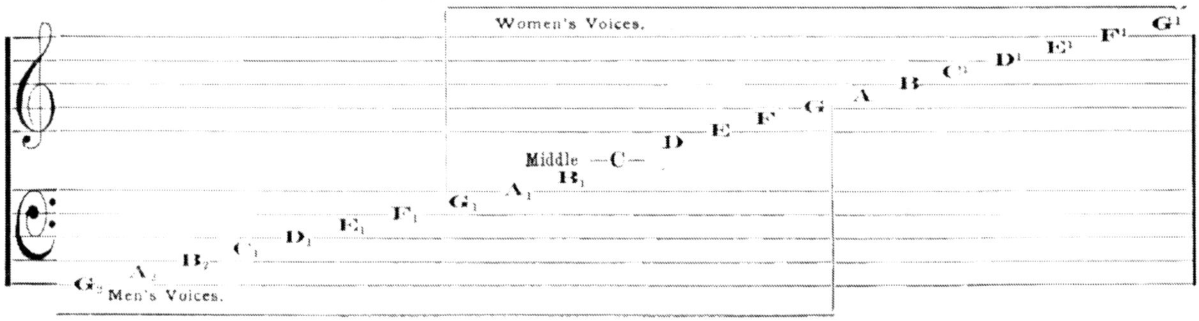

THE REAL PITCH OF THE CLEFS.

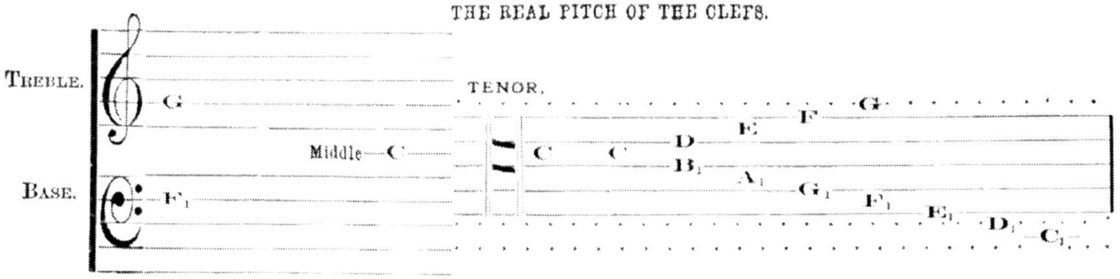

The Treble clef represents the G *above* Middle C. The Base clef represents the F *below* Middle C. The Tenor clef represents Middle C.

NOTE.—This use of the C clef is not the same as its use in orchestral scores. Its proper place is upon a line—the first line for Soprano, second line for Mezzo Soprano, third line for Contralto and fourth line for Tenor. It has been thought best to adopt the practice which is followed extensively in this country, and to place it in the third space, thus making the arrangement of the letters the same as that with the Treble clef and indicating the pitches which are really sung by the male voice when reading from the Treble clef.

The following five exercises are to be read by letter, not to be sung.

1.
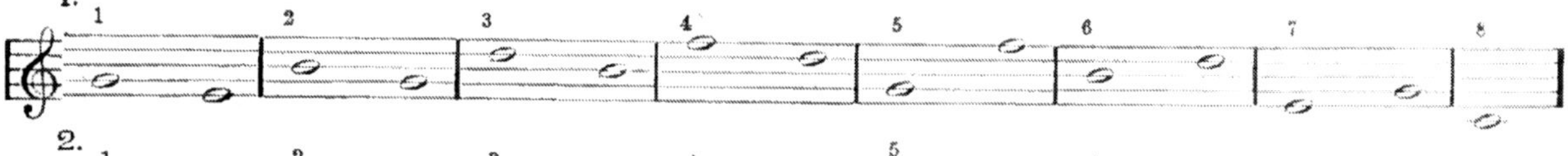

2.
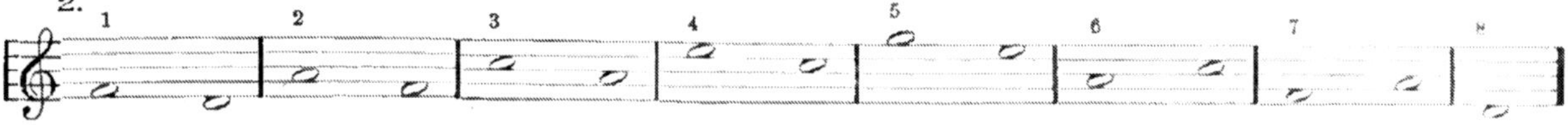

3.

5.
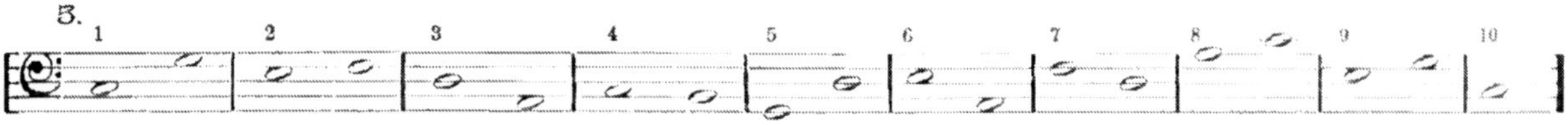

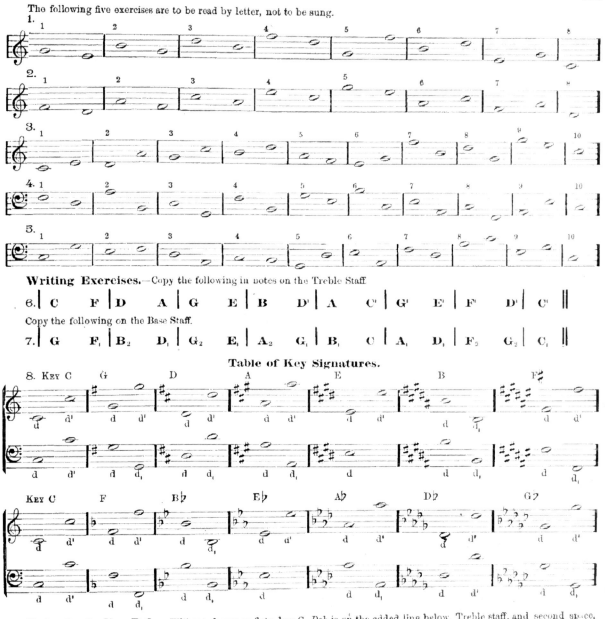

Writing Exercises.—Copy the following in notes on the Treble Staff.

6. | C F | D A | G E | B D' | A C' | G' E' | F' D' | C' ||

Copy the following on the Base Staff.

7. | G F, | B₂ D, | G₂ E, | A₂ G, | B, C | A, D, | F₂ G₂ | C, ||

Table of Key Signatures.

Rules for finding Doh.—Without sharps or flats, key C, *Doh* is on the added line below, Treble staff, and second space, Base staff. *With sharps,* the last sharp to the right is *Te. Doh* is on the next degree above. *With two or more flats,* the flat next to the last is *Doh.* With only one flat, that flat is *Fah, Doh* is on the fourth degree below.

MEMORY'S BELLS.

1.

1. Mem - 'rys bells are soft - ly chim - ing Thro' the years of long a - go,
2. There's a moth - er's fond ca - ress - ing, And a fa - ther's ten - der tone;
3. There were hours like jew - els wov - en In the gold - en web of day,
And I list - en to their rhym - ing, To each ca - dence soft and low,
Sis - ter's, broth - er's love - rich bless - ing, In those years were all my own.
Sor - rows which I since have prov - en Where my Fa - ther's bet - ter way.

2

O CARE! THOU WILT DISPATCH ME.

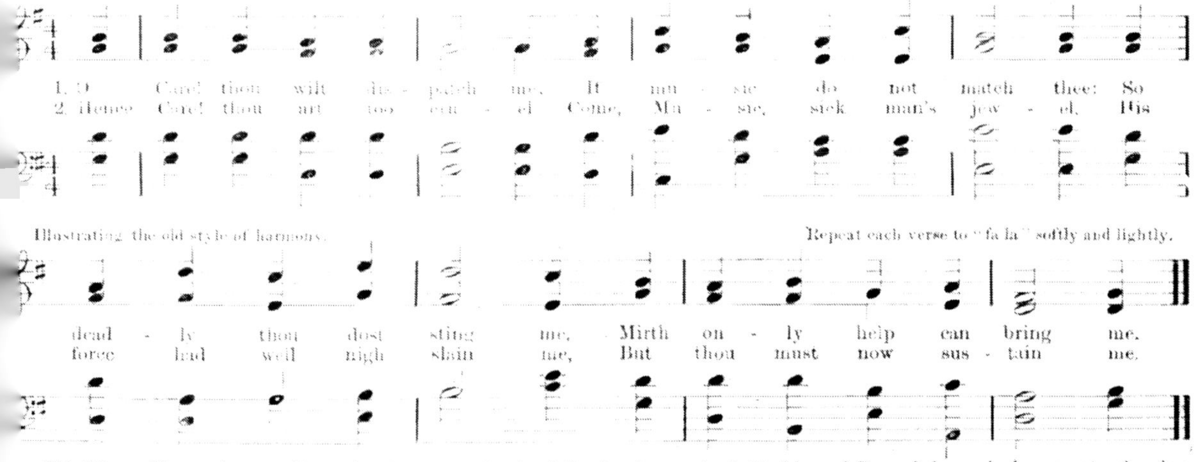
1. O Care! thou wilt dis - patch me, If mu - sic do not match thee: So
2. Hence Care! thou art too cru - el Come, Mu - sic, sick man's jew - el, His
Illustrating the old style of harmony.
Repeat each verse to "fa la" softly and lightly.
dead - ly thou dost sting me, Mirth on - ly help can bring me.
force had well nigh slain me, But thou must now sus - tain me.

Writing Exercises. Write the signatures for the following keys,—both Treble and Base clefs—and place a note showing the position of *Doh* or write the scale in each key—D, E, G, A, E♭, F, A♭, B♭.

Rests.—Silences are indicated by *Rests.* Each note has a rest of corresponding value.

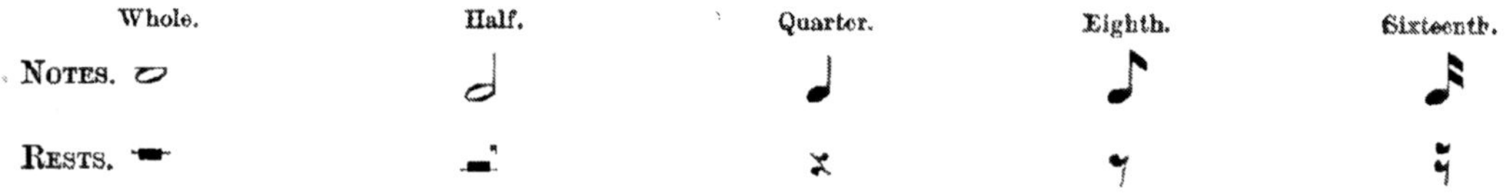

1.

2. **GLAD VOICES NOW ARE CALLING.**

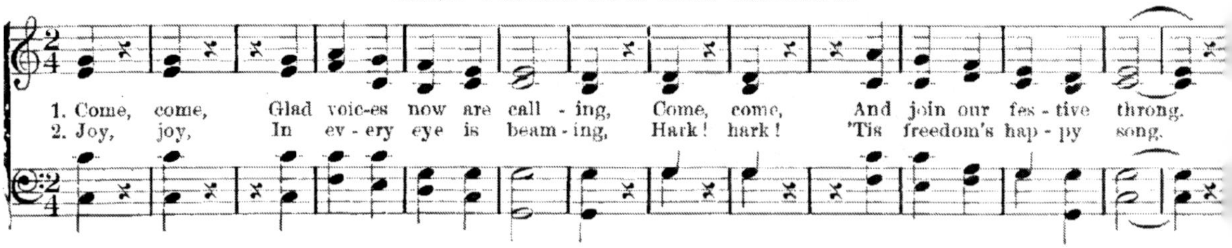

3. **SONG OF THE ECHO.**

1. Round for two parts.

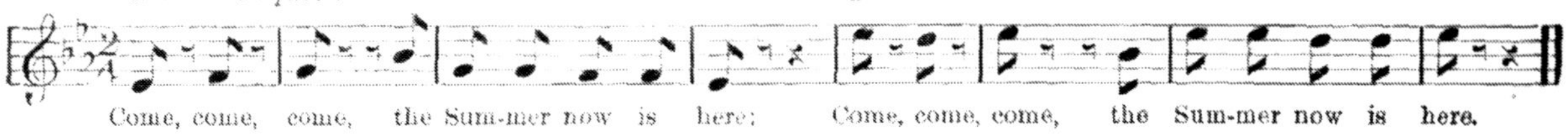
*
Come, come, come, the Sum-mer now is here; Come, come, come, the Sum-mer now is here.

Half-pulse Continuations.

2. *Quarter note to the pulse.*

TAA - AA - TAI TAA - AA - TAI

3. *Half-note to the pulse.*

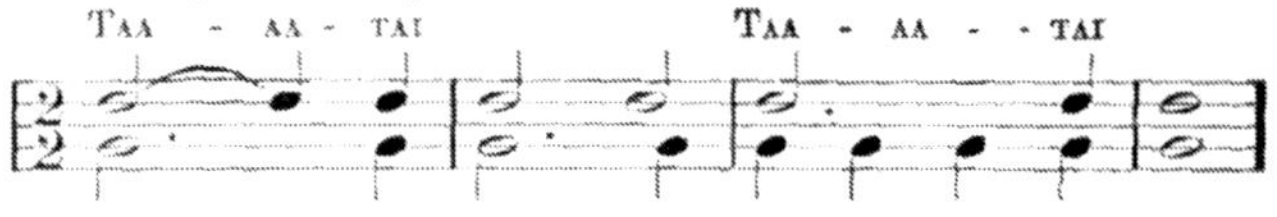
TAA - AA - TAI TAA - AA - - TAI

4. Round for three parts.

*
Nor love thy life nor hate, Nor love thy l fe nor hate, But what thou liv'st live well, But
what thou liv'st live well; How long or short per - mit, per - mit to heav'n.

THE GOLDEN CORN.

T. F. S.

1. Heap high the far - mer's win - try board! Heap high the gold - en corn!
2. Thro' vales of grass and meads of flow'rs, Our ploughs their fur - rows made,
3. All through the long bright days of June, Its leaves grew bright and fair,
4. And now with Au - tumn's moon - lit eves, Its har - vest time has come,
No rich - er gift has Au - tumn poured From out her lav - ish horn!
While on the hill the sun and show'rs Of change - ful A - pril played.
And waved in hot mid - sum - mer noon, Its soft and yel - low hair.
We pluck a - way its frost - ed leaves, And bear its treas - ures home.

1. **Quarter Pulses.**

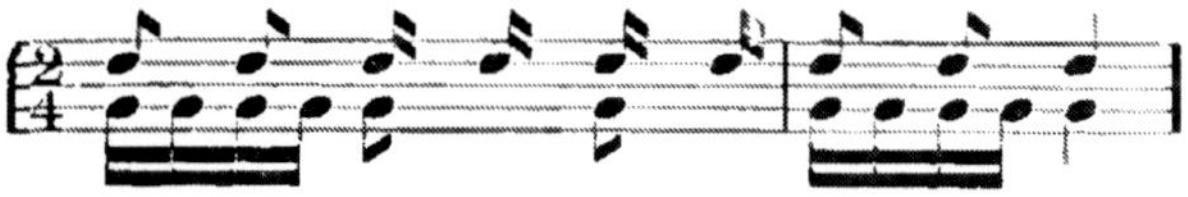
TAA TAI ta - fa - te - fe

2. **Quarter Continuations.**

TAA - te - fe TAA - e - fe

3.

4.

5. Round for three parts.

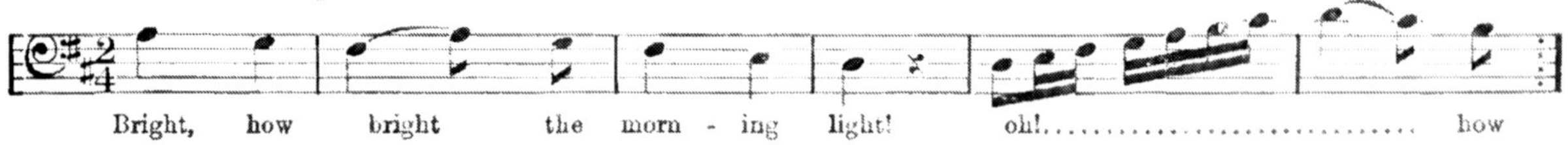
Bright, how bright the morn - ing light! oh!............................ how

6.

FINE.
D.C.

EVENING.

NAEGELI.

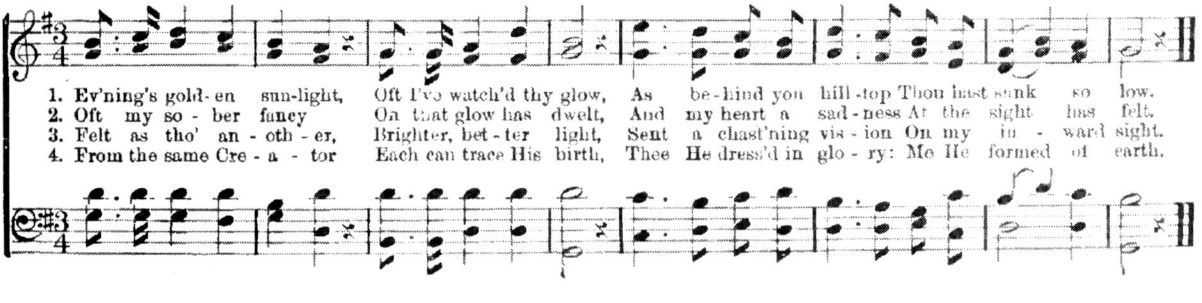
1. Ev'ning's gold- en sun-light, Oft I've watch'd thy glow, As be - hind yon hill - top Thou hast sunk so low.
2. Oft my so - ber fancy On that glow has dwelt, And my heart a sad - ness At the sight has felt.
3. Felt as tho' an - oth - er, Brighter, bet - ter light, Sent a chast'ning vis - ion On my in - ward sight.
4. From the same Cre - a - tor Each can trace His birth, Thee He dress'd in glo - ry: Me He formed of earth.

1.

FORTH WITH FOOTSTEPS LIGHT.

1. Forth, with foot - steps light, Up the mount-ain height; Winds fresh blow - ing, O - ders strew - ing,
2. See the sun in state Rise at heav - ens gate: Forth to meet him, And to greet him,
Cho.—Forth, forth, with foot - steps light, Let us scale the
Wait to greet us there.
Soars the war - bling lark.
Forth, come forth with foot - steps light, And let us scale the
mount - ain height; Fresh in the morn - ing air, Na - ture seems most fair.
mount - ain height, While fresh and bright in morn - ing air, All na - ture seems most fair.

2.

WHEN EARLY MORN SHALL WAKE US.

1. When ear - ly morn shall wake us To life and light a - new, Should drow - sy Sloth o'er-take us, Then
2. Birds war - ble their de - vo - tion In glad and thank-ful songs; Thro' wood, and field, and o - cean, All
Du - ty comes to shake us, And show us what to do,...... And show us what to do.
things are seen in mo - tion In gay and bus - y throngs, In gay and bus - y throngs.

FOURTH STEP.

Transition is sometimes indicated in the staff notation by a change of signature, but the general practice is to retain the old si nature and indicate the distinguishing tones of the new key (*Fe* or *Ta*) as they are needed by the use of Accidentals (♯ ♭, ♮).

Sharp Fah (*fe*) means the first sharp key and should be called *Te*, unless contradicted by *Fah*. In key C and all keys with sha signatures, *Fe* is expressed by a *sharp* on the degree that represents *Fah*. To restore *Fah* the natural is used. In all keys with fl signatures *Fe* is expressed by a *natural* on *Fah*. To restore *Fah* the flat is used.

Flat Te (*ta*) is the distinguishing tone of the first flat key and should be called *Fah*, unless contradicted by *Te*. In key C and keys with flat signatures *Ta* is expressed by a *flat* on the degree that represents *Te*. To restore *Te* a *natural* is used. In all sha keys *Ta* is indicated by a *natural* on *Te*. To restore *Te* a sharp is used,

Duration of Accidentals.—The influence of an accidental continues to the end of the measure in which it occurs, unless co tradicted by another sign. It affects the line or space upon which it is placed, not merely the note that follows it.

Cautionary Accidentals.—The pupil must be careful to distinguish between accidentals that are of *real* effect and those which a merely put in as a caution to the player. If an accidental, contradicting some other accidental in a *previous measure*, merely repea what is in the signature it is only cautionary.

1. *Fe* expressed by a ♯. *Fah* restored by a ♮. 2.

3. *Fe* expressed by a ♮. *Fah* restored by a ♭. 4.

5. *Ta* expressed by a ♭. *Te* restored by a ♮. 6.

7. *Ta* expressed by a ♮. *Te* restored by a ♯. 8.

9.

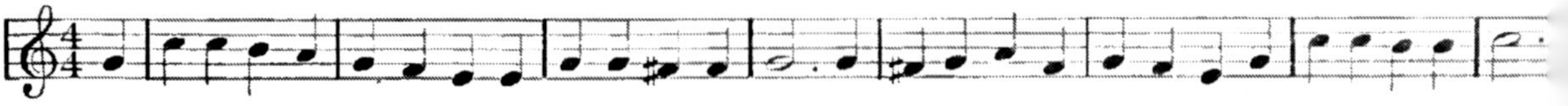

10.

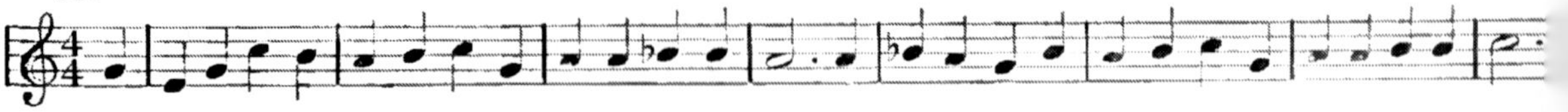

1. Transition with change of signature.

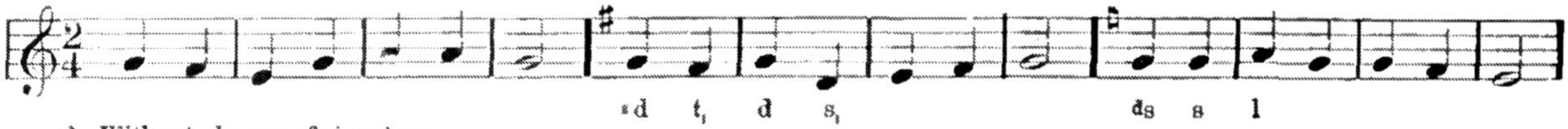

2. Without change of signature.

3.

4.

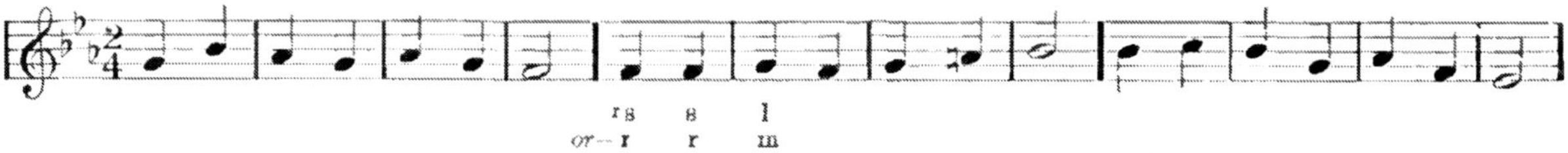

5. Should be sol-faed by both "perfect" and "imperfect" methods.

6.

7.

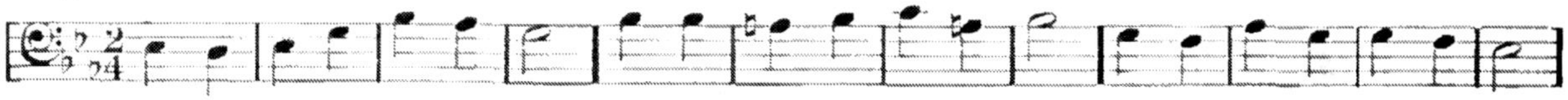

8.

10.

BARNARD. C. M.

B. C. UNSELD.

1. Come let us sing the song of songs— The saints in heav'n be - gan the strain,
2. To Him en - throned by fil - ial right, All pow'r in heav'n and earth pro - claim,
3. Long as we live, and when we die, And while in heav'n with Him we reign;
The hom - age which to Christ be - longs. "Wor - thy the Lamb, for He was slain."
Hon - or maj - es - ty and might, "Wor - thy the Lamb, for He was slain."
This song our song of songs shall be; "Wor - thy the Lamb, for He was slain."

SILVER SPRING. C. M.

DR. LOWELL MASON.

1. There is a name I love to hear, I love to sing its worth;
2. It tells me of a Sav - iour's love, Who died to set me free;
3. This name shall shed its fra - grance still A - long this thorn - y road;
It sounds like mu - sic in mine ear, The sweet - est name on earth.
It tells me of His pre - cious blood, The sin - ner's per - fect plea.
Shall sweet - ly smooth the rug - ged hill That leads me up to God.

1. **RELIANCE.** THEO. F. SEWARD, by per.

D.C. 1. O Je - sus! Friend un - fail - ing, How dear Thou art to me! Are cares or fears as -
2. Why should I droop in sor - row? Thou'rt ev - er by my side! Why, trembling, dread the
Fine.
sail - ing? I find my strength in Thee! Why should my feet grow wea - ry Of this my
mor - row, What ill can e'er be - tide? If I my cross have tak - en, 'Tis but to
D.C.
pil - grim way? Tho' rough the path and drea - ry, It ends in per - fect day!
fol - low Thee; If scorn'd, despised, for - sak - en, Naught sev - ers Thee from me!

2. **SUBMISSION.** DR. LOWELL MASON, by per.

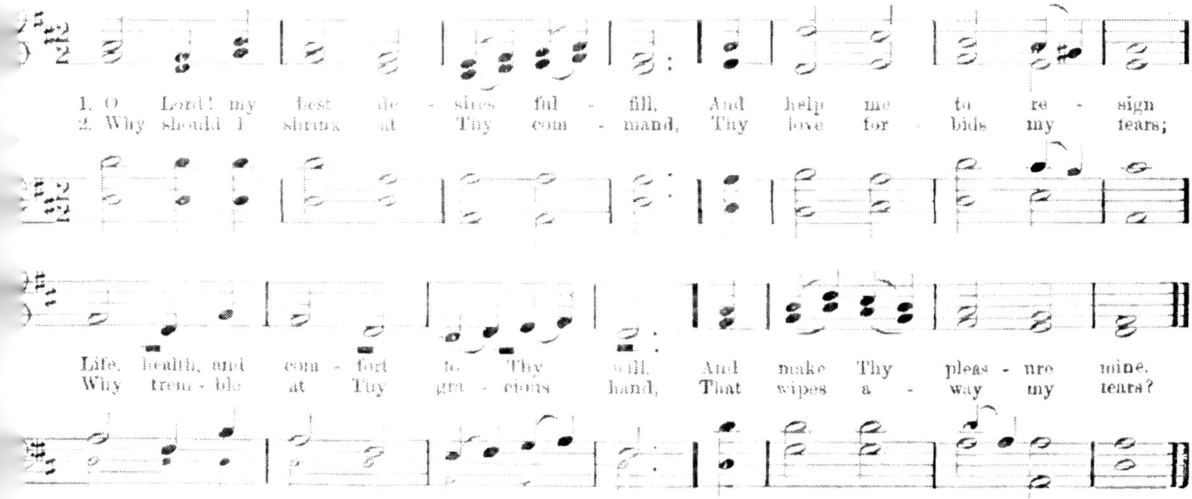
1. O Lord! my best de - sires ful - fill, And help me to re - sign
2. Why should I shrink at Thy com - mand, Thy love for - bids my tears;
Life, health, and com - fort to Thy will, And make Thy pleas - ure mine.
Why trem - ble at Thy gra - cious hand, That wipes a - way my tears?

1. **THERE'S A CHARM IN SPRING.** THEO. F. SEWARD, by per.

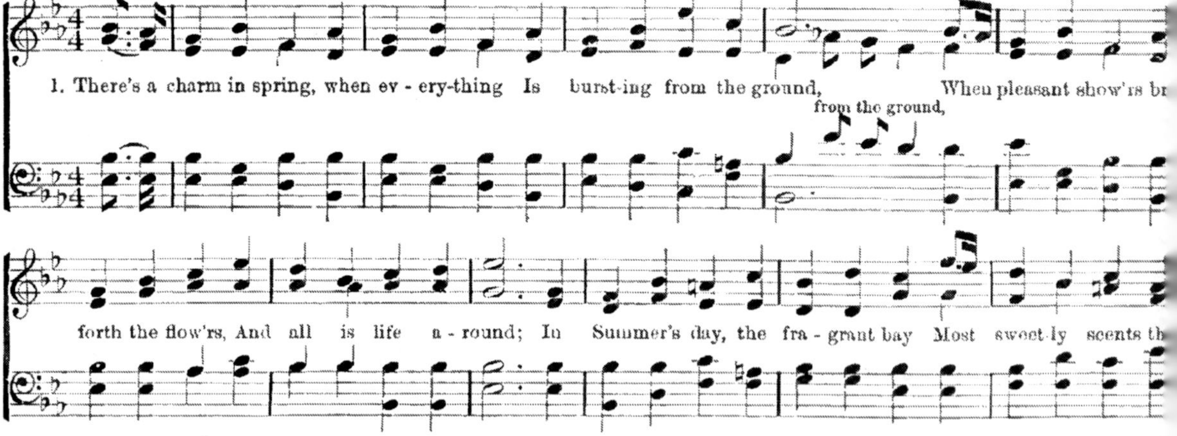

2.
When Autum's come, with rusty g
In quest of birds we roam;
Unerring aim, we mark the game,
And proudly bear it home.
Old Winter's night has its delight,
Around old stories go,
Old Winter's day we're blithe and
Defying ice and snow.

2. **SURRENDER.** CHESTER G. ALLEN, by per.

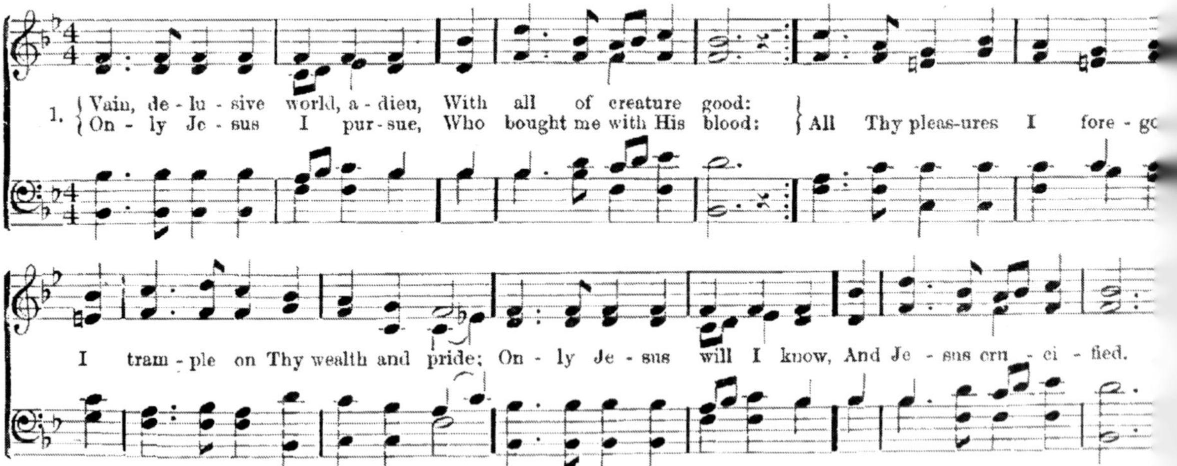

Writing Exercises.—Copy into Staff notation quarter-note to the pulse, with change of signature, Nos. 175 176, without change of signatures, Nos. 178, 179, 181, p. 68. Copy into Sol-fa, "perfect" method, Nos. 1, 5, 7; "imperfect" met Nos. 4, 6, 10, p. 208.

1. **Chromatic Scale.**

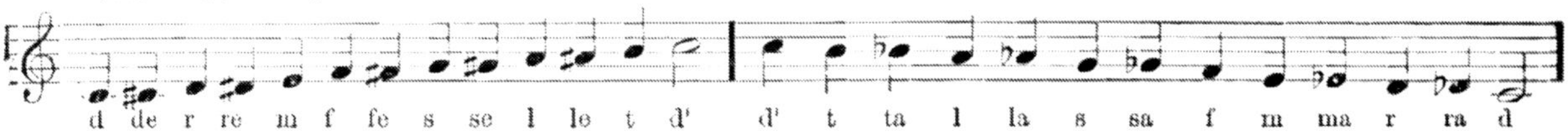

2.

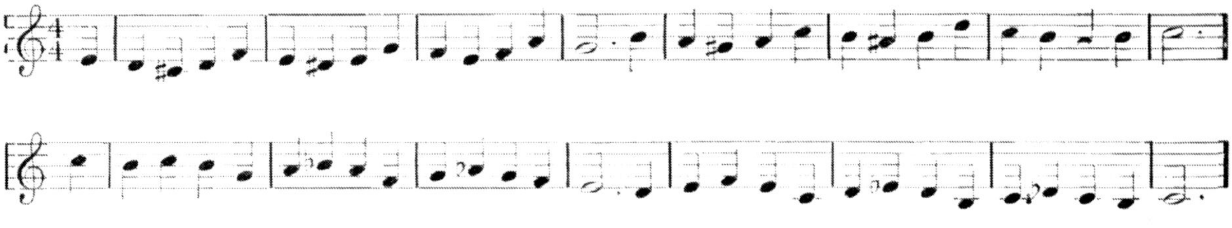

3. The ♮ as a ♯.

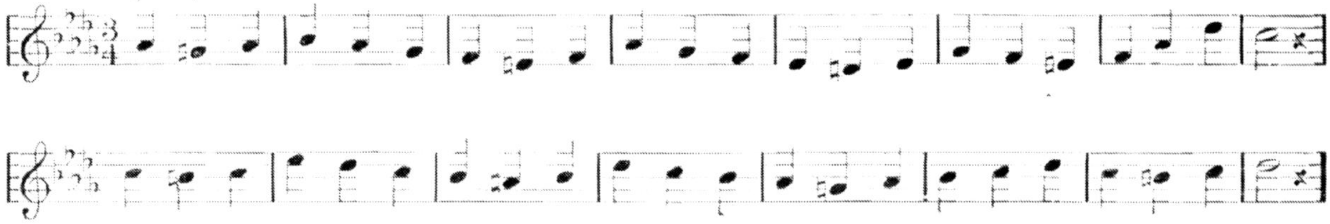

4.

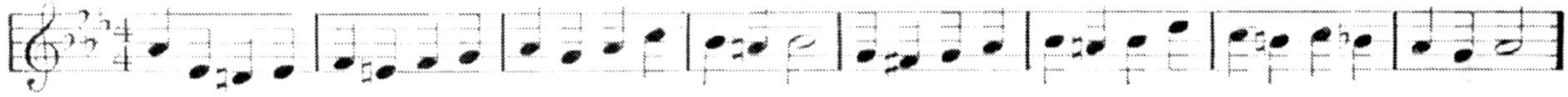

5. The ♮ as a ♭.

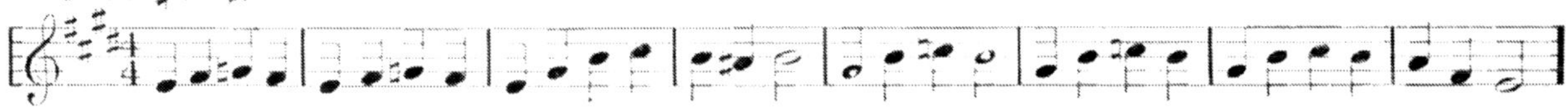

6.

7.

1.

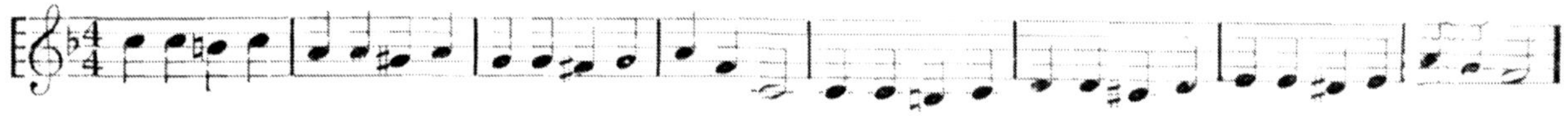

2.

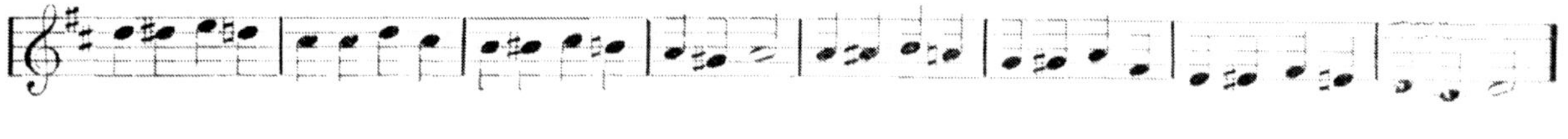

3. The × (Double Sharp) and its Cancel—♮♯

4. The ♭♭ (Double Flat) and its Cancel—♮♭.

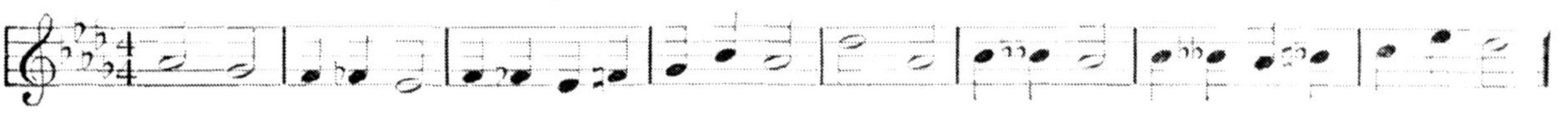

5.

Writing Exercises.—Copy into Staff notation, quarter note to the pulse, Nos. 220 in keys D and E, 221 in keys G and A♭, 225 in keys D and D♭, 227 in keys C, D♭ and E. Copy into Sol-fa notation Nos. 2, 3, 5, page, 212; Nos. 3 and 4, page, 213.

1. **WILBUR.** Theo. F. Seward, by per.

1. How ten - der is Thy hand, O Thou be - lov - ed Lord;
2. How gen - tle was the rod That chast - ened us for sin!
3 A Fa - ther's hand we felt, A Fa - ther's heart we knew;
Af - flic - tions come at Thy com - mand, And leave us at Thy word.
How soon we found a smil - ing God, Where deep dis - tress had been.
With tears of pen - i - tence we knelt, And found His word was true.

2. **CURTISS.** Wm. F. Sherwin, by per.

1. Cease, ye mourn - ers, cease to lan - guish O'er the grave of those you love;
2. While our si - lent steps are stray - ing, Lone - ly through night's deep - 'ning shade,
3. Light and peace at once de - riv - ing, From the hand of God most high,
Pain and death and night and an - guish En - ter not the world a - bove.
Glo - ry's bright - est beams are play - ing Round the hap - py Christ - ian's head.
In His glo - rious pres - ence liv - ing, They shall nev - er, nev - er die.

1. **Syncopation.**

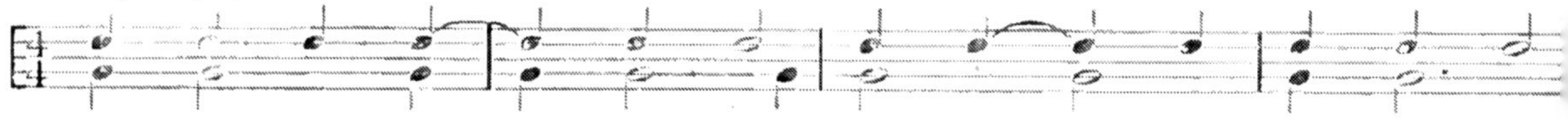

2.

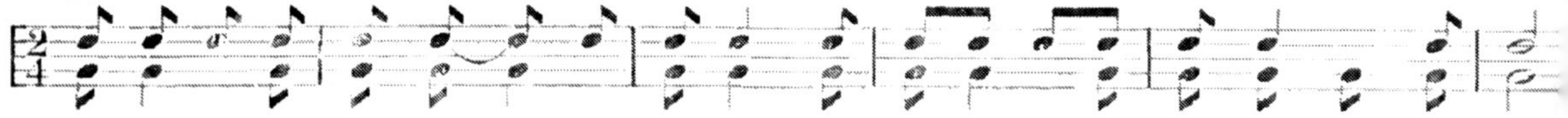

3. **IN GROVES OF FRAGRANT LARCHES.**

1. **Quarter-pulse Silence. Sixteenth Rest.**

2. **Thirds of a Pulse. Triplets.**

3
3
3
3
3

TRAVELING HOMEWARD.

F. J. Crosby. W. H. Doane.

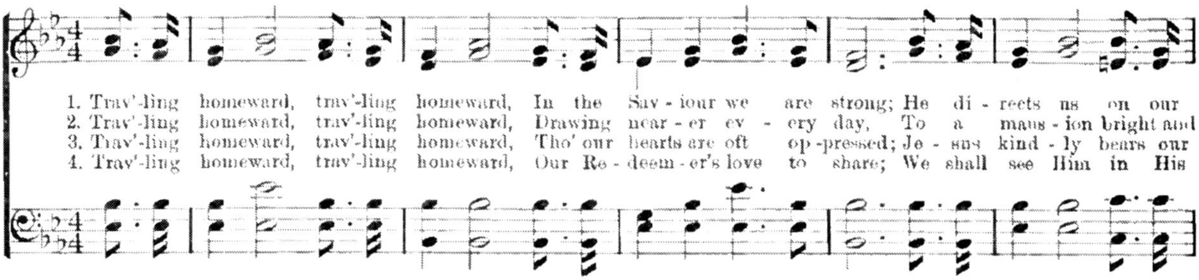
1. Trav'-ling homeward, trav'-ling homeward, In the Sav - iour we are strong; He di - rects us on our
2. Trav'-ling homeward, trav'-ling homeward, Drawing near - er ev - ery day, To a man - sion bright and
3. Trav'-ling homeward, trav'-ling homeward, Tho' our hearts are oft op-pressed; Je - sus kind - ly bears our
4. Trav'-ling homeward, trav'-ling homeward, Our Re - deem - er's love to share; We shall see Him in His

REFRAIN.
jour - ney, Fills our hearts with love and song.
glo - ry That shall nev - er fade a - way.
bur - dens, Gives the wea - ry spir - it rest.
king - dom, We shall dwell for - ev - er there.
Hal - le - lu - jah! Hal - le - lu - jah! Hal - le -
(sing)
(sing)

lu - jah! glad - ly sing; We are go - ing, we are go - ing To the pal - ace of a King.
(sing)

FIFTH STEP.

In the Staff notation the Minor Mode is represented as an appendage of the relative major. The minor mode is named from the pitch of the tone *Lah*. Thus the relative minor of the key C is *A minor;* the relative minor of the key G is *E minor*, and so on. Each signature indicates a major key and its relative minor. Thus the signature of one sharp indicates the keys of G major and *E minor*. The notational difficulties are with *Se* and *Ba*, chiefly with *Ba*.

The Sharp Seventh of the minor mode (*Se*) is always written as the sharp of *Soh*.

The Sharp Sixth of the minor mode (*Ba*) is always written as the sharp of *Fah*. There is no sign in the staff notation by which *Ba* can be distinguished from *Fe*. It is easily mistaken for *Fe* unless it stands in immediate relation with *Se*. When *Fah sharp* is followed by *Soh sharp*, and when *Soh sharp* is followed by *Fah sharp*, the *Fah sharp* must always be called *Ba*.

1.

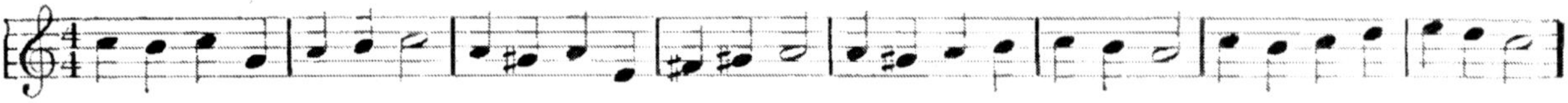

2.

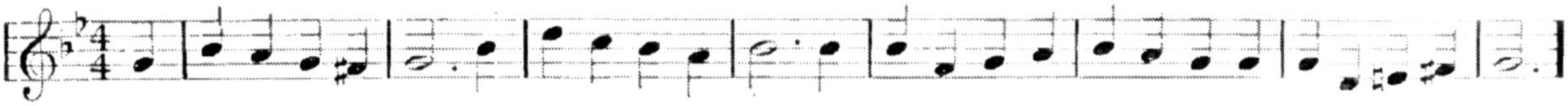

3.

4.

5.

6. Round for three parts.

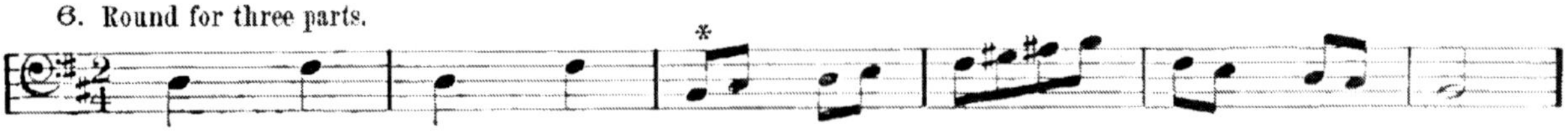

7. Round in four parts.

1.

2. Round for three parts.

3. Round for three parts.

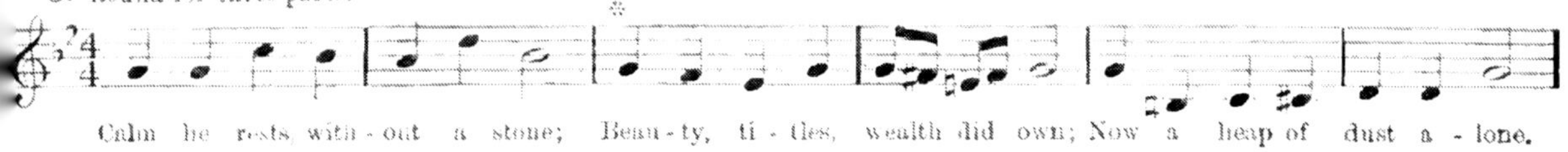

4. Round for four parts.

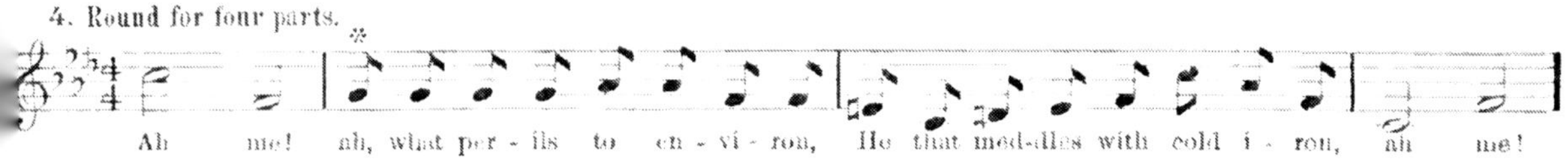

5. **ALL MY HOPE.**

Writing Exercises.—Copy into Staff notation, quarter note to the pulse, Nos. 272, 273, 280, 281, 283. Copy in Sol-fa notation, Nos. 2, 4, 5, page, 217.

SIXTH STEP.

Transitions of more distant removes.—Singing from the staff notation is easy so long as the music does not change key, or when there is a change of but one remove But reading remote transitions and modulations, in which the singer is confronted by a bewildering array of accidentals, is not easy The difficulty is to some extent in the music, but to a much greater extent in the notation Occasionally passages are met with which seem to be nothing but a wilderness of sharps, flats and naturals Nearly every note is altered, the signature is not the slightest guide to the key, and the singer is apt to despair of finding it Without a knowledge of harmony it is impossible to be perfectly certain in the power of deciding the key at a glance The harmonist reads the key most quickly by watching the movement of the Base, especially in cadences The ordinary singer, reading music at first sight, has not time to compare one part with another, to notice the movement of the Base, to mark the various accidentals and their resolutions He must watch for the characteristic melodic shapes and phrases All decided changes of key are felt most positively in cadences The mental affects are there most strongly asserted, therefore, by "looking ahead" to the close and noticing the mental effects, the singer will be aided in deciding the key The most expert readers sometimes find it necessary to analyze the whole phrase before they can be positively certain of the key

Rules for finding the key.—The order of the sharps or flats as they occur in signatures should be memorized A signature is the sharps or flats necessary in transitions from key C to other keys placed in *compact order;* the same sharps or flats occurring as accidentals are simply the *signature dispersed* It will be remembered that the last sharp in a signature is *Te*, the last flat is *Fah*, this same rule holds good in the case of accidentals (except as to chromatics, to be mentioned later)

Order of the sharps

1	2	3	4	5	6
F♯	C♯	G♯	D♯	A♯	E♯

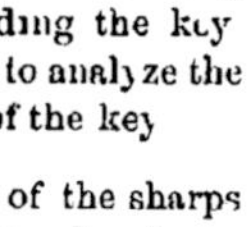

It should be remembered that the first sharp in the above table indicates the key G, the first and second key D, the first, second and third key A, and so on To adopt a convenient phrase, "C♯ is sharper than F♯, G♯ is sharper than C♯," and so on Or, we may say that F♯ is the nearest sharp, C♯ is a farther sharp G♯ a still farther sharp, and so on through the whole series From this we deduce the rule—"Find the *sharpest* or *farthest* sharp and call it *Te*."

Order of the flats

1	2	3	4	5	6
B♭	E♭	A♭	D♭	G♭	C♭

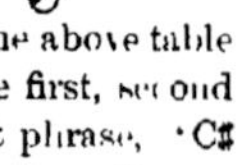

With the flats we notice that B♭ is the nearest flat, E♭ is farther flat, A♭ a still farther flat, and so on The rule for flats is —"Find the *flattest* or *farthest* flat and call it *Fah*"

Naturals in keys with flat signatures are the same as sharps and in keys with sharp signatures, naturals are the same as flats The rules of the *last sharp* and the *last flat* are now applied to the natural In flat signatures the last *natural* is *Te* In sharp signatures the last *natural* is *Fah* The last sharp or flat is the *farthest* one to the *right*, the last natural is the *nearest* one to the *left*

Order of naturals in keys with flat signatures

6	5	4	3	2	1
B♮	E♮	A♮	D♮	G♮	C♮

Order of naturals in keys with sharp signatures

6	5	4	3	2	1
F♮	C♮	G♮	D♮	A♮	E♮

The mode of search is now reversed In the above table it seen that the *farthest* natural is C♮, G♮ is a nearer natural, D♮ still nearer, and so on The rule is with flat signatures—"Find the *nearest* natural and call it *Te*" With sharp signatures—"Find the nearest natural and call it *Fah*" Another rule—The farthest sharp in the signature left uncancelled is *Te* The farthest flat left uncancelled is *Fah*

Sometimes, when a passage does not contain either a *Te* or *Fah* the rule of the farthest flat or sharp or nearest natural will not give the clue The key must then be decided by the melodic shape, the cadence and the mental effect of the passage

Chromatic Tones.—Care must be taken to distinguish between accidentals that indicate transition and those used for mere passing chromatic effects If an accidental is repeated through several measures, wherever the same tone occurs, no doubt the key is changed But if it is not repeated, or if it is contradicted, it is a chromatic tone, or a very brief transition If the farthest sharp or flat be immediately contradicted it is a chromatic tone, and the next farthest must be looked for to decide the key

Unmarked Accidentals.—In transition it sometimes happens that *Fe Ba*, and *Ta*, which would otherwise be expressed by a natural contradicting some sharp or flat in the signature, we have *nothing* to distinguish them, and are often a source of difficulty to the pupil *Fe* and *Ba* in all first flat removes are the same as *Te* of the old key and remain unmarked *Ta* in all first sharp removes is the same as *Fah* of the old key and remains unmarked

Sharp Removes, departing with sharps.

Flat Removes, returning with naturals.

Flat Removes, departing with flats.

Sharp Removes, returning with naturals.

1. Unmarked accidentals, *Fe, Ba, Ta.*

2.

3.

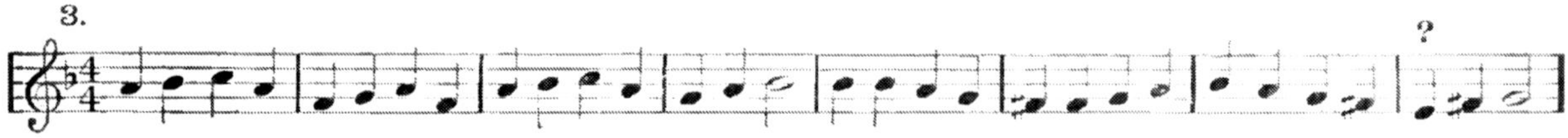

4.

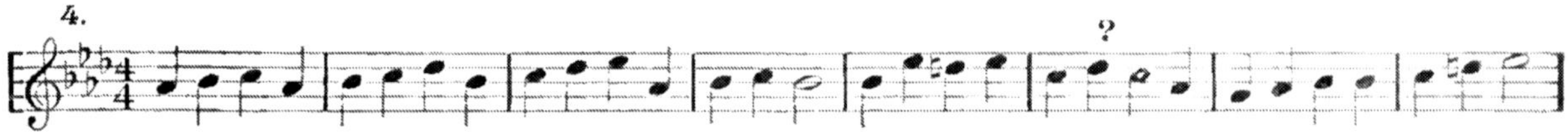

5. Transition—what Removes?

From J. Barnby.

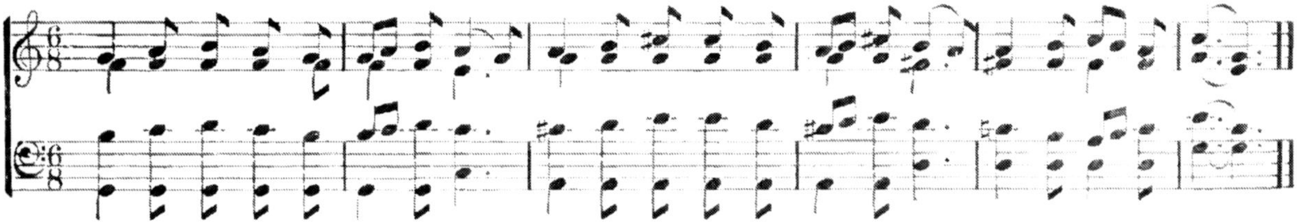

6.

From J. B. Dykes.

1.
f
m
f
2.
3.
4.
5.

1.

2.

3.

4.

Writing Exercises.—Copy into Staff notation, quarter note to the pulse, without change of signature. Nos. 328, 330, 333, 334, 346, 348, 347. Copy into Sol-fa notation, "perfect" method, Nos. 1, 2, 4, 5, 6, page, 221, Nos. 3 and 5, page, 2.2, 3 and 4, page, 223.

INDEX.—Part II.

For Index to Part I, see page 112.